Jesus and Muhammad

Their Messages, Side-by-Side

Louis St Michael

RISING MYRRH

Rising Myrrh Press
contact@risingmyrrhpress.com
www.risingmyrrhpress.com

In memory of my Father, who taught me about spirit, beauty and joy, and who never tired of my questions.

To my loving and caring spouse, who supports and encourages me to achieve my vision, always.

And to our dear young ones, who inspire us to blossom along with them.

Contents

"A very useful source-book and anthology of the core messages of Christianity and Islam respectively. The author has provided the reader with every conceivable source on a wide range of interesting subjects. Particularly interesting are the gaps between the messages where the reader can see the subjects about which Jesus expanded where Muhammad did not, and vice-versa. Relying upon the texts to speak for themselves, St. Michael has provided us with the essential messages of both religions so that everyone can judge them for these messages and by their fruits." — **David Cook, Ph.D.**, assistant professor of religious studies specializing in Islam at Rice University, author of *Studies in Muslim Apocalyptic*, *Understanding Jihad*, and *Contemporary Muslim Apocalyptic Literature*

"Many people today are being told that Christianity and Islam are essentially the same, but whether you are a Christian or a Muslim, comparing the words of the two founders makes it very clear that this is not the case. Certainly there are a number of similarities, such as a belief in one God only, seeking to live a pure life, and reaching out to help others. However, there are also some very great differences. For example, in the Fighting and Warfare chapter and the Miracles chapter of this book, it is eminently clear that Islam and Christianity are very different. This side-by-side comparison makes it easy to note the similarities as well as the differences, and in this way, the reader should gain a greater appreciation for the message from each religion. Another one of the helpful features is that the author allows the words of Jesus and the words of Allah (given to Muhammad) to be presented without the intrusion of the author's own interpretation or comments. Thus, readers are free to make their own judgments about the content. Is the God of Islam the same God of Christianity? Together with the format that collects the sayings under a number of subject headings, this structure provides a very useful resource book on Christianity and Islam. I highly recommend this book to anyone who wants to understand the core ideas of these two religions through a comparison of their teachings." — **Daniel Janosik, Ph.D.**, adjunct professor of Islamic Studies at Southern Evangelical Seminary and author of *John of Damascus, First Apologist to the Muslims*

"St Michael presents an interesting, useful and new approach to the comparative study of Christianity and Islam. Rather than subject readers to his particular interpretations of the various tenets and articles of the faiths, he chose major topics and arrayed the pertinent passages from the New Testament and Qur'an, accordingly. The selected passages reflect where the faiths agree or differ. This is important because in an atmosphere in which we tend to look for only the comfortable common ground, it is imperative that we also realize what profoundly separates the two faiths. The book additionally provides concise summaries of the early histories of the religions and succinct glossaries of technical terms and beliefs for each faith. *Jesus and Muhammad* is a valuable handbook for anyone interested in studying the history of these figures and faiths and the contacts and conflicts between the religions."— **Dr. William J. Neidinger**, archaeologist and historian associated with the Texas Foundation for Archaeological & Historical Research (tfahr.org). Dr. Neidinger has directed more than two dozen excavations in the Middle East, the Balkans and Europe at Biblical, classical, and medieval sites. His lectures are available worldwide on amazon.com and vimeo.com.

"This groundbreaking work provides a reference for those seeking to quickly compare Jesus' and Muhammad's approaches on various issues, as presented in the New Testament and the Qur'an. St Michael has done a great job in creating a parallel layout of texts, based on important themes, making it easy for anyone who wants to quickly investigate the two books. In addition, the historical, doctrinal and terminological sections provide valuable material for the serious reader. This book represents a commendable effort that paves the way to a deeper understanding of the similarities and differences of the various teachings found in Christianity and Islam."— **Fr. Panayiotis Papageorgiou, Ph.D.**, translator of *John Chrysostom: Homilies on Romans*

"I thoroughly appreciated the book *Jesus and Muhammad: Their Messages, Side-by-Side* by Louis St Michael. As a convert to Islam, I found the information and layout of the book very helpful, and it was easy to see the similarities and differences between these two great spiritual leaders and their individual and collective impact on humanity. The book is a good reference for people who are genuinely interested in studying the two religions or two historical figures side by side. I appreciated the fact that the author seems to be neutral in his overall viewpoint and tends to focus specifically on historical information of the two religions and factual similarities and differences between the Bible and the Quran. To my knowledge, I have not seen another book written quite like this one, in such a straightforward and simple way. . . . St Michael simply provides the quotes from the sources and leaves the interpretation to the reader with very little commentary. I have actually shared this book with my older children as a reference point, because half of their family is Christian and the other half is Muslim. . . . the idea that they can reference it at some point when questions arise is exciting. . . . I would highly recommend this book to not only individuals, but also to religious and community organizations that feel as if their congregation or members would be educated through the power of knowledge provided in this book. I appreciate the work that St Michael has put into this work and give it 5 stars."— Christi Lyle-Rasheed for ***Manhattan Book Review***, ★ ★ ★ ★ ★

"The often inflammatory arguments between ideological partisans of Christianity and Islam are rarely conducted by way of sober textual analysis. The complex doctrines of the two religions—as well as the prohibitive nature of the foreign languages in which their primary sources were written—make such comparisons less than accessible. St Michael aims to dismantle that barrier to understanding by supplying an impressively comprehensive catalog of the utterances of Jesus and Muhammad. . . . St Michael clearly wants the texts to speak for themselves. . . . For readers of either faith, such a lucid and unbiased record of the points of commonality and disagreement between Jesus and Muhammad is sure to be educational. And the entire book is scrupulously sourced, adding to the general air of transparency and scholarly rigor. . . . An exhaustive compilation of immense theological value, especially as a prologue to future study." — ***Kirkus Reviews***

"A thought-provoking book that establishes a unique form of dialogue between the two spiritual teachers whose messages are at the core of the two most powerful religions on Earth. . . . The reader can quickly do a comparison between the two sets of scriptures and understand the common lessons shared by the two and what makes their messages unique and different from each other. There is no doubt that this is a well-researched book, and both Christian and Muslim scholars will discover in this work an honest quest for the truth about what divides our world. The book is an in-depth exploration of the core messages of the spiritual guides whose works have been at the heart of some of the greatest revolutions and civilizations the world has ever known. The writer writes in a style that pays homage to the spiritual texts." — Romuald Dzemo for **Readers' Favorite**, ★ ★ ★ ★ ★

"What do Jesus and Muhammad have in common? What makes them different? What is it their followers need to know about their core messages? St Michael offers surprising answers to these questions and allows readers to get to the key messages of the two spiritual figures who have had great impact on human history and man's relationship with God and with fellow man, helping readers make comparisons between the two. . . . The author . . .makes it easy for readers to see the similarities and the differences in what they both taught. . . . The image of the God of Jesus and Muhammad comes out clearly in these passages, and it provokes serious reflection for readers who are engaged in honestly seeking answers to the religious divide that cripples contemporary society. A gift that curious minds as well as those hungry for the truth should read. . . . St Michael has done an incredible job in putting this book together, a great gift for humanity." — Christian Sia for **Readers' Favorite**, ★ ★ ★ ★ ★

"A very well-written and well-researched book. I appreciated the neutral point of view along with the exhaustive factual information presented from not only the Bible and the Koran, but also from historical sources. The writing is crisp and engaging, and there was plenty of information in this book that I wasn't aware of, so that was interesting to learn. . . . This is a book that I would recommend to anyone." — Gisela Dixon for **Readers' Favorite,** ★ ★ ★ ★ ★

"A great book in the area of philosophy and spirituality . . . offers readers a unique opportunity to study two great spiritual leaders of history by looking at their core messages placed side by side. . . . St Michael has done a great job in compiling these writings, and readers will also enjoy the relevant historical notes and references at the beginning of the book. . . . This is a gift for anyone who wants to deepen their understanding of the message of Jesus and Muhammad." — Divine Zape for **Readers' Favorite,** ★ ★ ★ ★ ★

"A thorough and painstakingly researched compilation of the lives and statements, as proclaimed in the Christian Bible and the Islamic Q'uran, of two of the world's most historically compelling men. . . . This is done with a scholarly and impartial aspect, without context or opinion, through the use of graphs, charts, outlines, and with unembellished backstory. *Jesus and Muhammad: Their Messages, Side-by-Side* by Louis St Michael is almost a marvel, and it's absolutely mind-boggling to imagine how St Michael was able to produce such a work in a clean and concise manner. It's been pigeonholed into the genre of religious and philosophical non-fiction, but truly, *Jesus and Muhammad: Their Messages, Side-by-Side* reads like an accessible piece of academia. The side-by-side format allows for instant comparison with little more than the flick of a page. I can see this book being very useful to anyone needing a quick, fact-based resource, as well as those with an interest in learning more about the two fastest growing, influential, and relevant religions of the world. That St Michael achieves this without the usual bias found in such works lends further credence to its usefulness in any conversation on the topic. Highly recommended, and I am grateful to have had the opportunity to read it." — Jamie Michele for **Readers' Favorite**, ★ ★ ★ ★ ★

Préface

One can learn a great deal about a religion by going to the unfiltered source and reading the words of the founder. However, it is clear to the author that no adherent to any religion, no matter how learned or devout, is familiar with all nuances and details of his or her religion. Indeed many followers simply have no access to the holy books of their religions, often written in a different language from their own, and they are dependent on their religious leaders and counsel to determine, interpret and teach the most important messages, as they see it.

This book is not meant to present information for judgement of the faithful of either religion, but rather to elucidate the foundations of the faiths. Faith is simply that, a leap of heart, and those who partake in faith are clearly and simply seeking God in their familiar locales and cultures. A book like this can help clear up misconceptions and lead to better understanding among people of different mind-sets.

What are the messages that Islam and Christianity share? And where do the messages diverge? We have gone to great lengths to gather each speaker's core messages and match them side-by-side, based on topic, so that you can thoughtfully answer these questions.

Since you have cracked open this book, you might know something or nothing about these religions. You're likely not conversant in both. And it will probably be tough for you to make sense of some of these passages, which might feel intimidating or foreign.

We have compiled vocabulary, timelines and life histories in the next pages, which gives valuable context. However, if you are inclined to dive in to the comparisons, feel free to skip ahead to "Purpose" on page 43.

Core messages

- We make every attempt to fully represent the core messages of each messenger.
- At the risk of repetition, we include seemingly similar messages (with discrete differences) to actualize each messenger's relative emphasis on some topics.

Order

- With respect for the Islamic concept that Qur'anic verses should be read in context and in order, within each chapter of this book we present the Qur'anic verses by order of sura (chapter) and aya (verse).
- While we recognize that the ayat are out of order from chapter-to-chapter, we feel that it is valuable to present the content by topic, in sections and chapters.

Matching

- Passages align side-by-side to indicate one of two things: the passages converge or the passages diverge.
- Matching in some cases is evident, and in others more obscure. Some passages simply have no match.

- Muhammad lived a longer life. He delivered the message of the Qur'an for about 20 years, whereas Christ delivered for about three. Thus this book includes more material from Muhammad.

Date Notation

- In the body of the text, Common Era notation is listed first, and then Hijri notation.

- Common Era notation is BCE/CE (Before Common Era/Common Era). This corresponds to the Christian notation BC/AD.

- Hijri notation is BH/AH (In English, Before Hijra/After Hijra). Hijra is the year of the Muslim migration from Mecca to Medina.

  1 AH roughly corresponds with 622 CE. However conversions are approximate, because the New Year begins on a different day for each notation system.

Speakers

- Most New Testament Bible verses in this book contain only Christ's words. If verses *partially* contain Christ's words, quotation marks indicate his words. A few chapters require a narrative (by Christ's apostles) to show a sequence of events: in these chapters, verses that contain *no* words of Christ are italicized.

- The Muslim faith attributes each Qur'anic aya to God. Islamic tradition holds that God directly speaks the words of the Qur'an, through the angel Gabriel, to Muhammad.

Translations

Bible

- Most scholars agree that Jesus primarily spoke Aramaic[1] and perhaps some Hebrew and Koine Greek. The majority agree that all of the books that form the New Testament were written in Koine Greek.[2]

  In this book, we used the New Testament in *The Holy Bible: New Heart English Bible*, edited by Wayne A. Mitchell. This Bible was adapted from the *World English Bible*, with consultation from the *Greek New Testament* (United Bible Societies, 5th ed.) and *Novum Testamentum Graece* (28th ed.)—a version of the *Greek New Testament*.

  The *Greek New Testament* is the original form of the Koine Greek New Testament. It was first compiled in English in 1516 from the *Textus Receptus*, the "received texts" that were the succession of printed Greek texts.

  If footnotes in the *New Heart English Bible* indicate a variance from the *Textus Receptus* source, we used the *Textus Receptus* source.

---

1 Allen C. Myers, ed., *The Eerdmans Bible Dictionary* (Grand Rapids: William B. Eerdmans, 1987) 72.

2 Kurt Aland and Barbara Aland, *The Text of the New Testament*, (Grand Rapids: William B. Eerdmans, 1995) 52.

Qur'an

- Muhammad spoke Arabic. Most scholars agree that the Qur'an was recorded in Arabic.

To compile this book, we used *The Holy Qur'an*, translated by Maulvi (Maulani) Muhammad Ali, originally published in 1917, re-printed in 1920.

We modernized this work, generally by adding pronouns and rearranging syntax for clarity. In keeping with other English translations, we changed "Apostle" to "Messenger" (the Prophet Muhammad) and his "communications" to "Signs" or "Verses." For easier comparison, we changed "Allah" to "God." We also changed archaic words to modern words defined with the same meaning.

In rare cases, we changed a word or added words, for meaning. We indicate such by *square brackets*. (Note that the *parentheses* are the original translator's). We carefully considered these changes, based on consulting the following popular English translators' versions: Saheeh International, Muhammad Marmaduke Pickthall, Abdullah Yusuf Ali, Muhammad Sarwar and A.J. Arberry. We also consulted http://corpus.quran.com/, an open source project (GNU General Public License) that applies natural language computing technology to analyze the Arabic text, word by word. For example, we changed "unjust" to "[wrongdoers]," to coincide with other translations.

When Maulvi Muhammad Ali's numbering of ayat (verses) varies from other commonly used modern Qur'an translations, we use the modern numbering.

Acknowledgements

The thrill of unveiling a book is initially realized when reviewers express interest in your content. My excitement was especially powerful, because the reviewers were enthusiastic, patient and generous.

Thank you, Dr. William Neidinger, for your early, spirited support and precise critique of terminology. Dr. Panayiotis Papageorgiou, you bore down on the history and doctrine, and you shared your valuable expertise and optimism. Dr. David Cook, your persistence, interest, keen eye and deep knowledge of Islam were the source of invaluable and precise feedback. Finally, Dr. Daniel Janosik, I so appreciate your encouragement, scholarship and dedication to reviewing this book.

Family, we burned the candle late into the morning as you offered your gut reactions and perspectives to some thick and complex material. Friends, you kept asking and assuring, heartening and buoying this author on a long quest. Thank you, Rex, for digging in.

I am grateful for all of you.

Introduction

Timeline

 Jesus

Muhammad

B C E	C E
	30-33 (610-607 BH)
7-2 (648-643 BH)	

	C E		C E
	570 (74 BH)		
			632 (11 AH)

Years before ministry (30)   **Years before ministry (42)**

Years of ministry (3)   **Years of ministry (11)**

Years of ministry + battles (9)

Lifespan: 33 years   **Lifespan: 62 years**

Life Stories

 Jesus' Life Story

The life of Christ is taken from the four Gospels (Matthew, Mark, Luke and John) in the New Testament Bible, written between 65-110 CE (574-528 BH). Tradition holds that four of Christ's apostles wrote the four Gospels. Christ died between the years 30-33 CE (610-607 BH).

Contemporary Political Structure

- The Holy Roman Emperor Caesar Augustus rules the Roman Empire, which includes the Judea and Galilee regions.
- Pontius Pilate is the governor of the Judea region. Bethlehem (in the present-day West Bank of Jordan) and Jerusalem (in present-day Israel) are cities in Judea. Herod Antipas is the tetrarch ruler of the Galilee region. Nazareth (in present-day Northern Israel) is a city in Galilee.

Bloodline

- Abraham and wife Sarah > Isaac > Jesus

Contemporary Regional Religions

- Judaism

Background and Birth

- The angel Gabriel announces the Virgin Mary's pregnancy to her: "Rejoice, you highly favored one. The Lord is with you. Blessed are you among women! Do not be afraid, Mary, for you have found favor with God. You will conceive in your womb and bring forth a son, and will call his name Jesus. He will be great, and will be called the Son of the Most High." Mary said, "How can this be, seeing I am a virgin?" Gabriel said, "The Holy Spirit will come on you, and the power of the Most High will overshadow you. Therefore also the Holy One who is born will be called the Son of God." Mary said, "See, the handmaid of the Lord; be it to me according to your word." (Luke 1:26-35, 38)

- Mary visits her cousin Elizabeth, who miraculously is with child at an advanced age, carrying John the Baptist. Without knowing of Mary's pregnancy, when Elizabeth hears Mary's voice, John the Baptist leaps for joy in her womb and the Holy Spirit fills her. She speaks loudly, "Blessed are you among women, and blessed is the fruit of your womb! Why am I so favored, that the mother of my Lord should come to me? Blessed is she who believed, for there will be a fulfillment of the things which have been spoken to her from the Lord." Mary said: "My soul magnifies the Lord, and my spirit rejoices in God my Savior. For He has looked at the humble state of His servant girl. For behold, henceforth all generations will call me blessed. For He who is mighty has done marvelous things for me, And holy is His name." (Luke 1:39-49)

- Mary's betrothed, Joseph, learns in a dream that Mary's son is conceived of the Holy Spirit, and is to be named Jesus (Yeshua in Hebrew, Isho in Aramaic), which means Savior or God is Savior.

- Mary and Joseph travel from Nazareth to Bethlehem, Judea, to register for the census. Jesus of Nazareth is born in Bethlehem.

- Nearby shepherds see an angel who tells them of the Savior's birth. They visit Jesus and pay homage.

- Magi, possibly Zoroastrian priests/astrologers from the East (perhaps Persia), observe the star of the prophesied Christ. They travel to Jerusalem and inquire about the whereabouts of the newborn King of the Jews, and they learn that prophets had foretold the Messiah's birth to be in Bethlehem. They follow the star, find Jesus and pay homage with gifts.

- In fear of a Jewish uprising, King Herod orders the death of all infant boys in the Bethlehem area. Joseph is warned in a dream to flee to Egypt, and later he dreams that it is safe to travel home to Nazareth.

Young Life

- According to Jewish custom, Jesus' parents present him to the Lord at the Jewish Temple. At the temple, his parents meet Simeon and Anna. Simeon is a just and devout man to whom the Holy Spirit had revealed that he would see the Lord's Christ before he died. Simeon recognizes Jesus as "a light to bring revelation to the Gentiles and the glory of your people Israel." Anna is an 84-year-old prophetess who serves God day and night in the temple. She also recognizes the Christ-child and gives thanks to the Lord.

- Jesus is raised in Nazareth.

- In a Jerusalem temple, after Passover, he remains behind for three days, listening to and questioning teachers. The teachers are astonished by his understanding.

- Jesus learns carpentry from his earthly father, Joseph.

- The New Testament Bible contains no information about Jesus' middle years.

Ministry

- The prophet John the Baptist baptizes Jesus in the River Jordan when Jesus is 30 years old. God speaks to those present: "This is My beloved son, in whom I am well pleased."

- Alone in the wilderness, Jesus fasts for 40 days and nights. Satan tempts him, Jesus triumphs over Satan, and angels minister to Jesus.

- In and around Galilee in Northern Jerusalem, Jesus recruits 12 disciples, some of whom are brothers. Many are fishermen, and Jesus tells some of them that he will make them "fishers of men." One is a tax collector.

- Jesus begins his ministry around Galilee, continues through Judea, and ends it in Jerusalem. He preaches and ministers to multitudes for three years, age 30-33.

- Jesus performs miracles of feeding the masses, healing the sick, expelling demons, discernment, raising the dead and defying nature.

- Jesus' transfiguration occurs on a mountain during prayer with three disciples. His face shines like the sun, and his robe becomes white and glistening. The prophets Moses and Elijah appear and speak of Jesus' upcoming passion and mission on Earth. God speaks: "This is My beloved son, in whom I am well pleased. Listen to him!"

- Jesus predicts his own betrayal and death.

Death

- Jewish chief priests and elders call for Jesus' crucifixion, and the Roman governor Pontius Pilate and soldiers carry it out. Jesus is crucified at age 33.

- On the cross, his final words are "Father, into Your hands I commit my spirit." When he dies, the sun darkens, the veil in the Jewish temple tears from top to bottom, the Earth quakes and rocks split. Saints who had died appear in the city to many.

- Pilate gives Christ's body to a rich disciple named Joseph, who lays it in a tomb hewn out of rock. Mary and other women followers anoint the body. A large stone is rolled against the tomb, and Roman soldiers seal the stone and guard the tomb.

- After three days, an angel appears before the guards, Christ's Mother Mary and His follower Mary Magdalene. The angel tells them that Christ has risen from the dead. The tomb is empty. Jewish elders pay the guards to keep it a secret.

- Jesus appears repeatedly (resurrected) over the next 40 days to his mother Mary and to his apostles. He shows them the crucifixion marks on his hands and side, and the apostle Thomas touches his flesh. He tells them to make disciples of all nations, and to tend to his followers.

- Before his ascension, Jesus' final words are "And look, I am with you every day, even to the end of the age."

- As Jesus blesses his disciples, he is carried up into Heaven.

Muhammad's Life Story

The following sections are sourced from *Muhammad* by Martin Lings, published by Inner Traditions International and Bear & Company, © 2006. All rights reserved. http://www.Innertraditions.com. Reprinted with permission of publisher.

Lings compiled his book from the sira literature, Arabic biographies of Muhammad written from 767 CE (149 AH) through the ninth-century (285 AH). Muhammad died in 632 CE (11 AH).

Contemporary Political Structure

- Mecca (a financial center for surrounding tribes) and Yathrib (an agricultural oasis, now called Medina) are cities in the Hejaz region of present-day Saudi Arabia.

- The polytheistic Quraysh tribe rules Mecca. They guard the Ka'bah (sanctuary).

- Jewish and Bedouin tribes rule Yathrib (Medina).

Bloodline

- Abraham and Egyptian handmaid Hagar > Ishmael > Muhammad

- Abraham's wife Sarah cannot conceive. Sarah sanctions Abraham's desire to marry and conceive a son with Hagar, Sarah's Egyptian handmaiden.

- An angel tells Hagar that God will multiply her seed exceedingly, and that she will bear a son and name him Ishmael, which means "God shall hear."

- Hagar bears Ishmael.

- God tells Abraham that Ishmael is blessed, and that God will make him a great nation, but that God's covenant is established with Isaac, whom Sarah will bear.

- Sarah later bears her first child Isaac, and bitterness arises between Sarah and Hagar.

- At Sarah's request and through God's counsel to Abraham, Hagar and Ishmael leave Abraham's household. They enter the desert and survive after the miraculous Well of Zamzam arises from the sand at the touch of Ishmael's heel. They settle near Mecca.

- Later in life, Abraham visits Ishmael and Hagar at Mecca. They build the Ka'bah near the Well of Zamzam, including in the foundation a black celestial stone that an angel brought to Abraham.

- Hagar and Ishmael are buried beneath stones of the Ka'bah.

Unless otherwise noted, the following sections are sourced from *The Life of Mohammad, From Original Sources* by Aloys Sprenger, M.D. published by Presbyterian Mission Press, Godabad, 1851. Public domain.

Sprenger studied medicine, natural sciences and Oriental languages at the University of Vienna. Throughout his career he lived in England, India, Switzerland and Germany, serving in various positions including the principal of Delhi College; examiner, official government interpreter, and secretary of the Asiatic Society of Calcutta; and professor of oriental languages at the University of Bern. He wrote, edited, cataloged and translated a large body of works regarding historical Middle Eastern and Asian figures, religions, philosophies, civilizations, battles, medicine, science and poetry, in various languages. Sprenger methodically studied and cataloged Muhammad's earliest biographers, including the earliest, Ibn Ishaq, who died in 768 CE (151 AH), 141 years after Muhammad's death.

Contemporary Regional Religions

- Polytheistic idol worship, Zoroastrianism, Judaism, Nestorian Christianity (a heretical movement, *see* page 490), Collyridians (a Christian heretical movement that worshipped the Virgin Mary as a goddess),[1] Ebionite Jewish-Christian movement (heretical per Early Christian Church Fathers),[2] Gnosticism (a syncretic religion with heretical Christian ideas, per Early Christian Fathers),[3] Sabianism and Arian Christians (heretical per Early Christian Fathers, *see* page 490).

- Gradually, Meccans allow the Ka'bah to serve as a temple to idols rather than the original Sanctuary of God. Pilgrims are mostly polytheistic idol worshippers: there are 360 idols in and around the Ka'bah.

- However some pilgrims are Christians and Jews who come to honor the Sanctuary of Abraham. There is even an icon of the Virgin Mary and Christ-child painted on a wall inside the Ka'bah.

---

1 Epiphanius, *The Panarion of Epiphanius of Salamis: Sects 47-80, De Fide*, (Cyprus: 374-377 CE), Frank Williams, trans, (Boston: Brill, 2012), 567, The Collyridian sect, who offer a loaf in the name of Mary on a certain set day of the year.

2 Irenaeus, *Against Heresies*, (Smyrna: 174-189 CE), (Pickerington: Beloved, 2015), 388, 428. Ebionites believed that Jesus was non-divine.

3 Ibid., 34-37,.74-78, 91, 125-126, 190, 211, 225, 229, 254, 292, 303, 310, 388, 399, 485-486.

Background and Birth

- Muhammad's grandfather, Abd al-Muttalib, prays only to God. Nevertheless he acts as Ka'bah host to the intertribal, polytheistic pilgrims. A dream-vision tells him to dig for the lost well Zamzam near the Ka'bah. He digs and restores the well.

- A light shines from the forehead of Muhammad's grandfather, and rays fall on the Ka'bah. He is known to have supernatural powers, and the ability to bring rain. Later writers comment that this shows the nobility of the prophet.

- Muhammad's father, 'Abd Allah, dies from illness on a trading trip to Syria, leaving a pregnant wife, Aminah. While pregnant, Aminah has visions that she will give birth to the lord and prophet of his nation, and that she is to name her child Muhammad.

- Two months after his father dies, Muhammad is born Muhammad ibn 'Abdullah in 570 CE (74 BH) in Mecca, Hejaz, Arabia. He belongs to a prominent clan in Mecca that is part of the Quraysh tribe.

- Shortly after she gives birth, Aminah dreams of an intense light shining within herself, illuminating the castles of Bostra in Syria. Hearing this, Muhammad's grandfather names him Muhammad, meaning "praised."

Young Life

- According to local custom for sons of great families in Arab towns, Muhammad's mother gives him to Bedouin tribes to be suckled and weaned. His four-year-old foster brother reports that when Muhammad is around age two, two angels split open his chest and wash his heart in snow.

- In fear that Muhammad is possessed by an evil spirit, his foster-parents return him to his mother in Mecca. When he is six years old, his mother dies.

- Muhammad's grandfather Abd al-Muttalib, the keeper of the Ka'bah, raises him and takes him to the Ka'bah daily.

- When his grandfather dies, his uncle Abu Talib, a merchant and leader of the Banu Hashim tribe, raises him. On a merchant trip with his uncle, a Nestorian monk recognizes Muhammad as a prophet. The monk has been identified as Bahira by Muslim historians and as Sergius by Christians.

- While no Arabic translation of the Bible exists, Muhammad is exposed to certain parts of Christian and Jewish theology from various orthodox and unorthodox sources.

Middle Years

- In his early twenties, Muhammad is a merchant.

- At age 25, he marries Khadijah, a wealthy merchant who had employed Muhammad to assist in her trade mission. She had been married twice; she is 40 years old.

- Khadijah bears two sons who die before the age of two and four daughters.

- During renovation of the Ka'bah, Meccan leaders cannot agree on which clan should have the honor of replacing the sacred Black Stone. They agree to ask the next man who walks through the gates, who is Muhammad.

- Before age 40, Muhammad devoutly worships the gods of his fathers. Yearly, he spends the month of Ramadan meditating in seclusion in a cave of Mount Hira, near Mecca, where the Quraysh tribe (and possibly a few Christians) goes for ascetic exercises (prayer, fasting, meditating, feeding the poor, and circling the Ka'bah seven times on the return trip home).

- At age 40, he begins to doubt idolatry. Alone in the cave, an angel Gabriel commands Muhammad to read. Muhammad protests that he is not a reader: the angel repeats the command and intensely squeezes him three times, telling him "Read in the name of your Lord, the Creator, who has created man of congealed blood. Read, for your Lord is most beneficent. It is He who has taught by the pen (has revealed the Verses); it is He who has taught man what he does not know."

- Muhammad doubts the soundness of his mind. He tells his wife that he hears a sound, sees a light and is afraid that there are Jinn in him. She tells him that he will be the prophet of his nation.

- After this revelation, there is a period of silence, which causes Muhammad distress. One day while melancholic, he intends to throw himself off of a mountain, near Mecca, where he often wanders. He hears a voice from Heaven and sees the angel Gabriel between Heaven and Earth: "Oh Muhammad, you are in reality the prophet of God, and I am Gabriel." After this, revelations come, one after another.

- Before revelations, he is despondent. He then shivers, hears bells or humming (like swarming bees), his lips quiver, his eyes become fixed and his head motions become convulsive. He perspires profusely and sometimes falls comatose to the ground.

- Gabriel teaches Muhammad prayer postures and worship purification.

Ministry

- From the age of 43 until his death at age 62, Muhammad speaks publicly and leads his followers. His First followers are family members. Soon others seek his advice. Followers gather in glens outside of Mecca to pray the ritual prayer.

- Muhammad takes the Night Journey, a dream-vision wherein Gabriel transports him to Jerusalem on a winged steed to "the farthest mosque," the Temple Mount (the site of the first and second Jewish Temples). The present-day Al-Aqsa Mosque is later built here, in 691 CE (71 AH). Abraham, Moses and Jesus gather behind Muhammad (their elder brother, and the greatest among them) in prayer, and then Muhammad and Gabriel ascend Jacob's ladder, on the steed, to tour the seven levels of Heaven. In the sixth level he meets Moses, who cries from jealousy that Muhammad surpassed him, and he meets the angel of Hell, Malik, who punishes the enemies of Islam. Muhammad requests to see the fires of Hell, which he sees when Malik briefly removes the cover over Hell. In the seventh level he meets Abraham. Finally, God tells him how many times per day his people should pray: God initially proclaims fifty, and He finally reduces it to five.

- Muhammad immediately repeats his revelations to his companions, who memorize and recite them, passing them mouth-to-mouth. The revelations later form the Qur'an.

- Polytheistic idolators ridicule Muhammad and his followers. At the Ka'bah, he insults their idols and attempts to convert them to Islam. Converts repeat "I testify that there is no god but God, and that Muhammad is the Messenger of God."

- As more convert, the Quraysh tribe's livelihood is threatened because polytheistic pilgrimages are curtailed and revenues go down. Hostilities grow toward Muhammad, and persecutions begin, so he sends his followers to Abyssinia (modern-day Eritrea and Ethiopia), where they live under the protection of a Christian emperor.

- After preaching for about nine years in Mecca and under political pressure and threats of assassination, Muhammad moves first his followers (later known as the Emigrants), and then himself, to Yathrib (contemporary Medina). A Jewish community lives there, so Yathrib Arabs accept monotheism more readily.

Expeditions Ordered by Muhammad

Unless otherwise cited, this section is sourced from *Military career of Muhammad: The Complete Guide*, a Wikipedia® Book, retrieved from https://en.wikipedia.org/wiki/Book:Military_career_of_Muhammad (accessed December, 2017).

- Muhammad orders 95-97 expeditions in his lifetime. He attends 26-27 of them:

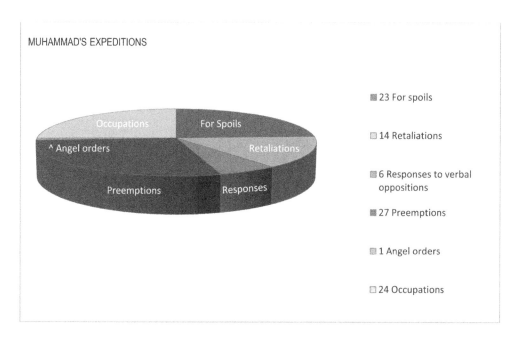

MUHAMMAD'S EXPEDITIONS

Occupations · For Spoils · Angel orders · Retaliations · Preemptions · Responses

- 23 For spoils
- 14 Retaliations
- 6 Responses to verbal oppositions
- 27 Preemptions
- 1 Angel orders
- 24 Occupations

- Muhammad's followers also take part in two additional battles that Muhammad did not initiate: The Expedition of Raji (5 Muslims die, 1 captured) and the Expedition of Bir Maona (40-70 Muslims die and 2 non-Muslims die). In these expeditions, Muhammad sends missionaries at the request of other tribes who express interest in Islam. Upon arrival, the "interested" tribes initiate battles.

- The expeditions begin in the year 623 CE (1 AH), after Muhammad and his followers migrate from Mecca to Medina.
- Initially, Muhammad unites the Medina-area Jewish and Arab tribes with the Meccan Emigrants under the Constitution of Medina. Together they fight the Meccan tribes for five years (623-628 CE/1-6 AH).
- In March of 628 CE (6 AH), Muhammad initiates the Treaty of Hudaybiyyah with Mecca. The treaty affirms a ten-year peace with Mecca and authorizes Muhammad and his followers to return to Mecca the following year in a peaceful pilgrimage to the Ka'bah (the Lesser Pilgrimage). In December of 629 CE (8 AH), an army of 10,000 Muslims marches on the city of Mecca and takes it with little bloodshed. They destroy the pagan idols in the city, and Muhammad sends troops to destroy all remaining temples in Eastern Arabia.
- Until his death in 632 CE (11 AH), Muhammad continues to initiate battles with other neighboring tribes.

EXPEDITIONS: RAIDS AND ATTACKS FOR SPOILS		
EXPEDITION (CE/AH YEAR)	DEATHS AND CAPTURES	CIRCUMSTANCE
Raids against Quraysh tribe caravans: Al Is Caravan Raid (623/1)[1] Batn Rabigh Caravan Raid (623/1)[2] Kharar Caravan Raid (623/1)[3] Invasion of Waddan (623/2) Invasion of Buwat (623/2) Invasion of Dul Ashir (623/2) Nakhla Raid (624/2) Battle of Badr (624/2) Nejd Caravan Raid (624/3) Invasion of Badr (625/4 or 626/4) Expedition of Zaid ibn Haritha (Al-Is) (627/6)	Cumulative this group: Muslims: 14 died Non-Muslims: 71 died, 73+ captured	Initially relieved poverty brought on by Muslim property loss in Mecca and emigration to Medina. Later furthered Muslim political, economic and military position.
Expedition of Zaid ibn Haritha (Al-Jumum) (627/6)	Non-Muslims: Some captured, one woman freed to marry a Muslim	Raided the Banu Salim tribe at Al-Jumum village. Muslims gained a lot of booty.
Expedition of Muhammad ibn Maslamah (627/6)	Non-Muslims: 10 died, 1 captured	Attacked the Bani Bakr tribe and retrieved plenty of booty.
Expedition of Ukasha bin Al-Mihsan (627/6)	None	The Banu Assad bin Qhusayma tribe fled, but the Muslims gained 200 camels

1 "Caravan Raids," *INFOGALACTIC*, https://infogalactic.com/info/Caravan_raids (accessed December 2017).

2 Ibid.

3 Ibid.

EXPEDITIONS: RAIDS AND ATTACKS FOR SPOILS (Con't)		
EXPEDITION (CE/AH YEAR)	DEATHS AND CAPTURES	CIRCUMSTANCE
Third Raid on Banu Thalabah (627/6)	None	The tribe had fled, but the Muslims captured their camels.
Expedition of Umar ibn al-Khatab (628/7)	None	Sent to attack the Banu Hawazin tribe, who fled, but the Muslims got booty.
Expedition of Bashir Ibn Sad al-Ansari (Fadak) (628/7)	Non-Muslims: Many died Muslims: 29 died	Attacked the Banu Murrah tribe, seized cattle and camels.
Expedition of Ghalib ibn Abdullah al-Laithi (Mayfah) (629/7)	Non-Muslims: Some died	Attacked the Banu 'Awal and Banu Thalabah tribes, took camels and flock.
Expedition of Ghalib ibn Abdullah al-Laithi (Al-Kadid) (629/8)	Non-Muslims: Large number died, 1 captured	Raided the Banu al-Mulawwih tribe, took great deal of booty.
Expedition of Shuja ibn Wahb al-Asadi (629/8)	Unknown	Raided and plundered camels and sheep.
Expedition of Abu Ubaidah ibn al Jarrah (629/8)	None	Sent to attack and chastise the Juhaynah tribe and observe a Quraysh caravan.
Expedition of Abu Qatadah ibn Rab'i al-Ansari (Batn Edam) (629/8)	Muslims:1 died by Muslims	Eight men attacked a caravan passing through Edam, to divert attention from Muhammad's intention to attack Mecca.
Expedition of Qutbah ibn Amir (630/9)	Non-Muslims: Many died, women captured Muslims: Many died	Attacked the Banu Khatham tribe as they slept, captured a large number of camels and goats.

EXPEDITIONS: RETALIATION OR REVENGE		
EXPEDITION (CE/AH YEAR)	DEATHS AND CAPTURES	CIRCUMSTANCE
Invasion of Safwan (623/2)	None	Sent to retaliate for looting. The tribe fled.
Invasion of Banu Qaynuqa (624/2)	None	A member of this Jewish tribe pinned the clothes of a Muslim woman, causing them to rip when she moved. Muslims invaded, the tribe surrendered and Muhammad was convinced to expel them (vs. kill them). He distributed their property to the Muslims and kept one fifth for himself.

EXPEDITIONS: RETALIATION OR REVENGE (Con't)

EXPEDITION (CE/AH YEAR)	DEATHS AND CAPTURES	CIRCUMSTANCE
Invasion of Sawiq (624/2)	Muslims: 2 died	Retaliated for the killing of two Muslims and the burning of a cornfield.
The Mission of Amr bin Umayyah al-Damri (627/6)	Non-Muslims: 3 died, 1 captured	Attempted to kill Abu Safyan of the Quraysh tribe, because the Quraysh had killed a Muslim (who had killed a Quraysh).
Second Raid on Banu Thalabah (627/6)	Non-Muslims: 1 captured	Retaliated for the first raid, where nine Muslims died.
Invasion of Banu Lahyan (627/6)	None	Sent to retaliate for the Expedition of Al Raji, where 10 Muslims died. The tribe fled.
Raid on al-Ghabah (627/6)	Muslims: 1 shepherd died, his wife was captured	Muhammad's commander pursued a shepherd who had seized 20 of Muhammad's camels. Muhammad sent reinforcements.
Expedition of Dhu Qarad (627/6)	Non-Muslims: 4 died Muslims: 4 died	Attacked a group who had raided the outskirts of Medina, seized 20 of Muhammad's camels, killed a shepherd and taken his wife.
Expedition of Zaid ibn Haritha (Hisma) (628/7)	Non-Muslims: Heavy casualties, 100 women and boys captured	Attacked robbers who had attacked Muhammad's envoy.
Second Expedition of Wadi al-Qura (628/6)	Non-Muslims: 30 warriors (including 1 woman) died, many captured	Raided Wadi al-Qura inhabitants because nine Muslims died when Muhammad raided them previously.
Expedition of Kurz bin Jabir Al-Fihri (628/6)	Non-Muslims: 8 tortured to death Muslims: 1 died	Response to eight who came to Muhammad seeking "conversion to Islam," and then killed a Muslim and stole Muhammad's camels.
Expedition of Ghalib ibn Abdullah al-Laithi (Fadak) (629/8)	Non-Muslims: Everyone who come into contact with Muslims died.	Attacked the Banu Murrah as revenge for Muslim deaths in a prior failed raid by Muslims.
Battle of Mu'tah (629/8)	Non-Muslims: Unknown Muslims: 12 died	Raided the inhabitants of Mu'tah, because one of Muhammad's messengers was killed by the Byzantine governor of Ma'ab or Mu'tah.
Expedition of Khalid ibn al-Walid (2nd Dumatul Jandal) (631/9)	Non-Muslims: All who resisted died	Invaded the city of Dumat Al-Jandal to retaliate for the killings of Muslim imams. Also demolished the idol Wadd, worshipped by the Banu Kilab tribe.

EXPEDITIONS /ASSASSINATIONS: RESPONSE TO VERBAL OPPOSITION

EXPEDITION (CE/AH YEAR)	DEATHS AND CAPTURES	CIRCUMSTANCE
Assassination of Asama bint Marwan (624/2)	Asama bint Marwan assassinated.	The assassinated opposed Muhammad with poetry and provoked others to attack Muhammad.
Assassination of Abu Afak (624/2)	Abu Afak assassinated.	The assassinated opposed Muhammad with poetry.
Assassination of Ka'b ibn al-Ashraf (624/2)	Ka'b ibn al-Ashraf assassinated.	The assassinated complained about Muhammad and composed verses about the Battle of Badr victims and insulting verses about Muslim women.
Expedition of 'Abdullah ibn 'Atik (624/2)	Abu Rafi' ibn Al-Huqaiq assassinated.	The assassinated mocked Muhammad with poetry and provided money and supplies to opposition troops.
Expedition of Abdullah Ibn Unais (625/4)	Khalid bin Sufyan assassinated.	The assassinated reportedly incited the people of Nakhla or Uranah.
Demolition of Masjid al-Dirar (630/8)	None, perhaps some burned	After people built the mosque to minister to the sick and poor, they asked Muhammad to come and pray for them. But he believed they promoted opposition to him, so he ordered his men to burn down the mosque.

EXPEDITIONS: PREEMPTION OF SUSPECTED ATTACKS

EXPEDITION (CE/AH YEAR)	DEATHS AND CAPTURES	CIRCUMSTANCE
Al Kudr Invasion (624/2)	Unknown	Surprise attack to preempt an alleged plot by the Banu Salim tribe to attack Medina.
Invasion of Dhi Amr (624/3)	Non-Muslims:1 captured	Invaded after receiving intelligence that the Banu Muharib and Banu Talabah tribes planned to raid the outskirts of Medina.
Invasion of Buhran (624/3)	None	A patrolling expedition because the Muslims heard that the Banu Sulaym were advancing on Medina.
Battle of Uhud (625/3)	Non-Muslims: 22-37 died Muslims: 70 died	Muslims were warned of the Quraysh army's approach: the Quraysh avenged the Battle of Badr.

EXPEDITIONS: PREEMPTION OF SUSPECTED ATTACKS (Con't)

EXPEDITION (CE/AH YEAR)	DEATHS AND CAPTURES	CIRCUMSTANCE
Invasion of Hamra al-Asad (625/3)	Non-Muslims: 2 captives die Muslims: 2 spies died	Invaded to prevent a Quraysh attack on the weakened Muslim army.
Expedition of Qatan (625/4)	Non-Muslims: 3 captured	Invaded to preempt an alleged plot by the Banu Asad bin Khuzaymah tribe, based on intelligence received.
Invasion of Banu Nadir (625/4)	Unknown	Attacked the Banu Nadir tribe after the angel Gabriel told Muhammad that some of them wanted to assassinate him.
Expedition of Dhat al-Riqa (625/5 or 627/7)	Non-Muslims: Many women captured	Attacked after hearing that the Banu Ghatafan tribe were suspiciously assembling at Dhat al-Riqa.
Invasion of Dumatil Jandal (626/5)	None	Invaded in response to intelligence that some tribes were prepared to attack Medina.
Battle of the Trench (627/5)	Non-Muslims: Heavy casualties Muslims: Light casualties	Defended against a potential attack by Jewish Banu Nadir and confederate tribes in alliance with the Quraysh tribe. Jewish tribes were vengeful for being expelled from Medina by Muhammad.
First Raid on Banu Thalabah (627/6)	Muslims: 10 died	Attacked the tribe because Muhammad suspected they would be tempted to steal his camels.
Expedition Zaid ibn Haritha (Wadi al-Qura) (627/6)	Muslims: 9 died	Surveyed the area and monitored the movements of Muhammad's enemies.
Invasion of Banu Mustaliq (627/6)	Non-Muslims: 10 died, 200 families captured Muslims: 1 died in friendly fire	In response to rumors that the tribe was gathering against the Muslims, the Muslims performed a surprise attack while the tribe watered its herds.
Expedition of Fadak (627/6)	Non-Muslims: 1 captured	Attacked the Banu Sad bin Bakr tribe in response to intelligence that the tribe was planning to help the Jews of Khaybar. Took 500 camels and 2,000 goats.
Expedition of Abdullah ibn Rawaha (628/6)	Non-Muslims: 30 died	Attacked the Al-Yusayr ibn Rizam group after hearing they were was preparing to attack Muslims.

EXPEDITIONS: PREEMPTION OF SUSPECTED ATTACKS (Con't)

EXPEDITION (CE/AH YEAR)	DEATHS AND CAPTURES	CIRCUMSTANCE
Expedition of Bashir Ibn Sad al-Ansari (Yemen) (628/7)	Non-Muslims: 1 died, 2 captured	Attacked a large group of polytheists whom Muslims believed had gathered to raid the outskirts of Medina.
Expedition of Ka'b ibn 'Umair al-Ghifari (629/8)	Muslims: 14 died	Attacked the Banu Quda'a tribe after receiving intelligence that the tribe had gathered a large number to attack Muslim positions.
Expedition of Amr ibn al-As (629/8)	Unknown	Rumors were that the Banu Qudah were preparing to attack Medina, so the Muslims tried to subjugate them.
Expedition of Abi Hadrad al-Aslami (629/7)	Non-Muslims: 1 beheaded, 4 women captured	Assassinated Rifa'ah bin Quays, because Muhammad heard that he was enticing people of Qais to fight the Muslims.
Expedition of Abu Qatadah ibn Rab'i al-Ansari (Khadirah) (629/8)	Non-Muslims: Some died, some captured	After hearing that the Banu Sulaym tribe were amassing troops, the Muslims attacked the tribe and captured large amounts of flock.
Battle of Hunayn (630/8)	Non-Muslims: 70 died, 6,000 women and children captured Muslims: Unknown large number	The Hawazin and Thaqif tribes were concerned about Muslim conversions all around them, and they were threatening to overwhelm the Muslims. Hearing this, 12,000 Muslims met and fought them and took enormous spoils, including 24,000 camels.
Battle of Autas (630/8)	Non-Muslims: Many died	With 12,000 fighters, defeated an alliance of tribes that formed in defense against Muhammad.
Expedition of Abu Amir Al-Ashari (630/8)	Non-Muslims: 9 died Muslims: 1 died	Preemptively chased survivors who had fled from the Battle of Hunayn. The expedition commander died.
Expedition of Abu Musa Al-Ashari (630/8)	Non-Muslims: 1 or more died. Men, women and children captured	Preemptively chased survivors who had fled from the Battle of Hunayn. Captured war booty.
Expedition to Tabouk (630/8)	None	In response to rumors of a possible attack by the Byzantine Emperor Heraclius, 30,000 Muslim troops captured Tabouk. No Byzantines were found.
Siege of Ta'if (630/8)	Non-Muslims: Unknown Muslims: 12 died	Survivors who had fled from the Battle of Hunayn were now in the city of Ta'if, preparing to attack the Muslims. The Muslims unsuccessfully used catapults to try to break through the fortress at Ta'if.
Expedition of Alqammah bin Mujazziz (630/9)	None	Sent to attack a group of Abyssinians (Ethiopians) whom Muhammad suspected were pirates. They fled.

EXPEDITIONS: BY ORDER OF THE ANGEL GABRIEL

EXPEDITION (CE/AH YEAR)	DEATHS AND CAPTURES	CIRCUMSTANCE
Invasion of Banu Qurayza (627/5)	Non-Muslims: 600-900 males and one female beheaded, remaining women/children captured Muslims: 2 died	Seized the Jewish Banu Qurayza tribe who had remained neutral in fighting between the Medina Muslims and the Meccans.

EXPEDITIONS: OCCUPATION, TAXATION AND/OR CONVERSION TO ISLAM

EXPEDITION (CE/AH YEAR)	DEATHS AND CAPTURES	CIRCUMSTANCE
Expedition of Abdur Rahman bin Auf (627/6)	None	700 went to the Arabian oasis Fadak, Khabar, to convert Christian King Al-Asbagh and his people to Islam within 3 days, or pay a tax. They paid.
Conquest of Fadak (628/7)	None	Forced the Jews of Fadak to surrender property and wealth, accept Muhammad's terms, or be attacked. They agreed to give half their property and wealth and continue to work the land to share the crop yield. Muhammad reserved the right to banish them, which occurred later (with restitution for half the land), under Caliph Umar.
Battle of Khaybar (628/7)	Non-Muslims: 93 Jews died Muslims: 16-18 died	Attacked the Jews of Khaybar. Confiscated their land and distributed their goods and weapons among Muslims. After the Jews pleaded, allowed them to remain under protection, practice their religion without military service, work the confiscated land, and give half of the yield to the Muslims. Later, Caliph Umar expelled them.
Third Expedition of Wadi al Qura (628/7)	Non-Muslims: 11 Jews died Muslims: 1 died	Invited the Jewish colony to embrace Islam, conquered their land with arrangements similar to Fadak and Khaybar.
Expedition of Abu Bakr As-Siddiq (628/7)	Non-Muslims: At least 7 families died, many prisoners	Attacked the Banu Kilab tribe.
Expedition of Ibn Abi Al-Awja Al-Sulami (629/8)	Non-Muslims: Most died, 2 captured Muslims: Most died	Demanded allegiance of the Banu Sulaym tribe to Islam. Tribe refused, fighting ensued.
Conquest of Mecca (630/8)	Non-Muslims: 19 died Muslims: 2 died	Conquered Mecca with little bloodshed. At the Ka'bah, broke idols and destroyed gods.

EXPEDITIONS: OCCUPATION, TAXATION AND/OR CONVERSION TO ISLAM (Con't)

EXPEDITION (CE/AH YEAR)	DEATHS AND CAPTURES	CIRCUMSTANCE
Expedition of Khalid ibn al-Walid (Nakhla) (630/8)	Non-Muslims: 1 woman died, said to be the idol goddess herself	Destroyed the temple of the idol goddess Al-Uzza.
Raid of Amr ibn al-As (630/8)	None	One man was sent to destroy the Suwa deity worshipped by the Banu Hudhail. The doorkeeper told him he would not be able to destroy it, but he did, so the doorkeeper became Muslim on the spot.
Raid of Sad ibn Zaid al-Ashhali (630/8)	Non-Muslims: 1 woman died, said to be the idol goddess herself	Destroyed the Manat goddess idol, which was worshipped by the Al-Aws and Al-Khazraj tribes.
Expedition of Khalid ibn al-Walid (Banu Jadhimah) (630/8)	Non-Muslims: Entire tribe initially taken as prisoners, some executed	Invited the Banu Jadhimah tribe to Islam. Some accepted, but Khalid captured all and executed some before he was stopped. Muslims paid the survivors blood money.
Expedition of Al-Tufail ibn 'Amr Ad-Dausi (630/8)	None	Destroyed the idol Yaguth, and secured conversion of the Banu Daws tribe, who lent catapults for use in the Seige of Taif.
Expedition of Uyainah bin Hisn (630/9)	Non-Compliant Muslims: 11 men, 22 women and 30 boys captured	A delegation went to collect tax from a sub-tribe of the (Muslim) Banu Tamim, but they drove away the Muslims. The Muslims returned with 50 fighters who attacked the sub-tribe and took captives. Tribal leaders went to Medina, begged forgiveness of Muhammad and recited poetry. Muhammad released the captives.
Expedition of Dahhak al-Kilabi (630/9)	Non-Muslims: 1 died as his Muslim son held him down.	Called the Banu Kilab tribe to embrace Islam. They refused, and fighting ensued.
Expedition of Ali ibn Abi Talib (630/9)	Non-Muslims: A number of men, women (including chief's sister) and children captives	Raided Christian Banu Tai tribe, some of whom also worshipped the idol al-Qullus. Destroyed the idol, took camels, sheep and armaments. Chief later converted to Islam.
Expedition of Ukasha bin Al-Mihsan (Udrah and Baliy) (630/9)	Unknown	Attacked the Christian Udhrah and Baliy tribes, some of whom also worshipped the idol al-Shams. Possibly some were disaffected Muslims.

EXPEDITIONS: OCCUPATION, TAXATION AND/OR CONVERSION TO ISLAM (Con't)		
EXPEDITION (CE/AH YEAR)	DEATHS AND CAPTURES	CIRCUMSTANCE
Expedition of Khalid ibn al-Walid (Dumatul Jandal) (630/8 or 631/9)	Non-Muslims: 1 died, 2 captured	Captured the Christian Prince of Duma and his brother, and killed another brother. Ransomed 2000 camels, 800 sheep, 400 armors and 400 lances. Exacted a tax on Dumat, Tabuk, Ailah and Taima.
Expedition of Abu Sufyan ibn Harb (630/9)	Unknown	Muhammad sent a few men to demolish the idol al-Lat and retrieve it's treasure and ornamentation. Used the treasure to pay back a debt owed by one of the men to Muhammad.
Expedition of Surad ibn Abdullah (631/10 or 632/10)	Non-Muslims: Heavy casualties among the people of Jurash	Muhammad ordered Surad ibn Abdullah (a new convert) to lead a battle against the non-Muslim tribes in his neighborhood.
Expedition of Khalid ibn al-Walid (Najran) (631/10)	None	Some of the Banu Harith tribe of Najran were Christian and some were polytheistic. A Christian bishop with delegation visited Muhammad, engaging him in a debate about the divinity of Christ. Muhammad ordered the tribe to pay the Jizyah (tax) and give Muhammad 2,000 garments in exchange for peace and security. One year later, Muhammad sent an expedition to Najran to offer the polytheists in the tribe to embrace Islam or fight the Muslims. They converted, and Muhammad told them that had they not, he would have beheaded them.
Expedition of Ali ibn Abi Talib (Mudhij) (631/10)	Non-Muslims: 20 died	Attacked the Banu Nakhla tribe, "Followers of the Book," for submission to Islam. After killing 20, they held back and offered conversion. The tribe converted, and the fighters returned with many spoils, including camels, flocks, women and children.
Expedition of Ali ibn Abi Talib (Hamdan) (631/10)	None	Called the people of Hamdan to embrace Islam: they did, after initially refusing for six months.
Demolition of Dhul Khalasa (632/10)	Non-Muslims: 300 died	Demolished and burned the cult Temple of Dhul Khalasa, worshipped by the Bahila, Khatham and Banu-Qubafah tribes.
Expedition of Usama bin Zayd (632/11)	Non-Muslims: Many die, many captured	As Muhammad was dying, 3,000 men followed his order to invade Palestine and attack the Balqa and Darum regions.

Marriages and Relationships

This section is largely sourced from *The Life of Mohammad, From Original Sources* by Aloys Sprenger, M.D. (Godabad: Presbyterian Mission Press, 1851) and *The Life of Muhammad: A Translation of Ibn Ishaq's Sirat Rasul God*, by A Guillaume, (Oxford: Oxford University Press, 2004).

- Muslims respectfully refer to Muhammad's wives and bondmaidens as the Mothers of the Faithful.

- After his first wife Khadijah dies after 25 years of marriage, Muhammad is married to multiple wives simultaneously. Each wife (or bondmaiden) has a separate apartment and appointed times with Muhammad.

- Muhammad has three sons (two with Khadijah and one with Mariyah), and he raises four daughters. All precede him in death (in childhood) except his daughter Fatimah. Most Shia Muslims accept only Fatimah as a true daughter, the other three having been part of Khadijah's household before Muhammad married her.

MUHAMMAD'S MARRIAGES AND RELATIONSHIPS		
WIFE	MARRIAGE AGE WIFE:MUHAMMAD	CIRCUMSTANCE
Khadijah bint Khuwaylid	40:25	She is a wealthy merchant who hires Muhammad as a trade agent. She had been married twice before, and she proposes to him and bares him two sons (Qasim dies before age two, Abdallah dies in childhood). They raise four daughters (Zaynab, Ruqayyah, Umm Kulthum and Fatimah). After 25 years of marriage, Khadijah dies when Muhammad is nearly 50 years old.
Sawdah bint Zam'a	30:50	Sawdah is one of the followers who goes to live in Abbysinia with her husband, who later dies. Muhammad marries her, a widow.
A'ishah bint Abi Bakr	9:53	She is the daughter of Abu Bakr, a devoted follower. He promises her to Muhammad at age 6, she marries him at age 9. She is his "favorite" after the death of his first wife, Khadijah.
Hafsah bint Umar	18:55	She is the widow of a follower who returned from Abbysinia. She is introduced to Muhammad by Umar, who later becomes a trusted companion of Muhammad and finally the second caliph of the four Rightly-guided Caliphs.
Zaynab bint Khuzayma	Late 20s:56	She is a Bedouin, whose husband dies in battle for Islam. She marries Muhammad a year after being widowed, and she dies eight months after the marriage.
Zaynab bint Jahsh	40:58	After she divorces Muhammad's adopted son, Muhammad receives a vision that (only) he can be married to more than four wives simultaneously, and that Zaynab will be a wife.

MUHAMMAD'S MARRIAGES AND RELATIONSHIPS

WIFE	MARRIAGE AGE WIFE:MUHAMMAD	CIRCUMSTANCE
Umm Salama (Hind bint Abi Umayya)	29:56	At marriage, she is four months a widow: After Khadijah, she is the most influential wife.
Juwayriyah bint al-Harith	20:59	She is a captive from a defeated Arab tribe and a daughter of the tribal leader. Because of her marriage, her kinsmen convert to Islam, and Muhammad releases them.
Umm Habiba (Ramlah bint Abi Sufyan)	34:59	Her husband, the Prophet's cousin, converts from Islam to Christianity while living in Abyssinia. She remains Muslim, her husband dies, and Muhammad marries her in absentia and sends for her.
Rayhana bint Zayd	Unknown:60	Muhammad's armies defeat the Jewish Banu Qurayza tribe. Rayhana is enslaved, and the men are executed. Initially she refuses to accept Islam, but she later converts. Muhammad offers to marry her, but she chooses to remain a maiden-slave, and she dies young, about five years after her capture.
Safiyyah bint Huyayy	17:60	Muhammad's armies defeat the Jewish Banu Nadir tribe in battle. Safiyyah's husband is tortured and dies. She is captured with all of the women, and Muhammad chooses her. She converts to Islam, and Muhammad marries her.
Maymunah bint al-Harith	Late 20s-Early 30s:61	During the Lesser Pilgrimage, a follower of Muhammad from the Quraysh tribe visits Muhammad's camp at the Ka'bah Mosque and offers his wife's sister in marriage to Muhammad. She is a widow.
Mariyah bint Shamun (Maria al-Qibtiyyah)	Unknown:61	In response to a summons to Islam by Muhammad, the Christian ruler of Egypt (Muqawqis) sends gold, gifts and Mariyah and her sister as slaves. Mariyah is beautiful, and he keeps her as a legally-acquired bondmaiden, in an apartment adjoining the mosque. He visits her day and night, and she bears him a son, Ibrahim, who dies at 18 months.

Death

This section is sourced from *The Life of Muhammad: A Translation of Ibn Ishaq's Sirat Rasul God*, by A Guillaume, (Oxford: Oxford University Press, 2004), 678-688.

- He suffers from head pain for a few days.
- He dies on June 8, 632 CE (11 AH) at age 62, with his head resting on his favorite wife's lap (Aisha).
- His final words are, "No, the most Exalted Companion is of Paradise."
- He is buried where he dies, in Aisha's house (the present-day Green Dome at al-Masjid an-Nabawi, Medina, Saudi Arabia).

Glossary

 ## Christian Terms

- **Apostle:** One sent out by Christ to spread the faith. The original twelve whom Jesus sent out are the Twelve Apostles, the closest disciples of Jesus during His life and ministry. The Seventy Apostles are also early emissaries of Jesus. (Luke 10:1-24) Jesus appoints them and sends them out in pairs on specific missions of healing.

- **Bible:** The Hebrew Bible is known by the Jewish people as the Tanakh. It includes the Written Torah, the Prophets and the Writings, and it was assembled as Jewish canon (Masoretic Text) between 7-10 CE (635-630 BH).

  The Christian Old Testament was taken from the Hebrew Bible and the Septuagint.[1] The Septuagint was the Hebrew text that was studied by Greek-speaking Jewish people throughout the Roman Empire at the time of Christ. The Septuagint is in Greek, translated by Jewish scholars of the day.

  The later New Testament describes Christ's life and mission, and it contains the four Gospels written (tradition holds) by four of Christ's apostles (Matthew, Mark, Luke, John).

- **Chapters and verses:** A chapter is akin to a sura in the Qur'an. A verse is akin to an aya in the Qur'an.

- **Disciple:** One who learns from another. The twelve students of Jesus during His ministry, known as the Twelve Disciples. They are Andrew, Bartholomew (Nathanael), James of Zebedee, James of Alphaeus, John, Judas Iscariot, Jude (Thaddaeus), Matthew, Peter (Simon Peter), Philip, Simon and Thomas. All but Judas Iscariot later become apostles—Matthias replaces the disciple Judas, after Judas betrays Christ.

- **False Prophets:** Christ said that many deceiving false prophets will come after Him, in sheep's clothing, some in His name, and that you will know them by their fruits.

- **He/His:** Capitalized, these words indicate God.

- **Holy Spirit:** The Spirit of Truth proceeds from God. (John 15:26) God gives the Holy Spirit (The Helper) to those who ask Him. (Luke 11:13) The Father sends the Helper in Christ's name, and He teaches you all things. (John 14:26) The Spirit of Truth enables God to abide with you forever. (John 14:16) John the Baptist baptized with water, but Christians are baptized with the Holy Spirit. (Acts 11:16) Baptize disciples of all nations in the name of the Father and of the Son and of the Holy Spirit. (Matthew 28:19)

- **Messiah:** The Hebrew term that means the "anointed one." Jewish prophets predict a messiah in many Hebrew Bible passages (see "Relationship to Earlier Faiths" on page 518). Angels proclaim Christ's messiahship to Mary and Joseph before His birth (Luke 1:26-38; Matthew 1:20) and at His birth (Luke 2:1-20), and God proclaims it at His baptism. (Matthew 3:16-17)

  Christ speaks with a woman who says, "I know that Messiah is coming" (who is called Christ). "When He comes, He will tell us all things." Jesus replies, "I who speak to you am He." (John 4:25-26)

---

1 Some later Old Testament versions exclude books taken from the Septuagint that are not shared by the Hebrew Bible.—Ed.

- **New Covenant:** In the Hebrew Bible, the Covenant (formal agreement) between God and His people includes worshipping only God and complying with His instructions and laws in exchange for God's reward. The Christian New Covenant fulfills the Hebrew Covenant by transforming people from within (writing the law on their hearts—Jeremiah 31:30-34) through the promised Messiah, Christ. Christ reconciles humanity with God and gives the capability of everlasting life to anyone with a heart open to the guidance of Christ and the Holy Spirit. With Christ's coming, the warfare of God's people as described in the Hebrew Bible is converted to spiritual warfare. (Ephesians 6:10-18)

- **Prophets:** Holy people inspired by God to deliver God's message about the present and the future and to direct people to God's will so that they can return to His ways. Christians believe that Christ is the Messiah, not merely a prophet.

- **Repent:** Translated from the Greek μετανoια (metanoia), which is defined as a transformative change of heart and mind.

- **Scribes and Pharisees:** In Israel during the time of Christ, scribes had knowledge of the law and could draft legal documents. The Pharisees were at various times a political party, a social movement, and a school of thought in the Holy Land. The Pharisees believed in resurrection and in following legal traditions ascribed to "the traditions of the fathers." They were legal experts.

- **Sin:** Translated from the Greek (amartia), meaning "missing the mark." All of humanity are sinners: as humans, we all miss the mark. God forgives every single sin through sincere repentance. The only unforgivable sin is blaspheme against the Holy Spirit. (Matthew 12:31-32; Mark 3:28-30, Luke 12:10) This is willful hardness of heart against the divine activity of the Holy Spirit, which is a refusal to accept God's forgiveness and mercy.[1]

- **Son of Man/Son of God:** Christ sometimes refers to Himself as the Son of Man, expressing His humanity and empathy with the Human race. He also refers to Himself as the Son of God. The First Council of Nicaea in 325 CE (306 BH), the Council of Ephesus in 431 CE (197 BH), and the Council of Chalcedon in 451 CE (176 BH) declared that Jesus was both fully God (begotten from the Father) and fully man (taking his flesh and human nature from the Virgin Mary). The term Son of God implies the unique relationship that Jesus has to God—it does not imply that God had sexual relations with the Virgin Mary, a blasphemy to Christians.

- **The Way:** The Way of God and Christ.

- **Trinity:** The Father, the Son and the Holy Spirit. The Father is the Godhead, eternal, not begotten. The Son is the Word of God (Logos), eternal, and begotten of the Father.[2] The Holy Spirit is eternal and proceeds from the Father. (*See* "The Holy Trinity" on page 519.)

---

1 Alan Wallerstedt, Joseph Allen, Th.D., Michel Najim, Ph.D., Jack Norman Sparks, Ph.D., and Theodore Stylianopoulis, Th.D., eds, *The Orthodox Study Bible: Old and New Testaments* (Nashville: Thomas Nelson, 2008) 35. (Hereafter cited as Wallerstedt et al, *Orthodox Bible: Old and New Testaments* 2008).

2 John 1:14: And the Word (Logos) became flesh and lived among us, and we saw his glory, such glory as of the one and only of the Father, full of grace and truth.

ﷺ Muslim Terms

- **Aya**: An aya is akin to a verse in the New Testament Bible.

- **Believers/Disbelievers**: Believers/Disbelievers in the Prophet Muhammad's message.

- **Day of Resurrection/Day of Judgment/Last Day/Latter Day/the Day/the Hour/Day of Gathering/Day of the Manifestation of Defects**: The day on which God gives the final assessment of humanity. All life on Earth is then annihilated, followed by its resurrection of the living and the dead. They are judged and sent to Paradise or Hell.

- **Emigrants**: Muhammad's initial followers who emigrated with him from the city of Mecca to the city of Medina (the Hijrah), in present-day Saudi Arabia.

- **Followers of the Book/Followers of the Reminder/Those Who Were Given the Knowledge Before**: Jews and Christians.

- **Hereafter:** Life after death, either Heaven or Hell.

- **His Messenger**: Muhammad (God's Messenger). When not capitalized, it refers to all prophets, including Jewish prophets and Jesus Christ.

- **Holy Spirit**: In the Qur'an, some scholars think the Holy Spirit refers to the angel Gabriel. There are instances in the Qur'an of the Holy Spirit strengthening Jesus and his mother, Mary.

- **Hypocrites**: Muslims who are half-hearted, imperfect or weak (including in warfare), and who work against the Islamic state. Non-Muslims who willfully reject Islam.

- **Iblis**: Satan.

- **Idolaters (polytheists)**: People who worshipped idols during the time of Muhammad. People in Mecca worshipped 360 idols (gods).

- **Islam**: The religion of Muslims. The Arabic translation of the word Islam is "submission" or "surrender."

- **Jinn**: Unseen beings that sometimes appear. God created Jinn from smokeless (intensely hot) fire. Jinn (like humankind) can be unbelievers, ordinary believers or the best of believers.

- **Muslim**: A person who submits to the will of God: a follower of Islam (the religion).

- **Prophets (Nabi)**: God enables prophets to deliver *new* scriptures from God, and He commissions messengers (Rasul) to confirm *existing* Scriptures. While Muhammad is a messenger, he is also a prophet, the *final* prophet.[1] (33:40)

- **Say, [Prophet]**: In the text of the Qur'an, God speaking to Muhammad, telling him to give the people the message that follows in the revelation.

- **Scripture/Book/Verses of God/Verses**: When capitalized, these terms refer to God's

---

1 "The Difference between Prophet and Messenger," *TRUE ISLAM*, http://www.Qur'an-islam.org/articles/prophet_and_ messenger_(P1161).html (accessed December, 2017)

revelation to Muhammad. When not capitalized, they include scriptures that came to the prophets before Muhammad (Jewish scriptures and the New Testament Bible).

- **Sin:** Disobeying the commands of God, a breach of the laws and standards laid down by religion. Muslims can eliminate their sin through repentance. However, claiming that God has equals is the only unforgivable sin. At the end of time, God weighs your sins and good deeds to determine if you are rewarded in Paradise or punished in Hell.[1]

- **Sura:** A sura is akin to a chapter in the New Testament Bible.

- **The Prophet (or Prophet):** Muhammad

- **The Reminder:** God's message to the people, the Qur'an.

- **Those whom your right hands possess:** Females taken prisoner in war, or male or female slaves.[2]

- **Trinity:** The Muslim faith describes the Christian Trinity as God, Jesus and *Mary*, whereas the Christian Trinity is Father, Son and *Holy Spirit*.

- **We, He and Us:** God. The words of the Qur'an are believed to be spoken by God. God refers to Himself as We, He or Us.

---

1 John L. Esposito, ed, "Sin" in *Oxford Islamic Studies Online*, http://www.oxfordislamicstudies.com/browse (accessed December, 2017).

2 Maulvi Muhammad Ali, trans, *The Holy Qur'an*, (Lahore: Ahmadiyya Anjuman-I-Ishaat-I-Islam, 1920), 106, 702, (Hereafter cited as Ali, M.M., *The Holy Qur'an*).

Purpose

Why I Came

 Jesus

And when his disciples James and John saw this, they said, "Lord, do you want us to command fire to come down from the sky and consume them, just as Elijah did?" But Jesus turned and rebuked them, and said, "You do not know of what kind of spirit you are. For the Son of Man did not come to destroy men's lives, but to save them. (Luke 9:54-56)

For the Son of Man came to seek and to save that which was lost. (Luke 19:10)

My food is to do the will of He who sent me, and to accomplish His work. (John 4:34)

I am the good shepherd. The good shepherd lays down his life for the sheep. He who is a hired hand and not a shepherd, who does not own the sheep, sees the wolf coming and leaves the sheep and runs away; and the wolf snatches them and scatters them. And the hired hand flees because he is a hired hand, and the sheep mean nothing to him. I am the good shepherd. I know my own, and my own know me; even as the Father knows me, and I know the Father. I lay down my life for the sheep. I have other sheep, which are not of this fold. I must bring them also, and they will hear my voice. They will become one flock with one shepherd. Therefore my Father loves me, because I lay down my life, that I may take it again. No one takes it away from me, but I lay it down by myself. I have power to lay it down, and I have power to take it again. I received this commandment from my Father. (John 10:11-18)

Thus it is written, and thus it was necessary, for the Messiah to suffer and to rise from the dead the third day, and that repentance for forgiveness of sins should be preached in his name to all nations, beginning at Jerusalem.[1] (Luke 24:46-47)

---

1 Spoken by the resurrected Jesus to His apostles during the 40-day period after his death, during which He appeared to them.—Ed.

This Book, there is no doubt about it, is a guide to those who guard (against evil), those who believe in the unseen and keep up prayer, and spend out of what We have given them. And who believe in what has been revealed to you and what was revealed before you, and they are sure of the Hereafter. (The Cow 2:2-4)

When your Lord said to the angels, I am going to place on the Earth one who will rule (on it), they said: What? Will You place on Earth one who makes mischief and sheds blood? We celebrate Your praise and extol Your holiness. He said: Surely, I know what you do not know. (The Cow 2:30)

Certainly, God bestowed a benefit on the believers when He raised a Messenger from among themselves, reciting His Verses to them, and purifying them, and teaching them the Book and the wisdom, although before that they were surely in obvious error. (The Family of Amran 3:164)

Oh, Followers of the Book![1] Indeed our Messenger has come to you, bringing clarity to you after a cessation of the messengers, for fear that you might say: neither a bearer of good news nor a warner came to us. So indeed, a bearer of good news and a warner has come to you. And God has power over all things. (The Food 5:19)

We have revealed to you the Book with the truth, verifying what came before it from the Book, and guarding over it. So judge between them by what God has revealed. Do not follow their low desires (to turn away) from the truth that has come to you. For each of you, We appointed a law and a way. If God had pleased, He would have made you (all) a single people, but He intended to test you in what He gave you. So strive with one another to hasten to virtuous deeds. You will all return to God, and then He will inform you about what you differed. (The Food 5:48)

This is a Blessed Book that We have revealed, verifying what came before it, so that you may warn the metropolis[2] and those who are around it. Those who believe in the Hereafter believe in it, and they attend to their prayers constantly. (The Cattle 6:92)

---

1 Followers of the Book: Christians and Jews.—Ed

2 Ali, M.M., *The Holy Qur'an*, 301. Mecca.

Jesus

As Moses lifted up the serpent in the wilderness, even so must the Son of Man be lifted up, so that whoever believes in him may have eternal life. For God so loved the world that He gave His only son, so that whoever believes in him will not perish, but have eternal life. For God did not send His son into the world to judge the world, but so that the world should be saved through him. (John 3:14-17)

So he came to Nazareth, where he had been brought up. He entered, as was his custom, into the synagogue on the Sabbath day, and stood up to read. The scroll of the prophet Isaiah was handed to him. He opened the scroll, and found the place where it was written, "The Spirit of the Lord is upon me, Because he has anointed me to preach the good news to the poor. He has sent me to heal the brokenhearted, to proclaim liberty to the captives, recovering of sight to the blind, to deliver those who are crushed, and to proclaim the acceptable year of the Lord." He closed the scroll, gave it back to the attendant, and sat down. The eyes of all in the synagogue were fastened on him. He began to tell to them, "Today, this Scripture has been fulfilled in your hearing." (Luke 4:16-21)

Go and learn what this means: I desire mercy, and not sacrifice. For I came not to call the righteous, but sinners, to repentance.[1] (Matthew 9:13)

As they were eating, Jesus took bread, gave thanks for it, and broke it. He gave to the disciples, and said, "Take, eat; this is my body." He took the cup, gave thanks, and gave to them, saying, "All of you drink it, for this is my blood of the new covenant, which is poured out for many for the remission of sins." (Matthew 26:26-28)

I came to throw fire on the Earth. I wish it were already kindled. But I have a baptism to be baptized with, and how distressed I am until it is accomplished. (Luke 12:49)

---

1 Repent is translated from the Greek μετανοια (metanoia), which has also been defined as a transformative change of heart and mind.—Ed.

Muhammad ﷺ

Say, [Prophet]: Surely my prayer and my sacrifice and my life and my death are (all) for God, the Lord of the Worlds. He has no associate—this I am commanded—and I am the first of those who submit. (The Cattle 6:162-163)

Certainly a Messenger has come to you from among yourselves, grievous about your falling into distress, most concerned about you. To the believers, (he is) compassionate, merciful. (The Immunity 9:128)

Certainly, We have revealed to you a Book, in which is your eminence. Will you not then understand? How many a wicked town did We demolish, and then afterwards raise up another people? When they felt Our punishment, lo! They began to flee from it. Do not flee (now) and return to the easy lives that you led, and to your dwellings: you might be questioned. They said: Oh, woe to us! Indeed, we were [wrongdoers]. This cry of theirs did not cease until We reaped them and made them extinct. (The Prophets 21:10-15)

[Prophet], We have sent you only as a giver of good news and as a warner. Say: I do not ask anything in return except that whoever wills may take the way to his Lord. (The Distinction 25:56-57)

Most surely this is a revelation from the Lord of the Worlds. The Faithful Spirit has descended with it upon your heart,[1] [Prophet], so that you may be one of the warners, in plain Arabic language. Most surely the same is in the Scriptures of the ancients. Isn't it a sign, that the learned men of the Israelites know it? (The Poets 26:192-197)

---

1 Ali, M.M., *The Holy Qur'an*, 739. The angel Gabriel.

Jesus

For the bread of God is that which comes down out of Heaven and gives life to the world. I am the bread of life. He who comes to me will not be hungry, and he who believes in me will never be thirsty. For I have come down from Heaven, not to do my own will, but the will of He who sent me. This is the will of the One who sent me, so that everyone who sees the Son and believes in him should have eternal life; and I will raise him up at the last day. This is the bread which comes down out of Heaven, so that anyone may eat of it and not die. (John 6:33, 35, 38, 40, 50)

Those who are healthy have no need for a physician, but those who are sick. I came not to call the righteous, but sinners to repentance. (Mark 2:17)

Pilate, therefore, said to him, "Are you king, then?" Jesus answered, "You say that I am a king. For this reason I have been born, and for this reason I have come into the world—to testify to the truth. Everyone who is of the truth listens to my voice." (John 18:37)

I have come as a light into the world, so that whoever believes in me may not abide in darkness. (John 12:46)

Muhammad ﷺ

You, [Prophet], were not on the western side when We revealed the commandment to Moses, nor were you among the witnesses. But We raised up generations and prolonged life for them. You were not dwelling among the people of Midian, reciting Our Verses to them, but We were the senders. You were not on this side of [Mount Sinai] when We called. But it is a mercy from your Lord that you may warn a people to whom no warner came before, so that they may be mindful. Thus, if a disaster should befall them because of their own deeds, they cannot say: Our Lord, why did You not send a messenger to us, so that we might have followed Your Verses and been of the believers? (The Narrative 28:44-47)

Oh, Prophet! Surely We have sent you as a witness, and as a bearer of good news, and as a warner. As one who invites to God, by His permission, and as a light-giving torch. Give to the believers the good news that they will have great grace from God. Do not be compliant to the unbelievers and the hypocrites, disregard their annoying talk, and rely on God. God is a sufficient Protector. (The Allies 33:45-48)

Surely, [Prophet], We have sent you with the truth, as a bearer of good news and as a warner. There is not a people for whom a warner has not gone among them. If they call you a liar, those before them also called their messengers liars—their messengers came to them with clear arguments, and with Scriptures, and with the illuminating Book. Then I [seized] those who disbelieved—so how was My disapproval? (The Originator 35:24-26)

Say, [Prophet]: I am only a warner; and there is no god but God, the One, the Subduer (of all): The Lord of the Heavens and the Earth and what is between them, the Mighty, the most Forgiving. Say: It is a message of importance, and you are turning aside from it. I had no knowledge of the exalted chiefs when they were disputing. Only this is revealed to me: I am a plain warner. (Sad 38:65-70)

A Revelation from the Lord of Mercy, the Giver of Mercy; a Scripture whose verses are made distinct—a Quran in Arabic for people who understand, giving good news and warning. Yet most of them turn away and so do not hear. (Ha Mim 41:2-4)

Thus, We reveal to you an inspired Book, by Our command. You did not know what the Book was, nor (what) the Faith (was), but We made it a light, guiding with it whom We please of Our servants. Most surely, [Prophet], you show the way to the right path. (The Counsel 42:52)

Jesus

I am the Alpha and the Omega, the First and the Last, the Beginning and the End. (Revelation 22:13)

Muhammad

Who is more [wrong] than he who invents a lie against God while he is invited to Islam? God does not guide the [wrongdoers]. They desire to put out the light of God with their mouths, but God will perfect His light, though the unbelievers may be averse. It is He who sent His Messenger with the guidance and the true religion, so that He may make it overcome the religions, all of them, though the polytheists may be averse. (The Ranks 61:7-9)

No! I call to witness the stars that run their course (and) hide themselves, and the night when it departs, and the morning when it brightens. Most surely it is the word of an honored Messenger, the possessor of strength, having an honorable place with the Lord of the Dominion, One (to be) obeyed, and trustworthy. Your companion [The Prophet] has not gone mad. Truly he saw him on the clear horizon.[1] Nor is he a concealer of the unseen. Nor is it the word of the cursed Devil.
(The Folding Up 81:15-25)

---

1 Most translations consider this a reference to the angel Gabriel.—Ed.

Prior Messengers

 Jesus

Do not think that I came to destroy the Law or the Prophets. I did not come to destroy, but to fulfill. For truly, I tell you, until Heaven and Earth pass away, not one iota or one dot will pass from the Law, until all things are accomplished. (Matthew 5:17-18)

What did you go out into the wilderness to see? A reed shaken by the wind? But what did you go out to see? A man clothed in soft clothing? Look, those who are gorgeously dressed, and live delicately, are in kings' courts. But what did you go out to see? A prophet? Yes, I tell you, and much more than a prophet. This is he of whom it is written, "Look, I send my messenger ahead of you, who will prepare your way before you." For I tell you, among those who are born of women there is none greater than John the Baptist, yet he who is least in the Kingdom of God is greater than he. (Luke 7:24-28)

When the men had come to him, they said, "John the Baptist has sent us to You, saying, 'Are you the one who is to come, or should we look for another?" In that hour he cured many diseases and plagues and evil spirits; and to many who were blind he gave sight. Jesus answered them, "Go and tell John the things that you have seen and heard: that the blind receive their sight, the lame walk, the lepers are cleansed, the deaf hear, the dead are raised up, and the poor have good news preached to them. Blessed is he who is not offended by me." (Luke 7:20-23)

Muhammad

Note: Muhammad refers to Christians and Jews as Followers of the Book and Followers of the Reminder.—Ed.

And when Abraham and Ishmael raised the foundations of the House,[1] they said: Our Lord! Accept from us. Surely You are the Hearing, the Knowing. Our Lord! Make us both submissive to You, and (raise) from our offspring a nation submissive to You, and show us our ways of devotion, and turn to us (mercifully). Surely You are the Oft-returning (to mercy), the Merciful. Our Lord! Raise up a Messenger from among them who will recite Your Verses, and teach them the Book, and the wisdom, and purify them. Surely You are the Mighty, the Wise. (The Cow 2:127-129)

The angels called to him as he stood praying in the sanctuary,[2] saying: God gives you the good news of John, an honorable and chaste prophet from among the good ones, who will verify a word from God. He said: My Lord! How can I have a son when old age has already come upon me, and my wife is barren? The angel said: Even thus does God do as He pleases. Zachariah said: My Lord! Give me a sign. The angel said: Your sign is that you will not speak to men for three days, except with gestures. Remember your Lord much, and glorify (Him) in the evening and early morning. (The Family of Amran 3:39-41)

The angels said: Oh Mary! Surely God gives you good news, with a word from Him whose name is the Messiah, Jesus son of Mary, worthy of regard in this world and the Hereafter, and of those who are near (to God). He will speak to the people when in the cradle and in old age, and (he will be) one of the good ones. Mary said: My Lord! How will a son be (born) to me when a man has not touched me? He said: Even so; God creates what He pleases. When He decrees a matter, He only says, Be, and it is. God will teach Jesus the Book, and the wisdom, and the Torah, and the Gospel, and (make him) a messenger to the Children of Israel, (saying): I have come to you with a sign from your Lord—I design for you, from clay, the form of a bird. Then I breathe into it and it becomes a bird with God's permission. I heal the blind and the leper, and I bring the dead to life with God's permission. I inform you of what you should eat and what you should store in your houses. Most surely there is a sign in this for you, if you are believers. (I) verify what came before me of the Torah, so that I may allow you part of what was forbidden to you. I have come to you with a sign from your Lord, so [fear] God, and obey me.[3] (The Family of Amran 3:45-50)

---

1 The Ka'bah—Ed.

2 Zachariah, John the Baptist's father—Ed.

3 This story of Jesus speaking in his cradle is also in the *Syriac (Arabic) Infancy Gospel*. The story of the bird is also in the *Infancy Gospel of Thomas*. *See* page 487.—Ed.

Jesus

If you believed Moses, you would believe me; for he wrote about me. But if you do not believe his writings, how will you believe my words? (John 5:46-47)

This is what I told you, while I was still with you, that all things which are written in the Law of Moses, the Prophets, and the Psalms concerning me must be fulfilled. (Luke 24:44)

Muhammad ﷺ

When Jesus perceived disbelief on their part, he said: Who will be my helpers in God's way? His disciples said: We are God's helpers—we believe in God, and we bear witness that we are submitting ones. Our Lord, we believe in what you have revealed, and we follow the messenger, so write us down with those who bear witness. (The Jews) planned, and God (also) planned. God is the best of planners. (The Family of Amran 3:52-54)

They do not assign to God the attributes due to Him when they say: God has not revealed anything to a mortal. Say, [Prophet]: Who revealed the Book that Moses brought, a light and a guidance to men, which you make into scattered papers that you show while you conceal much? You are taught what neither you nor your fathers knew. Say: God revealed it. Then leave them sporting in their vain discourse. (The Cattle 6:91)

When Moses came at Our appointed time, and his Lord spoke to him, he said: My Lord! Show me (Yourself), so that I may look at You. The Lord said: You cannot (bear to) see Me, but look at the mountain. If it remains firm in its place, you will see Me. So when his Lord revealed His glory to the mountain, He made it crumble, and Moses fainted. When he recovered, he said: Glory to You! I turn to You, and I am the first of the believers. (The Elevated Places 7:143)

Certainly, We sent messengers before you, and We gave them wives and children. It is not in (the power of) a messenger to bring a sign, except by God's permission. There is an appointment for every term. God eliminates what He pleases and establishes what He pleases, and the basis of the Book is with Him. (The Thunder 13:38-39)

Certainly, We sent (messengers) before you, among the sects of the nations of yore. And there never came a messenger whom they did not mock. This is how We make it enter the hearts of the guilty.[1] (The Rock 15:10-12)

[Prophet], We sent before you only men to whom We had sent revelation. So ask the Followers of the Reminder, if you do not know (The Bee:16:43)

---

1 Ali, M.M., *The Holy Qur'an*, 525. God brings unbelief into the hearts of mockers, because of their mockery.

Jesus

The Law and the Prophets were until John.[1] From that time the Good News of the Kingdom of God is preached, and everyone is forcing his way into it. (Luke 16:16)

---

1 John the Baptist—Ed.

Muhammad ﷺ

Certainly, We gave Moses nine clear signs; so ask the Children of Israel. When Moses came to them, Pharaoh said: Surely, Oh Moses, you are [bewitched]. Moses said: Truly you know that none but the Lord of the Heavens and the Earth has sent down these clear proofs; and surely, Oh Pharaoh, I believe you are given over to utter destruction. So Pharaoh desired to drive them off of Earth, but We drowned Pharaoh and all of those with him, together. (The Israelites 17:101-103)

We said, Oh John![1] Take hold of the Book, with strength! We granted him wisdom while he was just a child, and tenderness from Us, and purity, and he was one who guarded (against evil). He was dutiful to his parents, and not insolent, disobedient. Peace on him the day he was born, the day he died, and the day he is raised to life. (Mary 19:12-15)

[Prophet], mention Ishmael in the Book.[2] Surely he was truthful in his promise, and he was a messenger, a prophet. He directed his family in prayer and almsgiving, and he was one in whom his Lord was well-pleased. (Mary 19:54-55)

We did not send any with revelation before you who were not men; so ask the Followers of the Reminder, if you do not know. We did not give them bodies that did not eat food, and they were not immortal. Then We fulfilled Our promise to them: We delivered them and those whom We pleased, and We destroyed the extravagant. (The Prophets 21:7-9)

(We made) the wind (subservient) to Solomon, blowing violently, pursuing its course to the land by his command, which We had blessed. We are knower of all things. There were devils who dived for him and did other work besides that: We kept guard over them. (The Prophets 21:81-82)

Solomon was David's heir, and he said: Oh, men! We have been taught the language of the birds, and we have been granted abundance. Most surely this is evident grace. And Solomon's hosts of the Jinn and the men and the birds were gathered to him, and they were formed into groups. When they came to the valley of Naml, an [ant] said: Oh [ants]! Enter your houses, lest Solomon and his hosts crush you inadvertently. (The Naml 27:16-18)

1 John the Baptist—Ed.

2 Son of Abraham and Hagar.—Ed.

Jesus

The men of Nineveh will stand up in the judgment with this generation, and will condemn it, for they repented at the preaching of Jonah; and look, something greater than Jonah is here. The Queen of the South will rise up in the judgment with this generation, and will condemn it, for she came from the ends of the earth to hear the wisdom of Solomon; and look, someone greater than Solomon is here.
(Matthew 12:41-42)

Muhammad ﷺ

(We made) the wind (subservient) to Solomon; it made a month's journey in the morning and a month's journey in the evening. We made a fountain of molten brass flow out for him. There were some Jinn who worked before him, by the command of his Lord—whoever among them turned aside from Our command, We made him taste of the chastisement of burning. They made for him what he pleased: fortresses and images, and (large) bowls and watering troughs and cooking-pots that will not move from their place. Give thanks, oh family of David! But very few of My servants are grateful. (The Saba 34:12-13)

Alas for the servants! Never does a messenger come to them whom they do not mock. Don't they see how many generations We destroyed before them because they do not turn to the messengers? (Yasin 36:30-31)

When Abraham said to his father and his people: Surely I am clear of what you worship, except Him Who created me, for surely He will guide me. And he gave this word to continue in his posterity, so that they may return [to God]. (The Embellishment 43:26-28)

Those who disbelieve say concerning those who believe: If it had been good, they would not have preceded us to it. Because they do not seek to be rightly directed, they say: It is an old lie. Before it the Book of Moses was a guide and a mercy— this is a Book verifying (it) in the Arabic language, so that it may warn those who are unjust, and as good news for the doers of good. (The Sandhills 46:11-12)

Noah said: My Lord! Do not leave on the land any of the unbelievers. For surely if you leave them, they will lead astray Your servants, and they will beget only immoral, ungrateful (children). My Lord! Forgive me and my parents and he who enters my house believing, and the believing men and the believing women. And do not increase the [wrongdoers], except in destruction! (Noah 71:26-28)

Focus

Worship Only God

 Jesus

Call no man on the Earth your father; for One is your Father, He who is in Heaven. (Matthew 23:9)

And the devil, taking him up to a high mountain, showed him all of the kingdoms of the world in a moment of time. The devil said to him, "I will give you all of this authority, and their glory—for it has been delivered to me—and I give it to whomever I want. So if you will worship before me, it will all be yours." Jesus answered, and said to him, "Get behind me, Satan. It is written, 'You are to worship the Lord your God, and serve Him only.'" (Luke 4:5-8)

Truly, truly, I tell you, a servant is not greater than his master, neither is one who is sent greater than He who sent him. If you know these things, blessed are you if you do them. (John 13:16-17)

The greatest of all the commandments is: "Hear, Israel, the Lord our God, the Lord is one." (Mark 12:29)

It is not appropriate for a mortal to whom God gives the Book, the judgement and the prophethood to then say to men: Be my servants, rather than God's. Rather, (he would say): Worship the Lord, because you have been teaching the Book and reading it. (The Family of Amran 3:79)

Surely God does not forgive anything being associated with Him. Besides this, He forgives whom He pleases. Whoever associates anything with God indeed strays off into remote error. They only call on inanimate objects, and they do not call on anything but a devil devoid of all good. God cursed the Devil, so he said: Most certainly I will take an appointed portion of Your servants. Most certainly I will lead them astray and excite in them vain desires, and bid them so that they will slit the ears of the cattle. Most certainly I will bid them so that they will alter God's creation. Whoever takes the Devil rather than God for a guardian will indeed suffer a clear loss. He gives them promises and excites vain desires in them. The Devil promises them only to deceive. (The Women 4:116-121)

Say [Prophet]: Who is it who delivers you from the dangers of the land and the sea (when) you call upon Him, (openly) humiliating yourselves, and in secret? If He delivers us from this, we should certainly be of the grateful ones. God delivers you from them and from every distress, but again you set up others (with Him). (The Cattle 6:64)

They make the Jinn associates with God, though He created the Jinn, and they falsely attribute sons and daughters to God, without knowledge. Glory be to God! He is highly exalted above what they ascribe (to Him). (The Cattle 6:100)

Say, [Prophet]: Is there any one among your [associate-gods] who can bring into existence the creation in the first instance, and then reproduce it? Say: God brings creation into existence in the first instance, and then He reproduces it. So, how are you turned away? (Jonah 10:34)

He sends down the angels with the inspiration, by His commandment, to whom He pleases of His servants, saying: Give the warning that there is no God but Me, so [fear] Me. (The Bee 16:2)

Have they taken gods from the Earth who raise (the dead)? If there were any gods besides God [in the Heavens and on Earth], they would both certainly be in a state of disorder. So glory be to God, Lord of the Dominion, above what they attribute (to Him). (The Prophets 21: 21-22)

Jesus

Muhammad

So exalted is God, the True King. There is no god but Him, the Lord of the Honorable Dominion. Whoever invokes with God another god—he has no proof of this—his reckoning is only with his Lord. Surely the unbelievers will not be successful. (The Believers 23:116-117)

So, [Prophet], do not call not upon another god with God, lest you be of those who are chastised. Warn your nearest relations, and lower your wing over he who follows you of the believers. But if they disobey you, say: Surely I am clear of what you do. (The Poets 26:213-216)

Do not call on any other god with God. There is no god but Him. Everything is perishable but Him. The judgement is His, and you will be returned to Him. (The Narrative 28:88)

We have charged man to be good to his parents. But if your parents contend with you that you should associate (others) with Me, others of which you have no knowledge, do not obey them. Your return is to Me, and I will inform you of what you did. (The Spider 29:8)

Surely God knows whatever thing they call upon besides Him. And He is the Mighty, the Wise. (The Spider 29:42)

Oh, My servants who believe! Surely My Earth is vast, so you should serve Me, alone. Every soul must taste of death, and then you will be brought back to Us. (The Spider 29:56-57)

Among His Signs are the night and the day and the sun and the moon. Do not bow in worship to the sun or the moon, but bow in worship to God Who created them, if it is Him that you serve. (Ha Mim 41:37)

Certainly, We destroyed the towns that are around you, and We repeat Our communications, so that they might turn [to Me]. Why did the gods that they took to draw (them) near (to God) not help them? No! The gods were lost by the people. That was the people's lie, what they invented. (The Sandhills 46:27-28)

Jesus

Why do you call me good? No one is good except One—God. (Mark 10:18)

Muhammad ﷺ

He is God, besides Whom there is no god. The Knower of the unseen and the seen. He is the Beneficent, the Merciful. He is God, besides Whom there is no god. The King, the Holy, the Author of Peace, the Granter of Security, the Guardian over all, the Mighty, the Supreme, the Possessor of Every Greatness. Glory be to God from what they associate (with Him). He is God the Creator, the Maker, the Fashioner. His names are the most excellent. Whatever is in the Heavens and the Earth declares His glory; and He is the Mighty, the Wise. (The Banishment 59:22-24)

Say, [Prophet], Oh, unbelievers! I do not serve what you serve, nor do you serve He whom I serve, nor am I going to serve what you worship, nor are you going to serve He Whom I serve. You will have your recompense, and I will have my recompense. (The Unbelievers 109:1-6)

Follow Light

 Jesus

I am the light of the world. He who follows me will not walk in darkness, but will have the light of life. (John 8:12)

Jesus said to them, "For a little while the light is with you. Walk while you have the light, so that darkness does not overtake you. He who walks in the darkness does not know where he is going. While you have the light, believe in the light, that you may become children of light." Jesus said these things, and he departed and hid himself from them. (John 12:35-36)

For everyone who does evil hates the light and does not come to the light, lest his works would be exposed. But he who does the truth comes to the light, so that his works may be revealed, that they have been done in God. (John 3:20-21)

No one, when he has lit a lamp, puts it in a cellar or under a basket. Rather he puts it on a stand, so that those who come in may see the light. The lamp of the body is the eye. Therefore when your eye is good, your whole body is also full of light; but when it is bad, your body also is full of darkness. So see whether the light that is in you is not darkness. If your whole body is full of light, having no part dark, it will be wholly full of light, as when the lamp with its bright shining gives you light. (Luke 11:33-36)

While I am in the world, I am the light of the world. (John 9:5)

Oh, people! Surely convincing proof has come to you from your Lord, and We have sent you a clear light. He will admit those who believe in God and hold fast by Him into His mercy and grace, and He will guide them to Himself, on a right path. (The Women 4:174-175)

Oh, Followers of the Book! Indeed, Our Messenger has come to you, making clear to you much of what you concealed of the Book, and he overlooks much. Indeed, there has come to you light and a clear Book from God. With it, God guides those who follow His pleasure into the ways of peace, and He brings them out of utter darkness into light by His will, and He guides them to the right path. (The Food 5:15-16)

I am God, the Seeing. (This is) a Book that We have revealed to you, [Prophet], so that you may bring forth men, by their Lord's permission, from utter darkness into light—to the way of the Mighty, the Praised One. God is the One to whom belongs whatever is in the Heavens and whatever is in the Earth. Woe to the unbelievers for the severe chastisement! (Abraham 14:1-2)

God is the light of the Heavens and the Earth. His light is like a niche in which is a lamp, the lamp is in a glass, and the glass is as if it were a brightly shining star, lit from a blessed olive tree, neither of the East nor the West, the oil from which almost glows, even if fire does not touch it. Light upon light. God guides to His light whom He pleases. God sets forth parables for men, and God is Cognizant of all things. (The Light 24:35)

He sends down clear communications to His servant [The Prophet], so that he may bring you forth from utter darkness into the light. Most surely God is Kind, Merciful to you. (The Iron 57:9)

Discord and Peace

Persecution

 Jesus

He said to them, "When I sent you without money bag, and pack, and shoes, did you lack anything?" They said, "Nothing." Then he said to them, "But now, whoever has a money bag, let him take it, and likewise a pack. Whoever has none must sell his cloak and buy a sword. For I tell you that this which is written must still be fulfilled in me: 'He was numbered with the transgressors.' For that which concerns me has an end." They said, "Lord, look, here are two swords." He said to them, "That is enough."[1] (Luke 22:35-38)

They will put you out of the synagogues, but an hour is coming when whoever kills you will think that he is offering a service to God. They will do these things because they have not known the Father or me. (John 16:2-3)

But watch out for yourselves, for they will deliver you up to councils. You will be beaten in the synagogues. You will stand before rulers and kings for my sake, as a testimony to them. (Mark 13:9)

Blessed are you when men hate you, and when they exclude you and insult you, and throw out your name as evil, for the Son of Man's sake. Rejoice in that day, and leap for joy, for look, your reward is great in Heaven, for their fathers did the same thing to the prophets. (Luke 6:22-23)

Brother will deliver up brother to death, and the father his child. Children will rise up against parents, and cause them to be put to death. You will be hated by all men for my name's sake, but he who endures to the end will be saved. (Mark 13:12-13)

---

1 Jesus is speaking to his disciples in anticipation of their persecution after his arrest and Crucifixion.—Ed.

Fight in the way of God with those who fight you, and do not exceed the limits. Surely God does not love those who exceed the limits. And kill them wherever you find them, and drive them out from wherever they drove out you. Persecution is more severe than slaughter. Do not fight them at the Sacred Mosque until they fight with you in it, but if they do fight you, slay them. Such is the recompense of the unbelievers. But if they cease, surely God is Forgiving, Merciful. Fight them until there is no persecution and religion is only for God. But if they cease, there should be no hostility except against the oppressors. (The Cow 2:190-193)

[Prophet], they ask you concerning the sacred month—about fighting in it. Say: fighting in it is a grave matter. But hindering (men) from God's way and denying Him, and (hindering men from) the Sacred Mosque and turning people out of it are still graver with God. Persecution is greater than slaughter, and they will not stop fighting you until they turn you away from your religion, if they can. Whoever of you turns away from his religion and then dies while he is a disbeliever—his works will become worthless in this world and in the Hereafter. They are the inmates of the Fire: there they will abide. (The Cow 2:217)

Let those who sell this world's life for the Hereafter fight in the way of God. We will grant a mighty reward to whoever fights in the way of God, whether he is slain or victorious. What reason have you to not fight in the way of God for the weak among the men, women and children, who say: Our Lord! Cause us to go forth from this town whose people are oppressors, and give us a guardian from You, and give us a helper from You! Those who believe fight in the way of God, and those who disbelieve fight in the way of the Devil. So, fight against the friends of the Devil— surely the struggle of the Devil is weak. (The Women 4:74-76)

[Prophet], when those who disbelieved devised plans against you such that they might confine you or slay you or drive you away, they devised plans, and God had arranged a plan, too. God is the best of planners, so that He might separate the impure from the good, and put the impure one upon another, pile them up together, and then cast them into Hell. These are the losers. Fight them until there is no more persecution and all religion is only for God. But if they cease, then surely, God sees what they do. (The Accessions 8:30, 37, 39)

Jesus

Rejoice, and be exceedingly glad, for great is your reward in Heaven. For that is how they persecuted the prophets who were before you. (Matthew 5:12)

Look, I send you out as sheep in the midst of wolves. Therefore be wise as serpents and harmless as doves. But when they deliver you over, do not be anxious about how or what you will say, for it will be given to you in that hour what you will say. For it is not you who speak, but the Spirit of your Father who speaks in you.
(Matthew 10:16, 19-20)

Blessed are those who are persecuted for righteousness' sake, for theirs is the Kingdom of Heaven. Blessed are you when men insult you, persecute you, and say all kinds of evil against you falsely, for my sake. (Matthew 5:10-11)

To him who strikes you on the cheek, offer also the other; and from him who takes away your cloak, do not withhold your coat also. (Luke 6:29)

But Saul, still breathing threats and slaughter against the disciples of the Lord, went to the high priest and asked letters from him to the synagogues of Damascus, so that if he found any who were of the Way, whether men or women, he might bring them bound to Jerusalem. As he traveled, it happened that he got close to Damascus, and suddenly a light from the sky shone around him. He fell on the earth, and heard a voice saying to him, "Saul, Saul, why do you persecute me? It is hard for you to kick against the goads." And he said, "Who are You, Lord?" Then the Lord said, "I am Jesus, whom you are persecuting."[1] (Acts 9:1-5)

---

1 Saul of Tarsus, a devout Jew with Roman citizenship, had this experience a few years after Christ's death.—Ed

Alan Wallerstedt, Joseph Allen, Th.D., Michel Najim, Ph.D., Jack Norman Sparks, Ph.D., and Theodore Stylianopoulis, Th.D., eds, *The Orthodox Study Bible: New Testament and Psalms* (Nashville: Thomas Nelson, 1993) 290 (Hereafter cited as Wallerstedt et al., *Orthodox Bible*. Saul's purpose is to arrest and prosecute Jewish Christians. Goads are spikes: this expression implies the futility of Saul's action against an invincible force (Christ). Saul converted and became an apostle of Christ (the apostle Paul).

Muhammad ﷺ

If they break their oaths after their agreement and (openly) revile your religion, fight the leaders of disbelief—surely their oaths are nothing—so that they may cease. What? Will you not fight a people who broke their oaths and who aimed at the expulsion of the Messenger, who attacked you first? Do you fear them? But God is most deserving that you should fear Him, if you are believers. Fight them. God will chastise them by your hands, bring them to disgrace, assist you against them, and heal the hearts of a believing people—He will remove the rage of their hearts. God turns (mercifully) to whom He pleases, and God is Knowing, Wise.
(The Immunity 9:12-15)

Surely your Lord, with respect to those who emigrate after they are persecuted and then struggle hard and are patient, most surely your Lord after that is Forgiving, Merciful. (The Bee 16:110)

There is no way (to blame) whoever defends himself after being oppressed. The way (of blame) is only against those who oppress men and revolt on the Earth unjustly. These will have a painful chastisement. Whoever is patient and forgiving—that most surely is [behavior] that determines matters.
(The Counsel 42:41-43)

Surely those who persecute the believing men and the believing women and then do not repent will have the chastisement of Hell, and they will have the chastisement of the burning. (The Stars 85:10)

Jesus

If you were of the world, the world would love its own. But because you are not of the world, since I chose you out of the world, the world hates you. Remember the word that I said to you: "A servant is not greater than his master." If they persecuted me, they will also persecute you. If they kept my word, they will keep yours also. But all these things they will do to you because of my name, because they do not know He who sent me. If I had not come and spoken to them, they would not have had sin, but now they have no excuse for their sin. He who hates me hates my Father also. If I had not done among them the works which no one else did, they would have no sin. But now they have seen and also hated both me and my Father. This happened so that the word might be fulfilled which is written in their law, "They hated me without a cause." (John 15:19-25)

I have given them Your word. The world hated them because they are not of the world, even as I am not of the world. I pray not that You would take them from the world, but that You would keep them from the evil one.[1] (John 17:14-15)

---

1 Christ's prayer to God, about His disciples.—Ed

Muhammad ﷺ

Enemies

 Jesus

But I tell you, love your enemies, bless those who curse you, do good to those who hate you, and pray for those who mistreat you and persecute you, so that you may be children of your Father in Heaven. For He makes His sun rise on the evil and on the good, and He sends rain on the just and on the unjust. (Matthew 5:44-45)

The people said to them: Surely men have gathered against you, so fear them. But this increased their faith, and they replied: God is sufficient for us, and most excellent is the Protector. So they returned with favour from God, and (His) grace, and no evil touched them. They followed the pleasure of God. God is the Lord of Mighty Grace. It is only the Devil who causes you to fear his friends, so do not fear them. Fear Me, if you are believers. (The Family of Amran 3:173-175)

Do not be weak-hearted in pursuit of the enemy. If you suffer pain, surely they suffer pain as you suffer pain. You hope from God what they do not hope. God is Knowing, Wise. (The Women 4:104)

Oh, you who believe! Do not take My enemies and your enemies for friends. Would you offer them love while they deny the Truth that has come to you, driving out the Messenger and yourselves because you believe in God, your Lord? If you go forth struggling hard in My path and seeking My pleasure, would you show love to them? I know what you conceal and what you show. Whoever of you does this indeed strays from the straight path. If they find you, they will extend toward you their hands and their tongues with evil. They ardently desire that you disbelieve. (The Examined One 60:1-2)

Perhaps God will bring about friendship between you and those whom you hold to be your enemies among them. God is Powerful, and God is Forgiving, Merciful. God does not forbid you from respecting those who have not made war against you for your religion and have not driven you from your homes, so that you show them kindness and deal with them justly. Surely, God loves those who act justly. God only forbids you from respecting those who made war upon you because of (your) religion and drove you from your homes and supported (others) in your expulsion. Whoever makes friends with them are the [wrongdoers]. (The Examined One 60:7-9)

Oh, you who believe! Surely among your wives and your children there is an enemy to you, so beware. But if you pardon and forbear and forgive, surely God is Forgiving, Merciful. (The Manifestation of Defects 64:14)

Oh, you who believe! In the matter of the slain, retaliation is prescribed for you: the free for the free, and the slave for the slave, and the female for the female. But if any of you aggrieved brothers pardons the murderer, the murderer follows up with the suitable payment to the aggrieved, in a good manner. This is an alleviation from your Lord, and a mercy. Whoever exceeds the limit after accepting the blood-money will have a painful chastisement. There is life for you in (the law of) retaliation, Oh men of understanding, so that you may guard yourselves. (The Cow 2:178-179)

Retaliation

 Jesus

You have heard that it was said, "An eye for an eye and a tooth for a tooth." But I tell you, do not set yourself against the one who is evil. But whoever slaps you on your right cheek, turn to him the other also. And if anyone sues you and take away your coat, let him have your cloak also. (Matthew 5:38-40)

The sacred month for the sacred month, and all sacred things are (under the law of) retaliation. So whoever acts aggressively against you, inflict injury on him according to the injury that he inflicted on you, and [fear] God. Know that God is with those who [fear Him]. Spend in the way of God, and do not throw yourselves to perdition with your own hands, and do good (to others). Surely God loves the doers of good. (The Cow 2:194-195)

We prescribed in [the Torah] a life for a life, and an eye for an eye, and a nose for a nose, and an ear for an ear, and a tooth for a tooth, and for wounds, retaliation. But there will be an atonement for whoever forgoes this. Those who do not judge by what God has revealed are the [wrongdoers]. (The Food 5:45)

If you fear treachery from a people, throw back [their treaty] to them on terms of equality. Surely God does not love the treacherous. Do not let those who disbelieve think that they will come in first. Surely they will not escape. (The Accessions 8:58-59)

Permission (to fight) is given to those upon whom war is made, because they are oppressed. Most surely God is well able to assist them. Those who are expelled from their homes without just cause other than their saying: Our Lord is God. Had God not repelled some people by others, certainly monasteries, churches, synagogues and mosques in which God's name is much remembered would have been demolished. Surely God will help he who helps His cause. Most surely, God is Strong, Mighty. (The Pilgrimage 22:39-40)

God will certainly help whoever retaliates, in like manner, for his own affliction and oppression. Most surely God is Pardoning, Forgiving. (The Pilgrimage 22:60)

The recompense of an evil is an evil like it; but whoever forgives and amends will have his reward from God. Surely God does not love the [wrongdoers]. (The Counsel 42:40)

Fighting and Warfare

 Jesus

Now he who betrayed him gave them a sign, saying, "Whomever I kiss, He is the one. Seize him." Immediately he came to Jesus, and said, "Hail, Rabbi," and kissed Him. Jesus said to him, "Friend, why are you here?" Then they came and laid hands on Jesus, and took Him. And look, one of those who were with Jesus stretched out his hand and drew his sword, and struck the servant of the high priest, and cut off his ear. Then Jesus said to him, "Put your sword back into its place, for all who take the sword will die by the sword." (Matthew 26:48-52)

Fighting is prescribed for you, though you dislike it. It may be that you dislike a thing while it is good for you, and it may be that you love a thing while it is evil for you. God knows, while you do not know. (The Cow 2:216)

Fight in the way of God, and know that God is Hearing, Knowing. Who will offer to God a goodly gift, so that He will multiply it to him in many ways? God restricts and amplifies, and you will be returned to Him. (The Cow 2:244-245)

So they put them to flight, by God's permission. David slew Goliath, and God gave him kingdom and wisdom, and taught him what He pleased. Were it not for God's repelling some men by others, the Earth would certainly be in a state of disorder: but God is Gracious to the creatures. (The Cow 2:251)

Indeed there was a sign for you in the two armies that met in encounter—one group fighting in the way of God, and the other unbelievers. [The believers] saw twice as many of themselves with the sight of their eyes.[1] God strengthens with His aid whom He pleases. There is a lesson in this for those with vision. (The Family of Amran 3:13)

Yes! If you remain patient and [fear God], and they come upon you in a headlong manner, your Lord will assist you with five thousand of the havoc-making angels. God causes this only as good news for you, to ease your hearts. Victory is only from God, the Mighty, the Wise. So that He may cut off a portion from among those who disbelieve, or abase them so that they return disappointed about not attaining what they desired. (The Family of Amran 3:125-127)

God certainly fulfilled His promise to you when you slew them by His permission, until you became weak-hearted and disputed about the affair and disobeyed after He showed you that which you love. Some of you desired this world, and some of you desired the Hereafter. Then He diverted you from them, so that He might test you. He has indeed pardoned you. God is Gracious to the believers. When you ran off hastily and did not wait for anyone, and the Messenger was calling you from the rear. So He replaced your sorrow with another sorrow, so that you might not grieve at what had escaped you, nor (at) what befell you.[2] God is Aware of what you do. (The Family of Amran 3:152-153)

---

1 Ali, M.M., *The Holy Qur'an*, 148. This is in reference to the Battle of Badr. The believers saw twice as many as themselves, but in reality the enemy troops were more than three times the troops of the believers. So God gave them strength to fight.

2 Ali, M.M., *The Holy Qur'an*, 184. At the Battle of Uhud, some archers left their positions to take spoils, and the enemy was able to turn against the Muslims because of them leaving their posts. Thus they lost their booty, but they grieved more because they put the Prophet in the vulnerable position of having to call out to them.

Jesus

Muhammad ﷺ

Then after sorrow, He sent down security upon you: sleep overcoming a group of you, and another group who had made their own souls anxious—they quite unjustly entertained thoughts of ignorance about God. They said: We have no hand in this affair. Say, [Prophet]: Surely the affair is wholly (in the hands) of God. They conceal within their souls what they would not reveal to you. They say: Had we any hand in the affair, we would not have been slain here. Say: Had you remained in your houses, those for whom slaughter was decreed would certainly have gone toward the places where they would be slain, so that God might test what was in your breasts and purge what was in your hearts. God knows what is in the breasts. As for those who turned back on the day when the two armies met, only the Devil made them slip because of some deeds they had done, and certainly God has pardoned them. Surely God is Forgiving, Forbearing. (The Family of Amran 3:154-155)

Oh, you who believe! Do not be like those who disbelieve and say (this) of their brothers when they travel on Earth or engage in fighting: Had they been with us, they would not have died or been slain. God makes this an intense regret in their hearts. God gives life and causes death. And God sees what you do. (The Family of Amran 3:156)

If you are slain in the way of God, or if you die, certainly forgiveness from God and mercy are better than what others amass. (The Family of Amran 3:157)

[Prophet], fight in God's way. You are responsible only for yourself. Rouse the believers to zeal: maybe God will restrain the fighting of those who disbelieve, and God is strongest in prowess and strongest to give an exemplary punishment. (The Women 4:84)

Make exception for those who reach [out to] a people who share an alliance with you, or those who come to you, their hearts shrinking from fighting you or fighting their own people. If God had pleased, He would have given them power over you, so that they would have certainly fought you. So if they withdraw from you and do not fight you and offer you peace, God gives you no way against them. (The Women 4:90)

You will find others who desire to be safe from you and secure from their own people. But every time they are returned to the mischief, they are thrown into it headlong.[1] So if they do not withdraw from you and do not offer you peace and restrain their hands, seize them and kill them wherever you find them. We have given you a clear authority against them. (The Women 4:91)

---

1 ..Ali, M.M., *The Holy Qur'an*, 226. Though they show an inclination to remain at peace with the Muslims, they hastily fight them when their people call them to fight.

Jesus

While he was still speaking, look, a crowd came, and he who was called Judas, one of the twelve, was leading them. He came near to Jesus to kiss him. But Jesus said to him, "Judas, do you betray the Son of Man with a kiss?" When those who were around him saw what was about to happen, they said to him, "Lord, should we strike with the sword?" A certain one of them struck the servant of the high priest and cut off his right ear. But Jesus answered, "Let me at least do this"—and he touched his ear, and healed him. (Luke 22:47-51)

Muhammad ﷺ

Oh, you who believe! When you go to war in God's way, investigate, and do not, because you seek goods of this world's life, say to any one who offers you a peace salutation: You are not a believer. With God there are abundant gains. You too were once as they are—unbelievers, and then God conferred a benefit on you. Therefore, investigate. Surely God is Aware of what you do.[1] (The Women 4:94)

Believers without injury who hold back are not equal with those who strive in God's way with their wealth and their lives. God has made those who strive with their wealth and their lives excel to a high degree over those who hold back. God has promised good—but God will grant a mighty reward to the strivers over the holders back. (The Women 4:95)

The only punishment for those who wage war against God and His Messenger and strive to [spread corruption] in the land is that they should be murdered, or crucified, or their hands and their feet should be cut off on opposite sides, or they should be imprisoned. This will be a disgrace for them in this world, and in the Hereafter they will have a grievous chastisement, except those who repent before you overpower them. Know that God is Forgiving, Merciful. (The Food 5:33-34)

When God promised you that one of the two groups would be yours, and you [wished] that the one not armed would be yours, God desired to plainly show the Truth by His words, and to cut off the roots of the unbelievers. So that He may clearly show the Truth and show falsehood, even if the guilty disliked it. He caused calm to fall on you, a security from Him, and then He sent down water from the cloud on you, so that He may purify you and take away from you the uncleanness of the Devil, and fortify your hearts and steady your footsteps. (The Accessions 8:7-8, 11)

Your Lord revealed to the angels: I am with you, so make firm those who believe. I will cast terror into the hearts of those who disbelieve. So strike off their heads and strike off every finger-tip of them. This is because they acted adversely to God and His Messenger. Surely, God is severe in repaying (evil)for whoever acts adversely to God and His Messenger. This—so taste it, and (know) that the chastisement of fire is for the unbelievers. (The Accessions 8:12-14)

---

1 Ali, M.M., *The Holy Qur'an*, 228. Even if you doubt the sincerity of the greeting, you must deal with the greeter as a friend, not an enemy.

Jesus

My Kingdom is not of this world. If my Kingdom were of this world, then my servants would fight, so that I would not be delivered to the Jewish leaders. But now my Kingdom is not from here." (John 18:36)

Muhammad ﷺ

Oh, you who believe! When you meet those who disbelieve marching for war, do not turn your backs to them. Whoever turns his back to them on that day, except for the sake of fighting or to withdraw to a company, indeed becomes deserving of God's wrath, and his abode is Hell— an evil destination it will be. You did not slay them, God slew them, and you did not smite when you smote (the enemy), God smote, so that He might confer on the believers a good gift. Surely God is Hearing, Knowing. (The Accessions 8:15-17)

Know that one-fifth of anything you acquire in war is for God, the Messenger, the near of kin, the orphans, the needy and the wayfarer, if you believe in God and in what We revealed to Our servant, on the Day of the Distinction,[1] the day on which the two forces met. God has power over all things. (The Accessions 8:41)

Oh, you who believe! When you meet a [force], be firm, and remember God much, so that you may be successful. And obey God and His Messenger, and do not quarrel, for then you will be weak in hearts, and your power will depart. Be patient; surely God is with the patient. (The Accessions 8:45-46)

Surely, the vilest of animals in God's sight are the disbelievers, who will not believe. Those with whom you make an agreement, and then they break their agreement every time, and they do not [fear God]. So if you overtake them in fighting, scatter them by (making an example of) those who are in their rear, so that they may be mindful. (The Accessions 8:55-57)

Prepare against them what force you can. Tie horses at the frontier, to frighten the enemy of God and your enemy and others besides them whom you do not know. God knows them, and any thing that you spend in God's way will be paid back to you fully, and you will not be dealt with unjustly. If they incline to peace, then you also incline to it, and trust in God. Surely He is the Hearing, the Knowing. But if they intend to deceive you, surely God is sufficient for you. It was He who strengthened you with His help, and with the believers. (The Accessions 8:60-62)

Oh, Prophet! Urge the believers to war; if there are twenty patient ones among you, they will overcome two hundred, and if there are one hundred of you, they will overcome a thousand of those who disbelieve, because they are a people who do not understand. (The Accessions 8:65)

---

1 The Battle of Badr, a decisive battle that was an early turning point in Muhammad's struggle with his opponents among the Quraish in Mecca.—Ed.

Jesus

Muhammad

It is not fitting for a prophet to take captives of war unless he has fought and triumphed in the land. You desire the frail goods of this world, while God desires (for you) the Hereafter; God is Mighty, Wise. Were it not for a decree from God that had already gone forth, surely a great chastisement would have befallen you for what you took. So eat of the lawful and good (things) that you acquired in war, and [fear] God. Surely, God is Forgiving, Merciful. (The Accessions 8:67-69)

Certainly God helped you in many battlefields and on the day of Hunain, when your great numbers made you vain, but they availed you nothing. The Earth became constricted to you, in spite of its spaciousness, and you turned back, retreating. Then God sent down His tranquility on His Messenger and on the believers, and He sent down armies that you did not see, and chastised those who disbelieved— that is the reward of the unbelievers. (The Immunity 9:25-26)

Go forth light and heavy,[1] and strive hard in God's way with your wealth and your lives; this is better for you, if you know. (The Immunity 9:41)

[Prophet], only those who do not believe in God and the Latter Day ask leave of you; their hearts are in doubt, so they waver in their doubt. If they had intended to go forth, they would have certainly provided equipment for it. But God did not like their going forth, so He withheld them, and it was said (to them): Hold back with those who hold back. Had they gone forth with you, they would not have added to you except corruption, and they would have certainly hurried about among you, seeking (to sow) dissension. Among you are those who would have listened to them. God knows the [wrongdoers]. (The Immunity 9:45-47)

Those who were left behind were glad to sit behind God's Messenger, and they were averse from striving in God's way with their wealth and their lives. They said: Do not go forth in the heat. Say, [Prophet]: The Fire of Hell is much more severe in heat. If only they could understand. So they will laugh a little and then weep much, as a recompense for what they earned. (The Immunity 9:81-82)

---

1 Ali, M.M., *The Holy Qur'an*, 408. Whether it is easy or difficult, whether you are armed or unarmed.

Jesus

Muhammad ﷺ

[Prophet], if God brings you back to a group of them, and they ask your permission to go forth, say: By no means will you ever go forth with me, and by no means will you fight any enemy with me. Surely, you chose to sit the first time, so sit (now) with those who remain behind. Never offer prayer for any one of them who dies, and do not stand by his grave. Surely they disbelieve in God and His Messenger, and they will die while they are defiantly disobedient. Do not let their property and their children excite your admiration—God only wishes to chastise them with them in this world, and He wishes (that) their souls may depart while they are unbelievers. (The Immunity 9:83-85)

[Prophet], do they not see that We are bringing destruction upon the land by cutting away its borders? God pronounces a doom—there is no repeller of His decree, and He is swift to take account. (The Thunder 13:41)

Do they have gods who can defend them against Us? They will not be able to assist themselves, nor will they be defended from Us. No, We gave provision to them and their fathers until life was prolonged to them. Don't they see that We are visiting the land, reducing it from its borders? Shall they prevail? Say, [Prophet]: I warn you only by revelation; and the deaf do not hear the call when they are warned. If a blast of your Lord's chastisement were to touch them, they would certainly say: Oh, woe to us! Surely we were [wrongdoers]! (The Prophets 21:43-46)

Say, [Prophet]: Fleeing will not do you any good. If you flee from death or slaughter, you will be allowed to enjoy yourselves only a little. Say: Who can withhold you from God if He intends to do you evil, or if He intends to show you mercy? They will not find any guardian or helper besides God. God knows those among you who hinder others and those who say to their brethren, "Come to us"— they hardly ever come to the fight. (The Allies 33:16-18)

God turned back the unbelievers in their rage—they did not obtain any advantage. God is sufficient for the believers in fighting. God is Strong, Mighty. He drove down those among the Followers of the Book who backed [the unbelievers] from their fortresses, and He cast awe into their hearts. You killed some, and you took captive others. He made you heirs to their land and their dwellings and their properties, and (to) a land on which you had not yet walked. God has power over all things. (The Allies 33:25-27)

Jesus

Muhammad ﷺ

[Prophet], those who believe, say: Why has a chapter not been revealed? But when a decisive chapter is revealed, and fighting is mentioned in it, you see those with diseased hearts look at you with the look of one fainting, because of death. Woe to them! Obedience and a gentle word (was proper). But when the affair becomes settled, if they remain true to God, it will certainly be better for them. But if you had held command, you surely would have made mischief in the land and cut off the ties of kinship! God has cursed these: He has made them deaf and blinded their eyes. (Muhammad 47:20-23)

It was He who caused those who disbelieved of the Followers of the Book to go forth from their homes at the first exile.[1] You did not think that they would go, and they were certain that their fortresses would defend them against God. But God came to them when they did not expect it, and He cast terror into their hearts. They demolished their houses with their own hands and the hands of the believers. So take a lesson, oh you who have eyes! Had God not decreed the exile for them, He would certainly have chastised them in this world, and in the Hereafter they will have chastisement of the Fire, because they acted in opposition to God and His Messenger, and God is surely severe in retributing (evil) to whoever acts in opposition to Him. Whatever palm-tree you cut down or leave standing on its roots, it is by God's command, so that He may disgrace the defiantly disobedient. (The Banishment 59: 2-5)

Oh, you who believe! Why do you say what you do not do? It is most hateful to God that you say what you do not do. Surely, God loves those who fight in His way in ranks, as if they were a firm and compact wall. (The Ranks 61:2-4)

Have you not considered how your Lord dealt with the Possessors of the Elephant?[2] Did He not cause their war to end in confusion, and send down birds in flocks (to prey) upon them, casting them against hard stones, so that He rendered them like eaten-up straw? (The Elephant 105:1-5)

---

1 Ali, M.M., *The Holy Qur'an*, 1057. This refers to the forced exile by the Muslims of the Jewish clan Banu al-Nadir, who had repeatedly broken treaties with the Muslims.

2 Ali, M.M., *The Holy Qur'an*, 1224. This refers to the army of Abraha (a Christian ruler of Yemen), which marched to destroy the Ka'bah in Mecca and divert pilgrims to the new cathedral in San'aa in 570 CE, the year of the Prophet's birth. After the Meccan idolators prayed at the Ka'bah against the impending invasion, a virulent form of small-pox or some other pestilence broke out in Abraha's army with such severity that' the army retreated. Birds then feasted on their corpses, tearing off flesh from the dead bodies and casting it on stones.

Peace

 Jesus

Into whatever house you enter, first say, "Peace be to this house." If a peaceful person is there, your peace will rest on him; but if not, it will return to you. (Luke 10:5-6)

I have told you these things, so that in me you may have peace. In the world you will have oppression; but cheer up. I have overcome the world. (John 16:33)

Blessed are the peacemakers, for they will be called sons of God. (Matthew 5:9)

When he drew near, he saw the city and wept over it, saying, "If you, even you, had known today the things that make for peace! But now, they are hidden from your eyes. For the days will come on you, when your enemies will throw up a barricade against you, surround you, hem you in on every side, and dash you and your children within you to the ground. They will not leave in you one stone on another, because you did not know the time of your visitation." (Luke 19:41-44)

Peace I leave with you. My peace I give to you. I do not give to you as the world gives. Do not let your heart be troubled, neither let it be afraid. You have heard how I told you, "I am going away, and I will come to you." If you loved me, you would rejoice that I said I am going to my Father; for the Father is greater than I. (John 14:27-28)

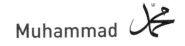
Do not make your swearing (by God) an obstacle to doing good, guarding (against evil) and making peace between men; God is Hearing, Knowing. (The Cow 2:224)

The servants of the Beneficent God are those who walk on the Earth in humbleness, and when the ignorant address them, they say: Peace. (The Distinction 25:63)

He sends His blessings on you, and (so do) His angels, so that He may bring you out of utter darkness into the light. He is Merciful to the believers. Their greeting on the day that they meet Him will be: Peace. He has prepared an honorable reward for them. (The Allies 33:43-44)

While you have the upper hand, do not be slack and call for peace. God is with you, and He will not count your deeds for nothing. The life of this world is only idle sport and play, and if you believe and (guard against) evil, He will give you your rewards, and He will not ask you for your possessions. (Muhammad 47:35-36)

It is God He who sent down tranquility into the hearts of the believers, so that they might have more faith added to their faith. The hosts of the Heavens and the Earth are God's, and God is Knowing, Wise. (The Victory 48:4)

Only the believers are brothers. So make peace between your brothers, and [fear] God, so that you may have mercy. (The Chambers 49:10)

Anger

 Jesus

You have heard that it was said to the ancient ones, "Do not murder," and "Whoever murders will be in danger of the judgment." But I tell you that everyone angry with his brother without a cause will be in danger of the judgement; and whoever will say to his brother, "good for nothing," will be in danger of the council; and whoever will say, "You fool," will be in danger of the fire of Hell. (Matthew 5:21-22)

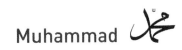

Those who spend (benevolently) during ease as well as limited times, and those who restrain (their) anger and pardon men—God loves the doers of good (to others).

(The Family of Amran 3:134)

Be Attentive

Believers and Disbelievers

 Jesus

Note: Jesus appeals to listeners: Believe in God, believe that Christ is the Son of God, and hear his message from God.—Ed.

And if anyone hears my words and does not believe, I do not judge him. For I came not to judge the world, but to save the world. He who rejects me and does not accept my words has One who judges him. The word that I spoke will judge him on the last day. For I spoke not from myself, but the Father who sent me. He gave me a commandment, what I should say, and what I should speak. I know that His commandment is eternal life. The things therefore that I speak, even as the Father has said to me, so I speak. (John 12:47-50)

To what then will I liken the people of this generation? What are they like? They are like children who sit in the marketplace, and call one to another, saying, "We played the flute for you, and you did not dance. We mourned for you, and you did not weep." For John the Baptist came neither eating bread nor drinking wine, and you say, "He has a demon." The Son of Man has come eating and drinking, and you say, "Look, a gluttonous man, and a drunkard; a friend of tax collectors and sinners." Wisdom is justified by all of her children. (Luke 7:31-35)

Muhammad ﷺ

Note: In some contexts, Muhammad refers to people who do not follow Islam as disbelievers or unbelievers, including Pagans, Christians and Jews.—Ed.

Whether you warn the disbelievers or do not warn them, it is the same to them. They will not believe. God has sealed their hearts and their hearing, and there is a covering over their eyes. There is a great chastisement for them (The Cow 2:6-7)

If you are in doubt about what We have revealed to Our servant, produce a chapter like it, and call on your helpers besides God, if you are truthful. But if you don't do (it)—and you never will do (it)—then be on guard against the Fire, its fuel of which is men and stones. It is prepared for the unbelievers. (The Cow 2:23-24)

Oh, Children of Israel! Remember My favour, which I bestowed on you, and be faithful to (your) covenant with Me. I will fulfil (My) covenant with you. And of Me, Me alone, should you be afraid. Believe in what I have revealed, verifying that which is with you. Do not be the first to deny it, and do not exchange My Signs for a small price, and Me, Me alone should you fear. Do not mix the truth with falsehood, and do not hide the truth while you know (it). (The Cow 2:40-42)

Evil is that for which they have sold their souls, so that they deny what God has revealed, out of envy that God would send down of His grace on whomever of His servants He pleases. So they have made themselves deserving of wrath upon wrath, and there is a disgraceful chastisement for the unbelievers. When it is said to them, Believe in what God has revealed, they say: We believe in what was revealed to us— and they deny anything besides that, while it is the truth verifying what they have. Say [Prophet]: Then why did you kill God's prophets before (this), if you were indeed believers? (The Cow 2:90-91)

The curse of God and the angels and men all together is surely on those who disbelieve and die while they are disbelievers. Abiding in it—their chastisement will not be lightened, nor will they be given respite. Your God is one God! There is no god but He; the Beneficent, the Merciful. (The Cow 2:161-162)

It is He who has revealed the Book to you. Some of its verses are decisive, they are the basis of the Book, and others are allegorical. Those with perversity in their hearts follow the part that is allegorical, seeking to mislead, and seeking to give it (their own) interpretation. But none know its interpretation except God and those who are firmly rooted in knowledge. Say: We believe in it, it is all from our Lord. None will heed except those who have understanding. (The Family of Amran 3:7)

Jesus

He said, "Truly I tell you, no prophet is acceptable in his hometown." (Luke 4:24)

But you are unwilling to come to me so that you may have life. I do not receive glory from men. But I know you, that you do not have God's love in yourselves. I have come in my Father's name, and you do not receive me. If another comes in his own name, you will receive him. How can you believe, you who receive glory from one another, and you do not seek the glory that comes from the only God? (John 5:40-44)

For the Kingdom of Heaven is like a man who was the master of a household, who went out early in the morning to hire laborers for his vineyard. When he had agreed with the laborers for a denarius a day, he sent them into his vineyard. He went out about the third hour, and saw others standing idle in the marketplace. He said to them, "You also go into the vineyard, and whatever is right I will give you." So they went their way. Again he went out about the sixth and the ninth hour, and did likewise. About the eleventh hour he went out, and found others standing idle. He said to them, "Why do you stand here all day idle?" They said to him, "Because no one hired us." He said to them, "You also go into the vineyard, and you will receive whatever is right." When evening had come, the lord of the vineyard said to his manager, "Call the laborers, and pay them their wages, beginning from the last to the first." When those who were hired at about the eleventh hour came, they each received a denarius. When the first came, they supposed that they would receive more; and they likewise each received a denarius. When they received it, they murmured against the master of the household, saying, "These last have spent one hour, and you have made them equal to us, who have borne the burden of the day and the scorching heat." But he answered one of them, "Friend, I am doing you no wrong. Did you not agree with me for a denarius? Take that which is yours, and go your way. It is my desire to give to this last just as much as to you. Is it not lawful for me to do what I want with what I own? Or is your eye evil, because I am good?" So the last will be first, and the first last; for many are called, but few are chosen. (Matthew 20:1-16)

Muhammad ﷺ

Announce a painful chastisement to those who disbelieve in the Signs of God, who slay the prophets unjustly, and who slay men who direct justice among the people. Their works will become null in this world and in the Hereafter, and they will have no helpers. (The Family of Amran 3:21-22)

Oh, you who believe! If you obey a group from among those who have been given the Book, they will turn you back as unbelievers after you have believed. How can you disbelieve as the Verses of God are recited to you, and His Messenger is among you? Whoever holds fast to God is indeed guided to the right path. (The Family of Amran 3:100-101)

(As for) those who disbelieve, surely neither their wealth nor their children will advantage them in the least against God. These are the inmates of the Fire, and they will abide in it. What they spend in this life is like an intensely cold wind that smites and destroys the harvest of a people who have done injustice to their own souls. God is not unjust to them; they are unjust to themselves. (The Family of Amran 3:116-117)

[Prophet], do not let those who hasten into unbelief grieve you. Surely, they can do no harm to God at all. God intends to not give them any portion in the Hereafter, and they will have a grievous chastisement. (The Family of Amran 3:176)

Do not let the unbelievers think that Our granting them respite is better for their souls. We grant them respite only so that they may add to their sins. They will have a humiliating chastisement. (The Family of Amran 3:178)

Do they envy the people for what God has given them of His grace? Indeed, We gave the Book and the wisdom to Abraham's children, and We gave them a grand kingdom. Some of them believe in him, and some of them turn away from him. Hell is sufficient to burn. We will make those who disbelieve in Our Signs enter fire—as often as their skins are thoroughly burned, We will change their skins for new skins, so that they may taste the chastisement. Surely God is Mighty, Wise. (The Women 4:54-56)

Surely, God will not forgive or guide to the (right) path those who believe, then disbelieve, again believe and again disbelieve, and then increase in disbelief. Announce to the hypocrites that there is a painful chastisement for them. (The Women 4:137-138)

Jesus

For the heart of this people has grown dull, and their ears are sluggish in hearing, and they have closed their eyes, otherwise they might see with their eyes, and hear with their ears, and understand with their heart, and turn back, and I would heal them. (Matthew 13:15)

Do not let your heart be troubled. Believe in God. Believe also in me. (John 14:1)

Muhammad ﷺ

Oh, you who believe! Whoever among you turns back from his religion, God will replace with other people: He will love them, and they will love Him. Lowly before the believers, and mightily against the unbelievers, they will strive hard in God's way and not fear the censure of a censurer. This is God's grace. He gives it to whom He pleases, and God is Ample-Giving, Knowing. (The Food 5:54)

Oh, you who believe! Do not ask questions about things that, if declared to you, might trouble you. If you question about them when the Qur'an is being revealed, they will be declared to you. God pardons this, and God is Forgiving, Forbearing. A people before you indeed asked such questions, and then they became disbelievers on account of the questions. (The Food 5:101-102)

Some listen to you, [Prophet], but We have cast veils over their hearts, lest they understand you, and a heaviness in their ears. Even if they see every sign, they will not believe in it. When they come to you, they only dispute with you; those who disbelieve say: This is nothing but the stories of the ancients. They prohibit (others) from it, and they keep far away from it, and they only bring destruction on their own souls, while they do not perceive. (The Cattle 6:25-26)

We send messengers only as announcers of good news and as givers of warnings. So whoever believes and acts right will have no fear, nor will they grieve. A chastisement will afflict those who reject Our Verses, because of their defiant disobedience. (The Cattle 6:48-49)

Leave those who take their religion for play and an idle sport, and those whom this world's life has deceived. Remind (them), lest a soul be given up to destruction for what it earned—it will not have any guardian or intercessor besides God. If it should seek to give every compensation, the compensation will not be accepted. These will be given up to destruction for what they earned. They will have a drink of boiling water and a painful chastisement because they disbelieved. (The Cattle 6:70)

In every town, We have made the great ones to be its guilty ones, so that they plan. But they only plan against their own souls, and they do not perceive. When a message comes to them, they say: We will not believe until we are given the like of what God's messengers are given. God knows best where He places His message. Humiliation and severe chastisement will fall on those who are guilty, for what they planned. (The Cattle 6:123-124)

Jesus

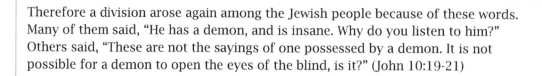

Therefore a division arose again among the Jewish people because of these words. Many of them said, "He has a demon, and is insane. Why do you listen to him?" Others said, "These are not the sayings of one possessed by a demon. It is not possible for a demon to open the eyes of the blind, is it?" (John 10:19-21)

The Father himself, who sent me, has testified about me. You have neither heard His voice at any time, nor seen His form. You do not have His word living in you; because you do not believe him whom He sent. You search the Scriptures, because you think that in them you have eternal life; and these are they which testify about me. (John 5:37-39)

Muhammad

I am God the Seeing. These are the verses of the wise Book. What? Is it a wonder to the people that We revealed to a man from among themselves, saying: Warn the people, and give good news to those who believe, that they have firm footing with their Lord. The unbelievers say: This is most surely an obvious enchanter. (Jonah 10:1-2)

This Qur'an could not be invented by those besides God, but it is a verification of what came before it, and it is a clear explanation of the Book. There is no doubt about it, it is from the Lord of the Worlds. Or do they say: He has invented it? Say, [Prophet]: Then bring a chapter like this, and invite whomever you can besides God, if you are truthful. (Jonah 10:37-38)

[Prophet], if they call you a liar, say: My work is for me and your work is for you. You are cleared of what I do, and I am cleared of what you do. (Jonah 10:41)

If you are in doubt about what We have revealed to you, ask those who read the Book before you. Certainly the truth has come to you from your Lord, so you should not be among the disputers. You should not be among those who reject the Signs of God, (for) then you would be one of the losers. (Jonah 10:94-95)

If your Lord had pleased, surely all of those on Earth would have believed, all of them. So, [Prophet], will you force men until they become believers? (Jonah 10:99-100)

[Prophet], do they say: He has invented it? Say: If I have invented it, my guilt is on me. But I am clear of that which you are guilty of. (Hud 11:35)

The parable of those who disbelieve in their Lord: Their actions are like ashes on which the wind blows hard, on a stormy day. They will not have power over anything that they have earned; this is the great error. Do you not see that God created the Heavens and the Earth with truth? If He pleases, He will remove you and bring a new creation. This is not difficult for God. (Abraham 14:18-20)

Often those who disbelieve wish that they had been Muslims. Leave them to eat and enjoy themselves, and [let] hope beguile them, for they will soon know. We never destroyed a town unless it had a term made known. No people can hasten their doom, nor can they postpone (it). (The Rock 15:2-5)

Jesus

Believe me that I am in the Father, and the Father is in me; or else believe me because of the works themselves. (John 14:11)

Jesus said, "I came into this world for judgment, that those who do not see may see; and that those who see may become blind." Those of the Pharisees who were with him heard these things, and said to him, "Are we also blind?" Jesus said to them, "If you were blind, you would have no sin; but since you say, 'We see,' your sin remains." (John 9:39-41)

Muhammad ﷺ

They do not believe in it, and indeed the example of the former people has passed. Even if We open a gateway of the Heaven to them, and they continuously ascend into it, they would certainly say: Our eyes have only been covered over. No, we are an enchanted people. (The Rock 15:13-15)

[Prophet], even if you desire their guidance, surely God does not guide those whom [He lets go] astray, nor will they have any helpers. They swear by God with their most energetic oaths that God will not raise up one who dies. Yes! It is a promise binding on Him, quite true, but most people do not know, so that He can make obvious to them that about which they differ, and so that those who disbelieve can know that they were liars. (The Bee 16:37-39)

Certainly We know that they say: Only a mortal teaches [Muhammad]. But the tongue of he whom they reproach is barbarous, and this [Qur'an] is clear Arabic tongue. (The Bee 16:103)

We reveal of the Qur'an what is a healing and a mercy to the believers, but it adds only to the utter destruction of the [wrongdoers]. (The Israelites 17:82)

Say, [Prophet]: If men and Jinn should combine together to bring the like of this Qur'an, they could not bring the like of it, even if some of them aided others. (The Israelites 17:88)

We send messengers only to give good news and warning. Those who disbelieve make a false debate, to invalidate the truth. They mock My Verses and warnings. (The Cave 18:56)

Whoever thinks that God will not assist him in this life and in the Hereafter, let him stretch a rope to the ceiling, and then let him cut off his breath, strangled. And then let him see if his struggle takes away what enrages him. Thus have We revealed clear Verses, because God guides whom He intends. (The Pilgrimage 22:15-16)

These are two adversaries who dispute about their Lord. There are cut out garments of fire for those who disbelieve. Boiling water will be poured over their heads, melting what is in their bellies and melting (their) skins. There are hooked rods of iron for them. Whenever they desire to go forth from it, from anguish, they will be turned back into it, to taste the chastisement of burning. (The Pilgrimage 22:19-22)

Jesus

Then Jesus shouted out and said, "Whoever believes in me, believes not in me but in He who sent me. And he who sees me sees He who sent me." (John 12:44-45)

Truly I tell you that the tax collectors and the prostitutes are entering into the Kingdom of God before you. For John came to you in the way of righteousness, and you did not believe him, but the tax collectors and the prostitutes believed him. When you saw it, you did not even repent afterward, so that you might believe him. (Matthew 21:31-32)

Muhammad ﷺ

[Prophet], When Our clear Verses are recited to those who disbelieve, you will recognize denial on their faces. They almost spring upon those who recite Our Verses to them. Say: Shall I inform you of what is worse than this? The Fire. God has promised it to those who disbelieve, and how evil the destination! (The Pilgrimage 22:72)

Is it that they do not recognize their Messenger, so that they deny him? Or do they say: There is madness in him? No! He has brought them the truth, and most of them are averse to the truth. (The Believers 23:69-70)

The deeds of those who disbelieve are like the mirage in a desert, which the thirsty man deems to be water. When he comes to it, he finds it to be nothing, and there he finds God, Who pays back to him his due, in full. God is quick in reckoning. Or like utter darkness in the deep sea: a wave covers it, above which is another wave, above which is a cloud, (layers of) utter darkness, one above another. When he holds out his hand, he is almost unable to see it. To whomever God does not give light, he has no light. (The Light 24:39-40)

Those who disbelieve, say: Why has the Qur'an not been revealed to him all at once? So that We may establish your heart by it, We arranged it well. They will not bring you any argument, but We bring you one with truth and the best significance. (The Distinction 25:32-33)

Kind and Gracious, Hearing God! These are the verses of the Qur'an, and the book that makes obvious a guidance and good news for the believers, those who keep up prayer and pay the poor-rate and believe with certainty in the Hereafter. (The Naml 27:2-3)

Nor can you lead the blind out of their error. You can not make any hear except those who believe in Our Verses—they will submit. It is God Who created you from a state of weakness, and then He gave strength, and then ordained weakness and gray hair after strength. He creates what He pleases, and He is the Knowing, the Powerful. (The Romans 30:53-54)

Is a believer like a defiantly disobedient one? They are not equal. As for those who believe and do good, the gardens are their home, an entertainment for what they did. And as for those who are defiantly disobedient, their abode is the Fire. Whenever they desire to go forth from it, they will be brought back into it, and it will be said to them: taste the chastisement of the Fire, which you called a lie. (The Adoration 32:18-20)

Jesus

Truly, truly, I tell you, we speak that which we know, and testify of that which we have seen, and you do not receive our witness. If I told you earthly things and you do not believe, how will you believe if I tell you heavenly things? (John 3:11-12)

Muhammad ﷺ

Those who disbelieve, say: Shall we point out to you a man who informs you that when you are scattered the utmost scattering, you will then most surely be (raised) into a new creation? He has invented a lie about God! Or is it madness in him? No! Those who do not believe in the Hereafter are in torment and great error. (The Saba 34:7-8)

When Our clear messages are recited to them, they say: This is only a man who desires to turn you away from what your fathers worshipped. They say: This is only a lie that is forged. Those who disbelieve say of the truth when it comes to them: This is only obvious magic. (The Saba 34:43)

We have placed chains on their necks, and these reach up to their chins, so their heads are raised aloft. We have made a barrier before them and a barrier behind them, and We have covered them so that they do not see. It makes no difference to them whether you warn them or not: they do not believe. You can only warn he who follows the Reminder and fears the Beneficent God in secret; so announce forgiveness and an honorable reward to him. (Yasin 36:8-11)

We have not taught the Prophet poetry, nor is it befitting for him; it is only a reminder and a plain Qur'an, so that it may warn he who would have life, and so (that) the word may prove true against the unbelievers. (Yasin 36:69-70)

Surely, they used to say: Had we a reminder from those of yore, we certainly would have been the servants of God—the purified ones. But (now) they disbelieve in it, so they will come to know. (The Rangers 37:167-170)

[Prophet], turn away from them for a time, and (then) see, for they too will see. (The Rangers 37:178-179)

Have you not seen those who dispute concerning the Signs of God, how they are turned away? Those who reject the Book and what We sent with Our Messenger? But soon they will come to know. When the restraints and the chains are on their necks, they will be dragged into hot water, and then they will be burned in the Fire. (The Believer 40:69-72)

Continue to remind, for by the grace of your Lord, you are not a soothsayer, or a madman. Or do they say: A poet for whom we await the evil accidents of time. Say, [Prophet]: Wait, for surely I too wait, with you. No! Do their mind's understandings urge them to say this? Or are they an inordinate people? Or do they say: He has forged it. No! They do not believe. Let them bring an announcement like it, if they are truthful. (The Mountain 52:29-34)

Jesus

Jesus answered them, "I told you, and you do not believe. The works that I do in my Father's name testify about me. But you do not believe, because you are not of my sheep, as I told you. My sheep hear my voice, and I know them, and they follow me. I give eternal life to them. They will never perish, and no one will snatch them out of my hand." (John 10:25-28)

For God did not send His son into the world to judge the world, but so that the world should be saved through him. He who believes in Him is not judged. He who does not believe has been judged already, because he has not believed in the name of the only Son of God. This is the judgement, that the light has come into the world, and men loved the darkness rather than the light; for their works were evil. (John 3:17-19)

Muhammad ﷺ

Have you not heard the story of those who disbelieved before, and then tasted the evil result of their affair and had a painful chastisement? That is because their messengers came to them with clear arguments, but they said: Shall mortals guide us? So, they disbelieved and turned away. God does not need (anything), and God is Self-sufficient, Praised. (The Manifestation of Defects 64:5-6)

Oh, Prophet! Strive hard against the unbelievers and the hypocrites, and be hard against them; their abode is Hell, and evil is the destination. (The Prohibition 66:9)

Those who disbelieve would almost smite you with their eyes when they hear the Reminder, and they say: Most surely he is mad. It is nothing but a Reminder to the nations. (The Pen 68:51-52)

What is the matter with those who disbelieve? They hasten around you, on the right hand and on the left, in various groups. Does every one of them desire to be admitted to the Garden of Bliss? By no means! Surely We have created them from what they know. But no! I call to witness the Lord of the Easts and the Wests—We are certainly able to replace them with others who are better than them, and We will not be overcome. So leave them alone to go on with their false discourse and to sport until they come face to face with that Day of theirs, with which they are threatened. (The Ways of Ascent 70:36-42)

[Prophet], bear patiently what they say, and avoid them graciously. Leave the rejecters to Me—the possessors of ease and plenty—respite them a little. Surely, with Us are heavy shackles and a flaming fire, and food that chokes, and a painful punishment. (The Wrapped Up 73:10-13)

But what is the matter with them, that they do not believe? When the Qur'an is recited to them, they do not make obeisance. No! Those who disbelieve give the lie to the truth. God knows best what they hide, so announce to them a painful chastisement. Except those who believe and do good; for them is a reward that will never be cut off. (The Bursting Asunder 84:20-25)

Surely they are scheming, but I too am scheming. So give the unbelievers a respite: leave them alone for a while. (The Night-Comer 86:15-17)

Surely those who disbelieve among the Followers of the Book and the polytheists will be abiding in the Fire of Hell; they are the worst of men. Surely those who believe and do good are the best of men. Their reward is with their Lord—Gardens of Perpetuity, beneath which rivers flow, abiding there forever. God is well pleased with them, and they are well pleased with Him. This is for him who fears his Lord. (The Clear Evidence 98:6-8)

Path of Life

 Jesus

Enter by the narrow gate; for wide is the gate and broad is the way that leads to destruction, and many enter by it. Because narrow is the gate and difficult is the way that leads to life. Few are those who find it. (Matthew 7:13-14)

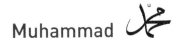

[Prophet], have you not considered Those to Whom a Portion of the Book Has Been Given?[1] They buy error and desire that you go astray from the way. (The Women 4:44)

Those who reject Our Verses are deaf and dumb, in utter darkness. God causes whom He pleases to err, and He puts on the right way whom He pleases. (The Cattle 6:39)

If you obey most of those on the Earth, they will lead you astray from God's way—they follow mere conjecture, and they only lie. Surely your Lord knows best who goes astray from His way, and He knows best those who follow the right course. (The Cattle 6:116-117)

God invites to the Abode of Peace, and He guides whom He pleases to the right path. Good (reward) and more is for those who do good. Neither blackness nor humiliation will cover their faces; these are the dwellers of the Garden—they will abide in it. (Jonah 10:25-26)

It rests upon God to show the right way, and there are some deviating (ways). If He pleased, He would certainly guide you all aright. (The Bee 16:9)

Most surely, [Prophet], you invite them to a right way. And most surely, those who do not believe in the Hereafter are deviating from the way. If We showed mercy to them and removed their distress, they would persist in their unregulated disorder, blindly wandering on. We already overtook them with chastisement, but they were not submissive to their Lord, nor did they humble themselves. Until We open a door of severe chastisement upon them. Behold! Then they will be in despair. (The Believers 23:73-77)

Certainly, We have revealed clear Verses, and God guides whom He pleases to the right way. (The Light 24:46)

Those who will be gathered to Hell on their faces are in a worse plight and straying farther away from the path. (The Distinction 25:34)

---

1 Christians and Jews.—Ed.

Jesus

Muhammad ﷺ

When they see you [Prophet], they take you for nothing but a mockery: Is this he whom God raised to be a messenger? He would have led us astray from our gods, had we not adhered to them patiently! They will know, when they see the chastisement, who is straying farther from the path. Have you seen he who takes his low desires for his god? Would you be a protector over him? Or do you think that most of them hear or understand? They are nothing but as cattle. No! They are straying farther from the path. (The Distinction 25:41-44)

Therefore, [Prophet], hold fast to what has been revealed to you; surely you are on the right path. (The Embellishment 43:43)

Who will be an army to assist you besides the Beneficent God? The unbelievers are only in deception. Or who will give you sustenance if He should withhold His sustenance? No! They persist in disdain and aversion. What! Is he who goes prone on his face better guided or he who walks upright on a straight path ? (The Kingdom 67:20-22)

By the grace of your Lord, [Prophet], you are not mad. Most surely you will have a reward never to be cut off. Surely you conform (yourself) to sublime morality. So you will see, and they (too) will see, which of you is afflicted with madness. Surely your Lord knows best he who errs from His way, and He knows best the followers of the right course. So do not yield to the rejecters. They wish you to be pliant, so that they (too) may be pliant. Do not yield to any mean swearer, defamer, going about with slander, a forbidder of good, outstepping the limits, sinful, ignoble, besides all that, known by his evil character, simply because he possesses wealth and sons. When Our Verses are recited to him, he says: Stories of those of yore. We will brand him on the nose. (The Pen 68:2-16)

Surely, this is a reminder, so that whoever pleases may take a way to his Lord. But you do not will it unless God wills it; surely God is Knowing, Wise. He admits whom He pleases into His mercy; but He has prepared a painful chastisement for the [wrongdoers]. (The Man 76:29-31)

Hear, See and Understand

 Jesus

Why do you not understand my speech? Because you cannot hear my word. You are of your father, the devil, and you want to do the desires of your father. He was a murderer from the beginning, and does not stand in the truth, because there is no truth in him. When he speaks a lie, he speaks on his own, for he is a liar, and its father. He who is of God hears the words of God. This is why you do not hear—because you are not of God. (John 8:43-44, 47)

Look, a farmer went out to sow. And as he sowed, some seeds fell by the roadside, and the birds came and devoured them. And others fell on rocky ground, where they did not have much soil, and they immediately sprang up, because they had no depth of earth. But when the sun had risen, they were scorched. Because they had no root, they withered away. Others fell among thorns, and the thorns grew up and choked them. Still others fell on good soil, and yielded fruit: some one hundred times as much, some sixty, and some thirty. He who has ears to hear, let him hear! (Matthew 13:3-9)

Take heed what you hear. With whatever measure you measure, it will be measured to you, and more will be given to you who hear. For whoever has, more will be given, and he who does not have, even that which he has will be taken away from him. (Mark 4:24-25)

Surely God is not ashamed to set forth any parable—that of a gnat, or anything below that. Those who believe know that it is the truth from their Lord. Those who disbelieve, say: What does God mean by this parable? He causes many to err by it, and He leads many aright by it, but He only causes the defiantly disobedient to err. The losers are those who break the Covenant of God after its confirmation. They cut apart what God has ordered to be joined, and they [spread corruption] in the land. (The Cow 2:26-27)

Do they not meditate on the Qur'an? If it were from any other than God, they would have found many a discrepancy in it. (The Women 4:82)

He causes the dawn to break, and He made the night for rest, and the sun and the moon for reckoning: this is an arrangement of the Mighty, the Knowing. It is He who made the stars for you, so that you may follow the right way in the darkness of the land and the sea. Truly, We have made plain the Signs for a people who know. It is He who brought you into being from a single soul, so there is (for you) a resting-place and a safe place. Indeed, We have made plain the Signs for a people who understand. (The Cattle 6:96-98)

We send down water from the cloud, and then We bring forth with it buds of all (plants). Then We bring forth from it green (foliage), from which We produce grain piled up (in the ear). And from the sheaths of the palm-tree come forth clusters (of dates), within reach. And gardens of grapes, and olives, and pomegranates, alike yet different. Behold its fruit when it yields, and the ripening. Most surely there are signs in this for a people who believe. (The Cattle 6:99)

The vegetation of the good land springs forth (abundantly) by the permission of its Lord, yet (the herbage) of inferior land comes forth scantily. This is how We repeat the Signs for a people who give thanks. (The Elevated Places 7:58)

Surely the vilest of animals, in God's sight, are the deaf, the dumb, who do not understand. (The Accessions 8:22)

Jesus

When it is evening, you say, "It will be fair weather, for the sky is red." In the morning, "It will be foul weather today, for the sky is red and threatening." Hypocrites. You know how to discern the appearance of the sky, but you cannot discern the signs of the times. (Matthew 16:2-3)

Everyone who hears these words of mine and does them, I will compare him to a wise man who built his house on a rock. And the rain came down, the floods came, and the winds blew and beat on that house; and it did not fall, for it was founded on the rock. And everyone who hears these words of mine and does not do them will be like a foolish man who built his house on the sand. And the rain came down, the floods came, and the winds blew, and beat on that house; and it fell—and great was its fall. (Matthew 7:24-27)

Hear, then, the parable of the farmer. When anyone hears the word of the Kingdom and does not understand it, the evil one comes and snatches away what has been sown in his heart. This is what was sown by the roadside. And what was sown on the rocky places, this is he who hears the word, and immediately receives it with joy; yet he has no root in himself, but endures only for a while. When oppression or persecution arises because of the word, immediately he stumbles. And what was sown among the thorns, this is he who hears the word, but the cares of the world and the deceitfulness of riches choke the word, and he becomes unfruitful. And what was sown on the good ground, this is he who hears the word, and understands it, who truly bears fruit, and brings forth, some one hundred times as much, some sixty, and some thirty. (Matthew 13:18-23)

Muhammad ﷺ

This world's life is only like water that We send down from the cloud, by which the herbage of the earth, of which men and cattle eat, grows luxuriantly. Until the Earth puts on its golden raiment and becomes garnished, and its people think that they have power over it. Then Our command comes by night or by day, and We render it as reaped harvest, as though it had not existed yesterday. Thus do We make clear the Signs for a people who reflect. (Jonah 10:24)

And on the Earth there are neighboring tracts, and gardens of grapevines and corn and palm-trees growing from a single root and (others) having distinct roots. They are watered with one water, but We make some of them excel in fruit over others: most surely there are signs in this for a people who understand. (The Thunder 13:4)

He sends down water from the cloud, and then watercourses flow, according to their measure, and the torrent moves along the swelling foam. From what they melt in the fire, to make ornaments or utensils, arises a scum like the swelling foam. Thus does God compare truth and falsehood; as for the scum, it passes away as a worthless thing, and as for what benefits the people, it remains in the earth. Thus God sets forth parables. (The Thunder 13:17)

Do not follow that of which you have no knowledge. Surely the hearing, the sight and the heart—you will be questioned about all of these. (The Israelites 17:36)

Man says: What? When I am dead, will I truly be brought forth alive? Does man not remember that We created him before, when he was nothing? So by your Lord! We will most certainly gather them with the devils, and then We will certainly bring around Hell, on their knees. Then We will most certainly draw forth, from every sect, those who were most exorbitantly rebellious against the Beneficent God. We certainly know best those who deserve most to be burnt. And there is not one of you who will not come to it; this is an unavoidable decree of your Lord. We will deliver those who [feared God], and We will leave the [wrongdoers] there, on their knees. (Mary 19:66-72)

Certainly, We have set forth for men every kind of parable in this Qur'an; but if you [Prophet] bring them a message, those who disbelieve will certainly say: You are nothing but falsifiers. This is how God seals the hearts of those who do not know. (The Romans 30:58-59)

Jesus

And when he was alone, those who were around him with the twelve asked him about the parables. And he said to them, "To you has been given to know the mystery of the kingdom of God, but to those who are outside, all things are done in parables, so that 'seeing they may see, and not perceive; and hearing they may hear, and not understand; lest perhaps they should turn and their sins be forgiven them.'"
(Mark 4:10-12)

Muhammad ﷺ

Certainly, We have set forth in this Qur'an similitudes of every sort for men, so that they may mind. An Arabic Qur'an without any crookedness, so that they may guard (against evil). (The Companies 39:27-28)

The blind and the seeing are not alike, nor the darkness and the light, nor the shade and the heat. Neither are the living and the dead alike. Surely God makes whom He pleases hear, and you can not make those who are in the graves hear. You are nothing but a warner. (The Originator 35:19-23)

He who says to his parents: Disgust to both of you! Do you threaten me that I will be brought forth [from my grave] when generations have passed away before me? And both [parents] call for God's aid: Woe to you! Believe, surely the promise of God is true. But he says: This is nothing but stories of the ancients. (The Sandhills 46:17)

Will they not consider the camels, how they are created? And the Heaven, how it is raised aloft? And the mountains, how they are set down, and the Earth, how it is made a vast expanse? (The Overwhelming Event 88:17-20)

Consider the fig and the olive, and Mount Sinai, and this city made secure. Certainly, We created man in the best of molds, and then We rendered him the lowest of the low, except those who believe and do good. They will have a reward never to be cut off. After (this), then, who can give you the lie about the judgment? Is not God the Best of the Judges? (The Fig 95:1-8)

Seek and Receive

 Jesus

Ask, and it will be given to you. Seek, and you will find. Knock, and it will be opened for you. For everyone who asks receives. He who seeks finds. To him who knocks it will be opened. Or who is there among you, who, if his son asks him for bread, will give him a stone? Or if he asks for a fish, who will give him a serpent? If you then, being evil, know how to give good gifts to your children, how much more will your Father who is in Heaven give good things to those who ask him. (Matthew 7:7-11)

All those whom the Father gives me will come to me. He who comes to me I will in no way throw out. (John 6:37)

If anyone is thirsty, let him come to me and drink. As the Scripture has said, rivers of living water will flow from within He who believes in me. (John 7:37b-38)

Look, I stand at the door and knock. If anyone hears my voice and opens the door, I will come in to him, and I will dine with him, and he with me. (Revelation 3:20)

Which of you, if you go to a friend at midnight, and tell him, "Friend, lend me three loaves of bread, for a friend of mine has come to me from a journey, and I have nothing to set before him," and he from within will answer and say, "Do not bother me. The door is now shut, and my children are with me in bed. I cannot get up and give it to you"? I tell you, although he will not rise and give it to him because he is his friend, yet because of his persistence, he will get up and give him as many as he needs. I tell you, ask, and it will be given to you. Seek, and you will find. Knock, and it will be opened to you. For everyone who asks receives. He who seeks finds. To him who knocks it will be opened. (Luke 11:5-10)

The one who has my commandments and keeps them is the one who loves me. And the one who loves me will be loved by my Father, and I will love him, and will reveal myself to him." (John 14:21)

And look, I am with you every day, even to the end of the age. Amen. (Matthew 28:20)

[Prophet], when My servants ask you about Me, surely I am very near. I answer the prayer of the supplicant when he calls on Me. So they should answer My call and believe in Me, so that they may walk in the right way. (The Cow 2:186)

Your Lord says: Call upon Me, I will answer you. Surely, those who are too proud for My service will soon enter Hell, abased. (The Believer 40:60)

Be Grateful to God

 Jesus

Even so, you also, when you have done all the things that are commanded of you, say, 'We are unworthy servants. We have done our duty." (Luke 17:10)

Remember Me, I will remember you, and be thankful to Me, and do not be ungrateful to Me. (The Cow 2:152)

A soul will not die without the permission of God; the term is fixed. Whoever desires the reward of the world, We will give him of it, and whoever desires the reward of the Hereafter, We will give him of it. We will reward the grateful. (The Family of Amran 3:145)

Why should God chastise you if you are grateful and believe? God is the Multiplier of Rewards, Knowing. (The Women 4:147)

We try some of them by others, so that they say: Are these the ones upon whom God has conferred benefit from among us? Does not God best know the grateful? (The Cattle 6:53)

[Iblis] said: Because You have caused me to remain disappointed, I will certainly lie in wait for them in Your straight path. Then I will certainly come to them from before them and from behind them, and from their right hand side and from their left-hand side. And You will not find most of them thankful. (The Elevated Places 7:16-17)

If We make man taste mercy from Us and then take it away from him, most surely he is despairing, ungrateful. (Hud 11:9)

If We make him taste a favour after distress has afflicted him, he will certainly say: The evils are gone away from me. Most surely he is exulting, boasting; Except those who are patient and do good—they will have forgiveness and a great reward. (Hud 11:10-11)

God sent down water from the cloud, and thereby gave life to the earth after its death. Most surely there is a sign in this for a people who would listen. Most surely there is a lesson for you in the cattle: We give you to drink of what is in their bellies—from between the bowels and the blood—pure milk, easy and agreeable to swallow for the drinkers. And from the fruits of the palms and the grapes, you take intoxicant and good provision; most surely there is a Sign in this for a people who ponder. Your Lord inspired the bee, saying: Make hives in the mountains and in the trees and in what they build. So eat of all the fruits, and walk in the ways of your Lord, submissively. There comes forth from the bees a beverage of many colours, in which there is healing for men. Most surely, there is a sign in this for a people who reflect. (The Bee 16:65-69)

Jesus

Muhammad ﷺ

God has brought you forth from the wombs of your mothers—you did not know anything—and He gave you hearing and sight and hearts, so that you may give thanks. (The Bee 16:78)

If they turn away, [Prophet], your duty is only the clear deliverance (of the message). They recognize the favour of God, yet they deny it, and most of them are ungrateful. (The Bee 16:82-83)

God sets forth a parable: (Consider) a town safe and secure, to which its means of subsistence come in abundance from every quarter. But it became ungrateful for God's favours, so God made it taste the utmost degree of hunger and fear because of what its people wrought. (The Bee 16:112)

When distress afflicts you at sea, those whom you call on go away, except Him. But when He brings you safe to the land, you turn away. Man is ever ungrateful. What? So do you feel secure that He will (not) make you disappear on a tract of land, or send a punishment against you, and then you will not find a protector for yourselves? Or, do you feel secure that He will (not) take you back into it again, and then send a fierce gale and drown you, because you disbelieved? And then you will not find any aider against Us in the matter. (The Israelites 17:67-69)

It is He who brought you to life, and then He will cause you to die, and then bring you to life (again); most surely, man is ungrateful. (The Pilgrimage 22:66)

It is He Who made for you ears and eyes and hearts for you: yet you give little thanks. And it is He it Who multiplied you on the Earth, and you will be gathered to Him. (The Believers 23:78-79)

They become ungrateful for what We have given them, so that they may enjoy; but soon they will know. (The Spider 29:66)

One of His signs is that He sends forth the winds bearing good news, and that He may make you taste of His mercy, and that the ships may run by His command, and that you may seek of His grace, and that you may be grateful. (The Romans 30:46)

Jesus

Muhammad ﷺ

If you are ungrateful, surely God is Self-sufficient, He is above all need of you. He does not like ungratefulness in His servants. If you are grateful, He likes it in you. No bearer of burden will bear the burden of another. To your Lord is your return; then will He inform you of what you did. Surely He is Cognizant of what is in the breasts. When distress afflicts a man he calls upon his Lord, turning to Him frequently. Then when God grants him a favour, he forgets what he called upon Him for before, and he sets up rivals to God so that he may cause (men) to stray off from God's path. Say: Enjoy yourself in your ungratefulness a little—surely you will be one of the inmates of the Fire. (The Companies 39:7-8)

When We show favour to man, he turns aside and withdraws himself. But when evil touches him, he makes lengthy, humble prayers. (Ha Mim 41:51)

But if they turn aside, We have not sent you as a watcher over them [Prophet]; on you is only to deliver (the message). Surely when We make man taste mercy from Us, he rejoices, but if evil afflicts them on account of what their hands have done, man is ungrateful. (The Counsel 42:48)

We have directed on man the doing of good to his parents; his mother bore him with trouble, and with trouble did she bring him forth. The bearing of him and the weaning of him was thirty months. When he attains his maturity and reaches forty years, he says: My Lord! Grant that I may give thanks for the favour that You have bestowed on me and on my parents, and that I may do good, which pleases You, and do good to me in respect of my offspring. Surely I turn to You, and surely I am of those who submit. We accept the best of what these have done, and We pass over their evil deeds. They are among the dwellers of the Garden—the promise of truth that they were promised. (The Sandhills 46:15-16)

We have ordained death among you, and We are not to be overcome. In order that We may transfigure you and make you grow into what you do not know. Certainly you know the first growth, so why do you not mind? Have you considered what you sow? Is it you who causes it to grow, or are We the causers of growth? If We pleased, We could have certainly made it debris, and then you would begin to lament, saying: Surely we are burdened with debt No! We are deprived. Have you considered the water that you drink? Is it you who sends it down from the clouds, or are We the senders? If We pleased, We could have made it salty; why then don't you give thanks? Have you considered the fire that you strike? Is it you who produces the trees for it, or are We the producers? We have made it a reminder and an advantage for the wayfarers of the desert. So, glorify the name of your Lord, the Great. (The Great Event 56:60-74)

Jesus

Muhammad ﷺ

We have created man from a small life-germ uniting (itself). We mean to try him, so We have made him hearing, seeing. Surely We have shown him the way, whether he be thankful or unthankful. (The Man 76:2-3)

Consider the runners, panting, and the producers of sparks, striking, and those who make raids at morn, raising dust, rushing on an assembly. Most surely man is ungrateful to his Lord. Most surely he is a witness of that. And most surely he is tenacious in the love of wealth. (The Assaulters 100:1-8)

Daily Living

Spirituality

 Jesus

It is written, "Man does not live by bread alone, but by every word that proceeds out of the mouth of God." (Matthew 4:4)

It happened as they went on their way, he entered into a certain village, and a certain woman named Martha received him into her house. She had a sister called Mary, who also sat at Jesus' feet, and heard his word. But Martha was distracted with much serving, and she came up to him, and said, "Lord, do you not care that my sister left me to serve alone? Ask her therefore to help me." But Jesus answered, and said to her, "Martha, Martha, you are anxious and troubled about many things, but one thing is needed. Mary has chosen the good part, which will not be taken away from her." (Luke 10:38-42)

Bear patiently what they say, and glorify your Lord by praising Him before the rising of the sun and before its setting. Also glorify (Him) during hours of the night and during parts of the day, so that you may be well pleased. And do not extend your eyes after what We have provided different classes of them, (of) the splendour of this world's life, so that We may try them. The sustenance (given) by your Lord is better and more abiding. (Ta Ha 20:130-131)

Whatever thing you are given is only a provision of this world's life. What is with God is better and more lasting for those who believe and rely on their Lord. (The Counsel 42:36)

No! You prefer the life of this world, while the Hereafter is better and more lasting. (The Most High 87:16-17)

Possessions and Wealth

 Jesus

Truly I say to you, a rich man will enter into the Kingdom of Heaven with difficulty. Again I tell you, it is easier for a camel to go through a needle's eye, than for a rich man to enter into the Kingdom of God. When his disciples heard it, they were exceedingly astonished, saying, "Who then can be saved?" Looking at them, Jesus said, "With men this is impossible, but with God, all things are possible." (Matthew 19:23-26)

Children, how hard it is for those who trust in riches to enter the Kingdom of God. (Mark 10:24)

But woe to you who are rich. For you have received your consolation. Woe to you, you who are full, for you will be hungry. Woe to you who laugh now, for you will mourn and weep. (Luke 6:24-26)

No one can serve two masters. Either he will hate the one and love the other, or he will be devoted to one and despise the other. You cannot serve both God and Mammon.[1] (Matthew 6:24)

Sell what you have, and give gifts to the needy. Make for yourselves purses that do not grow old, a treasure in the heavens that does not fail, where no thief approaches, nor moth destroys. For where your treasure is, there will your heart be also. (Luke 12:33-34)

---

1 From Aramaic, mammon is defined as "riches."—Ed.

The love of desires, of women and sons and hoarded treasures of gold and silver and well-bred horses and cattle and cultivated land, is made to seem fair to men. This is the provision of the life of this world. But with God is the good goal (of life). Say: Shall I tell you of what is better than these? For those who [feared] are gardens with their Lord, beneath which rivers flow, to abide in them, and pure mates, and God's pleasure. God sees the servants. Those who say: Our Lord! Surely we believe, so forgive us our faults, and keep us from the chastisement of the Fire. The patient, the truthful, the obedient, those who spend (benevolently), and those who ask forgiveness in the morning times. (The Family of Amran 3:14-17)

Oh, you who believe! Do not devour usury, doubling and redoubling [interest], and be careful of (your duty to) God, so that you may be successful. (The Family of Amran 3:130)

During their lives, We will pay in full for their deeds whoever desires this world's life and its finery. They will not be made to suffer loss in respect to their deeds. But there is nothing but Fire for them in the Hereafter, and what they wrought in [life] will count for nothing—what they do is vain. (Hud 11:15-16)

Whoever desires the reward of this world: with God is the reward of this world and the Hereafter. God is Hearing, Seeing. (The Women 4:134)

When We wish to destroy a town, We send our commandment to the people of it who lead easy lives, but they defiantly disobey. So the word comes into affect against the town, and We destroy it with utter destruction. How many of the generations We destroyed after Noah! Your Lord is a sufficient as Knowing and Seeing with regard to His servants' faults. (The Israelites 17:16-17)

Until We overtake with chastisement those who lead easy lives. Lo! They cry for relief. Do not cry for relief today; surely you will not be defended against Us. (The Believers 23:64-65)

He sets forth to you a parable relating to yourselves: Have you made partners among your slaves, in what We have given you for sustenance, so that you are equal in that respect? And do you fear them as you fear each other? Thus We make the Verses distinct for a people who understand. (The Romans 30:28)

Say [Prophet], surely my Lord amplifies the means of subsistence for whom He pleases of His servants and restricts for whom (He pleases), and whatever thing you spend, He exceeds it in reward. He is the best of Sustainers. (The Saba 34:39)

Jesus

Do not lay up treasures for yourselves on Earth, where moth and rust consume, and where thieves break through and steal. Rather lay up for yourselves treasures in Heaven, where neither moth nor rust consume, and where thieves do not break through and steal. For where your treasure is, there your heart will be also. (Matthew 6:19-21)

The ground of a certain rich man brought forth abundantly. He reasoned within himself, saying, "What will I do, because I do not have room to store my crops?" He said, "This is what I will do. I will pull down my barns, and build bigger ones, and there I will store all my grain and my goods. I will tell my soul, 'Soul, you have many goods laid up for many years. Take your ease, eat, drink, be merry.'" But God said to him, "You foolish one, tonight your soul is required of you. The things which you have prepared—whose will they be?" So is he who lays up treasure for himself, and is not rich toward God. (Luke 12:16-21)

Muhammad ﷺ

The life of this world is only idle sport and play, and if you believe and guard (against evil) He will give you your rewards, and will not ask of you your possessions. If He should ask you for it and urge you, you will withhold, and He will bring forth your malice. Behold! You are those who are called upon to spend in God's way, but among you are those who withhold, and whoever withholds, withholds against his own soul. God is Self-sufficient, and you have need (of Him), and if you turn back, He will bring in your place another people, and they will not be like you. (Muhammad 47:36-38)

The believers are only those who believe in God and His Messenger, and then do not doubt. And they struggle hard with their wealth and their lives in the way of God; they are the truthful ones. (The Chambers 49:15)

Know that this world's life is only sport and play and gaiety and boasting among yourselves, and a vying for the multiplication of wealth and children. Like the rain causing the vegetation to grow pleases the husbandmen, but then it withers away so that you will see it become yellow, and then it becomes dried up and broken down. In the Hereafter is a severe chastisement and (also) forgiveness from God, and (His) pleasure. This world's life is nothing but means of deception. (The Iron 57:20)

Your possessions and your children are only a trial. With God is a great reward. (The Manifestation of Defects 64:15)

By no means! Surely it is a flaming Fire. Dragging him by the head, it will claim he who retreats and turns his back, amasses wealth and hoards. (The Ways of Ascent 70:15-18)

Your striving is most surely diverse. We facilitate an easy end for those who give, those who [fear] and those who accept the best. We facilitate a difficult end for the miserly, those who consider themselves free from need (of God), and those who reject the best. Their wealth will not serve them when they perish. (The Night 92:4-11)

So I warn you of the Fire that flames. None will enter it but the most [wretched], who denied (the truth) and turned their backs. The one who guards most (against evil) will be kept away from it, who gives away his wealth, purifying himself. No one [expects] any favor for which he should be rewarded, but only seeks the pleasure of his Lord, the Most High. He will soon be well-pleased. (The Night 92:14-21)

Jesus

As some were talking about the temple and how it was decorated with beautiful stones and gifts, he said, "As for these things which you see, the days will come, in which there will not be left here one stone on another that will not be thrown down." They asked him, "Teacher, so when will these things be? What is the sign that these things are about to happen?" (Luke 21:5-7)

Muhammad ﷺ

Abundance diverts you, until you come to the graves. No! You will soon know. No! No! You will soon know. No! If you only knew with certainty—you will most certainly see Hell. You will most certainly see it with the eye of certainty. On that day, you will most certainly be questioned about the pleasures.

(The Multiplication of Wealth 102:1-8)

Diet and Cleanliness

 Jesus

That which enters into the mouth does not defile the man, but that which proceeds out of the mouth—this defiles the man. (Matthew 15:11)

Give for gifts to the needy those things that are within, and see, all things will be clean to you. (Luke 11:41)

Oh, men! Eat the lawful and good things out of the earth, and do not follow the footsteps of the Devil; surely, he is your open enemy. God only forbids you animals that died of themselves, and blood, and flesh of swine, and that over which any (name) other than God has been invoked. But no sin will be on whoever is driven by necessity, not desiring or exceeding the limit. Surely God is Forgiving, Merciful. (The Cow 2:168, 173)

They ask you, [Prophet], about intoxicants and games of chance. Say: In both of them is great sin and means of profit for men, but their sin is greater than their profit. And they ask you what they should spend. Say: What you can spare. Thus God makes clear to you the Verses, so that you may ponder. (The Cow 2:219)

They ask you, [Prophet], about menstruation. Say: It is slightly harmful; therefore keep aloof from the women during it, and do not approach them until they become clean. When they have cleansed themselves, go in to them as God has commanded you. Surely, God loves those who turn much (to Him), and He loves those who purify themselves. (The Cow 2:222)

Oh, you who believe! Do not go near prayer when you are intoxicated, until you know (well) what you say, nor when you are under an obligation to perform a total ablution[1]—unless (you are) travelling on the road—until you have washed yourselves. If you are ill, or on a journey, or one of you comes from the toilet, or you have touched the women, and you cannot find water, then take pure earth, and wipe your faces and your hands. Surely, God is Pardoning, Forgiving. (The Women 4:43)

Forbidden to you is what dies of itself, and blood, and flesh of swine, and that over which any name other than God has been invoked, and the strangled (animal) and that beaten to death, and that killed by a fall, and that killed by being gored by horns, and what wild beasts have eaten except what you slaughter, and what is sacrificed on stones set up (for idols) and that you divide by the arrows.[2] This is grave disobedience. (The Food 5:3a)

---

1 Ali, M.M., *The Holy Qur'an*, 214. The necessity to perform a total ablution arises in the case of sexual intercourse.

2 A Pagan tradition: divining arrows.—Ed.

Jesus

Do you also still not understand? Do you not understand that whatever goes into the mouth passes into the belly, and then out of the body? But the things which proceed out of the mouth come out of the heart, and they defile the man. For out of the heart come forth evil thoughts, murders, adulteries, sexual sins, thefts, false testimony, and blasphemies. These are the things which defile the man; but to eat with unwashed hands does not defile the man. (Matthew 15:16-20)

Muhammad ﷺ

Oh, you who believe! When you rise up to prayer, wash your faces and your hands as far as the elbows, and wipe your heads, and (wash) your feet to the ankles. If you are under an obligation to perform a total ablution, then wash (yourselves). If you are ill or on a journey, or if one of you come from the toilet, or if you have touched the women and you cannot find water, go to pure earth and wipe your faces and your hands with it. God does not desire to put on you any difficulty, but He wishes to purify you and to complete His favour on you, so that you may be grateful. (The Food 5:6)

Oh, you who believe! Intoxicants, games of chance, (sacrificing to) set-up stones and (dividing by) arrows[1] are only an uncleanness, the Devil's work. So shun it so that you may be successful. The Devil only desires to cause enmity and hatred to spring in your midst, by means of intoxicants and games of chance, and to hinder you from remembering God and from prayer. Will you desist? (The Food 5:90-91)

Oh, you who believe! God will certainly try you in respect to some game that your hands and your lances can reach, so that God might know who fears Him in secret. But whoever exceeds the limit after this will have a painful punishment. Oh, you who believe! Do not kill game while you are on pilgrimage, and whoever kills it intentionally, the compensation is the like of what he killed— from the cattle—as two just persons among you shall judge, as an offering to be brought to the Ka'ba, or the atonement (of it) is the feeding of the poor or the equivalent of it in fasting, so that he may taste the unwholesome result of his deed. God has pardoned what is gone by, but God will inflict retribution on whoever returns (to it). God is Mighty, Lord of Retribution. Lawful to you is the game of the sea and its food, a provision for you and for the travellers, and the game of the land is forbidden to you as long as you are on pilgrimage, and be careful of (your duty to) God, to whom you will be gathered. (The Food 5:94-96)

We made the camels among the symbols of God, for you. Therein is much good. So mention the name of God over them as they stand in a row, and then when they fall down, eat of them and feed the poor man who is contented and the beggar. We have made them subservient to you, so that you may be grateful. Neither their flesh nor their blood reach God, but your guarding against evil is acceptable to Him. He made them subservient to you, so that you may magnify God because He has guided you aright. Give good news to those who do good (to others). (The Pilgrimage 22:36-37)

---

1 Divining arrows—Ed.

Fasting

 Jesus

Moreover when you fast, do not be like the hypocrites, with sad faces. They disfigure their faces, so that they may be seen by men to be fasting. Truly I tell you, they have received their reward. But you, when you fast, anoint your head, and wash your face; so that you are not seen by men to be fasting, but by your Father who is in secret, and your Father, who sees in secret, will reward you. (Matthew 6:16-18)

Oh, you who believe! Fasting is prescribed for you, as it was prescribed for those before you, so that you may guard (against evil). (The Cow 2:183)

The month of Ramadan is the month in which the Qur'an was revealed, a guidance for men, and clear proofs of the Guidance and the Distinction. So whoever of you is present in the month shall fast during it, and whoever is sick or on a journey (shall fast) a (like) number of other days. God desires ease for you; He does not intend difficulty for you. (He desires) that you should complete the number, and that you should exalt the greatness of God for His having guided you, and that you may give thanks. (The Cow 2:185)

It is made lawful to you to go in to your wives on the nights of the fasting; they are an apparel for you, and you are an apparel for them. God knew that you acted unfaithfully to yourselves, so He turned to you (mercifully) and removed from you (this burden). So now be in contact with them, and seek what God has ordained for you. Eat and drink until the whiteness of the day becomes distinct from the blackness of the night at dawn, and then complete the fast until night, and do not have contact with them while you keep to the mosques. These are the limits of God, so do not go near them. Thus God makes clear His Verses for men, so that they may guard (against evil). (The Cow 2:187)

Accomplish the pilgrimage and the visit for God, but if you are prevented, (send) whatever offering is easy to obtain, and do not shave your heads until the offering reaches its destination. But whoever among you is sick or has an ailment of the head, he (should effect) a compensation by fasting or alms or sacrificing; then when you are secure, whoever profits by combining the visit with the pilgrimage (should take) whatever offering is easy to obtain. He who cannot find (any offering) should fast for three days during the pilgrimage and for seven days when you return—these (make) ten (days) complete; this is for him whose family is not present in the sacred mosque. Be careful (of your duty) to God, and know that God is severe in repaying (evil). (The Cow 2:196)

Associates

 Jesus

Can the blind guide the blind? Won't they both fall into a pit? (Luke 6:39)

Do not let the believers take the unbelievers for friends, rather than believers. Whoever does this will have nothing of God's (guardianship), unless you guard yourselves against them, guarding carefully. God makes you cautious of (retribution from) Himself; and to God is the eventual coming. (The Family of Amran 3:28)

Oh, you who believe! Do not take intimate friends from among those other than your own people.[1] They will not fall short of inflicting loss upon you; they love what distresses you. Vehement hatred has already appeared out of their mouths, and what their breasts conceal is greater still. Indeed, We have made the Verses clear to you, if you will understand. Lo! You are those who love them, while they do not love you. You believe in the Book, all of it. When they meet you, they say: We believe. But when they are alone, they bite their fingertips in rage against you. Say: Die in your rage. Surely God Knows what is in the breasts. If good befalls you, it grieves them, and if an evil afflicts you, they rejoice. If you are patient and guard yourselves, their scheme will not injure you in any way. Surely God comprehends what they do.
(The Family of Amran 3:118-120)

They wish that you would disbelieve as they have disbelieved, so that you (all) might be alike. So do not take friends from among them, until they flee (their homes) in God's way; but if they turn back, seize them and kill them wherever you find them, and do not take a friend or a helper from among them. (The Women 4:89)

Regarding those who take the unbelievers for [allies], rather than believers. Do they seek honour with them? Surely all honour is for God. Indeed, He has revealed to you in the Book that when you hear God's Verses disbelieved and mocked, do not sit with them until they enter into some other discourse. Surely then, you would be like them. Surely, God will gather together the hypocrites and the unbelievers, all in Hell.
(The Women 4:139-140)

Oh, you who believe! Do not take the unbelievers for guardians, rather than the believers. Do you wish to give God clear proof against yourselves? (The Women 4:144)

Oh, you who believe! Do not take the Jews and the Christians for friends; they are friends of each other. Whoever among you takes them for a friend surely is one of them. Surely God does not guide the [wrongdoers]. (The Food 5:51)

---

1 Ali, M.M., *The Holy Qur'an*, 176, Muslims.

Jesus

Muhammad ﷺ

Only God is your guardian, and His Messenger, and those who believe, and those who keep up prayer and pay the poor-rate, and bow down. Whoever takes God and His Messenger and those who believe for a guardian—the party of God—they are the triumphant. (The Food 5:55-56)

Oh, you who believe! Do not take guardians from among Those Who Were Given the Book Before You[1] and the unbelievers, those who take your religion as a mockery and a joke. Be care of (your duty to) God, if you are believers. (The Food 5:57)

When you see those who enter into false discourse about Our Verses, withdraw from them until they enter into some other discourse. If the Devil causes you to forget, after you recall, do not sit with the [wrongdoers]. (The Cattle 6:68)

Oh, you who believe! Do not take your fathers and your brothers for guardians if they love disbelief more than belief. Whoever takes them for guardians are the [wrongdoers]. Say, [Prophet]: If your fathers, sons, brothers, mates, kinsfolk, acquired property, trade about which you fear a decline, and dwellings that you like are dearer to you than God and His Messenger and striving in His way, wait until God brings about His command. God does not guide the defiantly disobedient people. (The Immunity 9:23-24)

Good and evil are not alike. Repel (evil) with what is best. And then, behold! The one with whom you had enmity will now be as if he is a warm friend. (Ha Mim 41:34)

Oh, you who believe! Do not befriend a people with whom God is intensely angry. Indeed, they despair of the Hereafter, just as the unbelievers despair of those in the tombs. (The Examined One 60:13)

---

1 Christians and Jews.—Ed.

Marriage

 Jesus

Moses allowed you to divorce your wives because of the hardness of your hearts, but from the beginning it has not been so. I tell you that whoever divorces his wife and marries another, except for sexual immorality, commits adultery. And he who marries her when she is divorced commits adultery. (Matthew 19:8-9)

Muhammad ﷺ

Do not marry the idolatresses until they believe. Certainly a believing maid is better than an idolatress woman, even if the idolatress pleases you. Do not give (believing women) in marriage to idolaters until they believe; certainly a believing servant is better than an idolater, even if the idolater pleases. These invite to the Fire, and God invites to the Garden and to forgiveness by His will, and He makes clear His Verses to men, so that they may be mindful. (The Cow 2:221)

Your wives are a tilth for you, so go in to your tilth as you like, and do good deeds beforehand for yourselves. And be careful (of your duty) to God, and know that you will meet Him, and give good news to the believers. (The Cow 2:223)

Divorced women should keep themselves in waiting for three menstrual periods, and it is not lawful for them to conceal what God has created in their wombs if they believe in God and the Last Day. Their husbands have a better right to take them back in this period if they wish for reconciliation; and the wives have rights similar to those of the men, in a just manner, but the men are a degree above them. God is Mighty, Wise. (The Cow 2:228)

Divorce may be (pronounced) twice; then keep the wife in good fellowship, or let her go with kindness. It is not lawful for husbands to take any part of what they have given wives, unless they both fear that they cannot keep within the limits of God. If they fear thus, there is no blame on either for what she gives up to become free. These are the limits of God, so do not exceed them. Whoever exceeds the limits of God are the [wrongdoers]. (The Cow 2:229)

(As for) those of you who die and leave wives behind, the wives should keep themselves in waiting for four months and ten days. When they have fully attained their term, there is no blame on you for what they do for themselves in a lawful manner. God is aware of what you do. (The Cow 2:234)

Those of you who die and leave wives behind, (make) a will in favour of your wives, with maintenance for a year without turning (them) out, and then if they themselves go away, there is no blame on you for what they do lawfully. God is Mighty, Wise. (The Cow 2:240-241)

If you fear that you cannot act equitably toward orphans,[1] marry such women as seem good to you, two and three and four. But if you fear that you will not do justice (between them), then (marry) only one, or marry those whom your right hands possess.[2] This is more proper, that you may not [oppress]. (The Women 4:3)

---

1 M.A.S. Abdel Haleem, trans., *The Qur'an* (New York: Oxford University Press, 2005) 50. (Hereafter cited as Haleem, *The Qur'an*). In pre-Islamic Arabia, some guardians of orphan girls married them to take their property.

2 Ali, M.M., *The Holy Qur'an*, 106. What your right hands possess means females who were taken prisoners in war.

Jesus

Whoever divorces his wife and marries another commits adultery against her. And if a woman divorces her husband and marries another, she commits adultery.
(Mark 10:11a-12)

Muhammad ﷺ

Oh, you who believe! It is not lawful for you to inherit women against (their) will;[1] and do not confine them in order to take part of what you have given them,[2] unless they are guilty of obvious indecency, and treat them kindly. If you hate them, it may be that you dislike a thing while God has placed abundant good in it. (The Women 4:19)

If you wish to have (one) wife in place of another, and you have given the original wife a heap of gold, do not take anything from it. Would you take it by slandering (her) and (doing her) obvious wrong? (The Women 4:20)

Do not marry women whom your fathers married, except what has already occurred; this was surely indecent and hateful, and it is an evil way. Forbidden to you are your mothers, your daughters, your sisters, your paternal aunts, your maternal aunts, your brothers' daughters and sisters' daughters, your mothers who have suckled you, your foster sisters, and mothers of your wives. Forbidden are your stepdaughters who are in your guardianship, (born) of your wives to whom you have gone in; but if you have not gone in to them, there is no blame on you (in marrying their daughters). Forbidden are the wives of your sons from your own loins, and two sisters together, except what has already occurred. Surely God is Forgiving, Merciful. Forbidden are all married women, except those whom your right hands possess.[3] (This is) God's ordinance to you; lawful for you are (all women) besides these, provided that you seek (them) with your wealth, taking (them) in marriage, not committing fornication. If you profit from a wife (by marrying), give her a dowry, as appointed; there is no blame on you for anything about what you mutually agree after the (dowry) is given. Surely God is Knowing, Wise. (The Women 4:22-24)

---

1 Ali, M.M., *The Holy Qur'an*, 205. Among the pre-Islamite Arabs, when a man died, his elder son or other relations had a right to possess his widow or widows, marrying them themselves if they pleased, without settling a dowry upon them, or marrying them to others, or prohibiting them from marriage altogether (Bkh, Rz).

2 Ali, M.M., *The Holy Qur'an*, 206. Husbands who were dissatisfied with their wives were inclined to give the wives trouble, so the wives would be forced to claim a divorce, and the husband could take back the dowry that they had paid to marry her (Rz).

3 Ali, M.M., *The Holy Qur'an*, 207-208. Those whom your right hands possess generally means those taken prisoner in war. Sometimes women taken prisoner converted to Islam, and they could not be sent back, so it was lawful to take them in marriage, even though they might not have been divorced formally by their former husbands.

Jesus

From the beginning of the creation, God made them male and female. For this cause a man will leave his father and mother, and will join to his wife, and the two will become one flesh, so that they are no longer two, but one flesh. Therefore, what God has joined together, let no man separate. (Mark 10:6-9)

Muhammad ﷺ

Whoever among you does not have ample means to marry free, believing women (may marry) your believing maidens from those whom your right hands possess. God knows best your faith. You are (sprung) one from the other; so marry them with the permission of their masters, and give them their dowries justly, they being chaste, not fornicating or receiving illicit lovers. When they are taken in marriage, if they are guilty of indecency, they will suffer half the punishment that is (inflicted) on free women. This is for he among you who fears falling into evil, but abstaining is better for you, and God is Forgiving, Merciful. (The Women 4:25)

Men are the maintainers of women, because God has made some of them excel over others, and because men spend out of their property. The good women are obedient, guarding the unseen, as God has guarded. (As for) those wives on whose part you fear desertion, admonish them, leave them alone in bed, and beat them. If they then obey you, do not seek a way against them. Surely God is High, Great. (The Women 4:34)

If you fear a breakup between a couple, appoint a judge from his people and a judge from her people. If they both desire agreement, God will effect harmony between them. Surely God is Knowing, Aware. (The Women 4:35)

If a woman fears ill treatment or desertion on the part of her husband, there is no blame on them if they effect a reconciliation between themselves, and reconciliation is better. Greed has been made to be present in (people's) minds. If you do good (to others) and guard (against evil), surely God is aware of what you do. (The Women 4:128)

You do not have it in your power to show justice between your wives, even though you wish justice. So do not be totally disinclined (from one), leaving her as if she is suspended. If you effect a reconciliation and guard (against evil), surely God is Forgiving, Merciful. If you separate, God will render you both free from want, out of His abundance. God is Ample-Giving, Wise. (The Women 4:129-130)

This day, (all) the good things are allowed for you. The food of those who were given the Book is lawful for you, and your food is lawful for them. The chaste believing women and the chaste among those who were given the Book before you (are lawful for you), when you have given them their dowries, taking (them) in marriage, not fornicating or taking them for illicit lovers in secret. The works of whoever denies faith is of no account, and in the Hereafter, he will be one of the losers. (The Food 5:5)

Jesus

Muhammad ﷺ

(As for) the fornicatress and the fornicator, flog each of them, (giving) one hundred lashes, and do not let pity for them detain you in the matter of obedience to God, if you believe in God and the Last Day. Let a group of believers witness their chastisement. The fornicator shall not marry anyone but a fornicatress or idolatress, and the fornicatress shall marry only a fornicator or an idolater. It is forbidden to the believers. (The Light 24:2-3)

He who accuses his wife and has no witnesses except himself, his testimony (should be taken) four times, bearing God to witness that he is most surely truthful, and the fifth (time) invoking the curse of God on himself if he is lying. And it will avert the chastisement from her if she testifies four times, bearing God to witness that he is most surely a liar, and the fifth (time) invoking the wrath of God on herself if he is truthful. (The Light 24:6-9)

Marry those among you who are single, and those who are fit among your male slaves and your female slaves. If they are needy, God will make them free from want, out of His grace; God is Amply-giving, Knowing. Let those who do not find a match keep chaste until God makes them free from want, out of His grace. (As for) those whom your right hands possess who ask for a writing [of emancipation] , give them the writing if you know any good in them, and give them of the wealth that God has given you. Do not compel your slave girls to prostitution, when they desire to keep chaste, in order to seek the frail good of this world's life. If anyone compels them [to prostitution], then surely after their compulsion, God is Forgiving, Merciful. (The Light 24:32-33)

The Prophet has a greater claim on the faithful than they have on themselves, and his wives are (as) their mothers.[1] (The Allies 33:6a)

Oh, Prophet! Say to your wives: If you desire this world's life and its ornamentation, then come, I will give you provision and allow you to depart a goodly departing. But if you desire God and His Messenger and the latter abode, surely God has prepared for the good-doers among you a mighty reward. (The Allies 33:28-29)

Oh, wives of the Prophet! Whoever of you commits an open indecency, the chastisement will be increased to you doubly; this is easy for God. We will give double reward to whoever of you is obedient to God and His Messenger and does good, and We have prepared for her an honorable sustenance. (The Allies 33:30-31)

---

1 Haleem, *The Qur'an*, 266. The Prophet's wives were given the title Mothers of the Believers.

Jesus

Muhammad ﷺ

Oh, wives of the Prophet! You are not like any other of the women. If you are on your guard, do not be soft in (your) speech, lest he in whose heart is a disease might yearn for you. Speak a good word. Stay in your houses, and do not display your finery like the displaying of the ignorance of yore. Keep up prayer, and pay the poor-rate, and obey God and His Messenger. God only desires to take away the uncleanness from you, Oh people of the household, and to purify you with a (thorough) purifying. (The Allies 33:32-33)

When you, [Prophet], said to Zaid, to whom God had shown favour and to whom you had shown a favour, keep your wife to yourself and be careful of (your duty to) God, you concealed in your soul what God would bring to light. You feared men, and God had a greater right that you should fear Him. So when Zaid ended his marriage to her, We gave her to you as a wife, so that there would be no discomfort for the believers concerning the wives of their adopted sons when the sons have ended their marriages. God's command will be performed.[1] (The Allies 33:37)

Oh, you who believe! When you marry the believing women, and then divorce them before you have touched them, they have no waiting period. So make some provision for them, and send them forth with a good sending. (The Allies 33:49)

Oh, Prophet! Surely We have made lawful to you your wives, whom you have given dowries, and those whom your right hand possesses from those whom God has given to you as prisoners of war, and the daughters of your paternal uncle, and the daughters of your paternal aunts, and the daughters of your maternal uncle, and the daughters of your maternal aunts who fled with you. And a believing woman if she gave herself to the Prophet, if the Prophet desired to marry her— only for you, not for the (rest of the) believers. We know what We have ordained for them concerning their wives and those whom their right hands possess, so that no blame may be on you. God is Forgiving, Merciful. It is not allowed for you, [Prophet], to take women afterwards, or to exchange them for other wives, even if their beauty is pleasing to you, except what your right hand possesses. God is Watchful over all things. (The Allies 33:50,52)

---

1 Ali, M.M., *The Holy Qur'an*, 824. Zaid was the adopted son of Muhammad. Zainab, Zaid's wife, was the daughter of the Prophet's aunt. The marriage was not a happy one. The Prophet advised Zaid not to divorce her, because he had arranged the marriage. But Zaid divorced Zainab. The Holy Prophet took her in marriage, that being the original wish of Zainab and her relatives before her marriage with Zaid. The Qur'an had declared against an adopted son being regarded as if he were a real son, and now there was an opportunity when the Holy Prophet could by his own example deal a death-blow to that custom.

Jesus

Muhammad ﷺ

[Prophet], you may put off whom you please of them and take to yourself whom you please. And take whom you desire of those from whom you had separated temporarily—no blame attaches to you. This is most proper, so that their eyes may be cool and they may not grieve, and that they should be pleased, all of them, with what you give them. God knows what is in your hearts. God is Knowing, Forbearing.
(The Allies 33:51)

(As for) those of you who put away your wives by likening their backs to the backs of your mothers,[1] they are not your mothers; your mothers are no other than those who gave birth to you. Most surely you utter hateful words and a falsehood, and most surely God is Pardoning, Forgiving. Retract what you said, and then free a captive before you touch each other—you are admonished (to conform) to this, and God is Aware of what you do. But whoever does not have the means, fast for two months successively before you touch each other. For him who is not able, feed sixty needy ones. This is so that you may have faith in God and His Messenger. These are God's limits, and the unbelievers will have a painful chastisement.
(The Pleading One 58:2-4)

Oh, you who believe! When believing women come fleeing to you, examine them; God knows best their faith. If you find them to be believing women, do not send them back to the unbelievers. They are not lawful wives for the unbelievers. Give the unbelievers what they have spent; no blame is attached to you for marrying them when you give them their dowries. Do not hold to the ties of marriage with unbelieving women, but ask for what you have spent, and let them ask for what they have spent. That is God's judgment; He judges between you. God is Knowing, Wise.
(The Examined One 60:10)

(As for) those of your women who have despaired of menstruation, if you have a doubt, their prescribed time [before divorce] shall be three months, and also those too who have not yet menstruated. (As for) the pregnant women, their prescribed time is when they deliver their burdens. God will make the affairs easy for whoever [fears] Him. (The Divorce 65:4)

---

1 Ali, M.M., *The Holy Qur'an*, 814. The custom was that when a man pronounced these words, the relation between husband and wife ended, but the woman was not at liberty to leave the husband's house. She was now treated as a deserted wife, the conjugal relation having ended forever.

Jesus

Muhammad ﷺ

Oh, Prophet! In your desire to please your wives, why do you forbid yourself what God has made lawful to you? Yet God is Forgiving and Merciful. God has indeed sanctioned for you a release from your oaths[1]—God is your Protector: He is the Knowing, the Wise. (The Prohibition 66:1-2)

When the Prophet secretly communicated a piece of information to one of his wives, and she informed (others) of it, God made him aware of it—he made known part of it and avoided part of it. So when the Prophet informed her of it, she said: Who informed you of this? He said: The Knowing, the One Aware informed me. If you both turn to God, indeed your hearts are inclined (to this). But if you back up each other against [The Prophet], surely God is his Guardian, and Gabriel, the believers who do good, the angels, and after that, his assistants. Maybe if his Lord divorces you, He will replace you with wives better than you: submissive, faithful, obedient, penitent, adorers, fasters, widows and virgins. (The Prohibition 66:3-5)

---

1 Ali, M.M., *The Holy Qur'an*, 1091. Possibly the Prophet had made an oath to abstain from conjugal relations with his wives for a month, perhaps because of jealousies among them.

Children

 Jesus

Whoever gives one of these little ones just a cup of cold water to drink, because he is a disciple, truly I tell you he will in no way lose his reward. (Matthew 10:42)

See that you do not despise one of these little ones, for I tell you that in Heaven their angels always see the face of my Father who is in Heaven. (Matthew 18:10)

Whoever receives one such little child in my name receives me, and whoever receives me does not receive me, but He who sent me. (Mark 9:37)

Whoever causes one of these little ones who believe in me to stumble, it would be better for him if he was thrown into the sea with a millstone hung around his neck. (Mark 9:42)

Allow the little children to come to me. Do not forbid them, for the Kingdom of God belongs to such as these. (Mark 10:14)

Mothers should suckle their children for two whole years, for he who desires to make complete the time of suckling. Their maintenance and their clothing must be borne by the father, fairly. No soul is burdened except to the extent of its capacity. Neither will a mother be made to suffer harm because of her child, nor a father because of his child, and a similar duty passes to the (father's) heir. But if both desire weaning by mutual consent and counsel, there is no blame on them, and if you wish to engage a wet-nurse for your children, there is no blame on you, as long as you pay what you promised, in a fair manner. Be careful of (your duty to) God, and know that God sees what you do. (The Cow 2:233)

Let those who fear leaving behind weak offspring have the same fear regarding the [orphans]. So let them be careful of (their duty to) God, and let them speak appropriate words. (The Women 4:9)

Oh, you who believe! Let those whom your right hands possess and those who have not attained puberty ask your permission [before entering your presence] at three times: before the morning prayer, when you put off your clothes at midday in summer, and after the prayer of nightfall. These are three times of privacy for you. Neither is it a sin for you, nor for them, besides these times. Some of you must go around (waiting) upon others. Thus does God make clear to you the Verses, and God is Knowing, Wise. When the children among you have attained puberty, let them seek permission as those before them sought permission. Thus God makes clear to you His Verses, and God is Knowing, Wise. (The Light 24:58-59)

Jesus

Muhammad ﷺ

Oh, you who believe! Do not let your wealth or your children, divert you from the remembrance of God. Those who do that are the losers. (The Hypocrites 63:9)

Lodge them where you lodge, according to your means, and do not injure them in order to restrict them. If they are pregnant, spend on them until they deliver their burden. And then if they suckle for you, give them their payment, and direct one another among you to do good. But if you disagree, another (woman) shall suckle on the father's behalf.[1] (The Divorce 65:6)

---

1 This aya appears in a sura (chapter) that deals with rules regarding divorce.—Ed.

Homosexuality

Jesus

As for those who are guilty of an indecency among your women,[1] call from among you four (witnesses) against them. If they bear witness, confine the women to their houses until death takes them or God opens some way for them. As for two [men] who are guilty of indecency among you, give them both a slight punishment; but if they repent and amend, turn aside from them. Surely God is Oft-Forgiving (to mercy), the Merciful. (The Women 4:15-16)

(We sent) Lot, when he said to his people: What? Do you commit an indecency that no one in the world has done before you? Most surely you come to males in lust, besides females. No, you are an extravagant people. His people answered only this: Drive them [Lot and his people] out of your town! Surely they are a people who seek to purify (themselves)! So We saved Lot and his family, except his wife: she remained behind. We rained upon them a rain; consider, then, the end of the guilty. (The Elevated Places 7:80-84)

When their brother Lot said to them: Will you not [fear God]? Surely I am a faithful messenger to you. So [fear] God, and obey me. I do not ask you any reward for it: my reward is only with the Lord of the Worlds. What? Do you come to the males among the creatures, and leave what your Lord has created for you—your wives? No, you are a people exceeding limits. They said: If you do not stop, Oh Lot, you will surely be of those who are expelled. He said: Surely I am of those who utterly abhor what you do. My Lord! Deliver me and my followers from what they do. So We delivered him and all of his followers, except an old woman, among those who remained behind. Then We utterly destroyed the others. We rained upon them a rain, and evil was the rain on those whom we warned. Most surely there is a sign in this, but most of them do not believe. (The Poets 26:161-174)

We sent Lot, when he said to his people: What? Do you commit indecency knowingly? What? Do you indeed approach men lustfully rather than women? No, you are a people who act ignorantly. But the answer of his people was only this: Turn out Lot's followers from your town! Surely they are a people who would keep pure! But We delivered him and his followers, except his wife. We ordained her to be of those who remained behind. And we rained on them a rain, and evil was the rain on those who were warned. (The Naml 27:54-58)

(We sent) Lot when he said to his people: Most surely you are guilty of an indecency that none of the nations has ever done before you: What? Do you approach the males, and commit robbery on the highway, and commit evil deeds in your assemblies? But his people answered nothing, except that they said: Bring on us God's chastisement, if you are one of the truthful. (The Spider 29:28-29)

---

1 Ali, M.M., *The Holy Qur'an*, 204. This signifies anything exceeding the bounds of rectitude (gross, immodest, lewd, obscene). The context shows that here it is used to signify any immoral conduct short of fornication.

Modesty

 Jesus

[Prophet], tell the believing men to lower their gaze and guard their private parts; that is purer for them. Surely God is Aware of what they do. Tell the believing women to lower their gaze and guard their private parts and not display their ornaments,[1] except what is apparent. Let them draw their head-coverings over their bosoms, and not display their ornaments except to their husbands or their fathers, or the fathers of their husbands, or their sons, or the sons of their husbands, or their brothers, or their brother's sons, or their sister's sons, or their women, or those whom their right hands possess, or the male servants not having need (of women), or the children who have not obtained knowledge of what is hidden of women. Do not let them stamp their feet to make known what they hide of their ornaments. Turn to God, all of you, Oh believers! So that you may be successful. (The Light 24:30-31)

(As for) women advanced in years who do not hope for a marriage, it is no sin for them if they take off their [outer] clothes without displaying their ornaments, but if they restrain themselves, it is better for them. God is Hearing, Knowing. (The Light 24:60)

There is no blame on [The Prophet's wives] in respect to their fathers, their sons, their brothers, their brothers' sons, their sisters' sons, their own women, or those whom their right hands possess. Be careful of (your duty to) God; surely God is a witness to all things (The Allies 33:55)

Oh, Prophet! Tell your wives and your daughters and the women of the believers to let down their over-garments upon themselves. This will be more proper, so that they may be known, and thus they will not be given trouble. God is Forgiving, Merciful. (The Allies 33:59)

---

1 Ali, M.M., *The Holy Qur'an*, 701. There is a difference of opinion as to what ztnat or ornament means. According to some it includes the beauty of the body, while according to others it is exclusively applied to external ornaments and adornments (Rz).

Finances

 Jesus

Someone in the crowd said to him, "Teacher, tell my brother to divide the inheritance with me." But he said to him, "Man, who made me a judge or an arbitrator over you?" (Luke 12:13-14)

Tell us, therefore, what do you think? Is it lawful to pay taxes to Caesar, or not?" But Jesus perceived their wickedness, and said, "Why do you test me, you hypocrites? Show me the tax money." So they brought him a denarius. He asked them, "Whose is this image and inscription?" They said to Him, "Caesar's." Then he said to them, "Give therefore to Caesar the things that are Caesar's, and to God the things that are God's." (Matthew 22:17-21)

When they had come to Capernaum, those who collected the didrachma coins came to Peter, and said, "Does not your teacher pay the didrachma?" He said, "Yes." When he came into the house, Jesus anticipated him, saying, "What do you think, Simon? From whom do the kings of the earth receive toll or tribute? From their children, or from strangers?" And Peter said to him, "From strangers." Jesus said to him, "Therefore the sons are exempt. But, lest we cause them to stumble, go to the sea, cast a hook, and take up the first fish that comes up. When you have opened its mouth, you will find a stater coin. Take that, and give it to them for me and you." (Matthew 17:24-27)

God directs you concerning your children: the male shall have the equal portion of two females. Then if they are more than two females, they shall have two-thirds of what the deceased left, and if there is one female, she shall have half. And as for the deceased's parents, each shall have one sixth of what he has left if he has a child, but if he has no child and (only) his two parents inherit him, then his mother shall have one third. If the deceased has brothers, his mother shall have one sixth after (the payment of) any bequest or debt. You do not know which of your parents and your children is nearer to you in usefulness. This is an ordinance from God: surely God is Knowing, Wise. (The Women 4:11)

Husbands shall have half of what their wives leave, if they have no child, but if they have a child, they shall have one fourth of what she leaves after (payment of) any bequest or debt. Wives shall have one fourth of what husbands leave, if they have no child, but if they have a child, they shall have one eighth of what you leave after (payment of) any bequest or debt. If a man or a woman does not leave property to be inherited by parents or offspring, and he (or she) has a brother or a sister, then each of them shall have one sixth, but if there are more siblings than that, they shall share one third, after (payment of) any bequest or debt, without being harmful. This is an ordinance from God: and God is Knowing, Forbearing. (The Women 4:12)

Distractions

Satan and Spirits

 Jesus

Just then, there was in their synagogue a man with an unclean spirit, and he shouted, saying, "Let us alone! What do we have to do with you, Jesus, Nazarene? Have you come to destroy us? I know who you are: the Holy One of God." Jesus rebuked him, saying, "Be quiet, and come out of him." The unclean spirit, convulsing him and crying with a loud voice, came out of him. (Mark 1:23-26)

Let your "Yes" be "Yes" and your "No" be "No." Whatever is more than these is of the evil one. (Matthew 5:37)

Again, the devil took him to a very high mountain, and showed him all the kingdoms of the world, and their glory. And he said to him, "I will give you all of these things, if you will fall down and worship me." Then Jesus said to him, "Get behind me, Satan. For it is written, 'You are to worship the Lord your God, and serve Him only.'" (Matthew 4:8-10)

Muhammad ﷺ

Note: Jinn are unseen beings who are made from smokeless fire or intensely hot fire. Iblis is Satan.—Ed.

The Devil threatens you with poverty and orders you to be miserly, and God promises you forgiveness from Himself, and abundance. God is Ample-giving, Knowing. (The Cow 2:268)

Even if We had sent down the angels to them, and the dead had spoken to them, and We had brought together all things before them, they would not believe unless God pleases, but most of them are ignorant. Thus We made an enemy for every prophet— devils from among men and Jinn, some of them suggesting to others varnished falsehood, to deceive them. Had your Lord pleased, they would not have done it. Therefore, leave them and what they invent. (The Cattle 6:111-112)

Oh, Children of Adam! We have indeed sent down to you clothing to cover your shame, and (clothing) for beauty. But the clothing that guards against evil—that is the best. This is from the Signs of God, so that they may be mindful. Oh, Children of Adam! Do not let the Devil cause you to fall into affliction, as he expelled your parents from the Garden, stripping from them their clothing to show them their evil inclinations. He surely sees you, he and his host, from where you cannot see them. Indeed, we have made the devils the guardians of those who do not believe. (The Elevated Places 7:26-27)

If a false suggestion from the Devil afflicts you, seek refuge in God; surely He is Hearing, Knowing. Indeed, when a visitation from the Devil afflicts those who guard (against evil), they become mindful, and then, lo! They see. And their brothers increase them in error, and they do not cease. (The Elevated Places 7:200-202)

(As for) those who have earned evil, the punishment for an evil is the like of it, and abasement will come upon them. They will have none to protect them from God—as if their faces had been covered with slices of the dense darkness of night. These are the inmates of the Fire, and they will abide in it. (Jonah 10:27)

The Devil will say, after the affair is decided: Surely, God promised you truth, and I gave you promises, and then I failed to keep them for you. I had no authority over you, except that I called you, and you obeyed me. So, do not blame me—blame yourselves. I cannot be your helper (now), nor can you be my helpers. Surely, I disbelieved in your associating me with God before. Surely, it is the [wrongdoers] who will have the painful chastisement. (Abraham 14:22)

Jesus

I saw Satan having fallen like lightning from Heaven. (Luke 10:18)

Look, I give you authority to tread on serpents and scorpions, and over all the power of the enemy, and nothing will in any way hurt you. Nevertheless, do not rejoice in this, that the spirits are subject to you, but rejoice that your names are written in Heaven.[1] (Luke 10:19-20)

He led him to Jerusalem, and set him on the pinnacle of the temple, and said to him, "If you are the Son of God, cast yourself down from here, for it is written, 'He will put his angels in charge of you, to guard you;' and, 'On their hands they will bear you up, lest perhaps you dash your foot against a stone.'" And Jesus, answering, said to him, "It is said, 'Do not test the Lord your God.'" (Luke 4:9-12)

When he came to the other side, into the country of the Gergesenes, two people possessed by demons met him there, coming out of the tombs, exceedingly fierce, so that nobody could pass that way. And look, they shouted, saying, "What do we have to do with you, Jesus, Son of God? Have you come here to torment us before the time?" Now there was a herd of many pigs feeding far away from them. And the demons begged him, saying, "If you cast us out, permit us to go away into the herd of pigs." And he said to them, "Go." And they came out, and went into the herd of pigs, and look, the whole herd of pigs rushed down the cliff into the sea, and died in the water. (Matthew 8:28-32)

---

1 Jesus is speaking to his first Seventy Apostles.—Ed.

Muhammad ﷺ

Certainly We created man from clay that gives forth sound, of black mud, fashioned in shape. We created the Jinn before, from intensely hot fire. Your Lord said to the angels: Surely, I am going to create a mortal out of the essence of black mud, fashioned in shape. When I make him complete, and breathe into him of My inspiration, fall down and bow to him. So the angels bowed, all of them together, except Iblis; he refused to be with those who bowed. The Lord said: Oh, Iblis! What excuse have you that you are not with those who make obeisance? Iblis said: I am not one to make obeisance to a mortal whom You created of the essence of black mud, fashioned in shape. The Lord said: Then get out of here, for surely you are driven away, and surely on you is the curse, until the Day of Judgment.[1] (The Rock 15:26-35)

Satan said: My Lord! Because You have made life evil to me, I will certainly make (evil) seem fair to those on Earth, and I will certainly cause them all to deviate, except Your servants among them, the chosen ones. God said: This is a right way to Me: Surely, you have no authority over My servants, except those of the deviators who follow you. (The Rock 15:39-42)

By God, most certainly We sent (messengers) to nations before you, but the Devil made their deeds fair-seeming to them, so he is their guardian today, and they will have a painful punishment. We have revealed the Book to you only so that you may make clear to them that about which they differ, and (as) a guidance and a mercy for a people who believe. (The Bee 16:63-64)

[Prophet], when you recite the Qur'an, seek refuge with God from the accursed Devil. Surely, he has no authority over those who believe and rely on their Lord. His authority is only over those who befriend him and those who associate others with Him. (The Bee 16:98-100)

[Prophet], do you not see that We have sent the devils against the unbelievers, inciting them by incitement? (Mary 19:83)

---

1 This story is also in the *Questions of Bartholomew*. See page 487.—Ed.

Jesus

Get behind me, Satan. You are a stumbling block to me, for you are not setting your mind on the things of God, but on the things of men. (Matthew 16:23)

But some of them said, "He casts out demons by Beelzebul, the prince of the demons." If Satan also is divided against himself, how will his kingdom stand? For you say that I cast out demons by Beelzebul. But if I cast out demons by the finger of God, then the Kingdom of God has come to you. (Luke 11:15, 18, 20)

Now is the judgment of this world. Now the prince of this world will be cast out.[1] (John 12:31)

When the sun was setting, all those who had any sick with various diseases brought them to him; and he laid his hands on every one of them, and healed them. Demons also came out from many, crying out, and saying, "You are Christ, the Son of God." But he rebuked them and did not allow them to speak, because they knew that he was the Messiah. (Luke 4:40-41)

---

1 Wallerstedt et al., *Orthodox Bible*, 247. Satan.

Muhammad ﷺ

[Prophet], regarding every messenger or prophet who We sent before you: When he had a desire, the Devil made a suggestion respecting his desire. But God annuls what Satan casts, and then God establishes His Verses. God is Knowing, Wise. God makes what Satan casts a trial for those whose hearts are diseased and those whose hearts are hard. Most surely, the [wrongdoers] are in a remote opposition. (The Pilgrimage 22:52-53)

The devils have not come down with [this Qur'an]. It is not advantageous to them, and they do not have not the power to do (it). Most surely they are far removed from hearing it. (The Poets 26:210-212)

Shall I inform you about whom the devils descend upon? They descend on every lying, sinful one. They incline their ears, and most of them are liars. (The Poets 26:221-223)

And on the Day when He will gather them all together, He will say to the angels: Did these [people] worship you? They will reply: Glory be to You! You are our Guardian, not they. No! They worshipped the Jinn; most of them were believers in them. (The Saba 34:40-41)

Oh, men! Surely the promise of God is true, so do not let the life of this world deceive you, and do not let the Arch-Deceiver deceive you, respecting God. Surely the Devil is your enemy, so take him for an enemy. He only invites his group, so that they may be inmates of the Burning Fire. (The Originator 35:5-6)

They assert a relationship between Him and the Jinn, yet the Jinn themselves know that they will be brought before Him. Glory be to God (for freedom) from what they describe. (The Rangers 37:158-159)

[The Lord] said: Oh, Iblis! What prevented you from bowing to him whom I created with My two hands? Are you proud, or are you of the exalted ones? Iblis said: I am better than him; You have created me of fire, and you created him of dust. God said: Then get out of here, for surely you are driven away, and surely My curse is on you to the Day of Judgment.[1] Iblis said: My Lord! Then delay for me, until the Day that they are raised. God said: Surely you are one of those in relief, until the period of the time is made known. Iblis said: Then by Your Might, I will surely make them all live an evil life, except Your servants, the purified ones. God said: Then the truth is—and I speak the truth—I will most certainly fill Hell with you and with all of those who follow you. (Sad 38:75-85)

---

1 This story is also in the *Questions of Bartholomew*. See page 487.—Ed.

Jesus

The unclean spirit, when he is gone out of the man, passes through waterless places, seeking rest, and does not find it. Then he says, "I will return into my house from which I came out," and when he has come back, he finds it empty, swept, and put in order. Then he goes, and takes with himself seven other spirits more evil than he is, and they enter in and dwell there. The last state of that man becomes worse than the first. Even so will it be also to this evil generation. (Matthew 12:43-45)

Muhammad ﷺ

We have appointed comrades for those who make what is before them and what is behind them seem pleasing. The word proved true against the nations of Jinn and men that have passed away before them—they will surely be losers. (Ha Mim 41:25)

We appoint a devil for whoever turns himself away from remembrance of the Beneficent God, so that the devil becomes his associate. Most surely the devils turn them away from the path, but they think that they are guided aright. (The Embellishment 43:36-37)

Most surely it is a knowledge of The Hour, so have no doubt about it, and follow me: this is the right path. Do not let the Devil prevent you; surely he is your open enemy. (The Embellishment 43:61-62)

[Prophet] we turned toward you a group of Jinn, who listened to the Qur'an. When they came to it, they said: Be silent. When it was finished, they turned back to their people, warning (them). The Jinn said: Oh, our people, we have listened to a Book, revealed after Moses, verifying what came before it, guiding to the truth and to a right path. Oh, our people! Accept the Divine caller, and believe in Him. He will forgive you of your faults and protect you from a painful chastisement. Whoever does not accept the Divine caller will not escape on the Earth, and he will not have guardians besides God. These are in obvious error. (The Sandhills 46:29-32)

Surely the Devil has [seduced] those who turned their backs after guidance became obvious to them, and God gives them respite. That is because they say to those who hate what God has revealed: We will obey you in some of the affairs—but God knows their secrets. So how will it be when the angels take them in death, striking their faces and their backs? (Muhammad 47:25-27)

I did not create the Jinn and the men except to serve Me. I do not desire any sustenance from them, and I do not desire that they feed Me. (The Scatterers 51:56-57)

He created man from dry clay, like earthen vessels, and He created the Jinn from a flame of fire. (The Beneficent 55:14-15)

Like the Devil, when he says to man: Disbelieve. But when he disbelieves, the Devil says: I am surely clear of you; surely I fear God, the Lord of the Worlds. So, the end of both is that they live in fire—that is the reward of the [wrongdoers]. (The Banishment 59:16-17)

Jesus

One out of the crowd answered, and said "Teacher, I brought you my son, who has a mute spirit; and wherever it seizes him, it throws him down, and he foams at the mouth, and grinds his teeth, and wastes away. I asked your disciples to cast it out, and they weren't able." Answering, he said to them, "You unbelieving generation, how long must I be with you? How long must I put up with you? Bring him to me." They brought him to him, and when he saw him, immediately the spirit convulsed him, and he fell on the ground, wallowing and foaming at the mouth. He asked his father, "How long has it been since this has come to him?" He said, "From childhood. And it has often cast him both into fire and into water, to destroy him. But if you can do anything, have compassion on us, and help us." Jesus said to him, "If you can believe, all things are possible to him who believes." Immediately the father of the child cried out and said with tears, "Lord, I believe. Help my unbelief." When Jesus saw that a crowd came running together, he rebuked the unclean spirit, saying to him, "You mute and deaf and mute spirit, I command you, come out of him, and never enter him again." Having screamed, and convulsed greatly, it came out of him. The boy became like one dead; so much that most of them said, "He is dead." But Jesus took him by the hand, and raised him up; and he arose. And when he had come into the house, his disciples asked him privately, "Why could we not cast it out?" And he said to them, "This kind can come out by nothing, except by prayer and fasting." (Mark 9:17-29)

Do not be afraid of the things that you are about to suffer. Look, the devil is about to throw some of you into prison, so that you may be tested; and you will have oppression for ten days. Be faithful until death, and I will give you the crown of life. (Revelation 2:10)

Muhammad ﷺ

We sought to reach Heaven, but we found it filled with strong guards and flames. We used to sit in some of the sitting-places there, to steal a listen, but anyone who (tries to) listen now will find a flame lying in wait for him. We don't know whether evil is meant for those on Earth or whether their Lord means to bring them good. Some of us are good and others of us are below that: we are sects following different ways. We know that we cannot escape God on the Earth, nor can we escape Him by flight.[1]

(The Jinn 72:8-12)

Say, [Prophet]: I seek refuge in the Lord of the dawn, from the evil of what He has created, and from the evil of the utterly dark night when it comes, and from the evil of those who [blow on knots],[2] and from the evil of the envious when he envies.

(The Dawn 113:1-5)

Say: I seek refuge in the Lord of Men, the King of Men, the God of Men, from the evil of the whisperings of the slinking (Devil), who whispers into the hearts of men among the Jinn and the men. (The Men 114:1-6)

---

1 This reveals a conversation among Jinn, after having listened to the *Qur'an*.—Ed.

2 A practice of witchcraft..—Ed.

Greed and Envy

 Jesus

Beware. Keep yourselves from all covetousness, for a man's life does not consist of the abundance of the things that he possesses. (Luke 12:15)

Oh, you who believe! Be careful of (your duty to) God, and give up what interest remains (due) to you, if you are believers. If you do not, be on notice of war from God and His Messenger. If you repent, you will have your principal. Do not make (the debtor) suffer loss, and you will not be made to suffer loss. And if (the debtor) has limited means, postpone payment until (he is in) ease. It is better for you if you remit (it) as alms, if you knew. Guard yourselves against a day in which you will be returned to God; every soul will be paid back is full what it has earned, and they will not be dealt with unjustly. (The Cow 2:278-281)

Among the Followers of the Book, there are some who, if you entrust one (of them) with a heap of wealth, he will pay it back to you. There are some among them who, if you entrust one (of them) with one silver coin, he will not pay it back to you unless you remain firm in demanding it—this is because they say: We are not accountable to the unlearned people. They knowingly tell a lie against God. Yes! Surely God loves those who fulfil their promises and [fear] Him. Those who exchange the covenant of God and their own oaths for a small price will have no portion in the Hereafter. God will not speak to them, nor will He look upon them on the Day of Resurrection, nor will He purify them, and they will have a painful chastisement.
(The Family of Amran 3:75-77)

Give to the orphans their property, do not substitute worthless (things) for (their) good (ones), and do not devour their property (as an addition) to your own property—this is surely a great crime. (As for) those who swallow the property of the orphans unjustly, surely they only swallow fire into their bellies, and they will enter burning Fire. (The Women 4:2,10)

Oh, you who believe! Do not devour your property among yourselves [unjustly], unless you are trading by mutual consent. And do not kill your people. Surely God is Merciful to you. (The Women 4:29)

Do not covet that by which God has made some of you excel over others. Men shall have the benefit of what they earn, and women shall have the benefit of what they earn. Ask God of His grace; surely, God knows all things. (The Women 4:32)

Jesus

Muhammad ﷺ

Whatever God has restored to His Messenger from the people of the towns is for God and for the Messenger, and for the near of kin and the orphans and the needy and the wayfarer, so that it may not be taken by turns among the rich among you. Whatever the Messenger gives you, accept it, and from whatever he forbids you, keep back, and be careful of (your duty to) God Surely God is severe in retributing (evil).[1]

(Greed and Envy 59:7)

Woe to the defrauders who, when they take the measure (of their dues) from men, take it fully, but when they measure out or weigh out for others, they are deficient. Do they not think that they will be raised again, on a mighty day?

(The Defaulters 83:1-5)

---

1 Ali, M.M., *The Holy Qur'an*, 1059. Possessions of the unbelievers restored to the Muslims, without war, or obtained after the laying down of arms.

Idle Words

Jesus

But I tell you that every idle word that men speak, they will give account of it in the day of judgment. For by your words you will be justified, and by your words you will be condemned. (Matthew 12:36-37)

There is no good tree that brings forth rotten fruit; nor a rotten tree that brings forth good fruit. For each tree is known by its own fruit. For people do not gather figs from thorns, nor do they gather grapes from a bramble bush. The good man out of the good treasure of his heart brings out that which is good, and the evil man out of the evil treasure of his heart brings out that which is evil, for out of the abundance of the heart, his mouth speaks. (Luke 6:43-45)

God does not love the public utterance of hurtful speech, unless (it is) by one to whom injustice has been done. God is Hearing, Knowing. (The Women 4:148)

When you heard it, why didn't you say: It is not becoming that we should speak of this. Glory be to You, [Oh, God]! This is a great slander! God admonishes you to not return to the like of this, ever again, if you are believers. God makes the Verses clear to you. God is Knowing, Wise. Regarding those who would love circulation of this scandal about those who believe—they will have a grievous chastisement in this world and the Hereafter. God knows, while you do not know.[1] (The Light 24:16-19)

Those who speak evil things of the believing men and the believing women without their having earned (it) are guilty indeed of a false accusation and a manifest sin. (The Allies 33:58)

Oh, you who believe! If an unrighteous man comes to you with a report, look carefully into it, lest you harm a people in ignorance and then be sorry for what you have done. (The Chambers 49:6)

Oh, you who believe! Do not let (one) people laugh at (another) people, perchance the others might be better than they. Do not let women (laugh) at (other) women, perchance the others might be better than they. Do not find fault with your own people, or call one another by [offensive] nicknames. Evil is a bad name after having faith, and whoever does not [repent] are the [wrongdoers]. (The Chambers 49:11)

Oh, you who believe! Avoid most suspicion, for surely, suspicion in some cases is a sin. Do not spy or let some of you backbite others. Would one of you like to eat the flesh of his dead brother? You would abhor it. Be careful of (your duty to) God, surely God is Oft-returning (to mercy), Merciful. (The Chambers 49:12)

Oh, you who believe! When you confer together in private, do not give each other counsel of sin, revolt and disobedience to the Messenger. Give each other counsel of goodness and guarding (against evil). Be careful of (your duty to) God, to whom you will be gathered together. Secret counsels are only (the work) of the Devil, so that he may cause grief to those who believe. But he cannot hurt them in the least, except with God's permission. Let the believers rely on God. (The Pleading One 58:9-10)

---

1 Ali, M.M., *The Holy Qur'an*, 697. This refers to an incident where the Prophet's wife Aisha lost a necklace while returning from an expedition. She went back to find it, and when she returned to camp, the group had inadvertently left her behind. Gossipers accused her of adultery, but there were no witnesses.

Jesus

Muhammad ﷺ

Woe to every slanderer, defamer, who amasses wealth and multiplies it. He thinks that his wealth will make him [immortal]. No! He will most certainly be hurled into the Crusher. What will make you realize what the Crusher is? It is the Fire kindled by God, which rises above the hearts. Surely it will close down upon them, in extended columns. (The Slanderer 104:1-9)

Divisiveness

 Jesus

And knowing their thoughts, Jesus said to them, "Every kingdom divided against itself is brought to desolation, and every city or house divided against itself will not stand." (Matthew 12:25)

Hold fast by the covenant of God, all together, and do not be disunited. Remember God's favour on you when you were enemies, when He united your hearts, so that by His favour you became brothers. You were on the brink of a pit of fire, and He saved you from it. This is how God makes clear to you His Verses, so that you may follow the right way. There should be a group from among you who invite to good and encourage what is right and forbid the wrong—these will be successful. Do not be like those who became divided and disagreed after clear arguments had come to them—these will have a grievous chastisement. (The Family of Amran 3:103-105)

Say: He has the power to send on you a chastisement from above you or from beneath your feet, or to throw you into confusion, (making you) of different [sects], and make some of you taste the fighting of others. See how We repeat the Signs, so that they may understand. (The Cattle 6:65)

Surely you have no concern with those who divided their religion into parts and became sects; their affair is only with God. He will inform them of what they did. (The Cattle 6:159)

Those who built a mosque to cause harm, unbelief and disunion among the believers, and as an ambushing [outpost] for whoever had warred against God and His Messenger before, will certainly swear: We did not desire anything but good. God bears witness that they are most surely liars. Never stand in it. Certainly a mosque founded on piety from the very first day is more deserving that you should stand in it—in it are men who love that they should be purified. God loves those who purify themselves.[1] (The Immunity 9:107-108)

Say, [Prophet]: Surely, I am the plain warner, like We sent down to the dividers, those who declared the Qur'an to be a lie. So, by your Lord, We will most certainly question them all about what they used to do. (The Rock 15:89-93)

[Prophet], tell My servants to speak what is best. Surely the Devil sows dissensions among them. Surely the Devil is an open enemy to man. (The Israelites 17:53)

Surely this is your religion, one religion (only), and I am your Lord. Therefore, serve Me. But they divided their [religion into sects] between them. All will come back to Us. (The Prophets 21:92-93)

---

1 Ali, M.M., *The Holy Qur'an*, 423. At the instigation of Abu Amir, who had fought against Muhammad for a long time, twelve hypocrites built a rival mosque. After Abu Amir died, they wanted Muhammad to bless it. Instead the mosque was demolished, because it was built in opposition to Islam.

Jesus

Do you think that I have come to give peace in the Earth? I tell you, no, but rather division. For from now on, there will be five in one house divided, three against two, and two against three. They will be divided, father against son, and son against father; mother against daughter, and daughter against her mother; mother-in-law against her daughter-in-law, and daughter-in-law against her mother-in-law. (Luke 12:51-53)

Do not think that I came to send peace on the Earth. I did not come to send peace, but a sword. For I came to set a man at odds against his father, and a daughter against her mother, and a daughter-in-law against her mother-in-law. And a man's foes will be those of his own household. (Matthew 10:34-36)

Muhammad ﷺ

Surely this religion of yours is one religion, and I am your Lord. So [fear] Me. But they became divided into [sects], each group rejoicing in what it has. Therefore [Prophet], leave them in their overwhelming ignorance for a time. (The Believers 23:52-54)

God has made plain to you the religion that We commanded upon Noah, revealed to you [Prophet], and commanded upon Abraham and Moses and Jesus—keep to obedience, and do not be divided. What you call the unbelievers to is difficult. God chooses for Himself whom He pleases, and He guides to Himself he who turns (to Him) frequently. They did not become divided until after knowledge came to them, out of envy among themselves. Had a word not gone forth from your Lord for an appointed term, certainly they would have judged between themselves. Those who were made to inherit the Book after them are most surely in disquieting doubt. (The Counsel 42:13-14)

When Jesus came with clear arguments, he said: Indeed, I have come to you with wisdom, so that I may make clear to you part of what you differ in. So be careful of (your duty to) God, and obey me. Surely God is my Lord and your Lord, therefore serve Him. This is the right path. But [factions] among them differed, so woe to the [wrongdoers], because of the chastisement of a painful day. (The Embellishment 43:63-65)

Disagreements

 Jesus

Why do you not judge for yourselves what is right? For when you are going with your adversary before the magistrate, try diligently on the way to be released from him, lest perhaps he drag you to the judge, and the judge deliver you to the officer, and the officer throw you into prison. I tell you, you will by no means get out of there, until you have paid the very last penny. (Luke 12:57-59)

If your brother sins against you, go, show him his fault between you and him alone. If he listens to you, you have gained back your brother. But if he does not listen, take one or two more with you, that at the mouth of two or three witnesses every word may be established. If he refuses to listen to them, tell it to the church. If he refuses to hear the church also, let him be to you as a Gentile or a tax collector. (Matthew 18:15-17)

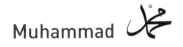

Oh, you who believe! Obey God and obey the Messenger and those in authority among you; and then if you quarrel about any thing, refer it to God and the Messenger. If you believe in God and the Last Day, this is better and very good in the end. (The Women 4:59)

If two people among the believers quarrel, make peace between them. But if one of them acts wrongfully toward the other, fight he who acts wrongfully until he returns to God's command. If he returns, make peace between them with justice, and act equitably. Surely God loves those who act equitably. (The Chambers 49:9)

Swearing and Oaths

 Jesus

Again you have heard that it was said to them of old time, "Do not make false vows, but fulfill your vows to the Lord." But I tell you, do not swear at all: neither by Heaven, for it is the throne of God; nor by the Earth, for it is the footstool of his feet; nor by Jerusalem, for it is the city of the great King. Neither should you swear by your head, for you cannot make one hair white or black. (Matthew 5:33-36)

God does not call you to account for unintentional swearing, but He will call you to account for what your hearts have earned. God is Forgiving, Forbearing. (The Cow 2:225)

God does not call you to account for what is thoughtless in your oaths, but He calls you to account for making deliberate oaths. So its atonement is the feeding of ten poor men out of the mediocre (food) that you feed your families, or clothing them, or the freeing a slave. But anyone who cannot find (means), fast for three days—this is the atonement of your oaths when you swear. Guard your oaths. Thus does God make clear to you His Verses, so that you may be grateful. (The Food 5:89)

When you have made a covenant with God, fulfill it. Do not break oaths after making them firm with God as a witness. Surely God knows what you do. Do not be like she who unravels her yarn, disintegrating it into pieces after she has spun it strongly, by making your oaths a means of deceit between you because (one) nation is more numerous than (another) nation. God only tests you by this. He will most certainly make clear to you, on the Resurrection Day, that about which you differed. (The Bee 16:91-92)

Do not make oaths a means of deceit between you, lest a foot should slip after its stability, and you should taste evil because you turned away from God's way. Grievous chastisement will be yours. (The Bee 16:94)

Have you not seen those who befriend a people with whom God is wrathful? They are neither with you nor with them, and they knowingly swear falsely. God has prepared a severe punishment for them. Surely what they do is evil. They make their oaths to serve as a cover so that they can turn away from God's way. So they will have an abasing punishment. (The Pleading One 58:14-16)

Arrogance and Pride

 Jesus

Two men went up into the temple to pray; one was a Pharisee, and the other was a tax collector. The Pharisee stood and prayed to himself like this: "God, I thank you, that I am not like the rest of men, extortioners, unrighteous, adulterers, or even like this tax collector. I fast twice a week. I give tithes of all that I get." But the tax collector, standing far away, would not even lift up his eyes to Heaven, but beat his breast, saying, "God, be merciful to me, a sinner." I tell you, this man went down to his house justified rather than the other; for everyone who exalts himself will be humbled, but he who humbles himself will be exalted. (Luke 18:10-14)

Beware of the scribes, who like to walk in long robes, and to get greetings in the marketplaces, and the best seats in the synagogues, and the best places at feasts: those who devour widows' houses, and for a pretense make long prayers. These will receive greater condemnation. (Mark 12:38b-40)

The life of this world is made to seem fair to those who disbelieve. They mock those who believe. Those who guard (against evil) will be above them on the Day of Resurrection, and God gives means of subsistence to whom He pleases, without measure. (The Cow 2:212)

By no means think that those who rejoice in what they have done and love to be praised for what they have not done are safe from the chastisement. They will have a painful chastisement. (The Family of Amran 3:188)

Serve God, and do not associate any thing with Him. Be good to the parents and to the near of kin, the orphans, the needy, the neighbour of (your) kin, the alien neighbour, the companion on a journey, the wayfarer and those whom your right hands possess. Surely God does not love he who is proud, boastful, those who are stingy and bid people to be stingy and hide what God has given them out of His grace. We have prepared for the unbelievers a disgraceful chastisement—those who spend their property (in alms) to be seen by the people and who do not believe in God or in the Last Day. As for he whose associate is the Devil, an evil associate is he! (The Women 4:36-38)

As for those who believe and do good, He will pay them fully their rewards and give them more out of His grace. As for those who disdain and are proud, He will chastise them with a painful chastisement. (The Women 4:173)

Oh, Children of Adam! Take your adornment at every place of prayer, and eat and drink and do not be extravagant. Surely He does not love the extravagant. (The Elevated Places 7:31)

Those who reject Our Verses and turn away haughtily from them are the inmates of the Fire, and they will abide in it. (The Elevated Places 7:36)

Surely the doors of Heaven will not be opened for those who reject Our Verses and turn away from them haughtily, nor will they enter the Garden until the camel passes through the eye of the needle. This is how We reward the guilty. (The Elevated Places 7:40)

When their eyes turn toward the inmates of the Fire, they will say: Our Lord! Do not place us with the unjust people. The dwellers of the most elevated places will call out to men whom they recognize by their marks, saying: Your amassings and your behaving haughtily are of no avail to you. (The Elevated Places 7:47-48)

Jesus

But he who is greatest among you will be your servant. (Matthew 23:11)

Woe to you when all men speak well of you, for their fathers did the same thing to the false prophets. (Luke 6:26)

Therefore, whoever humbles himself as this little child, the same is the greatest in the Kingdom of Heaven. (Matthew 18:4)

Muhammad ﷺ

I will turn away from My Signs those who are unjustly proud on the Earth. If they see every sign, they will not believe in it. And if they see the way of rectitude, they will not take it. If they see the way of error, they take it. This is because they rejected Our Signs and were heedless of them. Those who reject Our Signs and the meeting of the Hereafter, their deeds are null. Shall they be rewarded except for what they have done? (The Elevated Places 7:146-147)

Surely those who are with your Lord are not too proud to serve Him, and they declare His glory and throw themselves down in humility before Him. (The Elevated Places 7:206)

Your God is one God. The hearts of those who do not believe in the Hereafter are ignorant, and they are proud. Truly God knows what they hide and what they reveal. Surely He does not love the proud. (The Bee 16:22-23)

Do not go about the land exultingly, for you can not cut through the Earth, nor can you reach the mountains in height. (The Israelites 17:37)

And when We bestow favour on man, he turns aside and behaves proudly; and when evil afflicts him, he is despairing. Say: Every one acts according to his manner; but your Lord best knows who is best guided in the path. (The Israelites 17:83-84)

My messages were indeed recited to you, but you used to turn back on your heels, Haughtily discoursing about it, you withdrew yourselves to a distance. (The Believers 23:66-67)

And those who do not fear Our meeting, say: Why have angels not been sent down upon us, or (why) do we not see our Lord? Now certainly they are too proud of themselves and have revolted in great revolt. On The Day when they see the angels, there will be no good news for the guilty, and the angels will say: Let there be an inviolable obstruction: totally prohibited. (The Distinction 25:21)

(As for) the Abode of the Hereafter, We assign it to those who have no desire to exalt themselves on Earth, or to [spread corruption]. The good end is for those who guard (against evil). (The Narrative 28:83)

There are men who take frivolous discourse to lead astray from God's path, without knowledge, and they take it for a mockery. They will have an abasing chastisement. When Our Verses are recited to them, they turn away proudly, as if they had not heard them, as though heaviness were in their ears. Announce to them a painful chastisement. (Luqman 31:6-7)

Arrogance and Pride

 Jesus

When you are invited by anyone to a marriage feast, do not sit in the best seat, since perhaps someone more honorable than you might be invited by him, and he who invited both of you would come and tell you, "Make room for this person." Then you would begin, with shame, to take the lowest place. But when you are invited, go and sit in the lowest place, so that when he who invited you comes, he may tell you, "Friend, move up higher." Then you will be honored in the presence of all who sit at the table with you. For everyone who exalts himself will be humbled, and whoever humbles himself will be exalted. (Luke 14:8-11)

Muhammad ﷺ

Do not turn your face away from people, in contempt, or go about in the land exulting too much. Surely God does not love any self-conceited boaster. Pursue the right course in your going about, and lower your voice. Surely the most hateful of voices is the braying of the asses. (Luqman 31:18-19)

Surely they used to behave proudly when it was said to them: There is no god but God. They said: What? Shall we indeed give up our gods for the sake of a mad poet? No: He has come with the truth and verified the messengers. Most surely you will taste the painful chastisement. You will not be rewarded—except (for) what you did. (The Rangers 37:35-39)

Truthful God! Consider the Qur'an, possessing eminence. No! Those who disbelieve are in self-exaltation and opposition. (Sad 38:1-2)

Follow the best that has been revealed to you from your Lord, before chastisement comes to you, all of a sudden, while you do not even perceive. For fear that a soul should say: Oh, woe to me! I fell short in my duty to God, and I was one who laughed, to scorn. Or lest it say: Had God guided me, I would have guarded (against evil); Or lest it say, when it sees the chastisement: If only I could return, I would be a doer of good. Yes! My Verses came to you, but you rejected them, and you were proud, and you were one of the unbelievers. (The Companies 39:55-59)

On the Day of Resurrection, you will see those who lied against God. Their faces will be blackened. Is there not in Hell an abode for the proud? (The Companies 39:60)

Those who disbelieve will be driven to Hell in companies. When they come to it, its doors will open, and the keepers will say to them: Didn't messengers come to you from among yourselves, reciting to you the messages of your Lord and warning you of the meeting of this Day of yours? They will say: Yes! But the sentence of punishment was due against the unbelievers. It will be said: Enter the gates of Hell, to abide there. So evil is the abode of the proud. (The Companies 39:71-72)

It is greatly hated by God and by those who believe when people dispute concerning the Signs of God, without any authority given to them from God This is the way that God sets a seal over the heart of every proud, haughty one. (The Believer 40:35)

That is because you exulted in the land unjustly and because you behaved insolently. Enter the gates of Hell to abide. Evil is the abode of the proud. (The Believer 40:75-76)

Jesus

You know that they who are recognized as rulers over the nations lord it over them, and their great ones exercise authority over them. But it will not be so among you, for whoever wants to become great among you must be your servant. And whoever wants to be first must be bondservant of all. For the Son of Man also came not to be served, but to serve, and to give his life as a ransom for many. (Mark 10:42-45)

Muhammad ﷺ

When their messengers came to them with clear arguments, they exulted in what knowledge they had, so what they used to mock surrounded them. But when they saw Our punishment, they said: We believe in God alone, and we deny what we used to associate with Him. But their belief was not going to profit them when they had seen Our punishment; (this is) God's law, which indeed has preceded among His servants, and there the unbelievers are lost. (The Believer 40:83-85)

Woe to every sinful liar Who hears the Verses of God recited to him and then persists proudly, as though he had not heard them. Announce to him a painful chastisement. (The Kneeling 45:7-8)

On the day when those who disbelieve will be brought before the fire: You squandered your good things in your life of the world, and you enjoyed them for a while, so today you will be rewarded with the chastisement of abasement because you were unjustly proud in the land and because you exceeded all limits. (The Sandhills 46:20)

[Prophet], when you see them, they please you, and if they speak, you listen to their speech. (They are) like big pieces of wood, clad with garments. They think every cry to be against them. They are the enemy, so beware of them— May God destroy them—to where do they turn? When it is said to them, come, the Messenger of God will ask forgiveness for you, they turn back their heads, and you may see them turning away while they are big with pride. It is the same for them whether you beg forgiveness for them or do not beg forgiveness for them—God will never forgive them. Surely God does not guide the defiantly disobedient people. (The Hypocrites 63:4-6)

By no means! Surely he offers opposition to Our Verses. I will make a distressing punishment overtake him. Surely he reflected and plotted, but may he be cursed how he plotted. Again, may he be cursed how he plotted, and then he looked, frowned and scowled. Then he turned back and was big with pride. He said: This is nothing but magic, narrated (from others). This is nothing but the word of a mortal. I will cast him into Hell. And what will make you realize what Hell is? It leaves nothing, nor does it spare anything. It scorches the mortal. (The Clothed One 74:16-29)

No! When [the soul] comes up to the throat, and it is said: Who will be his charmer, now? He is sure that it is the (hour of) parting, and affliction is combined with affliction. You will be driven to your Lord on that day. He did not accept the truth, nor did he pray, but he called the truth a lie and turned back. Then he went to his followers, walking away in haughtiness. Nearer to you (is destruction), and nearer. Again, nearer to you and nearer. (The Resurrection 75:26-35)

Hypocrisy

 Jesus

Or how will you tell your brother, "Let me remove the speck from your eye;" and look, the log is in your own eye? You hypocrite. First remove the log out of your own eye, and then you can see clearly to remove the speck out of your brother's eye. (Matthew 7:4-5)

The scribes and the Pharisees brought to him a woman taken in adultery. Having set her in the midst, they told him, "Teacher, we found this woman in adultery, in the very act. Now in our Law, Moses commanded us to stone such. So what do you say?" But when they continued asking him, he looked up and said to them, "He who is without sin among you, let him throw the first stone at her." Jesus, standing up and having seen no one but the woman, said to her, "Woman, where are your accusers? Did no one condemn you?" She said, "No one, Lord." Jesus said, "Neither do I condemn you. Go your way. From now on, sin no more." (John 8:3-5, 7, 10-11)

And look, a certain man who had dropsy was in front of him. Jesus, answering, spoke to the Law scholars and Pharisees, saying, "Is it lawful to heal on the Sabbath?" But they were silent. He took him, and healed him, and let him go. He answered them, "Which of you, if your donkey or an ox fell into a well, would not immediately pull him out on a Sabbath day?" (Luke 14:2-5)

Many will tell me in that day, "Lord, Lord, did not we prophesy in your name, in your name cast out demons, and in your name do many mighty works?" And then I will tell them, "I never knew you. Depart from me, you who practice lawlessness." (Matthew 7:22-23)

Note: Hypocrites are the following:

- Muslims who are half-hearted, imperfect, weak (including in warfare) or pretending
- Non-Muslims who willfully reject Islam—Ed.

When they meet those who believe, they say: We believe. But when they are alone with their devils, they say: Surely we are with you, we were only mocking. God will pay them back for their mockery. He leaves them alone in their disorder, blindly wandering on. (The Cow 2:14-15)

The [hypocrites] wait for (some misfortune to befall) you; and then if you have a victory from God, they say: Were we not with you? And if there is a chance for the unbelievers, they say to them: Did we not have an advantage over you and defend you from the believers? So God will judge between you on the Day of Resurrection, and God will by no means give the unbelievers a way against the believers. (The Women 4:141)

Surely the hypocrites strive to deceive God, but He [deceives] them. When they stand up to prayer, they stand up sluggishly—they do it only to be seen by men, and they do not remember God, except a little. Wavering between that (and this), (belonging) to neither these nor those. You will not find a way for whoever God causes to err. (The Women 4:142-143)

Jesus

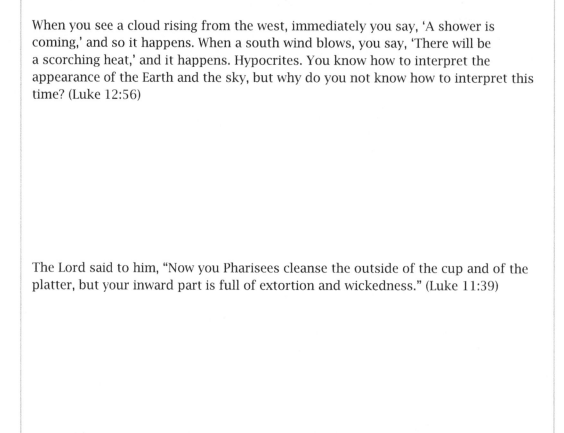

When you see a cloud rising from the west, immediately you say, 'A shower is coming,' and so it happens. When a south wind blows, you say, 'There will be a scorching heat,' and it happens. Hypocrites. You know how to interpret the appearance of the Earth and the sky, but why do you not know how to interpret this time? (Luke 12:56)

The Lord said to him, "Now you Pharisees cleanse the outside of the cup and of the platter, but your inward part is full of extortion and wickedness." (Luke 11:39)

But there is nothing covered up that will not be revealed, nor hidden that will not be known. Therefore whatever you have said in the darkness will be heard in the light. What you have spoken in the ear in the inner chambers will be proclaimed on the housetops. (Luke 12:2-3)

Woe to you, scribes and Pharisees, hypocrites. For you shut up the Kingdom of Heaven against men; for you do not enter in yourselves, neither do you allow those who are entering in to enter. (Matthew 23:14)

Muhammad ﷺ

Surely, the hypocrites are in the lowest depths of the fire, and you will not find a helper for them. (The Women 4:145)

The hypocrites and those in whose hearts was disease said: Their religion has deceived them. But whoever trusts in God, surely God is Mighty, Wise. If you could see how the angels will [take the souls] of those who disbelieve, smiting their faces and their backs, and (saying): Taste the punishment of burning! (The Accessions 8:49-50)

The hypocrites fear that a chapter will be sent down to them, telling them plainly what is in their hearts. Say, [Prophet]: Go on mocking, surely God will bring forth what you fear. If you question them, they will certainly say: We were only idly conversing and sporting. Say: Was it God and His Verses and His Messenger that you mocked? Do not make excuses; indeed you have denied after you had believed. If We pardon a group of you, We will chastise (another) group because they are guilty. (The Immunity 9:64-66)

The hypocritical men and the hypocritical women are all alike—they impose evil and forbid good and withhold their hands. They have forsaken God, so He has forsaken them. Surely the hypocrites are the defiantly disobedient. God has promised the hypocritical men and the hypocritical women and the unbelievers the Fire of Hell, to abide there—it is enough for them. God has cursed them, and they will have lasting chastisement. (The Immunity 9:67-68)

The dwellers of the desert are very hard in unbelief and hypocrisy, and they are more disposed to not know the limits of what God has revealed to His Messenger. God is Knowing, Wise. Of the dwellers of the desert are those who take what they spend to be a loss, and they wait for calamities to fall on you. But on them (will be) the evil calamity. God is Hearing, Knowing. (The Immunity 9:97-98)

Most certainly, God will know those who believe, and most certainly He will know the hypocrites. (The Spider 29:11)

Oh, Prophet! Be careful of (your duty to) God, and do not comply with (the wishes of) the unbelievers and the hypocrites; surely God is Knowing, Wise. (The Allies 33:1)

If the hypocrites and those in whose hearts is a disease and the agitators in the city do not desist, We will most certainly set you over them, and then they will be your neighbours only for a little while. Cursed! Wherever they are found, they will be seized and massacred, a (horrible) slaughter. (The Allies 33:60-61)

Jesus

Why do you also disobey the commandment of God because of your tradition? For God commanded, saying, "Honor your father and your mother," and, "He who speaks evil of father or mother, let him be put to death." But you say, "Whoever may tell his father or his mother, 'Whatever help you might otherwise have gotten from me is a gift devoted to God,' he is not to honor his father or his mother. You have made the word of God void because of your tradition. You hypocrites. Well did Isaiah prophesy of you, saying, "These people honor me with their lips; but their heart is far from me. And in vain do they worship me, teaching instructions that are the commandments of men." (Matthew 15:3-9)

You blind guides, who strain out a gnat, and swallow a camel. Woe to you, scribes and Pharisees, hypocrites. For you clean the outside of the cup and of the plate, but within they are full of extortion and self-indulgence. You blind Pharisee, first clean the inside of the cup and of the plate, so that its outside may become clean also. (Matthew 23:24-26)

Woe to you, scribes and Pharisees, hypocrites. For you are like whitened tombs, which outwardly appear beautiful, but inwardly are full of dead men's bones, and of all uncleanness. Even so you also outwardly appear righteous to men, but inwardly you are full of hypocrisy and iniquity. (Matthew 23:27-28)

Muhammad ﷺ

[Prophet] have you not seen those who have become hypocrites? They say to their brethren who disbelieve among the Followers of the Book: If you are driven forth, we will certainly go forth with you, and we will never obey any one concerning you. And if you are fought against, we will certainly help you. God bears witness that they are most surely liars. Certainly, if their brethren are driven out, they will not go out with them, and if they are attacked, they will not help them. Even if they help them, they will certainly turn (their) backs, so they will not be helped. You, [Prophet], are certainly greater feared in their hearts than is God; this is because they are a people who do not understand. They will not fight against you together, except in fortified towns or from behind walls. The fighting between them is severe. You may think of them as one body, but their hearts are disunited. That is because they are a people who have no sense. (The Banishment 59:11-14)

When the hypocrites come to you [Prophet], they say: We bear witness that you are most surely God's Messenger. God knows that you are most surely His Messenger, and God bears witness that the hypocrites are surely liars. They make their oaths a shelter, and then turn away from God's way. Surely evil is what they do. Because they believe, and then disbelieve, so a seal is set upon their hearts so that they do not understand. (The Hypocrites 63:1-3)

They are the ones who say: Do not spend on those who are with the Messenger of God, until they disband. And God's treasures are of the Heavens and the Earth, but the hypocrites do not understand. They say: If we return to Medina, the mighty will surely drive out the meaner. To God belongs the might, and to His Messenger and to the believers, but the hypocrites do not know. (The Hypocrites 63:7-8)

Temptation

 Jesus

But no one can enter into the house of the strong man to plunder, unless he first binds the strong man; and then he will plunder his house. (Mark 3:27)

Watch and pray, that you do not enter into temptation. The spirit indeed is willing, but the flesh is weak. (Matthew 26:41)

Oh, Messenger! Do not let those who hasten into unbelief grieve you, those who say with their mouths, We believe, and their hearts do not believe. And those among the Jews who are listeners for the sake of a lie, listeners for other people who have not come to you—they distort the words out of context, saying: If you are given this, take it, and if you are not given this, be cautious. As for he whose temptation God desires, you cannot control anything against God for him. God does not desire that these should purify their hearts; they will have disgrace in this world, and they will have a grievous punishment in the Hereafter. (The Food 5:41)

[Prophet], you should judge between them by what God has revealed, and do not follow their low desires, and be cautious of them, lest they seduce you from part of what God has revealed to you. But if they turn back, know that God desires to afflict them on account of some of their faults; and most surely many of the people are defiantly disobedient. (The Food 5:49)

It is He Who created the Heavens and the Earth in six periods—and His [throne] (extends) on the water, so that He might try you, which of you is best in action. (Hud 11:7)

[Prophet], surely they intended to tempt you away from what We have revealed to you, so that you should invent against Us something else, and then they would certainly have taken you for a friend. Had it not been that We had already [strengthened] you, you would certainly have nearly inclined to them a little. In that case We would certainly have made you taste a double (punishment) in this life and a double (punishment) after death, and then you would not have found any helper against Us. (The Israelites 17:73-75)

Every soul must taste of death; and We try you by evil and good as a trial; and you will be brought back to Us. (The Prophets 21:35)

Do men think that they will be left alone after saying, "We believe," and not be tested? Certainly We tested those before them, so God will certainly know those who are true, and He will certainly know the liars. (The Spider 29:2-3)

Blessed is He in whose hand is the Kingdom, and He has power over all things. Who created death and life so that He may try you—which of you is best in deeds. He is the Mighty, the Forgiving. (The Kingdom 67:1-2)

Fear

 Jesus

I tell you, my friends, do not be afraid of those who kill the body, and after that have no more that they can do. But I will warn you whom you should fear. Fear Him, who after He has killed, has power to cast into Hell. Yes, I tell you, fear Him. Are not five sparrows sold for two assaria coins? Not one of them is forgotten by God. But the very hairs of your head are all numbered. Therefore do not be afraid. You are of more value than many sparrows. (Luke 12:4-7)

If they have called the master of the house Beelzebul, how much more those of his household. Therefore do not be afraid of them, for there is nothing covered that will not be revealed; and hidden that will not be known. (Matthew 10:25-26)

Do not be afraid, only believe. (Mark 5:36b)

Do not be afraid, little flock, for it is your Father's good pleasure to give you the Kingdom. (Luke 12:32)

From wherever you come, turn your face toward the sacred Mosque. Wherever you are, turn your faces toward it, so that people will have no plea against you, except those who are [wrongdoers]. So do not fear them, fear Me, so that I may complete My favour on you, and so that you may walk on the right course. (The Cow 2:150)

Surely, those who believe and those who are Jews and Sabeans and Christians— whoever believes in God and the Last Day and does good—they will have no fear, nor will they grieve. (The Food 5:69)

Fear an affliction that might smite not only [wrongdoers]. Know that God is severe in requiting (evil). (The Accessions 8:25)

The faces will be humbled before the Living, Self-subsistent God, and he who bears iniquity is indeed undone. But whoever does good works and is a believer, he shall have no fear of injustice or of the withholding of his due. Thus have we sent down an Arabic Qur'an, and We have distinctly set forth threats in it, so that they may guard (against evil) or that it may produce a reminder for them. (Ta Ha 20:111-113)

Those who fear their Lord [unseen] will surely have forgiveness and a great reward. (The Kingdom 67:12)

What is the matter with them? They turn aside from the Reminder, like frightened asses who flee from a lion. No! Every one of them desires to be given pages, spread out. No! They do not fear the Hereafter. No! It is surely a reminder. So whoever pleases may pay heed to it. And they will not pay heed, unless God pleases. He is worthy to be feared, and worthy to forgive. (The Clothed One 74:49-56)

Protect Your Soul

 Jesus

I have said all these things to you so that you may be kept from stumbling. (John 16:1)

Woe to the world because of stumbling blocks. For there will always be something to cause people to stumble, but woe to the man through whom the stumbling block comes. (Matthew 18:7)

If you remain in my word, you are truly my disciples. You will know the truth, and the truth will make you free. Truly I tell you, everyone who commits sin is the bondservant of sin.[1] (John 8:31b-32, 34)

------

1 Translated from the Greek, sin (amartia) is defined as "missing the mark."—Ed.

God does not impose upon any soul a duty beyond the extent of its ability. The soul (will benefit from) what it has earned, and it will bear upon it (the evil of) what it has wrought. Our Lord! Do not punish us if we forget or make a mistake. Our Lord! Do not lay on us a burden, as You laid on those before us. Our Lord! Do not impose on us what we do not have the strength to bear. Pardon us, grant us protection and have mercy on us. You are our Patron, so help us against the unbelieving people. (The Cow 2:286)

Every soul will taste of death, and you will be paid fully your reward only on the Resurrection Day. Whoever is removed far away from the fire and is made to enter the Garden has indeed attained the object. The life of this world is nothing but a provision of vanities. (The Family of Amran 3:185)

Surely (as for) those whom the angels cause to die while they are unjust to their souls, the angels will ask: In what state were you? They will say: We were [oppressed] on the Earth. The angels will say: Was God's Earth not spacious, so that you should have migrated? These it is whose abode is Hell, and it is an evil resort. Except the weak from among the men and the women and the children who do not have the means or cannot find a way (to escape)—it may be that God will pardon them. God is Pardoning, Forgiving. (The Women 4:97-99)

[Prophet], do not plead on behalf of those who act unfaithfully to their souls—surely God does not love he who is treacherous, sinful. They hide themselves from men but do not hide themselves from God. He is with them when they meditate by night words that do not please Him, and God encompasses what they do. (The Women 4:107-108)

Whoever does evil or acts unjustly to his soul, and then asks forgiveness of God, will find God Forgiving, Merciful. Whoever commits a sin only commits it against his own soul; and God is Knowing, Wise. Whoever commits a fault or a sin, and then accuses an innocent of it, indeed takes upon himself the burden of slander and flagrant sin. (The Women 4:110-112)

Oh, you who believe! Take care of your souls. He who errs cannot hurt you when you are on the right way. To God is your return, all (of you): He will inform you of what you did. (The Food 5:105)

Jesus

If your hand causes you to stumble, cut it off. It is better for you to enter into life maimed, rather than having your two hands to go into Hell, into the unquenchable fire, where their worm does not die and the fire is not quenched. If your foot causes you to stumble, cut it off. It is better for you to enter into life lame, rather than having your two feet to be cast into Hell, into the fire that will never be quenched, where their worm does not die and the fire is not quenched. If your eye causes you to stumble, cast it out. It is better for you to enter into the Kingdom of God with one eye, rather than having two eyes to be cast into Hell fire, where their worm does not die, and the fire is not quenched. (Mark 9:43-48)

But know this, that if the master of the house had known in what watch of the night the thief was coming, he would have watched, and would not have allowed his house to be broken into. Therefore also be ready, for in an hour that you do not expect, the Son of Man will come. (Matthew 24:43-44)

When the strong man, fully armed, guards his own dwelling, his goods are safe. But when someone stronger attacks him and overcomes him, he takes from him his whole armor in which he trusted, and divides his spoils. (Luke 11:21-22)

Muhammad ﷺ

He takes your souls at night (in sleep), and He knows what you commit in the day. Then He raises you up, so that your appointed term is fulfilled. To Him is your return. He will inform you of what you did. He is the Supreme, above His servants, and He sends keepers over you until death comes to you. Our messengers take you, and they do not fail. You are then sent back to God, your Master, the True One. Surely, His is the judgment, and He is swiftest in taking account. (The Cattle 6:60-62)

They only wait for the angels to come to them, or that your Lord should come, or that some of the signs of your Lord should come. On the Day when some of the signs of your Lord will come, faith will not profit a soul that did not believe before or earn good through faith. Say: Wait—we too are waiting. (The Cattle 6:158)

Say, [Prophet]: What? Shall I seek a Lord other than God? When He is the Lord of all things? No soul earns (evil) except against itself, and no bearer of burden shall bear the burden of another. Your return is to your Lord, and He will inform you about that in which you differed. (The Cattle 6:164)

We have made every man's actions cling to his neck. On Resurrection Day, We will bring a record to him, which he will find wide open—read your record. Today you are sufficient as a reckoner against yourself. (The Israelites 17:13-14)

God takes souls at the time of their death, and He takes those of the living during their sleep. He withholds those on whom He has passed the decree of death, and He sends the others back until an appointed term. Most surely there are signs in this for people who reflect. (The Companies 39:42)

Whoever does good, it is for his own soul, and whoever does evil, it is against it. Your Lord is not in the least unjust to the servants. (Ha Mim 41:46)

Certainly, We created man, and We know what his [soul whispers] to him. We are nearer to him than his life-vein. When the two receivers receive, sitting on the right and on the left, he utters not a word, but there is an observer with him, ready [to record].[1] The stupor of death will come in truth; that is what you shunned! (Qaf 50:16-19)

---

1 Ali, M.M., *The Holy Qur'an*, 997. The yamin, or the right side, represents the good, and the shimdl, or the left side, the evil.

Jesus

Let your waist be girded and your lamps burning. Be like people watching for their lord, when he returns from the marriage feast; that, when he comes and knocks, they may immediately open to him. Blessed are those servants, whom the lord will find watching when he comes. Truly I tell you, that he will dress himself, and make them recline, and will come and serve them. And if he comes in the second watch, or comes in the third watch, and finds them so, blessed are those servants. (Luke 12:37-38)

By your endurance you will win your lives. (Luke 21:19)

What will it profit a man, if he gains the whole world, and forfeits his life? Or what will a man give in exchange for his life? (Matthew 16:26)

Muhammad ﷺ

Oh, you who believe! Be careful of (your duty to) God. Let every soul consider what it has sent ahead for tomorrow, and be careful of (your duty to) God. Surely God is aware of what you do. (The Banishment 59:18)

Every soul is held in pledge for what it earns, except the people of the right hand. In gardens, they will ask each other about the guilty: What has brought you into Hell? They will say: We were not of those who prayed, and we did not feed the poor. We needed to enter into vain discourse with those who entered into vain discourse. And we called the Day of Judgment a lie, until death overtook us. So the intercession of intercessors will not benefit them. (The Clothed One 74:38-48)

Do not be like those who forgot God, so He made them forget their own souls: these are the defiantly disobedient. (The Banishment 59:19)

Consider the Heaven and the Comer by Night. What will make you know how great the Comer by Night is? The star of piercing brightness. Over every soul is a keeper. (The Night-Comer 86:1-4)

But on that day, no one will punish with (anything like) His punishment, and no one will bind with (anything like) His binding. Oh, soul that is at rest! Return to your Lord, well-pleased (with Him), well pleasing (Him). Enter among My servants, and enter into My Garden. (The Daybreak 89:25-30)

Fundamentals

Greatest Commandments

 Jesus

"You are to love the Lord your God with all your heart, with all your soul, and with all your mind." This is the great and first commandment. A second likewise is this, "You are to love your neighbor as yourself." The whole Law and the Prophets depend on these two commandments. (Matthew 22:37-40)

This is my commandment, that you love one another, even as I have loved you. (John 15:12)

You know the commandments: Do not murder, do not commit adultery, do not steal, do not give false testimony, do not defraud, honor your father and mother. (Mark 10:19)

It is not in righteousness that you turn your faces toward the East and the West, but righteousness is that one should believe in God, the Last Day, the angels, the Book and the prophets. And give away wealth, out of love for Him, to the near of kin, the orphans, the needy, the wayfarer, the beggars and for (the emancipation of) the [slaves]. And keep up prayer, pay the poor-rate, perform your promise when you make one, and be patient in times of distress, affliction and conflict. These are true (to themselves), and these are the [God-fearing]. (The Cow 2:177)

A believer should not kill a believer. But whoever kills a believer by mistake should free a believing slave and pay blood-money to the deceased's people, unless they pardon the blood-money, as charity. But if the deceased believer is from a people who are hostile to you, freeing a believing slave (suffices). If he is from a tribe that has a covenant with you, pay the blood-money to his family, and free a believing slave. If you cannot find (a slave), fast for two months successively, a penance from God. God is Knowing, Wise. Whoever kills a believer intentionally, his punishment is Hell, and he will abide in it: God will send His wrath on him and curse him and prepare for him a painful chastisement. (The Women 4:92-93)

Say, [Prophet]: Come! I will recite what your Lord has forbidden you. Do not associate anything with God, show kindness to your parents, do not slay your children for (fear of) poverty—We provide for you and for them—and do not draw near to apparent or concealed indecencies. Do not kill the soul, which God has forbidden, except for the requirements of justice. This He orders you, so that you may understand. (The Cattle 6:151)

Do not approach the property of an orphan, except in the best manner, until he attains his maturity. Give full measure and weight, with justice. We do not impose on any soul a duty, except to the extent of its ability. When you speak, be just, even if it is (against) a relative. Fulfil God's covenant—with this He commands you, so that you may be mindful. (The Cattle 6:152)

Say, [Prophet]: My Lord has only prohibited indecencies, those that are apparent and those that are concealed, and sin and rebellion without justice, and that you associate with God anything for which He has not sent down authority, and that you say against God what you do not know. (The Elevated Places 7:33)

Jesus

"Why do you call me good? No one is good but one, that is, God. If you want to enter into life, keep the commandments." He said to him, "Which ones?" And Jesus said, "Do not murder. Do not commit adultery. Do not steal. Do not offer false testimony. Honor your father and mother. And, Love your neighbor as yourself." (Matthew 19:17-19)

Therefore, whoever breaks one of these least commandments, and teaches others to do so, will be called least in the Kingdom of Heaven; but whoever does and teaches them will be called great in the Kingdom of Heaven. (Matthew 5:19)

Muhammad ﷺ

Do not kill your children for fear of poverty—We give them sustenance, and yourselves (too)—surely to kill them is a great wrong.[1] Do not go near fornication; surely it is an indecency, and evil is the way. Do not kill any one whom God has forbidden, except for a just cause. We have indeed given authority to the heir of whomever is slain unjustly, but do not let the heir exceed the just limits in slaying; surely he is aided. Do not draw near to the property of the orphan, except in a goodly way, until he attains his maturity. Fulfil your promises; surely (every) promise will be questioned about. Give full measure when you measure out, and weigh with a true balance; this is fair and better in the end. (The Israelites 17:31-35)

Successful indeed are the believers, who are humble in their prayers, who keep aloof from vain [conversation], who act aiming for purification, who guard their private parts except before their mates or the [slaves] that their right hands possess, for they surely are not blameable. But whoever seeks to go beyond that exceeds the limits. Those who keep their trusts and their covenant, those who keep guard on their prayers, these are the heirs, who will inherit the Paradise; they will abide there. (The Believers 23:1-11)

---

1 Ali, M.M., *The Holy Qur'an*, 567. Infanticide, in the case of daughters, was met with among the Arabs, because the females could not go out to war and thus procure for themselves, by means of plunder, their means of subsistence (Rz).

Love One Another

 Jesus

You have heard that it was said, "Love your neighbor, and hate your enemy." For if you love those who love you, what reward do you have? Do not even the tax collectors do the same? And if you only greet your friends, what more do you do than others? Do not even the tax collectors do the same? (Matthew 5:43, 46-47)

And you shall love the Lord your God with all your heart, and with all your soul, and with all your mind, and with all your strength. This is the first commandment. The second is like this, 'You are to love your neighbor as yourself.' There is no other commandment greater than these. (Mark 12:30-31)

As you would like men to do to you, do the same to them. If you love those who love you, what credit is that to you? For even sinners love those who love them. (Luke 6:31-32)

And look, a woman in the city who was a sinner, when she knew that Jesus was reclining in the Pharisee's house, she brought an alabaster jar of ointment. Standing behind at his feet weeping, she began to wet his feet with her tears, and she wiped them with the hair of her head, kissed his feet, and anointed them with the ointment. Now when the Pharisee who had invited him saw it, he said to himself, "This man, if he were a prophet, would have perceived who and what kind of woman this is who touches him, that she is a sinner." Turning to the woman, he said to Simon, "Do you see this woman? I entered into your house, and you gave me no water for my feet, but she has wet my feet with her tears, and wiped them with her hair. You gave me no kiss, but she, since the time I came in, has not ceased to kiss my feet. You did not anoint my head with oil, but she has anointed my feet with ointment. Therefore I tell you, her sins, which are many, are forgiven, for she loved much. But to whom little is forgiven, the same loves little." He said to her, "Your sins are forgiven. Your faith has saved you. Go in peace." (Luke 7:37-39, 44-48, 50)

A new commandment I give to you, that you love one another. Just as I have loved you, you also must love one another. By this, everyone will know that you are my disciples, if you have love for one another. (John 13:34-35)

Even as the Father has loved me, I also have loved you. Remain in my love. If you keep my commandments, you will remain in my love; even as I have kept my Father's commandments, and remain in his love. I have spoken these things to you, that my joy may abide in you, and that your joy may be made full. (John 15:9-11)

One of His Signs is that He created mates for you from yourselves, that you may find quiet of mind in them, and He put between you love and compassion. Most surely there are Signs in this for a people who reflect. (The Romans 30:21)

Jesus

Greater love has no one than this, that someone lay down his life for his friends. You are my friends, if you do whatever I command you. No longer do I call you servants, for the servant does not know what his master is doing. But I have called you friends, for everything that I heard from my Father I have made known to you. (John 15:13-15)

Righteous Father, the world hasn't known You, but I knew You; and these knew that You sent me. I made Your name known to them, and I will make it known that the love with which You loved me may be in them, and I in them. (John 17:25-26)

I command these things to you, that you may love one another. If the world hates you, you know that it has hated me before it hated you. (John 15:17-18)

Muhammad ﷺ

(It is) for the poor who fled, those who were driven from their homes and their possessions, seeking grace of God, and (His) pleasure, and assisting God and His Messenger. It is these who are truthful. And those who made their homes in the city and in the faith, before them, love those who have fled to them.[1] They do not find in their hearts a need for what they are given, and they prefer (them) over themselves, even though poverty may afflict them. Whoever are preserved from the stinginess of their souls are the successful ones. (The Banishment 59:8-9)

---

1 Ali, M.M., *The Holy Qur'an*, 1060. The Helpers, i.e. the Muslim residents of Medina.

Forgive Others

 Jesus

For if you forgive men their trespasses, your heavenly Father will also forgive you. But if you do not forgive men their transgressions, neither will your Father forgive your trespasses. (Matthew 6:14-15)

Then Peter came to him and said, "Lord, how often can my brother sin against me, and I forgive him? Up to seven times?" Jesus said to him, "I do not tell you up to seven times, but up to seventy times seven." (Matthew 18:21-22)

Father, forgive them, for they do not know what they are doing. (Luke 23:34)

Watch yourselves. If your brother sins against you, rebuke him. If he repents, forgive him. And if he sins against you seven times in the day, and seven times in the day returns to you, saying, "I repent," you must forgive him. (Luke 17:3-4)

Many of the Followers of the Book wish to turn you back into unbelievers after your faith, out of selfish envy, (even) after the truth has become obvious to them. But pardon and forgive, until God brings about His command. Surely God has power over all things. (The Cow 2:109)

Kind speech and forgiveness is better than charity followed by injury. God is Self-sufficient, Forbearing. (The Cow 2:263)

If you do good openly or do it in secret or pardon an evil, surely God is Pardoning, Powerful. (The Women 4:149)

If you invite them to guidance, they do not hear; you see them looking toward you, yet they do not see. Take to forgiveness and enjoin good and turn aside from the ignorant. (The Elevated Places 7:198-199)

Ask forgiveness for them or do not ask forgiveness for them. Even if you ask forgiveness for them seventy times, God will not forgive them. This is because they disbelieved in God and His Messenger, and God does not guide the defiantly disobedient people. (The Immunity 9:80)

It is not (fit) for the Prophet and those who believe to ask forgiveness for the polytheists—even though they might be close relatives—after it has become clear that they are inmates of the Flaming Fire. Abraham asked forgiveness for his father only because of a promise that Abraham had made to him, but when it became clear that his father was an enemy of God, he declared himself to be clear of him. Most surely Abraham was very tender-hearted, forbearing. (The Immunity 9:113-114)

Jesus

Therefore the Kingdom of Heaven is like a certain king, who wanted to reconcile accounts with his servants. When he had begun to reconcile, one was brought to him who owed him ten thousand talents. But because he could not pay, his lord commanded him to be sold, with his wife, his children, and all that he had, and payment to be made. The servant therefore fell down and kneeled before him, saying, "Lord, have patience with me, and I will repay you all." The lord of that servant, being moved with compassion, released him, and forgave him the debt. But that servant went out, and found one of his fellow servants, who owed him one hundred denarii, and he grabbed him, and took him by the throat, saying, "Pay me what you owe."[1] So his fellow servant fell down at his feet and begged him, saying, "Have patience with me, and I will repay you all." He would not, but went and cast him into prison, until he should pay back that which was due. So when his fellow servants saw what was done, they were exceedingly sorry, and came and told to their lord all that was done. Then his lord called him in, and said to him, "You wicked servant. I forgave you all that debt, because you begged me. Should not you also have had mercy on your fellow servant, even as I had mercy on you?" His lord was angry, and delivered him to the tormentors, until he should pay all that was due to him. So my heavenly Father will also do to you, if you do not each forgive your brother, from your heart, for his misdeeds. (Matthew 18:23-35)

If therefore you are offering your gift at the altar, and there remember that your brother has anything against you, leave your gift there before the altar, and go your way. First be reconciled to your brother, and then come and offer your gift. (Matthew 5:23)

---

1 100 denarii was about one-sixtieth of a talent.—Ed.

Muhammad ﷺ

Those of you who possess grace and abundance: do not swear against giving to the near of kin, the poor and those who have fled in God's way. Rather, pardon and [overlook]. Do you not [wish] that God should forgive you? God is Forgiving, Merciful.
(The Light 24:22)

Those who shun the great sins and indecencies, who forgive whenever they are angry.
(The Counsel 42:37)

Say, [Prophet], to those who believe: Forgive those who do not fear the days of God, so that He may reward a people for what they earn. (The Kneeling 45:14)

Giving

 Jesus

Whoever compels you to go one mile, go with him two. Give to him who asks you, and do not turn away him who desires to borrow from you. (Matthew 5:41-42)

He called his disciples to himself, and said to them, "Truly I tell you, this poor widow gave more than all those who are giving into the treasury, for they all gave out of their abundance, but she, out of her poverty, gave all that she had to live on." (Mark 12:43-44)

Woe to you, scribes and Pharisees, hypocrites. For you tithe mint, dill, and cumin, and have left undone the weightier matters of the Law: justice, mercy, and faith. But you ought to have done these, and not to have left the other undone. (Matthew 23:23)

Be careful that you do not do your alms before men, to be seen by them, or else you have no reward from your Father who is in Heaven. (Matthew 6:1)

When you do merciful deeds, do not let your left hand know what your right hand does, so that your merciful deeds may be in secret. Then your Father who sees in secret will reward you. (Matthew 6:3-4)

Therefore when you do merciful deeds, do not sound a trumpet before yourself, as the hypocrites do in the synagogues and in the streets, that they may get glory from people. Truly I tell you, they have received their reward. (Matthew 6:2)

They said therefore to him, "What must we do, that we may work the works of God?" Jesus answered them, "This is the work of God, that you believe in him whom He has sent." (John 6:28-29)

They ask you what they should spend. Say, [Prophet]: Whatever wealth you spend, it is for the parents, the near of kin, the orphans, the needy and the wayfarer. Whatever good you do, God surely knows it. (The Cow 2:215)

They ask you what they should spend: say, "give what you can spare." This is how God makes His Verses clear to you, so that you may ponder. (The Cow 2:219b)

Oh, you who believe! Do not make your charity worthless by reproach and injury, like he who spends his property to be seen by men and does not believe in God and the Last Day. His parable is of a smooth rock with earth upon it, and then a heavy rain falls upon it and leaves it bare. They will not be able to gain anything of what they earned. God does not guide the unbelieving people. (The Cow 2:264)

Oh, you who believe! Spend (benevolently) of the good things that you earn and of what We have brought forth for you from the earth. Do not aim to spend (in alms) from what is bad, while you would not take it yourselves, [except with closed eyes]. Know that God is Self-sufficient, Praiseworthy. (The Cow 2:267)

If you give alms openly, it is good, but if you hide it and give it to the poor, it is better for you, and this will do away with some of your evil deeds. God is aware of what you do. (The Cow 2:271)

By no means will you attain righteousness until you spend (benevolently) out of what you love. Whatever thing you spend, God surely knows it. (The Family of Amran 3:92)

Say, [Prophet]: Spend willingly or unwillingly—it will not be accepted from you; surely you are a defiantly disobedient people. Nothing hinders their contributions being accepted from them except that they disbelieve in God and in His Messenger. They come to prayer only when they are sluggish, and they only spend unwilling. Do not let their property and their children excite your admiration. God only wishes to chastise them with these in this world's life, and (that) their souls may depart while they are unbelievers. (The Immunity 9:53-55)

Jesus

When you make a feast, ask the poor, the maimed, the lame, or the blind; and you will be blessed, because they do not have the resources to repay you. For you will be repaid in the resurrection of the righteous. (Luke 14:13-14)

Now there was a certain rich man, and he was clothed in purple and fine linen, living in luxury every day. A certain beggar, named Lazarus, was placed at his gate, full of sores, and desiring to be fed with the crumbs that fell from the rich man's table. Yes, even the dogs came and licked his sores. It happened that the beggar died, and that he was carried away by the angels to Abraham's bosom. The rich man also died, and was buried. In Hell, he lifted up his eyes, being in torment, and saw Abraham far off, and Lazarus at his bosom. He called out and said, "Father Abraham, have mercy on me, and send Lazarus, that he may dip the tip of his finger in water, and cool my tongue. For I am in anguish in this flame." But Abraham said, "Son, remember that you, in your lifetime, received your good things, and Lazarus, in like manner, bad things. But now here he is comforted, and you are in anguish. Besides all this, between us and you there is a great gulf fixed, so that those who want to pass from here to you are not able, and so that none may cross over from there to us." He said, "I ask you therefore, Father, that you would send him to my Father's house; for I have five brothers, so that he may testify to them, so they won't also come into this place of torment." But Abraham said to him, "They have Moses and the Prophets. Let them listen to them." He said, "No, Father Abraham, but if one goes to them from the dead, they will repent." He said to him, "If they do not listen to Moses and the Prophets, neither will they be persuaded if one rises from the dead." (Luke 16:19-31)

Blessed are the merciful, for they will obtain mercy. (Matthew 5:7)

Muhammad ﷺ

Alms are only for the poor and the needy, the officials (appointed) over them, those whose hearts are made to incline (to truth), the (ransoming of) captives, those in debt and the way of God, and the wayfarer. An ordinance from God. God is Knowing, Wise. (The Immunity 9:60)

It was not seemly for the people of Medina, and those around them of the Bedouins, to remain behind the Messenger of God. Nor should they prefer anything for themselves over the Messenger. Because a good work is recorded for them if they are afflicted by thirst or fatigue or hunger in God's way. Or if they tread a path that enrages the unbelievers, or attain from the enemy what they attain. Surely God does not waste the reward of the doers of good. Nor do they spend anything that may be spent, small or great, nor do they cross a valley, without it being written down to their credit, so that God may reward them with the best of what they have done. (The Immunity 9:120-121)

God has made some of you excel over others in the means of subsistence, but those who are made to excel [would] not give away their sustenance to those [slaves] whom their right hands possess, so that they would be equal. Is it then the favour of God that they deny? (The Bee 16:71)

We will most certainly make whoever is a believer and does good, whether male or female, live a happy life, and We will most certainly give him the reward for the best of what they did. (The Bee 16:97)

Jesus

But he, desiring to justify himself, asked Jesus, "Who is my neighbor?" Jesus answered, "A certain man was going down from Jerusalem to Jericho, and he fell among robbers, who both stripped him and beat him, and departed, leaving him half dead. By chance, a certain priest was going down that way. When he saw him, he passed by on the other side. In the same way a Levite also, when he came to the place, and saw him, passed by on the other side. But a certain Samaritan, as he traveled, came where he was. When he saw him, he was moved with compassion, came to him, and bound up his wounds, pouring on oil and wine. He set him on his own animal, and brought him to an inn, and took care of him. On the next day when he departed, he took out two denarii, and gave them to the host, and said to him, "Take care of him. Whatever you spend beyond that, I will repay you when I return." Now which of these three do you think seemed to be a neighbor to him who fell among the robbers?" He said, "He who showed mercy on him. Go and do likewise." (Luke 10:29-37)

If you want to be perfect, go, sell what you have and give to the poor, and you will have treasure in Heaven; and come, follow me. (Matthew 19:21)

It is more blessed to give than to receive. (Acts 20:35)

If you lend to those from whom you hope to receive, what credit is that to you? Even sinners lend to sinners, to receive back as much. (Luke 6:34)

Muhammad ﷺ

Your Lord has commanded that you not serve (any) but Him, and that you show goodness to your parents. If either or both of them reach old age with you, do not say to them (so much as) "Ugh," or chide them, and speak a generous word to them. Make yourself submissively gentle to them with compassion, and say: Oh, my Lord! Have compassion on them, as they brought me up (when I was) little. Your Lord knows best what is in your minds. If you are good, then He is surely Forgiving to those who turn (to Him) frequently. (The Israelites 17:23-25)

Give the near of kin his due, and the needy and the wayfarer, and do not spend wastefully. Surely the wasteful are the fellows of the devils, and the Devil is ever ungrateful to his Lord. If you turn away from them to seek mercy from your Lord, which you hope for, speak a gentle word to them.[1] (The Israelites 17:26-28)

Surely We have made whatever is on the Earth an embellishment for it, so that We may try them, to see which of them is best in works. Most surely We will make Earth barren. (The Cave 18:7-8)

Wealth and children are adornments of the life of this world, but ever-abiding good works are better with your Lord for reward and better in expectation. (The Cave 18:46)

The successful are those whose good deeds are heavy. As for those whose good deeds are light, they will have lost their souls, abiding in Hell. The fire will scorch their faces, and they will [grin with disfigured lips]. (The Believers 23:102-104)

Whatever you lend in usury, so that it may increase in the property of men, will not increase with God. Whatever you give in charity, desiring God's pleasure, you will get manifold. (The Romans 30:39)

---

1 Ali, M.M., *The Holy Qur'an*, 566. i.e. not having anything to give to the needy.

Jesus

If you do good to those who do good to you, what credit is that to you? For even sinners do the same. If you lend to those from whom you hope to receive, what credit is that to you? Even sinners lend to sinners, to receive back as much. (Luke 6:33-34)

He who receives a prophet in the name of a prophet will receive a prophet's reward. He who receives a righteous man because he is a righteous man will receive a righteous man's reward. (Matthew 10:41)

Give to everyone who asks you, and do not ask him who takes away your goods to give them back again. (Luke 6:30)

Give, and it will be given to you: good measure, pressed down, shaken together, and running over, will be poured into your lap. For with the same measure you measure it will be measured back to you. (Luke 6:38)

Therefore whatever you desire for men to do to you, do also to them; for this is the Law and the Prophets. (Matthew 7:12)

Muhammad ﷺ

[Regarding] those who are miserly and impose it on men, and whoever turns away—surely God is Self-sufficient, the Praised. (The Iron 57:24)

Blessed is He in whose hand is the Kingdom, Who has power over all things, Who created death and life so that He may try you—which of you is best in deeds? He is the Mighty, the Forgiving. (The Kingdom 67:1-2)

No! You do not honour the orphan, nor do you urge one another to feed the poor. You eat away the inheritance, devouring (everything) indiscriminately, and you love wealth with exceeding love. No! When the Earth crumbles to pieces, and your Lord comes, and the angels in ranks—Hell appears on that day. On that day man will be mindful, and how will being mindful serve him, (then)? (The Daybreak 89:17-23)

What will make you comprehend what the uphill road is? (It is) freeing a slave. Or feeding in a day of hunger, to an orphan near of kin, or to the poor man lying in the dust. To be of those who believe and charge one another to show patience and compassion. These are the people of the right hand. But those who disbelieve in Our messages are the people of the left hand. Fire is closed over on them. (The City 90:12-20)

Consider the early hours of the day, and the night when it covers with darkness. Your Lord has not forsaken you, nor has He become displeased. Surely what comes after is better for you than what has gone before. Soon your Lord will give to you, so that you will be well pleased. Did He not find you as an orphan and give you shelter? And find you unable to see and show the way? And find you in want and make you free from want? So, do not oppress the orphan. And do not chide he who asks. And announce the favour of your Lord. (The Early Hours 93:1-11)

[Prophet], have you considered he who calls the Judgment a lie? He is the one who treats the orphan with harshness and does not urge (others) to feed the poor. Woe to the praying ones who are unmindful of their prayers, who do (good) to be seen, who withhold alms. (The Alms 107:1-7)

Virtue and Justice

 Jesus

Do not judge according to appearance, but judge with righteous judgment. (John 7:24)

Blessed are those who hunger and thirst after righteousness, for they will be filled. (Matthew 5:6)

You judge according to the flesh. I judge no one. (John 8:15)

Woe to you Pharisees. For you tithe mint and rue and every herb, but you bypass justice and the love of God. You ought to have done these, and not to have left the other undone. (Luke 11:42)

Do not judge, and you won't be judged. Do not condemn, and you won't be condemned. Forgive, and you will be forgiven. (Luke 6:37)

Do not judge, so that you won't be judged. For with whatever judgment you judge, you will be judged; and with whatever measure you measure, it will be measured to you. (Matthew 7:1-2)

God commands you to return deposits to their owners, and when you judge between people, judge with justice. Surely God admonishes you with what is excellent; surely God is Seeing, Hearing. (The Women 4:58)

Oh, you who believe! Maintain justice, bear witness for God's sake, though it may be against yourselves or (your) parents or near relatives. Whether he is rich or poor, God is most competent (to deal) with them both. So do not follow (your) low desires, lest you deviate; and if you swerve or turn aside, surely God is aware of what you do. (The Women 4:135)

Oh, you who believe! Be upright for God, bearers of witness with justice, and do not let hatred of a people incite you to not act equitably. Act equitably, that is nearer to piety. [Fear] God. Surely God is aware of what you do. (The Food 5:8)

Cut off the hands of the man who steals and the woman who steals, as a punishment for what they have earned—an exemplary punishment from God. God is Mighty, Wise. (The Food 5:38)

Surely God commands doing justice and doing good (to others) and giving to kindred, and He forbids indecency and evil and rebellion; He admonishes you so that you may be mindful. (The Bee 16:90)

We sent Our messengers with clear arguments, and We sent down with them the Book and the measure (balance), so that men may conduct themselves with justice. And We made the iron, in which is great violence and advantages to men, so that God may know who helps Him and His messengers in the secret. Surely God is Strong, Mighty. (The Iron 57:25)

Imitate and Achieve

 Jesus

Therefore, you are to be perfect, as your heavenly Father is perfect. (Matthew 5:48)

A disciple is not above his teacher, but everyone, when he is fully trained, will be like his teacher. (Luke 6:40)

Why do you call me, "Lord, Lord," and do not do the things that I say? Everyone who comes to me, and hears my words, and does them, I will show you who he is like. He is like a man building a house, who dug and went deep, and laid a foundation on the rock. When a flood arose, the stream broke against that house, and could not shake it, because it was founded on the rock. But he who hears, and does not do, is like a man who built a house on the Earth without a foundation, against which the stream broke, and immediately it fell, and the ruin of that house was great. (Luke 6:46-49)

So when he had washed their feet, put his outer garment back on, and sat down again, he said to them, "Do you know what I have done to you? You call me, "Teacher" and "Lord." You say so correctly, for so I am. If I then, the Lord and the Teacher, have washed your feet, you also ought to wash one another's feet I have given you an example, so that you also should do as I have done to you." (John 13:12-15)

Heal the sick, raise the dead, cleanse the lepers, cast out demons. Freely you received, freely give. Do not take any gold, nor silver, nor bronze in your money belts. Take no bag for your journey, neither two coats, nor shoes, nor staff: for the laborer is worthy of his food. (Matthew 10:8-10)

Truly, truly, I tell you, he who believes in me, the works that I do, he will do also; and he will do greater works than these, because I am going to my Father. (John 14:12)

Purity

 Jesus

I thank you, Father, Lord of Heaven and Earth, that you hid these things from the wise and intelligent, and revealed them to little children. Yes, Father, for so it was well-pleasing in your sight. (Matthew 11:25-26)

The good man out of his good treasure brings out good things, and the evil man out of his evil treasure brings out evil things. (Matthew 12:35)

There is nothing from outside of the man, that going into him can defile him; but the things which proceed out of the man are what defile the man. If anyone has ears to hear, let him hear. That which proceeds out of the man, that defiles the man. For from within, out of the hearts of men, proceed evil thoughts, adulteries, sexual sins, murders, thefts, covetings, wickedness, deceit, lustful desires, an evil eye, blasphemy, pride, and foolishness. All these evil things come from within, and defile the man. (Mark 7:15-16, 20-23)

Either make the tree good, and its fruit good, or make the tree corrupt, and its fruit corrupt; for the tree is known by its fruit. (Matthew 12:33)

You are those who justify yourselves in the sight of men, but God knows your hearts. For that which is exalted among men is an abomination in the sight of God. (Luke 16:15)

The lamp of the body is the eye. If therefore your eye is sound, your whole body will be full of light. But if your eye is bad, your whole body will be full of darkness. If therefore the light that is in you is darkness, how great is the darkness. (Matthew 6:22-23)

[Prophet], have you not considered those who attribute purity to themselves? No, God purifies whom He pleases, and they will not be wronged so much as the husk of a date-stone. (The Women 4:49)

Now surely they fold up their breasts to conceal (their enmity) from Him. Surely, when they use their garments as a covering, He knows what they conceal and what they make public. Surely He knows what is in the breasts. (Hud 11:5)

We assigned to Abraham the place of the House, saying: Do not associate anything with Me, and purify My House for those who make the circuit and stand to pray and bow and prostrate themselves. (The Pilgrimage 22:26)

Oh, you who believe! Do not follow the footsteps of the Devil. Whoever follows the footsteps of the Devil surely bids the doing of indecency and evil. Were it not for God's grace on you, and His mercy, not one of you would have ever been pure. But God purifies whom He pleases. God is Hearing, Knowing. (The Light 24:21)

Do those with diseased hearts think that God will not expose their spite? (Muhammad 47:29)

No! I swear by the setting of the stars—and most surely it is a very great oath, if you only knew—most surely it is an honoured Qur'an. In a Book that is protected—none will touch it except the purified ones—is a revelation from the Lord of the Worlds. Do you hold this announcement in contempt? (The Great Event 56:75-81)

He knows what is in the Heavens and the Earth, and He knows what you hide and what you reveal. God is Cognizant of what is in the hearts. (The Manifestation of Defects 64:4)

He who purifies himself will indeed be successful, and he who magnifies the name of his Lord, and prays. (The Most High 87:14-15)

Jesus

Blessed are the pure in heart, for they will see God. (Matthew 5:8)

"I tell you that whoever divorces his wife, except for sexual immorality, and marries another, commits adultery. And he who marries her when she is divorced commits adultery." His disciples said to him, "If this is the case of the man with his wife, it is not expedient to marry." But he said to them, "Not all men can receive this saying, but those to whom it is given. For there are eunuchs who were born that way from their mother's womb, and there are eunuchs who were made eunuchs by men; and there are eunuchs who made themselves eunuchs for the Kingdom of Heaven's sake. He who is able to receive it, let him receive it." (Matthew 19:9-12)

You have heard that it was said to the ancients, "Do not commit adultery;" but I tell you that everyone who looks at a woman to lust after her has committed adultery with her already in his heart. (Matthew 5:27-28)

Do not give to the dogs what is holy, neither throw your pearls before the pigs, or they will trample them under their feet and turn and tear you to pieces. (Matthew 7:6)

Muhammad ﷺ

He who purifies [his soul] will indeed be successful, and he who corrupts it will indeed fail. (The Sun 91:9-10)

So I warn you of the Fire that flames. None will enter it but the most unhappy, who gives the lie (to the truth) and turns (his) back. The one who guards most (against evil) will be kept away from it— he who gives away his wealth, purifying himself. No one has any favors with him, for which a reward is expected. He only seeks the pleasure of his Lord, the Most High. He will soon be well pleased. (Purity 92:14-21)

Shine Your Light

 Jesus

You are the light of the world. A city located on a hill cannot be hidden. Neither do you light a lamp, and put it under a measuring basket, but on a stand; and it shines to all who are in the house. Even so, let your light shine before men; that they may see your good works, and glorify your Father who is in Heaven. (Matthew 5:14-16)

No one, when he has lit a lamp, covers it with a container, or puts it under a bed; rather, he puts it on a stand, so that those who enter may see the light. For nothing is hidden that will not be revealed; nor is anything secret that will not be known and come to light. (Luke 8:16-17)

Muhammad ﷺ

Lead by Serving

 Jesus

You know that the rulers of the nations lord it over them, and their great ones exercise authority over them. It will not be so among you, but whoever desires to become great among you must be your servant. And whoever desires to be first among you must be your bondservant, even as the Son of Man came not to be served, but to serve, and to give his life as a ransom for many.[1] (Matthew 20:25-28)

If any man wants to be first, he must be last of all, and servant of all. (Mark 9:35b)

For who is greater, one who sits at the table, or one who serves? Is it not he who sits at the table? But I am in the midst of you as one who serves. (Luke 22:27)

So when he had washed their feet, put his outer garment back on, and sat down again, he said to them, "Do you know what I have done to you? You call me, "Teacher" and "Lord." You say so correctly, for so I am. If I then, the Lord and the Teacher, have washed your feet, you also ought to wash one another's feet. (John 13:12-14)

---

1 Wallerstedt et al., *Orthodox Bible,* 56. In Aramaic, "for many" means "for all."

God's Will

 Jesus

It came to pass, as he said these things, a certain woman out of the crowd lifted up her voice, and said to him, "Blessed is the womb that bore you, and the breasts which nursed you." But he said, "On the contrary, blessed are those who hear the word of God, and keep it." (Luke 11:27-28)

For whoever does the will of my Father who is in Heaven, he is my brother, and sister, and mother. (Matthew 12:50)

"The time has come for the Son of Man to be glorified. Truly, truly, I tell you, unless a grain of wheat falls into the earth and dies, it remains by itself alone. But if it dies, it bears much fruit. He who loves his life will lose it, and he who hates his life in this world will keep it to eternal life. Now my soul is troubled And what should I say? 'Father, save me from this hour?' But for this cause I came to this hour. Father, glorify your name." Then there came a voice out of the sky, saying, "I have both glorified it, and will glorify it again." The crowd therefore, who stood by and heard it, said that it had thundered. Others said, "An angel has spoken to him." Jesus answered, "This voice hasn't come for my sake, but for your sakes. And I, if I am lifted up from the Earth, will draw everyone to myself." (John 12:23-30, 32)

Then Jesus came with them to a place called Gethsemane, and said to his disciples, "Sit here, while I go there and pray." Then Jesus said to them, "My soul is exceedingly sorrowful, even to death. Stay here, and watch with me." He went forward a little, fell on his face, and prayed, saying, "My Father, if it is possible, let this cup pass away from me; nevertheless, not what I desire, but what you desire."
(Matthew 26:36, 38-39)

My Father, if this cup cannot pass away from me unless I drink it, your desire be done.[1] (Matthew 26:42)

---

1 Christ's prayer as he prepared for apprehension by Roman soldiers, and death. —Ed.

Is he who follows the pleasure of God like he who makes himself deserving of God's displeasure, and his abode is Hell? It is a evil destination. There are (varying) grades with God, and God sees what they do. (The Family of Amran 3:162-163)

Do not say about anything: Surely I will do it tomorrow, [without adding] if God pleases. When you forget, remember your Lord, and say: Maybe my Lord will guide me to a nearer course to the right way. (The Cave 18:23-24)

If We had pleased, We certainly would have given every soul its guidance, but the word (which had gone forth) from Me was just: I will certainly fill Hell with the Jinn and the men, together. (The Adoration 32:13)

Oh, men! It is you who stand in need of God, and God is Self-sufficient, the Praised One. If He pleases, He will do away with you and bring a new generation. This is not hard for God. (The Originator 35:15-17)

Repent

 Jesus

What woman, if she had ten drachma coins, if she lost one drachma coin, would not light a lamp, sweep the house, and seek diligently until she found it? When she has found it, she calls together her friends and neighbors, saying, "Rejoice with me, for I have found the drachma which I had lost." Even so, I tell you, there is joy in the presence of the angels of God over one sinner repenting.[1] (Luke 15:8-10)

The time is fulfilled, and the Kingdom of God is near. Repent, and believe in the Good News. (Mark 1:15)

---

1 Repent is translated from the Greek μετανοια (metanoia), which has also been defined as a transformative change of heart and mind.—Ed.

Surely God will curse those who conceal the clear proofs and the guidance after We revealed it and made it clear for men in the Book. And those who curse will (also) curse them. Except those who repent and amend and openly declare (the truth). I turn (mercifully) to them, and I am the Oft-returning (to mercy), the Merciful.
(The Cow 2:159-160)

How will God guide a people who disbelieved after believing, and (after) they had borne witness that the Messenger is true, and clear arguments had come to them? God does not guide the [wrongdoers]. Their reward is the curse of God and the angels and men, all together. Abiding in it, their chastisement will not be lightened, and they will not have periods of relief, except those who repent after that, and amend. Surely God is Forgiving, Merciful. Surely repentance will not be accepted from those who disbelieve after believing, and then increase in unbelief—they go astray. Surely the Earth full of gold will [never] be accepted from one of those who disbelieves and dies while he is an unbeliever, even if he should offer to ransom himself with it. These will have a painful chastisement, and they will have no helpers.
(The Family of Amran 3:86-90)

Hasten to forgiveness from your Lord and to a Garden, the extensiveness of which is (as) the Heavens and the Earth. It is prepared for those who guard (against evil), those who spend (benevolently) in ease as well as in hardship, and those who restrain (their) anger and pardon men. God loves the doers of good (to others). And those who, when they commit an indecency or do injustice to their souls, remember God and ask forgiveness for their faults—who forgives faults but God? And those (who) do not knowingly persist in what they have done. Their reward is forgiveness from their Lord, and gardens beneath which rivers flow, to abide in them, and excellent is the reward of the labourers. (The Family of Amran 3:133-136)

Jesus

For the Kingdom of Heaven is like a man who was the master of a household, who went out early in the morning to hire laborers for his vineyard. When he had agreed with the laborers for a denarius a day, he sent them into his vineyard. When evening had come, the lord of the vineyard said to his manager, "Call the laborers and pay them their wages, beginning from the last to the first." When those who were hired at about the eleventh hour came, they each received a denarius. When the first came, they supposed that they would receive more; and they likewise each received a denarius. When they received it, they murmured against the master of the household, saying, "These last have spent one hour, and you have made them equal to we who have borne the burden of the day and the scorching heat." But he answered one of them, "Friend, I am doing you no wrong. Did you not agree with me for a denarius? Take that which is yours, and go your way. It is my desire to give to this last just as much as to you. Is it not lawful for me to do what I want to with what I own? Or is your eye evil, because I am good?" So the last will be first, and the first last; for many are called, but few are chosen. (Matthew 20:1-2, 8-16)

I tell you that even so there will be more joy in Heaven over one sinner who repents, than over ninety-nine righteous people who need no repentance. (Luke 15:7)

But what do you think? A man had two sons, and he came to the first, and said, "Son, go work today in my vineyard." He answered, "I will not," but afterward he changed his mind, and went. And he came to the second, and said the same thing. And he answered and said, "I go, sir," but he did not go. Which of the two did the will of his father?" They said to him, "The first." (Matthew 21:28-31)

Muhammad ﷺ

Repentance is only [accepted by] God from those who do evil in ignorance, and then turn (to God) soon. God turns (mercifully) to these, and God is ever Knowing, Wise. Repentance is not for those who go on doing evil deeds, until death comes to one of them, and he says: Surely now I repent. Nor (for) those who die while they are unbelievers. We have prepared a painful chastisement for these.
(The Women 4:17-18)

Surely God will turn (mercifully) to whoever repents after his iniquity and reforms (himself). Surely, God is Forgiving, Merciful. Do you not know that God—His is the Kingdom of the Heavens and the Earth—chastises whom He pleases and forgives whom He pleases? God has power over all things. (The Food 5:39-40)

An announcement from God and His Messenger to the people, on the Day of the Greater Pilgrimage: God and His Messenger are free from obligations to the idolaters. So if you repent, it will be better for you, and if you turn back, then know that you will not weaken God—announce painful punishment to those who disbelieve.
(The Immunity 9:3)

Do they not know that God accepts repentance from His servants and takes the alms, and that God is the Oft-returning (to mercy), the Merciful? (The Immunity 9:104)

Give good news to the believers! Those who turn (to God) [in repentance], who serve (Him), who praise (Him), who fast, who bow down, who prostrate themselves, who impose what is good and forbid what is evil, and who keep the limits of God.
(The Immunity 9:112)

Ask forgiveness of your Lord, and then turn to Him [in repentance]. He will provide you with good provision for an appointed term and bestow His Grace on everyone endowed with grace. But if you turn back, surely I fear for you the chastisement of a great day. (Hud 11:3)

Most surely I am most Forgiving to he who repents and believes and does good, and then continues to follow the right direction. (Ta Ha 20:82)

Jesus

Or those eighteen, on whom the tower in Siloam fell and killed them; do you think that they were worse offenders than all the men who dwell in Jerusalem? I tell you, no, and unless you repent, you will all perish in the same way. (Luke 13:4-5)

As many as I love, I rebuke and discipline. Therefore, be zealous, and repent. (Revelation 3:19)

Muhammad ﷺ

Those who, when they spend, are neither extravagant nor stingy, and who (keep) the just mean between these. Those who do not call upon another god with God and do not slay a soul—which God has forbidden, except in the requirements of justice—and those (who) do not commit fornication. Whoever does this will be compensated for his sin. The chastisement will be doubled for him on the Day of Resurrection, and he will abide there, humiliated. Except he who repents and believes and does good deeds. God changes the evil deeds of these to good deeds. God is Forgiving, Merciful. Whoever repents and does good [truly] turns to God. (The Distinction 25:67-71)

Do they not consider what is before them and what is behind them of the Heaven and the Earth? If We please, We will make them disappear in the land or bring down upon them a fragment from the heavens; most surely there is a sign in this for every servant turning (to God). (The Saba 34:9)

The revelation of the Book is from God, the Mighty, the Knowing, the Forgiver of faults and the Accepter of repentance, severe to punish, Lord of bounty; there is no god but He. To Him is the eventual coming. (The Believer 40:2-3)

Be patient, [Prophet]. Surely, the promise of God is true. Ask protection for your fault, and celebrate the praise of your Lord in the evening and the morning. (The Believer 40:55)

[Prophet], do they say: He has invented a lie against God? If God pleased, He would seal your heart. God will blot out falsehood and confirm truth with His words. Surely He is Cognizant of what is in the breasts. It is He Who accepts repentance from His servants and pardons the evil deeds, and He knows what you do. (The Counsel 42:24-25)

So, [Prophet], know that there is no god but God, and ask protection for your faults and for the faults of believing men and believing women. God knows your [movement] and your resting places. (Muhammad 47:19)

Surely, [Prophet], We have given you a clear victory. So that God may rectify your prior faults and those that remain [to come], and complete His favour on you, and guide you on a right way. (The Victory 48:1-2)

[Prophet], when God's help and the victory comes, and you see men entering the religion of God in companies, celebrate the praise of your Lord, and ask His forgiveness. Surely He is oft-returning (to mercy).[1] (The Help 110:1-3)

---

1 Ali, M.M., *The Holy Qur'an*, 1231. This sura, revealed at Mecca, may be said to be the last revelation of the Holy Prophet. It showed how those wonderful prophecies, announced in utter loneliness and helplessness, were now fulfilled at Mecca by the Prophet visiting that sacred city with over a hundred thousand followers. (i.e. the fall of Mecca—Ed.)

Endure

Trust, Don't Worry

 Jesus

But the boat was now in the midst of the sea, distressed by the waves, for the wind was against it. And in the fourth watch of the night, Jesus came to them, walking on the sea. And when the disciples saw him walking on the sea, they were troubled, saying, "It's a ghost," and they screamed with fear. But immediately Jesus spoke to them, saying "Cheer up. It is I. Do not be afraid." Peter answered him and said, "Lord, if it is you, command me to come to you on the waters." He said, "Come." Peter stepped down from the boat, and walked on the water and went toward Jesus. But when he saw the strong wind, he was afraid, and beginning to sink, he yelled, saying, "Lord, save me." Immediately Jesus stretched out his hand, took hold of him, and said to him, "You of little faith, why did you doubt?" When they got up into the boat, the wind ceased. Those who were in the boat came and worshiped him, saying, "You are truly the Son of God." (Matthew 14:24-33)

Therefore I tell you, do not be anxious for your life, what you will eat, nor yet for your body, what you will wear. Life is more than food, and the body is more than clothing. Consider the ravens: they do not sow, they do not reap, they have no warehouse or barn, and God feeds them. How much more valuable are you than birds. Which of you by being anxious can add a cubit to his height? If then you are not able to do even the least things, why are you anxious about the rest? Consider the lilies, how they grow. They do not toil, neither do they spin; yet I tell you, even Solomon in all his glory was not arrayed like one of these. But if this is how God clothes the grass in the field, which today exists, and tomorrow is cast into the oven, how much more will he clothe you, O you of little faith? (Luke 12:22-28)

When you went forth early in the morning from your family, to lodge the believers in encampments for war—and God is Hearing, Knowing. Two from among you determined that they should show cowardice, yet God was the guardian of them both. The believers should trust in God. (The Family of Amran 3:121-122)

If God assists you, no one can overcome you, and if He forsakes you, who can assist you after Him? The believers should rely on God. (The Family of Amran 3:160)

Whatever is in the Heavens and whatever is on the Earth is God's, and God is sufficient as a Protector. If He pleases, He can make you pass away, oh people! And bring others in your place. God has the power to do this. (The Women 4:132-133)

Oh, you who believe! Remember God's favour on you when a people had determined to stretch forth their hands against you, but He withheld their hands from you. And be careful of (your duty to) God; let the believers rely on God. (The Food 5:11)

They ask you about the accessions. Say, [Prophet]: The accessions are for God and the Messenger.[1] So be careful of (your duty to) God, and set aright matters of your difference, and obey God and His Messenger if you are believers. Believers are only those whose hearts become full of fear when God is mentioned, and when His messages are recited, they increase in faith, and they trust in their Lord—those who keep up prayer and spend (benevolently) out of what We have given them. (The Accessions 8:1-3)

---

1 Ali, M.M., *The Holy Qur'an*, 374. The most generally received opinion is that accessions means property acquired during war.

Jesus

Now it happened, on one of those days, that he entered into a boat, he and his disciples, and he said to them, "Let us go over to the other side of the lake." So they launched out. But as they sailed, he fell asleep. A wind storm came down on the lake, and they were taking on dangerous amounts of water. So they came to him and awoke him, saying, "Master, Master, we are dying." And he awoke, and rebuked the wind and the raging of the water, and they ceased, and it was calm. He said to them, "Where is your faith?" Being afraid, they marveled, saying one to another, "Who is this, then, that he commands even the winds and the water, and they obey him?" (Luke 8:22-25)

If God so clothes the grass of the field, which today exists, and tomorrow is thrown into the oven, won't he much more clothe you, you of little faith? Therefore do not be anxious, saying, "What will we eat?", "What will we drink?" or, "With what will we be clothed?" For the Gentiles seek after all of these things, for your heavenly Father knows that you need all of these things. But first seek the Kingdom of God and His righteousness, and all of these things will be given to you as well. Therefore do not be anxious for tomorrow, for tomorrow will be anxious for itself. Each day has enough trouble of its own. (Matthew 6:30-34)

Do not seek what you will eat or what you will drink; neither be anxious. For the nations of the world seek after all of these things, but your Father knows that you need these things. But seek God's Kingdom, and all of these things will be added to you. (Luke 12:29-31)

Muhammad

Although you will not aid [Muhammad], God certainly aided *him* when those who disbelieved expelled him. When they were both in the cave, he said to his companion (the second of the two): Grieve not, surely God is with us. So God sent down His tranquility on him and strengthened him with hosts that you did not see, and God made lowest the word of those who disbelieved. The word of God is the highest. God is Mighty, Wise.[1] (The Immunity 9:40)

Say [Prophet]: Nothing will afflict us except what God has ordained for us: He is our Patron. Let the believers rely on God. (The Immunity 9:51)

There is no moving creature on Earth that does not depend on God for sustenance, and He knows its resting-place and its depository. All (things) are in a clear [record]. (Hud 11:6)

And God's is the unseen in the Heavens and the Earth, and to Him is returned the whole of the affair. So serve Him, and rely on Him. Your Lord is not heedless of what you do. (Hud 11:123)

When you recite the Qur'an, seek refuge with God from the accursed Devil; Surely he has no authority over those who believe and rely on their Lord. His authority is only over those who befriend him and those who associate others with God. (The Bee 16:98-100)

[Prophet], recite what has been revealed to you of the Book of your Lord; none can alter His words. You will not find any refuge besides Him. (The Cave 18:27)

Rely on the Ever-living, Who does not die, and celebrate His praise. Sufficient is He at being aware of the faults of His servants, Who created the Heavens and the Earth and what is between them in six periods. He is firm in power, the Merciful God: so ask Him, One Aware. (The Distinction 25:58-59)

Say, [Prophet]: He is the Beneficent God, we believe in Him, and we rely on Him, so you will come to know who is in clear error. Have you considered, if your water should go down, who is it who will bring you flowing water? (The Kingdom 67:29-30)

Say, [Prophet]: Surely no one can protect me against God, nor can I find any place of refuge besides Him. (The Jinn 72:22)

Say [Prophet]: He, God, is One. God is He on whom all depend. (The Dawn 113:1-2)

---

1 Ali, M.M., *The Holy Qur'an*, 407. During the Prophet's flight from Mecca, he hid in a cave with only one companion, Abu Bakr. The believers are told that Allah saved the Prophet from his enemies amidst a whole nation of opponents.

Suffering and Hardship

 Jesus

Blessed are the poor in spirit, for theirs is the Kingdom of Heaven. Blessed are those who mourn, for they will be comforted. Blessed are the gentle, for they will inherit the Earth. (Matthew 5:3-5)

Therefore you have sorrow now, but I will see you again, and your heart will rejoice, and no one will take your joy away from you. (John: 16:22)

We will most certainly try you with something of fear and hunger and loss of property and lives and fruits. But give good news to the patient ones who, when a misfortune befalls them, say: Surely we are God's, and to Him we will return. They are the ones upon whom are blessings and mercy from their Lord, and they are the followers of the right course. (The Cow 2:155-157)

Do you think that you will enter the Garden when such trials of those who have passed away before you have not yet come upon you? Distress and affliction befell them, and they were shaken violently, so that the Messenger and those who believed with him, said: When will God's help come? Now surely the help of God is near! (The Cow 2:214)

Do not weaken, and do not grieve, and you will have the upper hand if you are believers. If a wound afflicts you, a wound like it has also afflicted the (unbelieving) people. We alternate these days among men, so that God may know those who believe and take [martyrs] from among you. God does not love the [wrongdoers]. And so that He may purge the believers, and [destroy] the unbelievers. Do you think that you will enter the Garden while God has not yet known who strove hard among you, and while (He has not) known the patient ones? (The Family of Amran 3:139-142)

Whatever benefit comes to you (oh, man!) is from God, and whatever misfortune befalls you is from yourself. We have sent you (oh, Prophet!) to mankind as a Messenger, and God is sufficient as a witness. (The Women 4:79)

If God touches you with affliction, there is no one to take it off except He. If He visits you with good, then He has power over all things. (The Cattle 6:17)

Certainly We sent (messengers) to nations before you, and then We seized the nations with distress and affliction so that they might humble themselves. Yet why did they not humble themselves when Our punishment came to them? Their hearts hardened, and the Devil made what they did seem fair to them. But when they neglected their admonishment, We opened the doors of all things for them, until they rejoiced in what they were given, and then We seized them suddenly. Then, lo! They were in utter despair. So the roots of the [wrongdoers] were cut off. All praise is due to God, the Lord of the Worlds. (The Cattle 6:42-45)

As for those in whose hearts is a disease, it adds uncleanness to their uncleanness and they die while they are unbelievers. Do they not see that they are tried once or twice in every year, yet they do not turn (to God) or heed. (The Immunity 9:125-126)

Jesus

Come to me, all you who labor and are heavily burdened, and I will give you rest.
Take my yoke upon you, and learn from me, for I am gentle and humble in heart;
and you will find rest for your souls. For my yoke is easy, and my burden is light.
(Matthew 11:28-30)

Blessed are you who are poor, for yours is the Kingdom of God. Blessed are you who
hunger now, for you will be filled. Blessed are you who weep now, for you will laugh.
(Luke 6:20-21)

Muhammad ﷺ

Even if there were a Qur'an by which the mountains were made to pass away, or the Earth was made to [split apart], or the dead were made to speak—No! The commandment is wholly God's. Do those who believe not yet know that if God pleased, He would certainly guide all the people? (As for) those who disbelieve, because of what they do, a repelling calamity will not cease to afflict them, or it will land close by their homes, until the promise of God comes about. Surely God will not fail in (His) promise. (The Thunder 13:31)

Whatever favour is (bestowed) on you, it is from God. Then when [adversity] afflicts you, you cry to Him for aid. Yet when He removes the adversity from you, lo! A group of you associate others with their Lord. (The Bee 16:53-54)

Do not consider the Messenger's calling (you) to be like your calling one to the other. God indeed knows those who steal away from among you, concealing themselves. So let those who go against the Prophet's order beware, lest a trial afflict them or lest a painful punishment befall them. (The Light 24:63)

Most certainly, We will make them taste of the nearer punishment before the greater punishment, so that by luck they may turn. (The Adoration 32:21)

When harm afflicts a man, he calls upon Us. Then, when We give him a favour, he says: I have been given it only because of my knowledge. No, it is a trial, but most of them do not know. (The Companies 39:49)

Man is never tired of praying for good, but if evil touches him, he despairs, hopeless. If We make him taste mercy from Us after distress has touched him, he would most certainly say: This is due to me, and I do not think The Hour will come to pass. If I am sent back to my Lord, I will have sure good with Him. But We will most certainly inform those who disbelieved of what they did, and We will most certainly make them taste of hard punishment. (Ha Mim 41:49-50)

No [disaster] falls on the Earth or on your own souls that is not [recorded] in a book before We bring it into existence. Surely that is easy for God, so that you may not grieve for what has escaped you or be exultant at what He has given you. God does not love any arrogant boaster. (The Iron 57:22-23)

No affliction comes about except by God's permission. God guides aright the heart of whoever believes in Him, and God is Cognizant of all things. Obey God and obey the Messenger, but if you turn back, Our Messenger's responsibility is only to clearly deliver (the message). (The Manifestation of Defects 64:11-12)

Jesus

Muhammad ﷺ

Surely man is created of a hasty temperament, being greatly grieved when evil afflicts him, and miserly when good befalls him. (The Ways of Ascent 70:19-21)

By the [father] and whom he begot, certainly We have created man to be in distress. Does he think that no one has power over him? (The City 90:3-5)

[Prophet], have We not expanded your breast for you, and taken off your burden from you, which pressed heavily on your back? And exalted for you your eminence? Surely with difficulty is ease. With difficulty surely is ease. So when you are free, strive hard, and make your Lord your exclusive object. (The Expansion 94:1-8)

Wandering, Lost and Astray

 Jesus

This is the will of my Father who sent me, that of all He has given to me, I should lose nothing, but should raise him up at the last day. (John 6:39)

For the Son of Man came to save what was lost. What do you think? If a man has one hundred sheep, and one of them goes astray, does he not leave the ninety-nine, go to the mountains, and seek that which has gone astray? If he finds it, truly I tell you, he rejoices over it more than over the ninety-nine which have not gone astray. Even so it is not the will of your Father who is in Heaven that one of these little ones should perish. (Matthew 18:11-14)

[Believers], what is the matter with you, that you have become two groups about the hypocrites, while God has made them return (to unbelief) for what they have earned? Do you wish to guide he whom God has caused to err? Whomever God causes to err, you will by no means find a way for him. (The Women 4:88)

Whomever God intends to guide aright, He expands his breast for Islam, and whomever He intends to err, He causes his breast to become constricted and narrow, as though he were ascending upwards. This is how God lays uncleanness on those who do not believe. (The Cattle 6:125)

[Prophet], recite to them the news of he to whom We give Our Verses, but he withdraws himself from the Verses, so Satan overtakes him, and he is of those who perish. If We had pleased, We would certainly have exalted him. But he clung to the Earth and followed his low desire. So his parable is like the parable of the dog: if you attack him, he pants, and if you leave him alone, he pants. This is the parable of the people who reject Our Signs. So relate the narrative, so that they may reflect. Evil is like the people who reject Our Signs and are unjust to their own souls. Whomever God guides, he is the one who follows the right way; and whomever He causes to err, these are the losers. Certainly, We have created many of the Jinn and the men for Hell; they have hearts with which they do not understand, they have eyes with which they do not see, and they have ears with which they do not hear. They are as cattle. No, they are in worse error; these are the heedless ones. (The Elevated Places 7:175-179)

We draw near (to destruction) those who reject Our messages, by degrees, without them knowing about it. I grant them respite; surely My scheme is effective. Do they not realize that their companion [the Prophet] does not have unsoundness of mind? He is only a plain warner. Do they not consider the Kingdom of the Heavens and the Earth and whatever things that God has created, and that maybe their doom shall have drawn near? What announcement would they believe in after this? There is no guide for whomever God causes to err. He leaves them alone in their disorder, blindly wandering on. (The Elevated Places 7:182-186)

God always makes clear to a people what they should guard against before He lets them go astray after He has guided them. Surely God knows all things. (The Immunity 9:115)

Jesus

Be careful that no one leads you astray. Many will come in my name, saying, "I am he," and will lead many astray. (Mark 13:5-6)

Muhammad ﷺ

If God were to hasten the evil to men as they desire the hastening on of good, their doom certainly would have been decreed for them. But We leave alone in their disorder those who do not hope for Our meeting, blindly wandering on. (Jonah 10:11)

Say, [Prophet]: Oh, people! Indeed, the truth from your Lord has come to you. So, whoever goes aright, goes aright only for the good of his own soul, and whoever goes astray, goes astray only to the detriment of it. I am not a custodian over you. (Jonah 10:108)

We sent each messenger with the language of his people, so that he might explain to them clearly. Then God makes whom He pleases err, and He guides whom He pleases. He is the Mighty, the Wise. (Abraham 14:4)

God will not guide those who do not believe in God's messages, and they will have a painful punishment. The lie is fabricated only by those who do not believe in God's communications; they are the liars. (The Bee 16:104-105)

This is because they love this world's life more than the Hereafter, and because God does not guide the unbelieving people. God has set a seal on their hearts and their hearing and their eyes. They are the heedless ones. No doubt that in the Hereafter, they will be the losers. (The Bee 16:107-109)

[Prophet], when you recite the Qur'an, We place a hidden barrier between you and those who do not believe in the Hereafter. We have placed coverings on their hearts and a heaviness in their ears, lest they understand it. When you mention your Lord alone in the Qur'an, they turn their backs in aversion. We know best what they listen to when they listen to you, and when they take counsel secretly, when the [wrongdoers] say: You follow only a man [bewitched]. See what they liken you to! They have gone astray and cannot find the way. (The Israelites 17:45-48)

Whomever God guides is a follower of the right way, and you will not find guardians besides Him for whomever He leads astray. We will gather them together on the Day of Resurrection on their faces, blind and dumb and deaf; their abode is Hell. Whenever it subsides, We will add to their burning. (The Night Journey 17:97)

Say, [Prophet]: The Merciful God will surely prolong the lives of those who remain in error, until they see what they were threatened with, either the chastisement or the Hour. Then they will know who is worse in plight and weaker in forces. God increases guidance for those who go aright, and ever-abiding good works are, with your Lord, best in recompense and best in yielding fruit. (Mary 19:75-76)

Jesus

A certain man had two sons. The younger of them said to his father, "Father, give me my share of your property." He divided his livelihood between them. Not many days after, the younger son gathered all of this together and traveled into a far country. There he wasted his property with riotous living. When he had spent all of it, there arose a severe famine in that country, and he began to be in need. He went and joined himself to one of the citizens of that country, and he sent him into his fields to feed pigs. And he wanted to fill his stomach with the carob pods that the pigs ate, but no one gave him any. But when he came to himself he said, 'How many hired servants of my father's have bread enough to spare, and I'm dying with hunger. I will get up and go to my father, and will tell him, "Father, I have sinned against Heaven, and in your sight. I am no longer worthy to be called your son. Make me like one of your hired servants." He arose, and came to his father. But while he was still far off, his father saw him, and was moved with compassion, and ran, and fell on his neck, and kissed him. The son said to him, "Father, I have sinned against Heaven, and in your sight. I am no longer worthy to be called your son." But the father said to his servants, "Bring out the best robe, and put it on him. Put a ring on his hand, and shoes on his feet. Bring the fattened calf, kill it, and let us eat, and celebrate; for this, my son, was dead, and is alive again. He was lost, and is found." They began to celebrate. Now his elder son was in the field. As he came near to the house, he heard music and dancing. He called one of the servants to him, and asked what was going on. He said to him, "Your brother has come, and your father has killed the fattened calf, because he has received him back safe and healthy." But he was angry, and would not go in. Therefore his father came out, and begged him. But he answered his father, "Look, these many years I have served you, and I never disobeyed a commandment of yours, but you never gave me a goat, that I might celebrate with my friends. But when this, your son, came, who has devoured your living with prostitutes, you killed the fattened calf for him." He said to him, "Son, you are always with me, and all that is mine is yours. But it was appropriate to celebrate and be glad, for this brother of yours was dead and is alive again; and he was lost, and is found." (Luke 15:11-32)

Muhammad ﷺ

Those who go astray follow the poets. Do you not see that they wander about bewildered in every valley? That they say what they do not do. (The Poets 26:224-226)

As for those who do not believe in the Hereafter, We have surely made their deeds seem fair to them, but they blindly wander on. They will have an evil chastisement, and in the Hereafter they will be the greatest losers. (The Naml 27:4-5)

So, [Prophet], rely on God; surely you are on the path to clear truth. Surely you do not make the dead hear, and you do not make the deaf hear the call when they turn back, retreating. Nor can you guide the blind out of their error; you can not make (anyone) hear except those who believe in Our messages, so they submit. (The Naml 27:79-81)

Surely you cannot guide whom you love; God guides whom He pleases, and He knows best the followers of the right way. (The Narrative 28:56)

Say, [Prophet]: Then bring some (other) book from God that is a better guide than both of them, so (that) I may follow it, if you are truthful. But if they do not answer you, then know that they only follow their low desires—who is more erring than he who follows his low desires without any guidance from God? Surely God does not guide the unjust people. (The Narrative 28:49-50)

We will most certainly guide in Our ways those who strive hard for Us. God is most surely with the doers of good. (The Spider 29:69)

What of he whose evil deed is made fairseeming to him, such that he considers it good? Now surely God makes err whom He pleases and guides aright whom He pleases. So do not let your soul waste away in grief for them. Surely God is Cognizant of what they do. (The Originator 35:8)

Jesus

A certain man made a great supper, and he invited many people. And he sent his servant at the hour for supper to tell those who were invited, "Come, for everything is ready now." They all as one began to make excuses. The first said to him, "I have bought a field, and I must go and see it. Please have me excused." Another said, "I have bought five yoke of oxen, and I must go try them out. Please have me excused." Another said, "I have married a wife, and therefore I cannot come." That servant came, and told his lord these things. Then the master of the house, being angry, said to his servant, "Go out quickly into the streets and lanes of the city, and bring in the poor, maimed, blind, and lame." The servant said, "Lord, it is done as you commanded, and there is still room." The lord said to the servant, "Go out into the highways and hedges, and compel them to come in, that my house may be filled. For I tell you that none of those men who were invited will taste of my supper." (Luke 14:16-24)

Muhammad ﷺ

What! Is he whose heart God has opened for Islam so that he is in a light from his Lord (like the hard-hearted)? No, woe to those whose hearts are hard against the remembrance of God—they are in clear error. God has revealed the best announcement, a Book consistent in its various parts, repeating. Causing the skin of those who fear their Lord to shudder, and then their skin and their hearts become pliant at the remembrance of God. This is God's guidance; He guides with it whom He pleases. (As for) he whom God makes err, there is no guide for him.
(The Companies 39:22-23)

Is God not sufficient for His servant? They seek to frighten you with those besides Him. Whomever God makes err, there is no guide for him, and whom God guides, there is none who can lead him astray. Is not God Mighty, the Lord of Retribution?
(The Companies 39:36-37)

Whomever God makes err has no guardian after God. You, [Prophet], will see the [wrongdoers], when they see the chastisement, saying: Is there any way to return?
(The Counsel 42:44)

[Prophet], what? Can you make the deaf hear or guide the blind and he who is in clear error? If We took you away, We would still inflict retribution on them. Rather, We will certainly show you what We have promised them; for surely We possess full power over them. So hold fast to what has been revealed to you [Prophet]; surely you are on the right path. (The Embellishment 43:40-43)

[Prophet], have you considered he who takes his low desire for his god, whom God has knowingly made err, and has sealed his hearing and his heart, and put a covering on his eyes. Who can guide him after God? Will you not be mindful?
(The Kneeling 45:23)

When Moses said to his people: Oh, my people! Why do you give me trouble, when you know indeed that I am God's messenger to you? When they turned aside, God made their hearts turn aside, and God does not guide the rebellious people.
(The Ranks 61:5)

God's Mercy

 Jesus

Won't God avenge his chosen ones, who are crying out to him day and night, and yet he exercises patience with them? I tell you that he will avenge them quickly. Nevertheless, when the Son of Man comes, will he find faith on the Earth? (Luke 18:7-8)

Say, [Prophet]: If you love God, then follow me. God will love you and forgive you your faults, and God is Forgiving, Merciful. (Family of Amran 3:31)

God desires to explain to you, and to guide you in the ways of those before you, and to turn to you (mercifully). God is Knowing, Wise. God desires to turn to you (mercifully), and those who follow (their) lusts desire you to deviate (with) a great deviation. God desires to make your burdens light, and man is created weak. (The Women 4:26-28)

When news of security or fear comes to them, they spread it abroad; and if they had referred it to the Messenger and to those in authority among them, those among them who can search out the knowledge of it would have known it. Were it not for the grace of God upon you, and His mercy, you would have certainly followed the Devil, except for a few. (The Women 4:83)

When those who believe in Our Verses come to you, say: Peace be on you, your Lord has ordained mercy on Himself, (so) if any one of you does evil in ignorance and then turns after that and acts right, He is Forgiving, Merciful. (The Cattle 6:54)

Your Lord is the Self-sufficient one, the Lord of mercy. If He pleases, He may remove you, and make whom He pleases successors after you, just as He raised you up from the seed of another people. (The Cattle 6:133)

This is a Book that We have revealed, blessed; so follow it, and guard against evil, so that mercy may be shown to you. (The Cattle 6:155)

Oh, you who believe! If you are careful of (your duty to) God, He will grant you a distinction and do away with your evils and forgive you. God is the Lord of mighty grace. (The Accessions 8:29)

And (as for) the believing men and the believing women, they are guardians of each other; they impose good and forbid evil and keep up prayer and pay the poor-rate, and obey God and His Messenger. God will show mercy to these; surely, God is Mighty, Wise. (The Immunity 9:71)

Others have confessed their faults. They have mingled a good deed and an evil one; maybe God will turn to them (mercifully). Surely, God is Forgiving, Merciful. [Prophet], take alms out of their property, to cleanse them and purify them, and pray for them. Surely your prayer is a relief to them. God is Hearing, Knowing. (The Immunity 9:102-103)

Jesus

Muhammad ﷺ

When We make people taste of mercy after an affliction touches them, lo! They devise plans against Our revelations. Say, [Prophet]: God is quicker to plan; surely Our messengers write down what you plan. (Jonah 10:21)

Oh, men! Indeed, there has come to you an admonition from your Lord, a healing for what is in the breasts, a guidance and mercy for the believers. Say, [Prophet]: Rejoice in the grace of God and in His mercy; it is better than what you gather. (Jonah 10:57-58)

If you were to count God's favours, you would not be able to number them; most surely God is Forgiving, Merciful. (The Bee 16:18)

Your Lord knows you best; He will have mercy on you if He pleases, or He will chastise you if He pleases. [Prophet], We have not sent you to be in charge of them. (The Israelites 17:54)

If We please, We could certainly take away what We have revealed to you, and then you would not find any protector against Us. But because of mercy from your Lord, surely His grace for you is abundant. (The Israelites 17:86-87)

[Prophet], We have sent you only as a mercy to the nations. (The Prophets 21:107)

Keep up prayer and pay the poor-rate and obey the Messenger, so that mercy may be shown to you. (The Light 24:56)

He chastises whom He pleases and has mercy on whom He pleases, and to Him you will return. You will not escape on the Earth or in the Heaven, and you have neither a protector nor a helper besides God. Those who disbelieve in the Signs of God and His meeting despair of My mercy, and they will have a painful chastisement. (The Spider 29:21-23)

Look at the Signs of God's mercy, how He gives life to the earth after its death. Most surely He gives life to the dead, and He has power over all things. (The Romans 30:50)

Whatever God grants men of (His) mercy, none can withhold it, and what He withholds, none can send it forth after that. He is the Mighty, the Wise. (The Originator 35:2)

Jesus

He spoke this parable. "A certain man had a fig tree planted in his vineyard, and he came seeking fruit on it, and found none. He said to the vine dresser, 'Look, three years I have come looking for fruit on this fig tree, and found none. Cut it down. Why does it waste the soil?' He answered, 'Lord, leave it alone this year also, until I dig around it, and fertilize it. And if it bears fruit, fine; but if not, next time you can cut it down.'" (Luke 13:6-9)

But love your enemies, and do good, and lend, expecting nothing back. Your reward will be great, and you will be children of the Most High; for He is kind toward the unthankful and the evil. Therefore be merciful, even as your Father is merciful. (Luke 6:35-36)

Muhammad ﷺ

Were God to punish men for what they earned, He would not leave any creature on the surface of Earth. But He grants respite to them until an appointed term. When their doom comes, surely God is Seeing with respect to His servants.
(The Originator 35:45)

Those who [bear the throne] and those around Him celebrate the praise of their Lord and believe in Him and ask [forgiveness] for those who believe. Our Lord! You embrace all things in mercy and knowledge, [forgive] those who [repent] and follow Your way, and save them from the punishment of the Hellfire. (The Believer 40:7)

The Heavens almost break apart from above them, and the angels celebrate the praise of their Lord and ask forgiveness for those on Earth. Surely God is the Forgiving, the Merciful. (As for) those who take guardians besides Him, God watches over them, and you, [Prophet], do not have charge over them.
(The Counsel 42:5-6)

If God amplified provision for His servants, they would certainly revolt on Earth. But He sends provision down according to a measure, as He pleases. Surely He is Aware of, Seeing, His servants. It is He Who sends down the rain after they despair, and He unfolds His mercy. He is the Guardian, the Praised One. (The Counsel 42:27-28)

Whatever affliction befalls you, it is because of what your hands have wrought, yet He pardons most (of your faults). You cannot escape on the Earth, and you will not have a Guardian or a Helper besides God. Among His Signs are the ships in the sea, like mountains: if He wills, He causes the wind to become still, so that they lie motionless on its surface. Most surely there are Signs in this for every patient, grateful person. Or, He could make them sink for what they earned, but (even then), He pardons most. (The Counsel 42:30-34)

They think that they have done you a favor, Prophet, by becoming Muslims. Say: Do not consider your Islam a favor to me. Rather, God does you a favor by guiding you to the faith, if you are truthful. Surely God knows the unseen things of the Heavens and the Earth, and God sees what you do. (The Chambers 49:17-18)

The Beneficent God taught the Qur'an, He created man, and taught him the mode of expression. (The Beneficent 55:1-4)

Jesus

Muhammad ﷺ

Oh, you who believe! Be careful of (your duty to) God, and believe in His Messenger. He will give you two portions of His mercy, and make a light for you with which you will walk, and forgive you. God is Forgiving, Merciful. (The Iron 57:28)

Oh, Prophet! When believing women come to you giving you a pledge that they will not associate anything with God, nor steal, nor commit fornication, nor kill their children, nor bring a slander that they have invented between their hands and feet,[1] nor disobey you in what is good, accept their pledge, and ask forgiveness for them from God. Surely God is Forgiving, Merciful. (The Examined One 60:12)

It is He who raised among the illiterates a Messenger from among themselves, who recites to them His messages and purifies them, and teaches them the Book and the Wisdom, although they were certainly in clear error before. And others from among them who have not yet joined them. He is the Mighty, the Wise—that is God's grace; He grants it to whom He pleases, and God is the Lord of mighty grace. (The Congregation 62:2-4)

---

1 Lie about who is the father of their children.—Ed.

God and Messenger

Submit to God

 Jesus

Oh, you who believe! Enter into complete submission, and do not follow the footsteps of the Devil; surely he is your open enemy. But if you slip after clear arguments have come to you, then know that God is Mighty, Wise. (The Cow 2:208-209)

But if they dispute with you, say [Prophet]: I have submitted myself entirely to God, and (so has) every one who follows me. Say to those who have been given the Book and to the unlearned people: Do you submit yourselves? So if they submit, then indeed they follow the right way; and if they turn back, you are responsible only to deliver the message—God sees the servants. (The Family of Amran 3:20)

Remember the favour of God on you and His covenant with which He bound you firmly, when you said: We have heard and we obey. Be careful of (your duty to) God, surely God knows what is in the breasts. (The Food 5:7)

Say: Surely, if I disobey my Lord, I fear the chastisement of a grievous day. God indeed has shown mercy on he from whom chastisement is averted on that day. This is the clear achievement. (The Cattle 6:15-16)

Whoever is in the Heavens and on Earth bows to God only, willingly or unwillingly, and their shadows too, at morn and eve. (The Thunder 13:15)

Whatever creature is in the Heavens and on the Earth bows to God (only), and the angels (too), and they do not show pride. They fear their Lord supreme, and they do what they are commanded. (The Bee 16:49-50)

Say, [Prophet]: It is only revealed to me that your God is one God—will you then submit? (The Prophets 21:108)

Do you not see that whoever is in the Heavens and whoever is on the Earth [bows to] God, and the sun and the moon and the stars, and the mountains and the trees, and the animals and many of the people. But there are many against whom punishment is necessary. No one can make honourable whomever God humiliates. Surely God does what He pleases. (The Pilgrimage 22:18)

Jesus

Muhammad ﷺ

When the believers saw the allies, they said: This is what God and His Messenger promised us, and God and His Messenger spoke the truth. It only increased them in faith and submission. Of the believers are men who are true to the covenant that they made with God: some accomplished their vows, and others yet wait, and they have not changed in the least.[1] This was so that God may reward the truthful for their truth, and punish the hypocrites if He pleases, or turn to them (mercifully). Surely God is Forgiving, Merciful. (The Allies 33:22-24)

Say, [Prophet]: I am commanded to serve God, to be sincere to Him in obedience. And I am commanded to be the first of those who submit. Say: I fear the chastisement of a grievous day if I disobey my Lord, . Say: It is God (Whom) I serve, being sincere to Him in my obedience. Serve then what you like, besides Him. Say: The losers surely are those who will lose themselves and their families on the Day of Resurrection: Surely that is the clear loss. They will have coverings of fire above them and coverings beneath them This is how God frightens His servants. So [fear] Me, Oh My servants! (The Companies 39:11-16)

Say: Oh, My servants who have acted extravagantly against their own souls, do not despair of the mercy of God. Surely, God forgives the faults altogether; surely He is the Forgiving, the Merciful. Return to your Lord, time after time, and submit to Him before the chastisement comes to you. Then you will not be helped. (The Companies 39:54)

Say, [Prophet]: I am forbidden to serve those whom you call on besides God when clear proofs have come to me from my Lord, and I am commanded to submit to the Lord of the Worlds. (The Believer 40:66)

Surely Hell lies in wait, a place of resort for the exceedingly disobedient, living there for long years. They will not taste cool or drink, but boiling water and [pus]. A corresponding recompense. Surely they did not fear the account, and they called Our Verses a lie, giving the lie (to the truth). We have recorded everything in a book. So, taste! We will add only chastisement to you. (The Announcement 78:21-30)

---

1 Ali, M.M., *The Holy Qur'an*, 820. Some of the believers had become martyrs in the cause of truth; others yet waited, anxious to lay down their lives in the same cause.

Obey and Honor God and Messenger

 Jesus

For the Father judges no one, but he has given all judgment to the Son, so that all may honor the Son, even as they honor the Father. Whoever does not honor the Son does not honor the Father who sent him. (John 5:22-23)

The Messenger believes in what has been revealed to him from his Lord, and (so do) the believers. They all believe in God and His angels and His Books and His messengers, saying: We make no difference between any of His messengers. We hear and obey, our Lord! Your forgiveness (do we crave), and to You is the eventual course.[1] (The Cow 2:285)

Say, [Prophet]: Obey God and the Messenger; but if they turn back, surely God does not love the unbelievers. (Family of Amran 3:32)

Obey God and the Messenger, so that you may be shown mercy. (The Family of Amran 3:132)

Oh, you who believe! Obey God and obey the Messenger and those in authority among you. If you quarrel about any thing, refer it to God and the Messenger, if you believe in God and the Last Day. This is best, and very good in the end. (The Women 4:59)

But no, [Prophet]! By your Lord! They will not believe (in reality) until they make you a judge between them regarding their matters of disagreement, and find no discomfort in their hearts as to what you decide, and then submit with entire submission. If We had prescribed for them: Lay down your lives or go forth from your homes, they would not have done it, except a few of them. If they had done what they were admonished, it would have certainly been better for them and best in strengthening (them)—then We would have certainly given them a great reward. And We would have certainly guided them on the right path. Whoever obeys God and the Messenger are those upon whom God has bestowed favours from among the prophets and the truthful and the faithful and the good, and good company are they. (The Women 4:65)

Whoever obeys the Messenger, he indeed obeys God. We have not sent you as a keeper over those who turn their backs. (The Women 4:80)

[Prophet], they say: Obedience! But when they go away from your presence, a group of them decides by night to do other than what you say. God writes down what they decide by night, so turn aside from them, and trust in God. God is a sufficient protector. (The Women 4:81)

---

1 Martin Lings, *Muhammad, His Life Based on the Earliest Sources* (Rochester, Vermont: Inner Traditions and Bear and Company, 2006), 105 (Hereafter cited as Lings, *Muhammad*). This Revelation contains the Creed of Islam.

Jesus

A prophet is not without honor, except in his own country, and among his own relatives, and in his own house. (Mark 6:4)

Muhammad ﷺ

Certainly, messengers before you were mocked [Prophet], but the scoffers were surrounded by what they mocked. Say: Travel in the land, and see what was the end of the rejecters. (The Cattle 6:10-11)

There are some who molest the Prophet, and say, He is one who believes everything that he hears. Say: He is a hearer of good for you; he believes in God and believes the faithful, and he is a mercy for those of you who believe. Those who molest the Messenger of God will have a painful chastisement. (The Immunity 9:61)

Do they not know that whoever acts in opposition to God and His Messenger will surely abide in the Fire of Hell? That is the grievous abasement. (The Immunity 9:63)

Messengers before you were certainly mocked, but I gave respite to those who disbelieved, and then I destroyed them. How, then, was My requital (of evil)? (The Thunder 13:32)

Those who obey God and His Messenger, and fear God, and are careful of (their duty to) Him—these are the achievers. Say, [Prophet]: Obey God and obey the Messenger. But if you turn back, that which is imposed on you rests on you, and that which is imposed on me rests on me. If you obey me, you are on the right way. Nothing rests on the Messenger except clear delivery of (the message). (The Light 24:52, 54)

Believers are only those who believe in God and His Messenger, and when they are with his Messenger for a momentous affair, they do not go away until they have asked the Messenger's permission. [Prophet], those who ask your permission believe in God and His Messenger. So when they ask your permission for some affair of theirs, give it to whom you please, and ask forgiveness for them from God. Surely God is Forgiving, Merciful. (The Light 24:62)

It is not proper for a believing man and a believing woman to have any choice in their matter when God and His Messenger have decided the matter. Whoever disobeys God and His Messenger surely strays off into clear [error]. (The Allies 33:36)

Jesus

Then the Judeans answered him, "Do not we say well that you are a Samaritan, and have a demon?" Jesus answered, "I do not have a demon, but I honor my Father, and you dishonor me. But I do not seek my own glory. There is One who seeks and judges." (John 8:48-50)[1]

If anyone serves me, let him follow me; and where I am, there will my servant also be. If anyone serves me, the Father will honor him. (John 12:26)

---

1 Wallerstedt et al., *Orthodox Bible*, 236. Samaritans were viewed as demon-possessed heretics.

Muhammad ﷺ

Oh, you who believe! Do not enter the houses of the Prophet unless permission is given to you for a meal. Do not wait for the cooking to be finished—but when you are invited, enter, and when you have taken the food, disperse, not seeking to listen to conversation. Surely this gives the Prophet trouble, but he endures you, but God does not endure before the truth. And when you ask for any goods, ask from behind a curtain. This is purer for your hearts and (for) their hearts. It is not proper for you to give trouble to the Messenger of God, nor should you marry his wives after him, ever. Surely this is grievous in the sight of God. (The Allies 33:53)

Surely God and His angels bless the Prophet. Oh, you who believe! Call for (Divine) blessings on him, and salute him with a (becoming) salutation. Surely God has cursed in this world and the Hereafter those who speak evil things of God and His Messenger, and He has prepared for them a disgraceful chastisement. (The Allies 33:56-57)

On the day when their faces will be turned back into the fire, they will say: Oh, if only we had obeyed God and obeyed the Messenger! (The Allies 33:66)

Say, [Prophet]: I exhort you only to one thing: Rise up for God's sake, in twos and singly, and then ponder—there is no madness in your fellow-citizen [the Prophet]. He is only a warner to you, before a severe chastisement. (The Saba 34:46)

Be patient, [Prophet], as were the steadfast messengers. Do not seek to hasten (their doom) for them. On the Day that they see what they were promised, it will seem to them as if they had not tarried but an hour of a day. A sufficient exhibition. Will any be destroyed besides the defiantly disobedient people? (The Sandhills 46:35)

Surely those who disbelieve and turn away from God's way and oppose the Messenger after guidance has become clear to them cannot harm God in any way, and He will make null their deeds. Oh, you who believe! Obey God and obey the Messenger, and do not make your deeds of no effect. (Muhammad 47:32-33)

[Prophet], surely We have sent you as a witness and as a bearer of good news, and as a warner, so that you may believe in God and His Messenger, and aid Him and revere Him, and declare His glory, morning and evening. [Prophet], surely those who swear allegiance to you swear allegiance only to God. The hand of God is over their hands. So whoever breaks (his faith), breaks it only to the injury of his own soul, and God will grant a mighty reward to whoever fulfils his covenant with God. (The Victory 48:8-10)

Jesus

Then the Judeans said to him, "Now we know that you have a demon. Abraham died, and the prophets; and you say, 'If a man keeps my word, he will never taste of death.' Are you greater than our father, Abraham, who died? The prophets died. Who do you make yourself out to be?" Jesus answered, "If I glorify myself, my glory is nothing. It is my Father who glorifies me, of whom you say 'He is our God.' You have not known Him, but I know Him. If I said, 'I do not know Him,' I would be like you, a liar. But I know Him, and keep His word. Your father Abraham rejoiced to see my day. He saw it, and was glad." (John 8:52-56)

Muhammad ﷺ

Oh, you who believe! Do not raise your voices above the voice of the Prophet, and do not speak loud to him as you speak loud to one another, lest your [good] deeds become null while you do not perceive. (The Chambers 49:2)

Know that among you is God's Messenger. If he obeyed you in many a matter, you would surely fall into distress, but God has endeared the Faith to you, and made it seemly in your hearts. He has made hateful to you unbelief and transgression and disobedience—these are the followers of a right way. (The Chambers 49:7)

The dwellers of the desert say: We believe.[1] Say, [Prophet]: You do not believe—rather say, We submit, for faith has not yet entered into your hearts. If you obey God and His Messenger, He will not diminish any of your deeds. Surely, God is Forgiving, Merciful. (The Chambers 49:14)

[Prophet], haven't you seen those who are forbidden secret counsels, and then they return to what they are forbidden and hold secret counsels for sin, revolt and disobedience to the Messenger? When they come to you, they greet you with a greeting with which God does not greet you, and they say among themselves: Why does God not chastise us for what we say? Hell is enough for them—they will enter it, and evil is the destination. (The Pleading One 58:8)

Oh, you who believe! When you consult the Messenger, offer something in charity before your consultation. That is better for you, and purer. But if you do not find [the means], surely God is Forgiving, Merciful. (The Pleading One 58:12)

Surely those who oppose God and His Messenger will be among the most humiliated. God has written: I will most certainly prevail, I and My messengers. Surely God is Strong, Mighty. (The Pleading One 58:20-21)

Most surely, [this Qur'an] is the word of an honoured Messenger. It is not the word of a poet—little do you believe. Nor the word of a soothsayer— little do you take heed. It is a revelation from the Lord of the Worlds. And if [the Prophet] had invented, against Us, some of the sayings, We would have certainly seized him by the right hand. Then, We would certainly have cut off his aorta. And not one of you could have withheld Us from him. Most surely it is a reminder for those who guard (against evil). And most surely We know that some of you are rejecters. And most surely it is a great grief to the unbelievers. Most surely it is the true certainty. (The Sure Calamity 69:40-51)

---

1 Bedouin Arabs—Ed.

Jesus

Muhammad ﷺ

(It is) only a delivering (of communications) from God, and His messages. Whoever disobeys God and His Messenger will surely have the fire of Hell, to abide there for a long time. (The Jinn 72:23)

Damnation overtake both hands of the father of the flame: he will perish. His wealth and what he earned will not benefit him. He will soon burn in Fire that flames. And his wife, the [carrier of firewood]: upon her neck will be a halter of strongly twisted rope.[1] (The Flame 111:1-5)

---

1 Ali, M.M., *The Holy Qur'an*, 1233-1234. This sura refers to the Prophet's uncle, who severely opposed him, as did his wife. He followed the Prophet while he preached, telling the people that the Prophet was his mad relative. She spread slander about the Prophet and threw bunches of thorns tied with ropes into the Prophet's way.

Miracles

 Jesus

Note: The italicized verses in this chapter do not contain any of Christ's words. These verses are included to narrate the story of Christ's miracles.—Ed.

Feeding the Masses

"I have compassion on the crowd, because they have stayed with me now three days, and they have nothing to eat. If I send them away fasting to their homes, they will faint on the way, for some of them have come a long way." His disciples answered him, "From where could one satisfy these people with bread, here in a deserted place?" He asked them, "How many loaves do you have?" They said, "Seven." He commanded the crowd to sit down on the ground, and he took the seven loaves. Having given thanks, he broke them, and gave them to his disciples to serve, and they served the crowd. They had a few small fish. Having blessed them, he said to serve these also. They ate, and were filled. They took up seven baskets of broken pieces that were left over. Now they who had eaten were about four thousand. Then he sent them away. (Mark 8:2-9)

He entered into one of the boats, which was Simon's, and asked him to put out a little from the land. He sat down and taught the crowds from the boat. When he had finished speaking, he said to Simon, "Put out into the deep, and let down your nets for a catch." *Simon answered him, "Master, we worked all night, and took nothing; but at your word I will let down the net." When they had done this, they caught a great multitude of fish, and their net was breaking. They beckoned to their partners in the other boat, that they should come and help them. They came, and filled both boats, so that they began to sink. But Simon Peter, when he saw it, fell down at Jesus' knees, saying, "Depart from me, for I am a sinful man, Lord." For he was amazed, and all who were with him, at the catch of fish that they had caught; and so also were James and John, sons of Zebedee, who were partners with Simon.* Jesus said to Simon, "Do not be afraid. From now on you will be catching men." *When they had brought their boats to land, they left everything, and followed him.* (Luke 5:3-11)

But Jesus said to them, "They do not need to go away. You give them something to eat." *And they told him, "We only have here five loaves and two fish."* So he said, "Bring them here to me." *Then he commanded the crowds to sit down on the grass; and he took the five loaves and the two fish, and looking up to heaven, he blessed, broke and gave the loaves to the disciples, and the disciples gave to the crowds. And they all ate and were filled, and they took up twelve baskets full of that which remained left over from the broken pieces. Now those who ate were about five thousand men, besides women and children.* (Matthew 14:16-21)

Muhammad

Note: Considering that Muhammad was an "unlettered prophet," Islam considers the Quran itself to be a miracle, as evidenced by these passages: 2:23 (see page 103), 10:37-38 (see page 109) and 17:88 (see page 111).—Ed.

When the disciples said: Oh Jesus, son of Mary! Will your Lord consent to send down to us food from Heaven? He said: Be careful of (your duty to)God, if you are believers. They said: We desire to eat of it, so that our hearts would be at rest, knowing that you have indeed spoken the truth to us, and so that we may be witnesses to it. Jesus the son of Mary said: Oh God, our Lord! Send down to us food from Heaven, which should be to us an ever-recurring happiness, to the first of us and to the last of us, and a sign from You. Grant us means of subsistence—You are the best of the providers. God said: I will send it down to you, but whoever disbelieves among you afterwards, surely I will chastise him with a chastisement by which I have not chastised anyone among the nations. (The Food 5:112-115)

Jesus

And the third day there was a wedding in Cana of Galilee, and the mother of Jesus was there. Now Jesus also was invited, with his disciples, to the wedding. When the wine ran out, Jesus' mother said to him, "They have no wine." Jesus said to her, "Woman, what does that have to do with you and me? My hour has not yet come." His mother said to the servants, "Whatever he says to you, do it." Now there were six water pots of stone set there after the Jewish manner of purifying, containing two or three metretes apiece.[1] Jesus said to them, "Fill the water pots with water." They filled them up to the brim. He said to them, "Now draw some out, and take it to the ruler of the feast." So they took it. When the ruler of the feast tasted the water now become wine, and did not know where it came from (but the servants who had drawn the water knew), the ruler of the feast called the bridegroom, and said to him, "Everyone serves the good wine first, and when the guests have drunk freely, then that which is worse. You have kept the good wine until now." This beginning of his signs Jesus did in Cana of Galilee, and revealed his glory; and his disciples believed in him. (John 2:1-11)

Simon Peter said to them, "I'm going fishing." They told him, "We are also coming with you." Immediately they went out, and entered into the boat. That night, they caught nothing. But when day had already come, Jesus stood on the beach, yet the disciples did not know that it was Jesus. Jesus therefore said to them, "Children, have you anything to eat?" They answered him, "No." He said to them, "Cast the net on the right side of the boat, and you will find some."They cast it therefore, and now they weren't able to draw it in for the multitude of fish. That disciple therefore whom Jesus loved said to Peter, "It's the Lord." (John 21:3-7)

Healing People

He stretched out his hand, and touched him, saying, "I am willing. Be cleansed." And immediately his leprosy was cleansed. And Jesus said to him, "See that you tell nobody, but go, show yourself to the priest, and offer the gift that Moses commanded, as a testimony to them." (Matthew 8:3-4)

Then one possessed by a demon, blind and mute, was brought to him and he healed him, so that the blind and mute man spoke and saw. And all the crowds were amazed, and said, "Can this be the son of David?" (Matthew 12:22-23)

When the people of that place recognized him, they sent into all that surrounding region, and brought to him all who were sick, and they begged him that they might just touch the fringe of his garment. As many as touched it were made whole. (Matthew 14:34-36)

---

1 Two to three metretes is about 20 to 30 U. S. Gallons, 16 to 25 imperial gallons, or 75 to 115 litres.—Ed.

Muhammad ﷺ

When God will say: Oh Jesus, son of Mary! Remember My favour on you and on your mother, when I strengthened you with the Holy Spirit. You spoke to the people [when you were] in the cradle and in old age, and when I taught you the Book and the wisdom and the Torah and the Gospel. And when you made out of clay the form of a bird, by My permission, and then you breathed into it, and it became a bird by My permission.[1] And you healed the blind and the leprous by My permission, and when you brought forth the dead by My permission. And when I withheld the Children of Israel from you, when you came to them with clear arguments. Those who disbelieved among them said: This is nothing but clear enchantment. And when I revealed to the disciples, saying, Believe in Me and My messenger, they said: We believe and bear witness that we submit (ourselves)—[we are Muslims].

(The Food 5:110-111)

---

1 This story of Jesus speaking in his cradle is also in the *Syriac (Arabic) Infancy Gospel.* The story of the bird is also in the *Infancy Gospel of Thomas. See* page 487.—Ed.

Jesus

And when Jesus came into Capernaum, a centurion came to him, asking him, and saying, "Lord, my servant lies in the house paralyzed, grievously tormented." And Jesus said to him, "I will come and heal him." And the centurion answered, "Lord, I'm not worthy for you to come under my roof. Just say the word, and my servant will be healed. For I am also a man under authority, having under myself soldiers. I tell this one, 'Go,' and he goes; and tell another, 'Come,' and he comes; and tell my servant, 'Do this,' and he does it." And when Jesus heard it, he marveled, and said to those who followed, "Truly I tell you, I have not found so great a faith with anyone in Israel." And Jesus said to the centurion, "Go your way. Let it be done for you as you have believed." And his servant was healed in that hour. "And I tell you that many will come from the East and the West, and will sit down with Abraham, and Isaac, and Jacob in the Kingdom of Heaven, but the sons of the kingdom will be thrown out into the outer darkness. There will be weeping and gnashing of teeth."[1] (Matthew 8:5-13)

And look, they brought to him a man who was paralyzed, lying on a bed. And Jesus, seeing their faith, said to the paralytic, "Son, cheer up. Your sins are forgiven." And look, some of the scribes said to themselves, "This man blasphemes." But Jesus, knowing their thoughts, said, "Why do you think evil in your hearts? For which is easier, to say, 'Your sins are forgiven;' or to say, 'Get up, and walk?' But that you may know that the Son of Man has authority on Earth to forgive sins." (Then he said to the paralytic), "Get up, and take up your mat, and go up to your house." And he arose and departed to his house. (Matthew 9:2-7)

A woman who had a flow of blood for twelve years (who had spent all her living on physicians) and could not be healed by any, came behind him, and touched the fringe of his cloak, and immediately the flow of her blood stopped. Jesus said, "Who touched me?" When all denied it, Peter and those with him said, "Master, the crowds press and jostle you, and you say, 'Who touched me?'" But Jesus said, "Someone did touch me, for I perceived that power has gone out of me." When the woman saw that she was not hidden, she came trembling, and falling down before him declared to him in the presence of all the people the reason why she had touched him, and how she was healed immediately. He said to her, "Daughter, take courage, your faith has made you well. Go in peace." (Luke 8:43-48)

And when evening came, they brought to him many possessed with demons. He cast out the spirits with a word, and healed all who were sick. (Matthew 8:16)

---

1 Wallerstedt et al., *Orthodox Bible*, 24. Jesus praises the centurion, a Gentile, and lifts him up as a model of faith, saying that many from other nations will share Heaven with the Jewish patriarchs.

Wallerstedt et al, *Orthodox Bible: Old and New Testaments* 2008, 1280. The sons of the Kingdom are both the Jews who deny Christ and those raised in the Church who do not live their faith.

Muhammad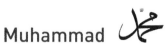

Jesus

When he had come into the house, the blind men came to him, and Jesus said to them, "Do you believe that I am able to do this?" They told him, "Yes, Lord." Then he touched their eyes, saying, "According to your faith, be it done to you." And their eyes were opened. And Jesus strictly commanded them, saying, "See that no one knows about this." (Matthew 9:28-30)

And look, there was a man with a withered hand. They asked him, "Is it lawful to heal on the Sabbath day?" that they might accuse him. And he said to them, "What man is there among you, who has one sheep, and if this one falls into a pit on the Sabbath day, won't he grab on to it, and lift it out? Of how much more value then is a man than a sheep. Therefore it is lawful to do good on the Sabbath." Then he told the man, "Stretch out your hand." And he stretched it out, and it was restored whole, just like the other. (Matthew 12:10-13)

They brought to him one who was deaf and had an impediment in his speech. They begged him to lay his hand on him. He took him aside from the crowd, privately, and put his fingers into his ears, and he spat, and touched his tongue. Looking up to Heaven, he sighed, and said to him, "Ephphatha." That is, "Be opened." And immediately, his ears were opened, and the impediment of his tongue was released, and he spoke clearly. He commanded them that they should tell no one, but the more he commanded them, so much the more widely they proclaimed it. (Mark 7:32-36)

As he passed by, he saw a man blind from birth. His disciples asked him, "Rabbi, who sinned, this man or his parents, that he was born blind?" Jesus answered, "Neither did this man sin, nor his parents; but, that the works of God might be revealed in him. I must work the works of He who sent me, while it is day. The night is coming, when no one can work. When he had said this, he spat on the ground, made mud with the saliva, anointed the blind man's eyes with the mud, and said to him, "Go, wash in the pool of Siloam" (which means "Sent"). So he went away, washed, and came back seeing. (John 9:1-4, 6-7)

Jesus asked him, "What do you want me to do for you?" The blind man said to him, "Rabboni, that I may see again." Jesus said to him, "Go your way. Your faith has made you well." And immediately he received his sight, and followed Jesus on the road. (Mark 10:51-52)

He was teaching in one of the synagogues on the Sabbath day. And look, a woman who had a spirit of infirmity eighteen years, and she was bent over, and could in no way straighten herself up. When Jesus saw her, he called her, and said to her, "Woman, you are freed from your infirmity." He laid his hands on her, and immediately she stood up straight, and glorified God. (Luke 13:10-13)

Jesus

He came to Bethsaida. They brought a blind man to him, and begged him to touch him. He took hold of the blind man by the hand, and brought him out of the village. When he had spit on his eyes, and laid his hands on him, he asked him if he saw anything. He looked up, and said, "I see men; they look like trees, walking." Then again he laid his hands on his eyes. He made him look up, and was restored, and saw everything clearly. He sent him away to his house, saying, "Do not enter into the village, or tell anyone in the village." (Mark 8:22-26)

As he entered into a certain village, ten men who were lepers met him, who stood up, at a distance. They lifted up their voices, saying, "Jesus, Master, have mercy on us." When he saw them, he said to them, "Go and show yourselves to the priests." It happened that as they went, they were cleansed. One of them, when he saw that he was healed, turned back, glorifying God with a loud voice. He fell on his face at Jesus' feet, giving him thanks; and he was a Samaritan. Jesus answered, "Weren't the ten cleansed? But where are the nine? Were there none found who returned to give glory to God, except this stranger?" Then he said to him, "Get up, and go your way. Your faith has healed you." (Luke 17:12-19)

The nobleman said to him, "Sir, come down before my child dies." Jesus said to him, "Go your way. Your son lives." The man believed the word that Jesus spoke to him, and he went his way. As he was now going down, his servants met him and reported, saying "Your son lives!" So he inquired of them the hour when he began to get better. They said to him, "Yesterday at the seventh hour, the fever left him." The father knew that it was at that hour in which Jesus said to him, "Your son lives." He believed, as did his whole house. (John 4:49-53)

Now in Jerusalem by the sheepgate, there is a pool, which is called in Hebrew Bethzatha, having five porches. In these lay a great multitude of those who were sick, blind, lame, or paralyzed. A certain man was there, who had been sick for thirty-eight years. When Jesus saw him lying there, and knew that he had been sick for a long time, he asked him, "Do you want to be made well?" The sick man answered him, "Sir, I have no one to put me into the pool when the water is stirred up, but while I'm coming, another steps down before me." Jesus said to him, "Arise, take up your mat, and walk." Immediately, the man was made well, and took up his mat and walked. (John 5:2-9)

See also Luke 14:2-5 on page 218.
See also Luke 22:47-51 on page 86.

 **Jesus**

Expelling Demons

In the synagogue there was a man who had a spirit of an unclean demon, and he shouted with a loud voice, saying, "And what have we to do with you, Jesus, Nazarene? Have you come to destroy us? I know you who you are: the Holy One of God." Jesus rebuked him, saying, "Be silent, and come out of him." When the demon had thrown him down in their midst, he came out of him, having done him no harm. Amazement came on all, and they spoke together, one with another, saying, "What is this word? For with authority and power he commands the unclean spirits, and they come out." (Luke 4:33-36)

When Jesus stepped ashore, a certain man out of the city who had demons for a long time met him. He wore no clothes, and did not live in a house, but in the tombs. When he saw Jesus, he shouted, and fell down before him, and with a loud voice said, "What do I have to do with you, Jesus, you Son of the Most High God? I beg you, do not torment me." For Jesus was commanding the unclean spirit to come out of the man. For the unclean spirit had often seized the man. He was kept under guard, and bound with chains and fetters. Breaking the bands apart, he was driven by the demon into the desert. Jesus asked him, "What is your name?" He said, "Legion," for many demons had entered into him. They begged him that he would not command them to go into the abyss. Now there was there a herd of many pigs feeding on the mountain, and they begged him that he would allow them to enter into those. He allowed them. The demons came out from the man, and entered into the pigs, and the herd rushed down the steep bank into the lake, and were drowned. When those who fed them saw what had happened, they fled, and told it in the city and in the country. (Luke 8:27-34)

And as they went out, look, a mute man who was demon possessed was brought to him. And when the demon was cast out, the mute man spoke. And the crowds marveled, saying, "Nothing like this has ever been seen in Israel." (Matthew 9:32-33)

Muhammad ﷺ

Jesus

Calming Storms

And leaving the crowd, they took him with them, even as he was, in the boat. And other small boats were also with him. And a big wind storm arose, and the waves beat into the boat, so much that it was already filled. And he himself was in the stern, asleep on the cushion, and they woke him up, and told him, "Teacher, do you not care that we are dying?" And he awoke, and rebuked the wind, and said to the sea, "Peace. Be still." And the wind ceased, and there was a great calm. And he said to them, "Why are you so afraid? How do you still have no faith?" And they were greatly afraid, and said to one another, "Who then is this, that even the wind and the sea obey him?" (Mark 4:36-41)

And immediately he made his disciples get into the boat, and to go ahead to the other side, to Bethsaida, while he himself was sending the crowd away. After he had taken leave of them, he went up the mountain to pray. When evening had come, the boat was in the midst of the sea, and he was alone on the land. He saw them distressed in rowing, for the wind was against them, about the fourth watch of the night he came to them, walking on the sea, and he would have passed by them, but they, when they saw him walking on the sea, supposed that it was a ghost, and began to scream; for they all saw him, and were troubled. But he immediately spoke with them, and said to them, "Cheer up. It is I. Do not be afraid." And he got into the boat with them, and the wind ceased. And they were completely profusely astonished among themselves, and marveled. (Mark 4:45-51)

Muhammad ﷺ

Jesus

Raising Dead

While he told these things to them, look, a ruler came and worshiped him, saying, "My daughter has just died, but come and lay your hand on her, and she will live." And Jesus got up and followed him, as did his disciples. And when Jesus came into the ruler's house, and saw the flute players, and the crowd in noisy disorder, he said to them, "Go away, for the girl is not dead, but asleep." And they laughed at him. But when the crowd was put out, he entered in, took her by the hand, and the girl arose. (Matthew 9:18-19, 23-25)

When he drew near to the gate of the city, then look, a man who was dead was carried out, the only son of his mother, and she was a widow; and a large crowd from the city was with her. When the Lord saw her, he had compassion on her and said to her, "Do not cry." He came near and touched the coffin, and the bearers stood still. He said, "Young man, I tell you, arise." He who was dead sat up and began to speak. And he gave him to his mother. (Luke 7:12-15)

Jesus said, "Take away the stone." Martha, the sister of the dead man, said to him, "Lord, by this time there is a stench, for he has been dead four days." Jesus said to her, "Did I not tell you that if you believed, you would see God's glory?" So they took away the stone from the place where the dead was lying. And Jesus lifted up his eyes, and said, "Father, I thank you that you listened to me. I know that you always listen to me, but because of the crowd that stands around I said this, that they may believe that you sent me." When he had said this, he shouted with a loud voice, "Lazarus, come out." The man who had died came out, bound hand and foot with wrappings, and his face was wrapped around with a cloth. Jesus said to them, "Free him, and let him go." (John 11:39-44)

Muhammad ﷺ

Seeking Miracles

 Jesus

This is the work of God, so that you believe in him whom He has sent.[1] (John 6:29)

Then the devil took him into the holy city. He set him on the pinnacle of the temple and said to him, "If you are the Son of God, throw yourself down, for it is written, 'He will put his angels in charge of you' and, 'In their hands they will lift you up, so that you will not strike your foot against a stone.' Jesus said to him, "Again, it is written, 'Do not test the Lord, your God.'" (Matthew 4:5-7)

An evil and adulterous generation seeks after a sign, but no sign will be given except the sign of Jonah the prophet. For as Jonah was three days and three nights in the belly of the great fish, so will the Son of Man be three days and three nights in the heart of the Earth. (Matthew 12:39-40)

Blessed are your eyes, for they see; and your ears, for they hear. For truly I tell you that many prophets and righteous men desired to see the things that you see and did not see them, and to hear the things that you hear and did not hear them. (Matthew 13:16-17)

---

1 Spoken after Jesus materialized on the other side of the Sea of Galilee, at Capernaum.—Ed.

And those who have no knowledge, say: Why does God not speak to us or a sign come to us? Those before them said the same—their hearts are all alike. Indeed We have made the signs clear for a people who are sure. [Prophet], We have sent you with the truth as a bearer of good news and as a warner, and you will not be called on to answer for the companions of the Flaming Fire. (The Cow 2:118-119)

Whoever disputes with you [Muhammad] in this matter, after what has come to you of knowledge, then say: Come! Let us call our sons and your sons and our women and your women and our people and your people, and let us be earnest in prayer, and pray for the curse of God on the liars. Most surely this is the true explanation, and there is no god but God. Most surely God is the Mighty, the Wise. But if they turn back, surely God knows the mischief-makers. (The Family of Amran 3:61-63)

If We had sent to you writing on a paper, and then they had touched it with their hands, certainly those who disbelieve would have said: This is nothing but clear enchantment. They say: Why has an angel not been sent down to him? Had We sent down an angel, the matter would have been decided: their punishment would not have been delayed. If We had made him an angel, We would certainly have made him appear as a man, thus confusing for them what they now confuse. (The Cattle 6:7-9)

If their turning away is hard on you, [Prophet], then if you can, seek an tunnel (to go down) into the Earth or a ladder (to ascend up) to Heaven so that you bring them a sign. If God had pleased, He would have certainly gathered them all on guidance—so do not be of the ignorant. (The Cattle 6:35)

And they swear by God, with their strongest oaths, that if a sign came to them, they would most certainly believe in it. Say, [Prophet]: Signs are only with God. But what will make you realize that even when it comes, they will not believe? We will turn away their hearts and their sight, just as they did not believe it the first time, and We will leave them in their disorder, blindly wandering. Even if We had sent down to them the angels, and the dead had spoken to them, and We had gathered all things before them, they would not believe unless God pleases, but most of them are ignorant. (The Cattle 6:109-111)

When they said: Oh, God! If this is the truth from You, rain stones on us from Heaven, or inflict on us a painful punishment. But God was not going to chastise them while you were among them, nor is God going to chastise them while they still ask for forgiveness. But what (excuse) have they that God should not chastise them while they hinder (men) from the Sacred Mosque? They are not (fit to be) guardians of it; its guardians are only those who guard (against evil), but most of them do not know. (The Accessions 8:32-34)

Jesus

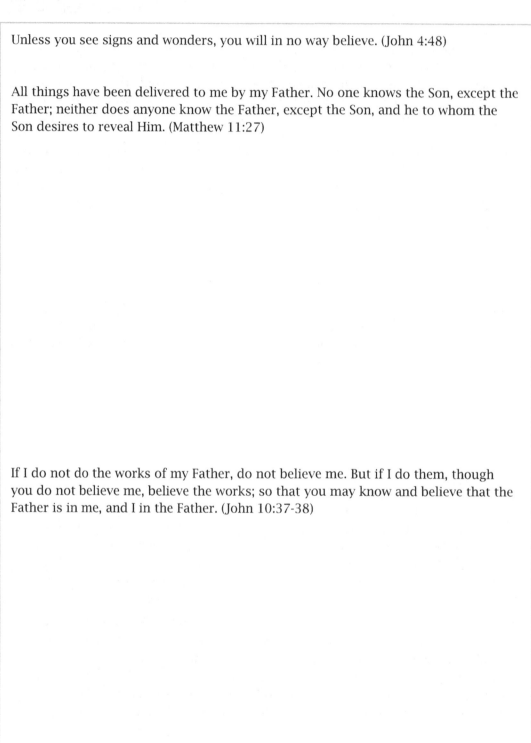

Unless you see signs and wonders, you will in no way believe. (John 4:48)

All things have been delivered to me by my Father. No one knows the Son, except the Father; neither does anyone know the Father, except the Son, and he to whom the Son desires to reveal Him. (Matthew 11:27)

If I do not do the works of my Father, do not believe me. But if I do them, though you do not believe me, believe the works; so that you may know and believe that the Father is in me, and I in the Father. (John 10:37-38)

Muhammad ﷺ

They say: Why is a sign not sent to him from his Lord? Say, [Prophet]: The unseen is only for God, so wait. Surely I too wait with you. (Jonah 10:20)

Then, may it be that you will give up part of what is revealed to you and your breast will become constricted by it because they say: Why has no treasure been sent down on him or an angel come with him? You are only a warner, and God is custodian over all things. Or, do they say: He has fabricated it. Say [Prophet]: Then bring ten fabricated chapters like it, and call upon whom you can besides God, if you are truthful. But if they do not answer you, then know that it is revealed by God's knowledge, and that there is no god but He. Will you then [be Muslims]? (Hud 11:12-14)

Those who disbelieve, say: Why has a sign not been sent down upon him from his Lord? [Prophet], you are only a warner, and there is a guide for every people. (The Thunder 13:7)

And those who disbelieve, say: Why is a sign not sent down upon him by his Lord? "Say, [Prophet]: Surely God makes he whom he wills go astray, and guides to Himself those who turn (to Him). (The Thunder 13:27)

They say: Oh, you to whom the Reminder has been revealed! You are most surely insane. Why do you not bring the angels to us if you are truthful? We only send the angels with truth, and then the unbelievers would not have a delay in punishment. (The Rock 15:6-8)

They say: Why does he not bring us a sign from his Lord? Has there not come to them a clear evidence of what is in the previous books? (Ta Ha 20:133)

Whenever a new reminder from their Lord comes to them, they listen to it while they ridicule, their hearts frivolous. They counsel together in secret: He is nothing but a mortal like yourselves. What? Will you then yield to enchantment while you see it? [The Prophet] said: My Lord knows what is spoken in the Heaven and the Earth, and He is the Hearing, the Knowing. No! say they. Medleys of dreams. No! He has invented it. No! He is a poet. Let him bring us a sign, like those sent with former (prophets). No town that We destroyed before them believed: Will they then believe? (The Prophets 21:2-6)

Jesus

The Pharisees came out and began to question him, seeking from him a sign from Heaven, and testing him. He sighed deeply in his spirit, and said, "Why does this generation seek a sign? Truly I tell you, no sign will be given to this generation." (Mark 8:11-12)

Therefore when Mary came to where Jesus was and saw him, she fell down at his feet, saying to him, "Lord, if you would have been here, my brother would not have died." Jesus wept. The Judeans therefore said, "See how he loved him." But some of them said, "Could not this man, who opened the eyes of him who was blind, have also kept this man from dying?" The man who had died came out, bound hand and foot with wrappings, and his face was wrapped around with a cloth. (John 11:32, 35-37, 44)

Then, John answered him, saying, "Teacher, we saw someone casting out demons in your name; and we forbade him, because he does not follow us." But Jesus said, "Do not forbid him, for there is no one who will do a mighty work in my name, and be able quickly to speak evil of me. For whoever is not against us is for us." (Mark 9:38-40)

But the testimony that I have is greater than that of John,[1] for the works that the Father gave me to accomplish— the very works that I do— testify about me, that the Father has sent me. (John 5:36)

Truly, truly, I tell you, the Son can do nothing by himself, only what he sees the Father doing. For whatever things He does, these the Son also does. For the Father has affection for the Son, and shows him all things that He Himself does. He will show him greater works than these, so that you may marvel. For as the Father raises the dead and gives them life, even so the Son also gives life to whom he desires. (John 5:19-21)

---

1 John the Baptist—Ed.

Muhammad ﷺ

They say: What is the matter with this Messenger, that he eats food and goes about in the markets? Why has an angel not been sent down to him, so that he would have a warner with him? Why is a treasure not sent down to him, or why does he not have a garden from which he could eat? The [wrongdoers] say: You are only following a man [bewitched]. See what they liken you to— they have gone astray. Therefore, they will not be able to find a way. (The Distinction 25:7-9)

[Prophet], perhaps you will kill yourself with grief because they do not believe. If We willed, We could send down a sign from the Heaven to them, so that their necks would bow. They turn aside from every new reminder that comes from the Beneficent God. They have indeed rejected (the truth). Therefore, the news from that which they mock will soon come to them. (The Poets 26:3-6)

They say: Why are no Signs sent down on him from his Lord? Say, [Prophet]: The Signs are only with God, and I am a plain warner. Is it not enough for them that We have revealed to you the Book that is recited to them? Most surely there is mercy in this, and a reminder for a people who believe. (The Spider 29:50-51)

Prophet or Messiah

 Jesus

Note: Jesus' followers gave him the surname Christ. The word "Christ" is the Greek translation of the Hebrew word מָשִׁיחַ (Mashiach) or Messiah, meaning the anointed one of God as the subject of Hebrew Bible prophecies.—Ed.

Jesus came to them and spoke to them, saying, "All authority has been given to me in Heaven and on Earth. (Matthew 28:18)

No one can come to me unless the Father who sent me draws him, and I will raise him up in the last day. It is written in the Prophets, "And they will all be taught by God." Therefore everyone who hears from the Father, and has learned, comes to me. Not that anyone has seen the Father, except he who is from God. He has seen the Father. (John 6:44-46)

Now when Jesus came into the parts of Caesarea Philippi, he asked his disciples, saying, "Who do men say that I, the Son of Man, am?" They said, "Some say John the Baptist, some, Elijah, and others, Jeremiah, or one of the prophets." He said to them, "But who do you say that I am?" Simon Peter answered, "You are the Messiah, the Son of the living God." And Jesus answered him, "Blessed are you, Simon Bar Jonah, for flesh and blood has not revealed this to you, but my Father who is in Heaven. Then he commanded his disciples that they should tell no one that he is Jesus the Messiah. (Matthew 16:13-17, 20)

All things have been delivered to me by my Father. No one knows who the Son is, except the Father, and who the Father is, except the Son, and he to whomever the Son desires to reveal Him. (Luke 10:22)

My teaching is not mine, but His who sent me. If anyone desires to do His will, he will know about the teaching, whether it is from God, or if I am speaking from myself. He who speaks from himself seeks his own glory, but he who seeks the glory of He who sent him is true, and no unrighteousness is in him. (John 7:16-18)

The woman said to him, "I know that Messiah comes," (he who is called Christ). "When he has come, he will declare to us all things." Jesus said to her, "I am he, the one who speaks to you." (John 4:25-26)

"Do you believe in the Son of God?" He answered, "Who is he, Lord, that I may believe in him?" Jesus said to him, "You have both seen him, and it is he who speaks with you." (John 9:35b-37)

Muhammad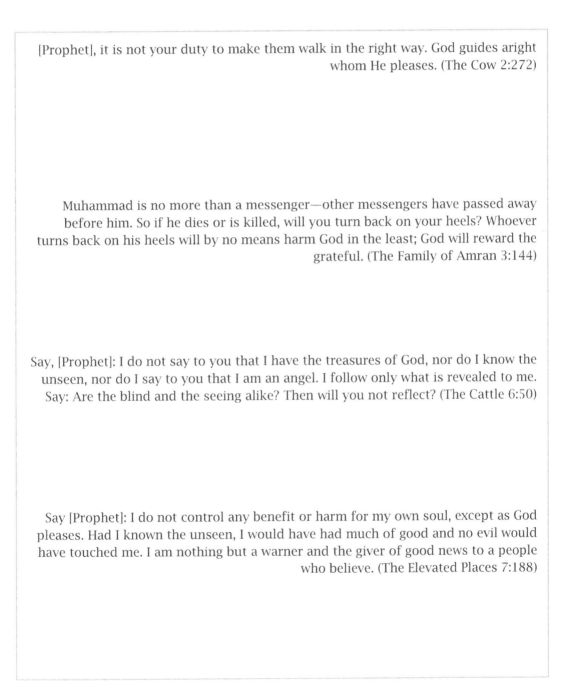

[Prophet], it is not your duty to make them walk in the right way. God guides aright whom He pleases. (The Cow 2:272)

Muhammad is no more than a messenger—other messengers have passed away before him. So if he dies or is killed, will you turn back on your heels? Whoever turns back on his heels will by no means harm God in the least; God will reward the grateful. (The Family of Amran 3:144)

Say, [Prophet]: I do not say to you that I have the treasures of God, nor do I know the unseen, nor do I say to you that I am an angel. I follow only what is revealed to me. Say: Are the blind and the seeing alike? Then will you not reflect? (The Cattle 6:50)

Say [Prophet]: I do not control any benefit or harm for my own soul, except as God pleases. Had I known the unseen, I would have had much of good and no evil would have touched me. I am nothing but a warner and the giver of good news to a people who believe. (The Elevated Places 7:188)

Jesus

"If you are the Messiah, tell us." But he said to them, "If I tell you, you won't believe, and if I ask, you will not answer me or let me go. From now on, the Son of Man will be seated at the right hand of the power of God." They all said, "Are you, then, the Son of God?" He said to them, "You say that I am." They said, "Why do we need any more witness? For we ourselves have heard from his own mouth." (Luke 22:67-71)

No one has ascended into Heaven, but he who descended out of Heaven, the Son of Man who is in Heaven. (John 3:13)

I know Him, because I am from Him, and He sent me. (John 7:29)

Again the high priest asked him, "Are you the Messiah, the Son of the Blessed One?" Jesus said, "I am. You will see the Son of Man sitting at the right hand of Power, and coming with the clouds of the sky." (Mark 14:61-62)

For God so loved the world that He gave His only Son, so that whoever believes in him will not perish, but have eternal life. (John 3:16)

I am the Alpha and the Omega, the First and the Last, the Beginning and the End.[1] Do not be afraid. I am the first and the last, and the living one. I was dead, but look, I am alive forevermore. Amen. I have the keys of death and of Hell.
(Revelation 22:13, 1:17b-18)

And it happened in those days, that Jesus came from Nazareth of Galilee, and was baptized by John in the Jordan. Immediately coming up from the water, he saw the heavens parting, and the Spirit descending on him like a dove. And a voice came out of the sky, "You are my beloved Son, in whom I am well pleased." And immediately the Spirit drove him out into the wilderness. And he was in the wilderness forty days tempted by Satan. He was there with the wild animals; and the angels were serving him. Now after John was taken into custody, Jesus came into Galilee, proclaiming the Good News of the Kingdom of God, and saying, "The time is fulfilled, and the Kingdom of God is near. Repent, and believe in the Good News." (Mark 1:9-14)

I glorified You on the Earth. I have accomplished the work that You have given me to do. Now, Father, glorify me with Your own self, with the glory that I had with You before the world existed. (John 17:4-5)

Do you not believe that I am in the Father, and the Father is in me? The words that I say to you I do not speak from myself; but the Father who lives in me does the works. (John 14:10)

---

1 Alpha and Omega are the first and last letters of the Greek alphabet.—Ed.

Muhammad

They say: We will by no means believe in you until you cause a fountain to gush forth from the earth for us. Or you have a garden of palms and grapes, in the midst of which you cause rivers to flow forth, gushing out. Or you cause the Heaven to come down on us in pieces, as you [have claimed], or bring God and the angels face to face (with us). Or you have a house of gold. Or you ascend into Heaven—but we will not believe in your ascension until you bring down to us a book that we may read. Say, [Prophet]: Glory be to my Lord; am I nothing but a mortal messenger?
(The Israelites 17:90-93)

Say, [Prophet]: I am only a mortal, like you. It is revealed to me that your god is one God. Therefore, whoever hopes to meet his Lord should do good deeds, and not associate any one with his Lord, in service. (The Cave 18:110)

Muhammad is not the father of any of your men, but he is the Messenger of God and the seal of the prophets. God is Cognizant of all things (The Allies 33:40)

Jesus

If God were your Father, you would love me, for I came out and have come from God. For I have not come of myself, but He sent me. (John 8:42)

I came forth from the Father and have come into the world. Again, I leave the world and go to the Father. (John 16:28)

If you have known me, you will know my Father also. From now on you do know Him and have seen Him. (John 14:7)

He who sent me is with me. The Father hasn't left me alone, for I always do the things that are pleasing to Him. (John 8:29)

I and the Father are one. (John 10:30)

You are from beneath. I am from above. You are of this world. I am not of this world. I said therefore to you that you will die in your sins; for unless you believe that I am he, you will die in your sins. (John 8:23-24)

Truly, truly, I tell you, before Abraham came into existence, I AM. (John 8:58)

For whoever will give you a cup of water to drink in my name, because you belong to the Messiah, truly I tell you, he will in no way lose his reward. (Mark 10:41)

Father, I desire that they also whom You have given me be with me where I am, so that they may see my glory, which You have given me, for You loved me before the foundation of the world. Righteous Father, the world hasn't known You, but I knew You; and these knew that You sent me. (John 17:24-25)

Muhammad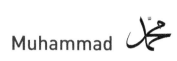

Say, [Prophet]: I am only a mortal like you. It is revealed to me that your God is one God. Therefore, follow the right way to Him, and ask His forgiveness. Woe to the polytheists. (Ha Mim 41:6)

It is not for any mortal that God should speak to him, except by revelation or from behind a veil, or by sending a messenger and revealing by His permission what He pleases. Surely, He is High, Wise. (The Counsel 42:51)

Say [Prophet]: I am not the first of the messengers, and I do not know what will be done with me or with you. I do not follow any thing but that which is revealed to me, and I am nothing but a plain warner. (The Sandhills 46:9)

Jesus

After six days, Jesus took with him Peter, James, and John his brother, and brought them up into a high mountain by themselves. He was transfigured before them. His face shone like the sun, and his garments became as white as the light. And look, Moses and Elijah appeared to them, talking with him. Peter answered, and said to Jesus, "Lord, it is good for us to be here. If you want, let us make three tents here: one for you, one for Moses, and one for Elijah." While he was still speaking, look, a bright cloud overshadowed them. And look, a voice came out of the cloud, saying, "This is My beloved Son, in whom I am well pleased. Listen to him." When the disciples heard it, they fell on their faces and were very afraid. Jesus came and touched them and said, "Get up, and do not be afraid." And when they lifted up their eyes, they saw no one except Jesus alone. As they were coming down from the mountain, Jesus commanded them, saying, "Do not tell anyone what you saw, until the Son of Man has risen from the dead." (Matthew 17:1-9)

I tell you, after this you will see the Son of Man sitting at the right hand of Power, and coming on the clouds of the sky. (Matthew 26:64)

Muhammad

Consider the star when it sets. Your companion [Muhammad] does not err, nor does he deviate. Nor does he speak out of desire. It is nothing but revelation that is revealed. The Lord of Mighty Power has taught him, the Lord of Strength. So he [Muhammad] attained completion. So he was in the highest part of the horizon. Then be drew near, [and came down]. He was at a distance of two bow-lengths, or closer still. And He revealed to His servant what He revealed.[1] The [Prophet's] heart did not lie in what it saw. What? Do you then dispute with him about what he saw? Certainly he saw him in another descent, at the farthest lote tree, near the Garden of Abode. When that which covers, covered the lote-tree. The [Prophet's] eyes did not turn aside, nor did they exceed the limit. Certainly he saw of the greatest Signs of his Lord. (The Star 53:1-18)

Therefore, [Prophet], do remind, for you are only a reminder. You are not a watcher over them. But God will chastise, with the greatest chastisement, whoever turns back and disbelieves. Surely to Us is their return. (The Overwhelming Event 88:21-24)

---

1 The angel Gabriel—Ed.

Crucified, Resurrected & Ascended

 Jesus

Note: The italicized verses in this chapter do not contain any of Christ's words. These verses are included to narrate the story of Christ's crucifixion, resurrection and ascension.—Ed.

Foretelling

"Did not Moses give you the Law, and yet none of you keeps the Law? Why do you seek to kill me?" *The crowd answered, "You have a demon. Who seeks to kill you?" Therefore some of them of Jerusalem said, "Is not this he whom they seek to kill? Look, he speaks openly, and they say nothing to him. Can it be that the rulers indeed know that this is truly the Messiah? But many in the crowd believed in him. They said, "When the Messiah comes, he won't do more signs than those which this man has done, will he?" The Pharisees heard the crowd murmuring these things concerning him, and the chief priests and the Pharisees sent officers to arrest him. Many of the crowd therefore, when they heard these words, said, "This is truly the Prophet." Others said, "This is the Messiah." But some said, "What, does the Messiah come out of Galilee? Hasn't the Scripture said that the Messiah comes of the seed of David, and from Bethlehem, the village where David was?" So there arose a division in the crowd because of him. Some of them would have arrested him, but no one laid hands on him. The officers therefore came to the chief priests and Pharisees, and they said to them, "Why did you not bring him?" The officers answered, "No one ever spoke like this man."* (John 7:19-20, 25-26, 31-32, 40-46)

In that same hour some Pharisees came, saying to him, "Get out of here, and go away, for Herod wants to kill you." And he said to them, "Go and tell that fox, 'Look, I cast out demons and perform cures today and tomorrow, and the third day I complete my mission. Nevertheless I must go on my way today and tomorrow and the next day, for it cannot be that a prophet perish outside of Jerusalem." (Luke 13:31-33)

He took the twelve aside, and said to them, "Look, we are going up to Jerusalem, and all the things that are written through the prophets concerning the Son of Man will be completed. For he will be delivered up to the Gentiles, will be mocked, treated shamefully, and spit on. They will scourge and kill him. On the third day, he will rise again." (Luke 18:31-33)

You know that after two days the Passover is coming, and the Son of Man will be delivered up to be crucified. (Matthew 26:2)

Muhammad ﷺ

Jesus

While he was at Bethany, in the house of Simon the leper, as he was reclining, a woman came having an alabaster jar of ointment of pure nard—very costly. She broke the jar, and poured it over his head. But there were some who were indignant among themselves, and saying, "Why has this ointment been wasted? For this ointment might have been sold for more than three hundred denarii, and given to the poor." They grumbled against her. But Jesus said, "Leave her alone. Why do you trouble her? She has done a good work for me. For you always have the poor with you, and whenever you want to, you can do them good; but you will not always have me. She has done what she could. She has anointed my body beforehand for the burying. Truly I tell you, wherever this Good News may be preached throughout the whole world, that which this woman has done will also be spoken of for a memorial of her." (Mark 14:3-9)

Simon Peter said to him, "Lord, where are you going?" Jesus answered, "Where I am going, you cannot follow now, but you will follow afterwards." (John 13:36)

Now I have told you before it happens so that, when it happens, you may believe. I will not speak with you much longer, for the ruler of this world is coming, and he has no hold on me.[1] But that the world may know that I love the Father, and as the Father commanded me, so I do. Arise, let us go from here. (John 14:30-31)

He said to them, "I have earnestly desired to eat this Passover with you before I suffer, for I say to you, I will not eat of it again until it is fulfilled in the Kingdom of God." (Luke 22:15-16)

When Jesus had said this, he was troubled in spirit, and testified, "Truly, truly, I tell you that one of you will betray me. It is he to whom I will give this piece of bread when I have dipped it." So when he had dipped the piece of bread, he gave it to Judas, the son of Simon Iscariot. After the piece of bread, then Satan entered into him. Then Jesus said to him, "What you do, do quickly." (John 13:21, 26-27)

As they were eating, Jesus took bread, and when he had blessed, he broke it, and gave to them, and said, "Take, eat; this is my body." He took the cup, and when he had given thanks, he gave to them. They all drank of it. He said to them, "This is my blood of the new covenant, which is poured out for many. Truly I tell you, I will no more drink of the fruit of the vine, until that day when I drink it anew in the Kingdom of God."[2] (Mark 14:22-25)

---

1 Wallerstedt et al., *Orthodox Bible*, 253. The ruler of this world, the Devil.

2 ibid, 122. This Passover meal is the first Eucharist (Communion), the heart of Christian worship, which celebrates the New Covenant and sacramental union with Christ.

Muhammad ﷺ

Jesus

He took bread, and when he had given thanks, he broke it, and gave to them, saying, "This is my body which is given for you. Do this in remembrance of me." Likewise, he took the cup after they had eaten, saying, "This cup is the New Covenant in my blood, which is poured out for you. But look, the hand of him who betrays me is with me on the table. The Son of Man indeed goes, as it has been determined, but woe to that man through whom he is betrayed." (Luke 22:19-22)

All of you will be made to stumble because of me tonight, for it is written, "I will strike the shepherd, and the sheep of the flock will be scattered." But after I am raised up, I will go before you into Galilee. (Matthew 26:31-32)

He said, "I tell you, Peter, the rooster will by no means crow today before you deny that you know me three times."[1] (Luke 22:34)

I will not leave you orphans. I will come to you. Yet a little while, and the world will see me no more; but you will see me. Because I live, you will live also. In that day you will know that I am in my Father, and you in me, and I in you. (John 14:18-20)

A little while, and you will no longer see me. Again a little while, and you will see me, because I go to the Father. Truly, truly, I tell you, that you will weep and lament, but the world will rejoice. You will be sorrowful, but your sorrow will be turned into joy. I came forth from the Father and have come into the world. Again, I leave the world, and go to the Father. (John 16:16, 20, 28)

Betrayal

He came out, and went, as his custom was, to the Mount of Olives. His disciples also followed him. When he was at the place, he said to them, "Pray that you do not enter into temptation." He was withdrawn from them about a stone's throw, and he knelt down and prayed, saying, "Father, if you are willing, remove this cup from me. Nevertheless, not my will, but yours, be done." And an angel from Heaven appeared to him, strengthening him. (Luke 22:39-43)

---

1 Peter was one of Christ's Twelve Disciples.—Ed.

Muhammad ﷺ

Jesus

While he was still speaking, look, a crowd came, and he who was called Judas, one of the twelve, was leading them. He came near to Jesus to kiss him. But Jesus said to him, "Judas, do you betray the Son of Man with a kiss?" When those who were around him saw what was about to happen, they said to him, "Lord, should we strike with the sword?" A certain one of them struck the servant of the high priest, and cut off his right ear. But Jesus answered, "Let me at least do this"—and he touched his ear, and healed him. Jesus said to the chief priests, captains of the temple, and elders, who had come against him, "Have you come out as against a robber, with swords and clubs? When I was with you in the temple daily, you did not stretch out your hands against me. But this is your hour, and the power of darkness." (Luke 22:47-53)

Do you think that I could not ask my Father, and he would even now send me more than twelve legions of angels? How then would the Scriptures be fulfilled that it must be so? (Matthew 26:53-54)

Then Judas, who betrayed him, when he saw that Jesus was condemned, felt remorse, and returned the thirty pieces of silver to the chief priests and elders, saying, "I have sinned in that I betrayed innocent blood." But they said, "What is that to us? You see to it." He threw down the pieces of silver in the sanctuary, and departed. He went away and hanged himself. (Matthew 27:3-5)

Arrest

They seized him, and led him away, and brought him into the high priest's house. But Peter followed from a distance. When they had kindled a fire in the middle of the courtyard, and had sat down together, Peter sat among them. A certain servant girl saw him as he sat in the light, and looking intently at him, said, "This man also was with him." But he denied it, saying, "Woman, I do not know him." After a little while someone else saw him, and said, "You also are one of them." But Peter answered, "Man, I am not." After about one hour passed, another confidently affirmed, saying, "Truly this man also was with him, for he is a Galilean." But Peter said, "Man, I do not know what you are talking about." Immediately, while he was still speaking, a rooster crowed. The Lord turned, and looked at Peter. Then Peter remembered the Lord's word, how he said to him, "Before the rooster crows today, you will deny me three times." And Peter went out, and wept bitterly. The men who held Jesus mocked him and beat him. (Luke 22:54-63)

Muhammad ﷺ

Jesus

The whole company of them rose up and brought him before Pilate. They began to accuse him, saying, "We found this man perverting the nation, forbidding paying taxes to Caesar, and saying that he himself is the Messiah, a king." Pilate asked him, "Are you the King of the Jews?" He answered him, "You say so." Pilate said to the chief priests and the crowds, "I find no basis for a charge against this man." But they insisted, saying, "He stirs up the people, teaching throughout all Judea, beginning from Galilee even to this place." (Luke 23:1-5)

Pilate, wishing to please the crowd, released Barabbas to them, and handed over Jesus, when he had flogged him, to be crucified. The soldiers led him away within the court, which is the Praetorium; and they called together the whole cohort. They clothed him with purple, and weaving a crown of thorns, they put it on him. They began to salute him, "Hail, King of the Jews." They struck his head with a reed, and spat on him, and bowing their knees, did homage to him. When they had mocked him, they took the purple off of him, and put his own garments on him. They led him out to crucify him. (Mark 15:15-20)

Then Pilate went out again, and said to them, "Look, I am bringing him out to you, so that you may know that I find no basis for a charge against him." Then Jesus came out, wearing the crown of thorns and the purple garment. Pilate said to them, "Look, here is the man." So when the chief priests and the officers saw him, they shouted, saying, "Crucify. Crucify." Pilate said to them, "Take him yourselves, and crucify him, for I find no basis for a charge against him." The Jewish leaders answered him, "We have a law, and by our law he ought to die, because he made himself the Son of God." So when Pilate heard this saying, he was more afraid. He entered into the Praetorium again, and said to Jesus, "Where are you from?" But Jesus gave him no answer. Pilate therefore said to him, "Are you not speaking to me? Do you not know that I have power to release you, and have power to crucify you?" Jesus answered, "You would have no power at all against me, unless it were given to you from above. Therefore he who delivered me to you has greater sin." (John 19:4-11)

When they led him away, they grabbed one Simon of Cyrene, coming from the country, and placed on him the cross, to carry it after Jesus. A large crowd of the people followed him, including women who also mourned and lamented him. But Jesus, turning to them, said, "Daughters of Jerusalem, do not weep for me, but weep for yourselves and for your children. For look, the days are coming in which they will say, 'Blessed are the barren, the wombs that never bore, and the breasts that never nursed.' Then they will begin to tell the mountains, 'Fall on us,' and tell the hills, 'Cover us.' (Luke 23:26-30)

Jesus

So Pilate, seeing that nothing was being gained, but rather that a disturbance was starting, took water and he washed his hands before the crowd, saying, "I am innocent of the blood of this righteous man. You see to it." (Matthew 27:24)

Crucifixion

He went out, carrying the cross himself, to the place called "The Place of a Skull," which is called in Hebrew, "Golgotha," where they crucified him, and with him two others, on either side one, and Jesus in the middle. Pilate wrote a title also, and put it on the cross. There was written, "JESUS OF NAZARETH, THE KING OF THE JEWS." (John 19:17-19)

Then the soldiers, when they had crucified Jesus, took his clothes and made four parts, to every soldier a part; and also the tunic. Now the tunic was without seam, woven from the top throughout. Then they said to one another, "Let us not tear it, but cast lots for it to decide whose it will be," so that the Scripture might be fulfilled, which says, "They divided my clothes among them, and for my clothing they cast lots." Therefore the soldiers did these things. (John 19:23-24)

One of the criminals who hung there insulted him, saying, "If you are the Messiah, save yourself and us." But the other answered, and rebuking him said, "Do you not even fear God, seeing you are under the same condemnation? And we indeed justly, for we receive the due reward for our deeds; but this man has done nothing wrong." And he said to Jesus, "Lord, remember me when you come into your Kingdom." And Jesus said to him, "Assuredly I tell you, today you will be with me in Paradise." (Luke 23:39-43)

It was now about the sixth hour, and darkness came over the whole land until the ninth hour. The sun was darkened, and the veil of the temple was torn in two. And Jesus, crying with a loud voice, said, "Father, into your hands I commit my spirit." Having said this, he breathed his last. When the centurion saw what was done, he glorified God, saying, "Certainly this was a righteous man." (Luke 23:44-47)

Now from the sixth hour there was darkness over all the land until the ninth hour. About the ninth hour, Jesus called out with a loud voice, saying, "Eli, Eli, lema sabachthani?" That is, "My God, my God, why have you forsaken me?"[1] (Matthew 27:45-46)

---

1 From noon until 3 PM. Amos, a Jewish prophet, predicted through a vision in Amos 8:9: "It will happen in that day," says the Lord GOD, "that I will cause the sun to go down at noon, and I will darken the Earth in the clear day.—Ed.

Jesus

And Jesus cried out again with a loud voice, and yielded up his spirit. And look, the veil of the temple was torn in two from the top to the bottom. The Earth quaked and the rocks were split. The tombs were opened, and many bodies of the saints who had fallen asleep were raised; and coming out of the tombs after his resurrection, they entered into the holy city and appeared to many. (Matthew 27:50-53)

Burial

Joseph took the body, and wrapped it in a clean linen cloth, and placed it in his own new tomb, which he had cut out in the rock, and he rolled a great stone to the door of the tomb, and departed. Mary Magdalene was there, and the other Mary, sitting opposite the tomb. Now on the next day, which was the day after the Preparation Day, the chief priests and the Pharisees were gathered together to Pilate, saying, "Sir, we remember what that deceiver said while he was still alive: 'After three days I will rise again.' Command therefore that the tomb be made secure until the third day, lest perhaps his disciples come at night and steal him away, and tell the people, 'He is risen from the dead;' and the last deception will be worse than the first." Pilate said to them, "You have a guard. Go, make it as secure as you can." So they went with the guard and made the tomb secure, sealing the stone. (Matthew 27:59-66)

Resurrection

Now after the Sabbath, as it began to dawn on the first day of the week, Mary Magdalene and the other Mary came to see the tomb. And look, there was a great earthquake, for an angel of the Lord descended from the sky, and came and rolled away the stone from the door, and sat on it. His appearance was like lightning, and his clothing white as snow. For fear of him, the guards shook, and became like dead men. The angel answered the women, "Do not be afraid, for I know that you seek Jesus, who has been crucified. He is not here, for he has risen, just like he said. Come, see the place where the Lord was lying. Go quickly and tell his disciples, 'He has risen from the dead, and look, he goes before you into Galilee; there you will see him.' See, I have told you." They departed quickly from the tomb with fear and great joy, and ran to bring his disciples word. (Matthew 28:1-8)

And as they went to tell his disciples, suddenly Jesus met them, saying, "Rejoice." They came and took hold of his feet, and worshiped him. Then Jesus said to them, "Do not be afraid. Go tell my brothers that they should go into Galilee, and there they will see me." (Matthew 28:9-10)

Muhammad ﷺ

For their unbelief, and for their having uttered against Mary a grievous slander, saying: Surely we have killed the Messiah, Jesus son of Mary, the messenger of God. They did not kill him, nor did they crucify him, but (the matter) was made [to appear so] to them. Most surely those who differ about it are only in doubt about it—they have no knowledge regarding it, but only follow conjecture. They did not kill him, for sure. No! God [raised him up to Himself]; God is Mighty, Wise.

(The Women 4:156-158)

Jesus

Now while they were going, look, some of the guards came into the city, and told the chief priests all the things that had happened. When they were assembled with the elders, and had taken counsel, they gave a large amount of silver to the soldiers, saying, "Say that his disciples came by night, and stole him away while we slept. If this comes to the governor's ears, we will persuade him and make you free of worry." So they took the money and did as they were told. This saying was spread abroad among the Jewish people, and continues until this day. (Matthew 28:11-15)

But Mary was standing outside at the tomb weeping. So, as she wept, she stooped and looked into the tomb, and she saw two angels in white sitting, one at the head, and one at the feet, where the body of Jesus had lain. They told her, "Woman, why are you weeping?" She said to them, "Because they have taken away my Lord, and I do not know where they have put him." When she had said this, she turned around and saw Jesus standing, and did not know that it was Jesus. Jesus said to her, "Woman, why are you weeping? Who are you looking for?" She, supposing him to be the gardener, said to him, "Sir, if you have carried him away, tell me where you have put him, and I will take him away." Jesus said to her, "Mary." She turned and said to him, "Rabboni," which is to say, "Teacher." Jesus said to her, "Do not touch me, for I have not yet ascended to my Father; but go to my brothers, and tell them, 'I am ascending to my Father and your Father, to my God and your God.'" Mary Magdalene came and told the disciples that she had seen the Lord, and that he had said these things to her. (John 20:11-18)

So when it was evening on that day, the first day of the week, and when the doors were locked where the disciples were assembled, for fear of the Jewish leaders, Jesus came and stood in the midst, and said to them, "Peace be to you." When he had said this, he showed them his hands and his side. The disciples therefore were glad when they saw the Lord. Jesus therefore said to them again, "Peace be to you. As the Father has sent me, even so I send you." When he had said this, he breathed on them, and said to them, "Receive the Holy Spirit. Whoever's sins you forgive, they are forgiven them. Whoever's sins you retain, they have been retained." But Thomas, one of the twelve, called Didymus, was not with them when Jesus came. The other disciples therefore said to him, "We have seen the Lord." But he said to them, "Unless I see in his hands the print of the nails, and put my hand into his side, I will not believe." (John 20:19-25)

After eight days again his disciples were inside, and Thomas was with them. Jesus came, the doors being locked, and stood in the midst, and said, "Peace be to you." Then he said to Thomas, "Put your finger here, and observe my hands. Reach out your hand, and put it into my side; and do not be unbelieving, but believing." Thomas answered and said to him, "My Lord and my God." Jesus said to him, "Because you have seen me, you have believed. Blessed are those who have not seen, and have believed." (John 20:26-29)

Muhammad ﷺ

Jesus

As they said these things, Jesus himself stood among them, and said to them, "Peace be to you." But they were terrified and filled with fear, and supposed that they had seen a spirit. He said to them, "Why are you troubled? Why do doubts arise in your hearts? See my hands and my feet, that it is truly me. Touch me and see, for a spirit does not have flesh and bones, as you see that I have." When he had said this, he showed them his hands and his feet. While they still did not believe for joy, and wondered, he said to them, "Do you have anything here to eat?" And they gave him a piece of a broiled fish and some honeycomb. And he took it and ate in front of them. (Luke 24:36-43)

Simon Peter said to them, "I'm going fishing." They told him, "We are also coming with you." They immediately went out, and entered into the boat. That night, they caught nothing. But when day had already come, Jesus stood on the beach, yet the disciples did not know that it was Jesus. Jesus therefore said to them, "Children, have you anything to eat?" They answered him, "No." He said to them, "Cast the net on the right side of the boat, and you will find some." They cast it therefore, and now they weren't able to draw it in for the multitude of fish. That disciple therefore whom Jesus loved said to Peter, "It's the Lord." So when Simon Peter heard that it was the Lord, he wrapped his coat around him (for he was naked), and threw himself into the sea. But the other disciples came in the little boat (for they were not far from the land, but about two hundred cubits away), dragging the net full of fish. (John 21:3-8)

So when they got out on the land, they saw a fire of coals there, and fish placed on it, and bread. Jesus said to them, "Bring some of the fish which you have just caught." Simon Peter went up, and drew the net to land, full of great fish, one hundred fifty-three; and even though there were so many, the net was not torn. Jesus said to them, "Come and eat breakfast." None of the disciples dared inquire of him, "Who are you?" Knowing that it was the Lord. Then Jesus came and took the bread, gave it to them, and the fish likewise. This is now the third time that Jesus was revealed to his disciples, after he had risen from the dead. (John 21:9-14)

Ascension

He led them out as far as Bethany, and he lifted up his hands, and blessed them. It happened, while he blessed them, that he departed from them, and was carried up into Heaven. They worshiped him, and returned to Jerusalem with great joy, and were continually in the temple, praising and blessing God. Amen. (Luke 24:50-53)

Muhammad ﷺ

Life Outside of Time

Heaven

 Jesus

And again he said, "To what can I compare the Kingdom of God? It is like yeast, which a woman took and hid in three measures of flour, until it was all leavened." (Luke 13:20-21)

In my Father's house are many dwelling places. If it weren't so, I would have told you; for I am going to prepare a place for you. (John 14:2)

For when they will rise from the dead, they neither marry, nor are given in marriage, but are like angels in Heaven. (Mark 12:25)

Their cry there will be: Glory to You, Oh God! Their greeting there will be: Peace. And the last of their cry will be: Praise be to God, the Lord of the Worlds. (Jonah 10:10)

We made [constellations] in the Heaven, and We made it beautiful to the beholders. We guard it against every accursed devil, except he who steals a hearing—so there follows him a visible flame. (The Rock 15:16-18)

Surely those who guard (against evil) will be in the midst of gardens and fountains. Enter them in peace, secure. We will root out whatever rancour is in their breasts— (they will be) as brothers, on raised couches, face to face. Toil will not afflict them, nor will they ever be ejected from it. Inform My servants that I am the Forgiving, the Merciful, and that My chastisement is the painful chastisement. (The Rock 15:45-50)

See how We have made some excel over others. Certainly the Hereafter is much superior in degrees and much superior in excellence. (The Israelites 17:21)

Certainly We made seven ways above you, and We are never heedless of creation. (The Believers 23:17)

God has settled us in a house abiding forever, out of His grace. Toil will not touch us there, nor will fatigue afflict us. (The Originator 35:35)

We have adorned the nearest Heaven with an adornment, the stars, and (there is) a safeguard against every rebellious devil. They cannot listen to the exalted assembly, and they are pelted from every side. Driven off, for them is a perpetual punishment. Except he who snatches off but once—a brightly shining flame follows him. (The Rangers 37:6-10)

Except the servants of God, the purified ones. For them is a known sustenance, fruits, and they will be highly honoured, in gardens of pleasure, on thrones, facing each other. A bowl will be circulated among them, from water running out of springs, white, delicious to those who drink. There will be no trouble from it, nor [intoxication]. (The Rangers 37:40-47)

Those who believed in Our messages and were submissive: Enter the Garden, you and your wives. You will be made happy. (The Embellishment 43:69-70)

Jesus

Again, the Kingdom of Heaven is like a treasure hidden in the field, which a man found, and hid. In his joy, he goes and sells all that he has, and buys that field. Again, the Kingdom of Heaven is like a man who is a merchant seeking fine pearls, and having found one pearl of great price, he went and sold all that he had, and bought it. (Matthew 13:44-46)

I will give to you the keys of the Kingdom of Heaven, and whatever you bind on Earth will be bound in Heaven, and whatever you loose on Earth will be loosed in Heaven. (Matthew 16:19)

To what will we liken the Kingdom of God? Or with what parable will we use for it? It's like a grain of mustard seed, which, when it is sown in the earth, though it is less than all the seeds that are on the Earth, yet when it is sown, grows up, and becomes greater than all the herbs, and puts out great branches, so that the birds of the sky can lodge under its shadow. (Mark 4:30-32)

Muhammad ﷺ

Golden bowls and drinking-cups will be sent around to them, and what their souls yearn after and that in which their eyes delight will be there, and you will abide there. This is the Garden that you are given as an inheritance, on account of what you did. For you are many fruits that you will eat there. (The Embellishment 43:71-73)

A parable of the Garden, which those guarding (against evil) are promised: There are rivers of water that are unaltered, and rivers of milk, the taste which does not change, and rivers of wine delicious to those who drink, and rivers of clarified honey. For them there are all fruits and protection from their Lord. (Are these) like those who abide in the Fire, and who are made to drink boiling water that tears apart their bowels into pieces? (Muhammad 47:15)

Reclining on thrones set in lines, We will unite them to large-eyed ones. And (as for) those who believe and their offspring follow them in faith, We will unite them with their offspring. We will not diminish for them any of their works; every man is responsible for what he wrought. We will provide them with fruit and flesh, such as they desire. They will pass cup, from one to another. There will be nothing vain there, nor any sin. Their boys will circulate among them, as if they were hidden pearls. And some of them will approach others, inquiring, saying: Surely we feared before, on account of our families. But God has been gracious to us, and He has saved us from the chastisement of the hot wind. We called on Him before: Surely He is the Benign, the Merciful. (The Mountain 52:20-28)

There will be [maidens] who restrain their glances—neither man nor Jinn have touched them before. Which then of the bounties of your Lord will you [both] reject? As if they were rubies and pearls. Which then of the favors of your Lord will you [both] deny?[1] (The Beneficent 55:56-59)

And besides these two are two (other) gardens: Which then of the bounties of your Lord will you [both] reject? Both inclining to blackness. Which then of the bounties of your Lord will you [both] reject? In both of them are two springs gushing forth. Which then of the bounties of your Lord will you [both] reject? In both are fruits and palms and pomegranates. Which then of the bounties of your Lord will you [both] reject? In them are goodly things, beautiful ones. Which then of the bounties of your Lord will you [both] reject? Pure ones confined to the pavilions. Which then of the bounties of your Lord will you [both] reject? Man has not touched them before, nor Jinn. Which then of the bounties of your Lord will you [both] reject? Reclining on green cushions and beautiful carpets. Which then of the bounties of your Lord will you [both] reject? (The Beneficent 55:62-77)

---

1 Haleem, *The Qur'an*, 353. Both refers to mankind and Jinn.

Jesus

Concerning the resurrection of the dead, have you not read that which was spoken to you by God, saying, "I am the God of Abraham, and the God of Isaac, and the God of Jacob?" God is not the God of the dead, but of the living. (Matthew 22:31-38)

Muhammad

Then the companions of the right—who are the companions of the right? And the companions of the left—who are the companions of the left? And the foremost are the foremost, these are the nearest ones (to God), in the Gardens of Bliss. A numerous group from the first, and a few from among the latter. On decorated thrones, reclining on them, facing one another. Immortal [boys] will circulate among them, with goblets and jugs and a cup of pure drink. They will not be affected with headache from it, nor will they get [intoxicated]. And fruits such as they choose, and the flesh of fowls, such as they desire. And pure, beautiful ones, like hidden pearls. A reward for what they used to do. They will not hear vain talk or sinful discourse, only the word: Peace, peace. (The Great Event 56:8-26)

God is He who created seven Heavens, and of the Earth the like of them. The decree continues to descend among them, so that you may know that God has power over all things and that God indeed encompasses all things in (His) knowledge. (The Divorce 65:12)

Surely for those who guard (against evil) is achievement, gardens and vineyards. And those showing freshness of youth, equals in age, and a full cup. They will not hear any vain words or lying. A reward from your Lord, a gift according to a reckoning— the Lord of the Heavens and the Earth and what is between them, the Beneficent God. They will not be able to address Him. (The Announcement 78:31-37)

Entering Heaven

 Jesus

Truly, truly, I tell you, he who believes in me has eternal life. I am the bread of life. Your fathers ate the manna in the wilderness, and they died. This is the bread that comes down out of Heaven, so that anyone may eat of it and not die. (John 6:47-50)

Truly I tell you, unless you turn, and become as little children, you will in no way enter into the Kingdom of Heaven. Whoever therefore humbles himself as this little child, the same is the greatest in the Kingdom of Heaven. Whoever receives one such little child in my name receives me. (Matthew 18:3-5)

Not everyone who says to me, "Lord, Lord," will enter into the Kingdom of Heaven; but he who does the will of my Father who is in Heaven. (Matthew 7:21)

Surely those who believe, and those who are Jews, and the Christians, and the Sabians—whoever believes in God and the Last Day and does good—they will have their reward with their Lord, and there is no fear for them, nor will they grieve. (The Cow 2:62)

Yes! Whoever earns evil and his sins surround him, these are the inmates of the fire: They will live in it. (As for) those who believe and do good deeds, these are the dwellers of the Garden: They will live in it. (The Cow 2:81-82)

Do not speak of those who are slain in God's way as dead. No, (they are) alive, but you do not perceive it. (The Cow 2:154)

And how many a prophet has fought alongside many worshippers of the Lord. They did not become weak-hearted because of what befell them in God's way, nor did they weaken or lower themselves. God loves the patient. And their saying was only this: Our Lord! Forgive us our faults and our extravagance in our affairs, and make firm our feet, and help us against the unbelieving people. So God gave them the reward of this world and better reward of the Hereafter. God loves those who do good (to others). (The Family of Amran 3:146-148)

Do not think of those who are killed in God's way as dead. No, they are alive, and they are provided sustenance from their Lord, rejoicing in what God has given them out of His grace. They rejoice for those who are (left) behind, who have not yet joined them, that they will have no fear, nor will they grieve. (The Family of Amran 3:169-170)

So their Lord accepted their prayer: I will not waste the works of the worker among you, whether male or female, each of you from the other. Therefore those who fled and were turned out of their homes and persecuted in My way, and who fought and were slain, I will most certainly cover their evil deeds, and I will most certainly admit them to gardens, beneath which rivers flow—a reward from God, and with God is yet better reward. (The Family of Amran 3:195)

Those who are careful of (their duty to) their Lord will have Gardens beneath which rivers flow, abiding in them; an entertainment from their Lord. What is with God is best for the righteous. (The Family of Amran 3:198)

These are God's limits. Whoever obeys God and His Messenger, He will cause him to enter Gardens beneath which rivers flow, to abide in them. This is the great achievement. (The Women 4:13)

Jesus

They were bringing to him little children, that he should touch them, but the disciples rebuked those who were bringing them. But when Jesus saw it, he was moved with indignation, and said to them, "Allow the little children to come to me. Do not forbid them, for the Kingdom of God belongs to such as these. Truly I tell you, whoever will not receive the Kingdom of God like a little child, he will in no way enter into it." And he took them in his arms, laying his hands on them, and blessed them. As he was going out into the way, one ran to him, knelt before him, and asked him, "Good Teacher, what must I do that I may inherit eternal life?" Jesus said to him, "Why do you call me good? No one is good except one—God. You know the commandments: 'Do not commit adultery,' 'Do not murder,' 'Do not steal,' 'Do not give false testimony,' 'Do not defraud,' 'Honor your father and mother.'" And he said to him, "Teacher, I have kept all these things from my youth." Jesus looking at him loved him, and said to him, "One thing you lack. Go, sell whatever you have, and give to the poor, and you will have treasure in Heaven; and come, follow me, taking up the cross." (Mark 10:13-21)

Strive to enter in by the narrow gate, for many, I tell you, will seek to enter in, and will not be able. When once the master of the house has risen up, and has shut the door, and you begin to stand outside, and to knock at the door, saying, "Lord, Lord, open to us," He will answer and tell you, "I do not know you or where you come from." Then you will begin to say, "We ate and drank in your presence, and you taught in our streets." He will say, "I tell you, I do not know where you come from. Depart from me, all you workers of iniquity." There will be weeping and gnashing of teeth, when you see Abraham, Isaac, Jacob, and all the prophets, in the Kingdom of God, and yourselves being thrown outside. They will come from the East, West, North, and South, and will sit down in the Kingdom of God. And look, there are some who are last who will be first, and there are some who are first who will be last. (Luke 13:24-30)

Muhammad ﷺ

If you shun the great things that you are forbidden, We will do away with your evil [deeds] and admit you to an honourable entrance.
(The Women 4:31)

(As for) those who believe and do good deeds, We will make them enter Gardens beneath which rivers flow, to live in them forever; they will have there pure mates. We will admit them in dense shade. (The Women 4:57)

[Prophet], have you not considered those to whom it was said: Withhold your hands, and keep up prayer, and pay the poor-rate? But when fighting is prescribed for them, lo! A group of them feared men as they should have feared God, or (even) with a greater fear, and they say: Our Lord! Why have You ordained fighting for us? Why don't You grant us a delay for a while? Say: The [enjoyment] of this world is short, and the Hereafter is better for he who guards against evil. You will not be wronged so much as the husk of a date-stone. (The Women 4:77)

Whoever emigrates in God's way will find many a place of refuge and abundant resources on the Earth. Whoever goes forth from his house as an emigrant for God and His Messenger, and then death overtakes him, his reward is indeed with God, and God is Forgiving, Merciful. (The Women 4:100)

(As for) those who believe and do good, We will make them enter into Gardens beneath which rivers flow, to abide there forever. (It is) a promise of God, true (indeed)—who is truer of word than God? (This) will not be in accordance with your vain desires nor in accordance with the vain desires of the Followers of the Book. Whoever does evil will be reunited with it, and he will find for himself neither a guardian nor a helper besides God. And whoever does good deeds, whether male or female, and he (or she) is a believer—these will enter the Garden, and they will not be dealt unjustly by as much as the speck [on a date seed]. (The Women 4:122-124)

Jesus

For God so loved the world that He gave his only Son, so that whoever believes in him will not perish, but have eternal life. (John 3:16)

Do not work for the food that perishes, but for the food that remains to eternal life, which the Son of Man will give to you. For God the Father has sealed him. (John 6:27)

This is eternal life, so that they may know You, the only true God, and him whom You sent, Jesus Christ. (John 17:3)

My sheep hear my voice, and I know them, and they follow me. I give eternal life to them. They will never perish, and no one will snatch them out of my hand. That which my Father has given me is more important than anything. No one is able to snatch them out of my Father's hand. (John 10:27-29)

I am the living bread which came down out of Heaven. If anyone eats of this bread, he will live forever; and the bread which I will give for the life of the world is my flesh. This is the bread which came down out of Heaven—not as our fathers ate the manna, and died. He who eats this bread will live forever. It is the spirit who gives life. The flesh profits nothing. The words that I speak to you are spirit, and are life. (John 5:51, 58, 63)

Truly, truly, I tell you, if a person keeps my word, he will never see death. (John 8:51)

Muhammad ﷺ

If the Followers of the Book had believed and guarded (against evil), We certainly would have covered their evil deeds, and We would have certainly admitted them to gardens of bliss. If they had observed the Torah and the Gospel and what was revealed to them from their Lord, they would have certainly eaten from above and from beneath their feet. There is a group of them keeping to the moderate course, but (as for) most of them, evil is what they do. (The Food 5:65-66)

This world's life is nothing but a play and an idle sport. Certainly the abode of the Hereafter is better for those who guard (against evil). Do you not then understand? (The Cattle 6:32)

This is the path of your Lord, (a) right (path). Indeed, We have made the Verses clear for a people who take heed. They will have the Abode of Peace with their Lord, and He is their guardian because of what they did. (The Cattle 6:126-127)

Oh, you who believe! What excuse have you, when it is said to you, Go forth in God's way, you incline heavily to the Earth? Are you contented with this world's life instead of the Hereafter? The provision of this world's life compared with the Hereafter is but little. If you do not go forth, He will chastise you with a painful chastisement, and replace you with a people other than yourselves, and you will do Him no harm. God has power over all things. (The Immunity 9:38-39)

God has promised to the believing men and the believing women Gardens, beneath which rivers flow, to abide in them. And goodly dwellings in Gardens of Perpetual Abode. Best of all is God's goodly pleasure—that is the grand achievement. (The Immunity 9:72)

Surely, God has bought from the believers their lives and their wealth for this: that they will have the Garden. They fight in God's way, so they slay and are slain—a promise that is binding on Him in the Torah and the Gospel and the Qur'an. Who is more faithful to his covenant than God? So rejoice in the pledge that you have made; that is the mighty achievement. (The Immunity 9:111)

Surely, the friends of God will have no fear, nor will they grieve. Those who believe and guard (against evil) will have good news in this world's life and in the Hereafter. There is no changing the words of God—this is the mighty achievement. (Jonah 10:62-64)

Jesus

Truly, truly, I tell you, the hour comes, and now is, when the dead will hear the Son of God's voice; and those who hear will live. For as the Father has life in himself, even so he gave to the Son also to have life in himself. He also gave him authority to execute judgment, because he is a Son of Man. (John 5:25-27)

Truly, truly, I tell you, unless one is born of water and the Spirit he cannot enter into the Kingdom of God. That which is born of the flesh is flesh. That which is born of the Spirit is spirit. Do not marvel that I said to you, "You must be born again." The wind blows where it wants to, and you hear its sound, but do not know where it comes from and where it is going. So is everyone who is born of the Spirit. (John 3:5-8)

Whoever drinks of the water that I will give him will never thirst again; but the water that I will give him will become in him a well of water springing up to eternal life. (John 4:14)

Muhammad ﷺ

Say, [Prophet]: This is my way—I call to God, I and those who follow me being certain, glory to God. I am not one of the polytheists. We have sent before you only men from (among) the people of the towns, to whom We sent revelations. Have they not travelled in the land and seen the end of those before them? Certainly the abode of the Hereafter is best for those who [fear] God; do you not understand? (Joseph 12:108-109)

Those who fulfill the promise of God and do not break the covenant. Those who join what God has bid to be joined and have awe of their Lord and fear the Evil Reckoning. Those who are constant, seeking the pleasure of their Lord, and who keep up prayer and spend (benevolently) out of what We have given them. Who secretly and openly repel evil with good. These will have the (happy) issue of the abode, the Gardens of Perpetual Abode that they will enter along with those who do good among their parents, spouses and offspring. The angels will enter upon them from every gate. (The Thunder 13:20-23)

God confirms those who believe in the Sure Word, in this world's life and in the Hereafter, and God causes the unjust to go astray. God does what He pleases. (Abraham 14:27)

It is said to those who guard (against evil): What has your Lord revealed? They say: Good. Good is for those who do good in this world, and certainly the Abode of the Hereafter is better. Certainly most excellent is the abode of those who guard (against evil). They will enter the Gardens of Perpetuity, with rivers flowing beneath them. They will have in them what they please. Thus does God reward those who guard (against evil), those whom the angels cause to die in a good state, saying: Peace be on you, enter the Garden for what you did. (The Bee 16:30-32)

Those who emigrate for God's sake after they are oppressed, We will most certainly give them a good abode in the world, and the reward of the Hereafter is certainly much greater: if they only knew. Those who are patient and rely on their Lord. (The Bee 16:41-42)

Whoever desires the Hereafter and strives for it as he ought to strive, and he is a believer, his striving will be gratefully accepted. (The Israelites 17:19)

Jesus

This is the will of the One who sent me, that everyone who sees the Son, and believes in him, should have eternal life; and I will raise him up at the last day. (John 6:40)

Truly, truly, I tell you, he who hears my word, and believes Him who sent me, has eternal life, and does not come into judgment, but has passed out of death into life. (John 5:24)

Muhammad ﷺ

Surely God will make those who believe and do good deeds enter Gardens beneath which rivers flow. They will be adorned with bracelets of gold and (with) pearls, and their garments will be of silk. (The Pilgrimage 22:23)

God will most certainly grant a good sustenance to those who fled in God's way and then were slain or died. Most surely, God is the best giver of sustenance. He will certainly admit them to an entrance that they will be well pleased with. Most surely God is Knowing, Forbearing. (The Pilgrimage 22:58-59)

Maybe he who repents and believes and does good will be among the successful. Your Lord creates and chooses whom He pleases—they have no choice. Glory be to God, and exalted is He, above what they associate (with Him). Your Lord knows what their breasts conceal and what they declare. (The Narrative 28:67-69)

Those who believe and do good, We will certainly give them abode in the high places in Gardens beneath which rivers flow, abiding there. How good is the reward of the workers—those who are patient and rely on their Lord. (The Spider 29:58-59)

Then, we are not going to die, except our previous death? And we will not be chastised? Most surely this is the mighty achievement. For the like of this then, let the workers work. Is this better entertainment, or the Tree of Zaqqum? Surely We have made [the tree] as a trial for the [wrongdoers]. Indeed it is a tree that grows in the bottom of Hell; its produce is like the heads of the serpents. Then most surely they will eat it and fill (their) bellies, and then most surely afterward they will drink a mixture prepared with boiling water. Then most surely their return will be to Hell. (The Rangers 37:58-68)

Those who are careful of (their duty to) their Lord will be conveyed to the Garden in groups. When they arrive, its doors will open, and the keepers of it will say to them: Peace be on you, you shall be happy; so enter, to abide. And they will say: (All) praise is due to God, Who has made good to us His promise. He has made us inherit the land— we may abide in the Garden where we please; so excellent is the reward of the workers. And you will see the angels going round about the throne, glorifying the praise of their Lord. Judgment will be given between them, with justice, and it will be said: All praise is due to God, the Lord of the Worlds. (The Companies 39:73-75)

The angels descend on those who say: Our Lord is God, and then continue in the right way. The angels say: Do not fear or grieve. Receive the good news of the Garden, which you were promised. We are your guardians in this world's life and in the Hereafter, and you will have there whatever your souls desire and what you ask for— an entertainment by the Forgiving, the Merciful. (Ha Mim 41:30-32)

Jesus

It is like a man, going on a journey, who called his own servants, and entrusted his goods to them. To one he gave five talents, to another two, to another one; to each according to his own ability. Then he went on his journey. Immediately the one who received the five talents went and traded with them, and made another five talents. In like manner he who got the two gained another two But he who received the one went away and dug in the earth, and hid his lord's money. Now after a long time the lord of those servants came, and reconciled accounts with them. And he who received the five talents came and brought another five talents, saying, "Lord, you delivered to me five talents. See, I have gained another five talents." His lord said to him, "Well done, good and faithful servant. You have been faithful over a few things, I will set you over many things. Enter into the joy of your lord." And he also who had the two talents came and said, "Lord, you delivered to me two talents. See, I have gained another two talents besides them." His lord said to him, "Well done, good and faithful servant. You have been faithful over a few things, I will set you over many things. Enter into the joy of your lord." He also who had received the one talent came and said, "Lord, I knew you that you are a hard man, reaping where you did not sow, and gathering where you did not scatter. I was afraid, and went away and hid your talent in the earth. See, you have what is yours.' But his lord answered him, 'You wicked and slothful servant. You knew that I reap where I did not sow, and gather where I did not scatter. You ought therefore to have deposited my money with the bankers, and at my coming I should have received back my own with interest. Take away therefore the talent from him, and give it to him who has the ten talents. For to everyone who has will be given, and he will have abundance, but from him who does not have, even that which he has will be taken away. Throw out the unprofitable servant into the outer darkness, where there will be weeping and gnashing of teeth." (Matthew 25:14-30)

Muhammad ﷺ

We will give whoever desires the gain of the Hereafter more of that gain. We will give of this world whoever desires the gain of this world, and he has no portion in the Hereafter. (The Counsel 42:20)

So when you meet those who disbelieve in battle, strike their necks until you have overcome them, and then make them prisoners, and afterwards either set them free as a favour, or let them ransom (themselves) until the war ends. That (shall be so). If God had pleased, He certainly could have taken retribution on them, but He tests some of you by means of others. Regarding those who are slain in the way of God— He will by no means cause their deeds to perish. He will guide them and improve their condition and admit them to the Garden, which He has made known to them. (Muhammad 47:4-6)

Surely, God will make those who believe and do good enter Gardens beneath which rivers flow; and those who disbelieve enjoy themselves and eat as the beasts eat, and the Fire is their abode. (Muhammad 47:12)

Say to those of the Bedouins who were left behind: You will soon be invited (to fight) against a people possessing mighty prowess. You will fight against them until they submit. If you obey, God will grant you a good reward, but if you turn back as you turned back before, He will chastise you with a painful chastisement. There is no blame on the blind, the lame, or the sick (if they do not go forth). God will admit whoever obeys God and His Messenger to Gardens beneath which rivers flow, but He will chastise whoever turns back, with a painful chastisement. (The Victory 48:16-17)

This is what you were promised—(it is) for every one who turns frequently (to God) and keeps (His limits). Who fears the Beneficent God in secret and comes with a penitent heart: Enter it in peace, that is the Day of [Eternity]. They have what they wish there, and with Us is more yet. (Qaf 50:32-35)

Surely those who guard (against evil) will be in gardens and fountains, taking what their Lord gives them. Surely they were the doers of good. They used to sleep little in the night, and in the morning they asked forgiveness. In their wealth was a portion due to he who begs and he who is [deprived]. (The Scatterers 51:15-19)

Jesus

Whoever believes in the Son has eternal life, but whoever refuses to believe in the Son won't see life, but the wrath of God remains on him. (John 3:36)

Then the King will tell those on his right hand, "Come, blessed of my Father, inherit the Kingdom prepared for you from the foundation of the world; for I was hungry, and you gave Me food to eat. I was thirsty, and you gave Me drink. I was a stranger, and you took Me in. I was naked, and you clothed Me. I was sick, and you visited Me. I was in prison, and you came to Me." Then the righteous will answer Him, saying, "Lord, when did we see You hungry, and feed You; or thirsty, and give You a drink? When did we see You as a stranger, and take You in; or naked, and clothe You? When did we see You sick, or in prison, and come to You?" The King will answer them, "Truly I tell you, inasmuch as you did it to one of the least of these My brothers, you did it to Me." (Matthew 25:34-40)

The Kingdom of God is as if a man should scatter seed on the earth, and should sleep and rise night and day, and the seed should spring up and grow, he does not know how. The earth bears fruit, first the blade, then the ear, then the full grain in the ear. But when the fruit is ripe, immediately he puts forth the sickle, because the harvest has come. (Mark 4:26-29)

Muhammad ﷺ

What reason have you to not spend in God's way? God's is the inheritance of the Heavens and the Earth. Those among you who spent before the victory and fought are not alike with (those who did not).[1] Those who spent before and fought are more exalted in rank than those who spent and fought afterwards. God has promised good to all, and God is Aware of what you do. Who will offer to God a good gift, so that He will double it for him, and he will have an excellent reward. On that Day, you will see the faithful men and women—their lights running before them and on their right hand—good news for you today. Gardens beneath which rivers flow, to live there, that is the grand achievement. (The Iron 57:10-12)

Hasten to forgiveness from your Lord and to a Garden, as extensive as the Heaven and the Earth. It is prepared for those who believe in God and His messengers— that is the grace of God. He gives it to whom He pleases, and God is the Lord of mighty grace. (The Iron 57:21)

You will not find a people who believe in God and the Latter Day [loving] those who act in opposition to God and His Messenger, even if they are their (own) fathers, or their sons, or their brothers, or their kinsfolk. These are those into whose hearts He has impressed faith, and whom He has strengthened with a [spirit] from Him. He will cause them to enter Gardens beneath which rivers flow, abiding there. God is well-pleased with them, and they are well-pleased with Him. These are God's party— surely, the party of God are the successful ones. (The Pleading One 58:22)

Believe in God and His Messenger, and struggle hard in God's way with your wealth and your lives. That is better for you, if only you knew! He will forgive you your faults and admit you into Gardens beneath which rivers flow, and to goodly dwellings in Gardens of Eternity; that is the mighty achievement. (The Ranks 61:11-12)

Therefore believe in God and His Messenger and the Light which We have revealed; God is aware of what you do. On the day that He gathers you for the Day of Gathering, that is the Day of the Manifestation of Defects. Whoever believes in God and does good, He will remove from him his evil and cause him to enter Gardens beneath which rivers flow, to abide there forever. That is the great achievement. (The Manifestation of Defects 64:8-9)

---

1 Ali, M.M., *The Holy Qur'an*, 1044. The victory is the conquest of Mecca.

Jesus

He entered and was passing through Jericho. And look, there was a man named Zacchaeus. He was a chief tax collector, and he was rich. He was trying to see who Jesus was, and could not because of the crowd, because he was short. He ran on ahead, and climbed up into a sycamore tree to see him, for he was to pass that way. When Jesus came to the place, he looked up and saw him, and said to him, "Zacchaeus, hurry and come down, for today I must stay at your house." He hurried, came down, and received him joyfully. And when they saw it, they all murmured, saying, "He has gone in to lodge with a man who is a sinner." And Zacchaeus stood and said to the Lord, "Look, Lord, half of my goods I give to the poor. If I have wrongfully exacted anything of anyone, I restore four times as much." Jesus said to him, "Today, salvation has come to this house, because he also is a son of Abraham. (Luke 19:1-9)

Muhammad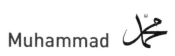

Oh, you who believe! Turn to God with sincere [repentance]—maybe your Lord will remove from you your evil and cause you to enter Gardens beneath which rivers flow, on the Day on which God will not disgrace the Prophet and those who believe with him. Their light will run before them and on their right. They will say: Our Lord! Make our light perfect, and grant us [forgiveness]—surely You have power over all things. (The Prohibition 66:8)

As for he who fears to stand in the presence of his Lord and forbids the soul from low desires, surely the Garden—that is the abode. (The Drawers 79:40-41)

Oh, soul that is at rest! Return to your Lord, well-pleased, well pleasing. Enter among My servants, and enter into My Garden. (The Daybreak 89:27-30)

End Times

 Jesus

You will hear of wars and rumors of wars. See that you are not troubled, for all this must happen, but the end is not yet. For nation will rise against nation, and kingdom against kingdom; and there will be famines and earthquakes in various places. But all these things are the beginning of birth pains. Then they will deliver you up to oppression, and will kill you. You will be hated by all of the nations for my name's sake. Then many will stumble, and will deliver up one another, and will hate one another. Many false prophets will arise, and will lead many astray. And because lawlessness is multiplied, the love of many will grow cold. But he who endures to the end, the same will be saved. This Good News of the Kingdom will be preached in the whole world for a testimony to all the nations, and then the end will come. (Matthew 24:6-14)

But immediately after the oppression of those days, the sun will be darkened, the moon will not give its light, the stars will fall from Heaven, and the powers of the heavens will be shaken; and then the sign of the Son of Man will appear in the sky. Then all the tribes of the Earth will mourn, and they will see the Son of Man coming on the clouds of the sky, with power and great glory. He will send out his angels with a loud trumpet blast, and they will gather together his chosen ones from the four winds, from one end of the sky to the other. Now from the fig tree learn this parable. When its branch has now become tender, and puts forth its leaves, you know that the summer is near. Even so you also, when you see all these things know that it is near, even at the doors. (Matthew 24:29-33)

Again, the Kingdom of Heaven is like a dragnet, that was cast into the sea, and gathered some fish of every kind, which, when it was filled, they drew up on the beach. They sat down, and gathered the good into containers, but the bad they threw away. So will it be in the end of the world. The angels will come forth, and separate the wicked from among the righteous, and will cast them into the furnace of fire. There will be the weeping and the gnashing of teeth. (Matthew 13:47-50)

But when the Son of Man comes in his glory, and all the holy angels with him, then he will sit on the throne of his glory. Before him all the nations will be gathered, and he will separate them one from another, as a shepherd separates the sheep from the goats. He will set the sheep on his right hand, but the goats on the left. (Matthew 25:31-33)

God said: Oh, Jesus! I will cause you to die, and [raise you to Myself], and clear you of those who disbelieved, and I will make those who follow you above those who disbelieve, to the Day of Resurrection. Then to Me is your return, and I will decide between you concerning that in which you differed. (The Family of Amran 3:55)

On the Day when (some) faces will turn white and (some) faces will turn black— to those whose faces turn black: Did you disbelieve after believing? Taste the chastisement because you disbelieved. But as for those whose faces turn white, they will be in God's mercy. They will abide in it. (The Family of Amran 3:106-107)

How will it be, then, when We bring from every people a witness, and We bring you, [Oh, Muhammad], as a witness against them? On that Day, those who disbelieve and disobey the Messenger will wish that the Earth be leveled with them. They will not be able to hide any word from God. (The Women 4:41-42)

Jesus

For the Son of Man will come in the glory of his Father with his angels, and then he will render to everyone according to his deeds. (Matthew 16:27)

But of that day or the hour no one knows, not even the angels in Heaven, nor the Son, but only the Father. (Mark 13:32)

But know this, that if the master of the house had known in what hour the thief was coming, he would have watched and not have allowed his house to be broken into. Therefore be ready also, for the Son of Man is coming in an hour that you do not expect him. (Luke 12:39-40)

The days will come, when you will desire to see one of the days of the Son of Man, and you will not see it. And they will tell you, "Look, there," or "Look, here." Do not go away or follow after them, for as the lightning, when it flashes out of the one part under the sky, shines to the other part under the sky; so will the Son of Man be in his day. (Luke 17:22-24)

And if I go and prepare a place for you, I will come again, and will receive you to myself; that where I am, you may be there also. And you know where I am going, and you know the way." (John 14:3-4)

Muhammad ﷺ

Most certainly, We will question those to whom (the messengers) were sent, and most certainly, We will also question the messengers. We will relate to them with knowledge. We were not absent. The measuring out on that Day will be just. As for those whose measure (of good deeds) is heavy, they will be successful; and as for those whose measure (of good deeds) is light, they have made their souls suffer loss because they disbelieved in Our Verses. (The Elevated Places 7:6-9)

For every nation is a doom. So when their doom comes, they will not remain behind the least while, nor will they go before. (The Elevated Places 7:34)

The inmates of the Fire will call out to the dwellers of the Garden, saying: Pour on us some water or some of what God has given you. The dwellers will say: Surely God has prohibited them both to the unbelievers, who took their religion for an idle sport and play, and who were deceived by this life's world. So today, We forsake them, as they neglected the meeting of this, their Day, and they denied Our Verses. (The Elevated Places 7:50-51)

Every nation has a messenger. When their messenger came, the matter was decided between them with justice, and they will not be dealt with unjustly. They say: When will this threat come about, if you are truthful? Say, [Prophet]: I do not control any harm or any benefit for myself, except what God pleases. Every nation has a term; when their term comes, they will not remain behind for an hour, nor can they go before (their time). (Jonah 10:47-49)

We will deliver Our messengers and those who believe—it is binding on Us (that) We deliver the believers. (Jonah 10:103)

Jesus

Likewise, even as it happened in the days of Lot: they ate, they drank, they bought, they sold, they planted, they built; but in the day that Lot went out from Sodom, it rained fire and sulfur from the sky, and destroyed them all. It will be the same way in the day that the Son of Man is revealed. In that day, he who will be on the housetop, and his goods in the house, let him not go down to take them away. Let him who is in the field likewise not turn back. Remember Lot's wife. Whoever seeks to keep his life will lose it, but whoever loses it will preserve it. I tell you, in that night there will be two people in one bed. The one will be taken, and the other will be left. There will be two grinding grain together. One will be taken, and the other will be left.
(Luke 17:28-36)

Do not marvel at this, for the hour comes, in which all that are in the tombs will hear His voice, and will come out; those who have done good, to the resurrection of life; and those who have done evil, to the resurrection of judgment. I can of myself do nothing. As I hear, I judge, and my judgment is righteous; because I do not seek my own will, but the will of the my Father who sent me. (John 5:28-30)

Muhammad ﷺ

Most surely there is a sign in this for those who fear the chastisement of the Hereafter; this is a Day on which the people will be gathered, and this is a day that will be witnessed. We do not delay it, except to an appointed term. When the Day comes, no soul will speak, except with His permission. (Some) of them will be the unhappy, and others happy. Those who are unhappy will be in the Fire; for them will be sighing and groaning, abiding there as long as the Heavens and the Earth endure, except as your Lord pleases. Surely your Lord is the mighty doer of what He intends. Those who are happy will be in the Garden, abiding in it as long as the Heavens and the Earth endure, except as your Lord pleases—a gift that will never be cut off. (Hud 11:103-108)

Do not think that God will fail to keep His promise to His messengers; surely God is Mighty, the Lord of Retribution. On the Day when the Earth will be changed into a different Earth, and the Heavens (as well), they will come before God, the One, Supreme. You will see the guilty on that Day, linked together in chains. Their shirts made of pitch, and the fire covering their faces, so that God may repay each soul for what it earned. Surely God is swift in reckoning. (Abraham 14:47-51)

On the Resurrection Day, He will disgrace them, and say: Where are the associates that you gave Me, for whose sake you became hostile? Those who are given the knowledge will say: Surely the disgrace and the evil are upon the unbelievers this Day—those whom the angels cause to die while they are unjust to themselves. Then they will offer submission: We did not do any evil. Yes! Surely God knows what you did. So enter the gates of Hell, to abide there; certainly evil is the dwelling place of the proud. (The Bee 16:27-29)

On the Day when We will raise up in every people a witness against them from among themselves, and bring you [Muhammad,] as a witness against them. We have revealed the Book to you clearly explaining everything, and as a guidance, mercy and good news for those who submit. (The Bee 16:89)

They ask you about the mountains. Say: My Lord will [blast] them [into particles], and then leave a plain, smooth and level. You will not see any crookedness or unevenness. On that day they will follow the Inviter, there is no crookedness in him, and the voices will be low before the Beneficent God, so that you will hear only a soft sound. On that Day, no intercession will be an advantage, except from him whom the Beneficent God allows, and whose word He is pleased with. (Ta Ha 20:105-109)

Jesus

Then two men will be in the field: one will be taken and one will be left; two women grinding at the mill, one will be taken and one will be left. Watch therefore, for you do not know on what hour your Lord comes. (Matthew 24:40-42)

But when you see Jerusalem surrounded by armies, then know that its desolation is near. Then let those who are in Judea flee to the mountains. Let those who are in the midst of her depart. Let those who are in the country not enter therein. For these are days of vengeance, that all things which are written may be fulfilled. Woe to those who are pregnant and to those who nurse infants in those days. For there will be great distress in the land, and wrath to this people. They will fall by the edge of the sword, and will be led captive into all the nations. Jerusalem will be trampled down by the Gentiles, until the times of the Gentiles are fulfilled. There will be signs in the sun, moon, and stars; and on the Earth anxiety of nations, in perplexity for the roaring of the sea and the waves; men fainting for fear, and for expectation of the things which are coming on the world: for the powers of the heavens will be shaken. Then they will see the Son of Man coming in a cloud with power and great glory. But when these things begin to happen, look up, and lift up your heads, because your redemption is near. (Luke 21:20-28)

The Son of Man will send out his angels, and they will gather out of his Kingdom all things that cause stumbling, and those who do iniquity, and will cast them into the furnace of fire. There will be weeping and the gnashing of teeth. Then the righteous will shine forth like the sun in the Kingdom of their Father. He who has ears to hear, let him hear. (Matthew 13:41-43)

Muhammad ﷺ

We will set up a just balance on the Day of Resurrection, so that no soul will be dealt with unjustly in the least. If there is even the weight of a mustard seed, We will bring it. Sufficient are We to take account. (The Prophets 21:47)

On the Day, We will roll up Heaven, like the rolling up of the scroll for writings. We originated the first creation, (so) We will reproduce it—a promise (binding) on Us. Surely We will bring it about. (The Prophets 21:104)

Oh, people! Guard against (the punishment from) your Lord; surely the violence of the hour is a grievous thing. On the Day when you will see it, every woman giving suck will quit in confusion over what she suckled, and every pregnant woman will lay down her burden, and you will see men intoxicated, but they will not be intoxicated. The chastisement of God will be severe. (The Pilgrimage 22:1-2)

Surely those who believe and those who are Jews and the Sabeans and the Christians and the Magians and those who are polytheists, surely God will decide between them on the Day of Resurrection. Surely God is a witness over all things. (The Pilgrimage 22:17)

They reject the Hour, and We have prepared a burning Fire for those who reject the Hour. When it comes into their sight from a distant place, they will hear its vehement raging and roaring. And when they are cast into a narrow place in it, bound, they will call out for destruction. (The Distinction 25:11-13)

On the Day when the Heaven will burst apart with the clouds, and the angels will be sent down, the Kingdom on that day will rightly belong to the Beneficent God, and it will be a hard day for the unbelievers. The Day when the [wrongdoer] will bite his hands, saying: Oh! If only I had taken a way with the Messenger! Oh, woe is me! If only I had not taken that one for a friend! Certainly he led me astray from the Reminder after it had come to me. The Devil fails to aid man. (The Distinction 25:25-29)

When the word comes to pass against them, We will bring forth for them a creature from the Earth that will wound them, because people did not believe in Our messages. (The Naml 27:82)

Jesus

The Kingdom of Heaven is like a man who sowed good seed in his field, but while people slept, his enemy came and sowed tares also among the wheat, and went away. But when the blade sprang up and brought forth fruit, then the tares appeared also. So the servants of the householder came and said to him, "Sir, did you not sow good seed in your field? Where did these tares come from?" And he said to them, "An enemy has done this." And the servants asked him, "Then do you want us to go and gather them up?" But he said, "No, lest perhaps while you gather up the tares, you root up the wheat with them. Let both grow together until the harvest, and in the harvest time I will tell the reapers, 'First, gather up the tares, and bind them in bundles to burn them; but gather the wheat into my barn.'" (Matthew 13:24-30)

The one who sows the good seed is the Son of Man, and the field is the world; and the good seed, these are the sons of the Kingdom; and the tares are the sons of the evil one, and the enemy who sowed them is the devil, and the harvest is the end of the age, and the reapers are angels. As therefore the tares are gathered up and burned with fire; so will it be at the end of the age. (Matthew 13:37-40)

Muhammad ﷺ

On the Day when the trumpet is blown, those who are in the Heavens and those who are on the Earth will be terrified, except such as God pleases, and all will come to Him, humbled. You see the mountains and think they are solid, but they will pass away as the passing of a cloud—the handiwork of God, Who has made every thing thoroughly. Surely He is Aware of what you do. Whoever brings good will have better than it, and will be secure from terror on that day. Whoever brings evil will be thrown down on their faces into the fire. Will you be rewarded (for) anything other than what you did ? (The Naml 27:87-90)

Surely, your Lord will judge between them, on the Day of Resurrection, concerning that in which they differ. (The Adoration 32:25)

Those who disbelieve, say: The Hour will not come upon us. Say: Yes! By my Lord, the Knower of the Unseen, it will certainly come upon you. Not even the weight of an atom escapes from Him, in the Heavens or on the Earth, and neither less than that nor greater. (All) is in a clear book, so that He may reward those who believe and do good. For these is forgiveness and an honourable sustenance. (As for) those who strive hard in opposing Our Verses, there will be a painful punishment of an evil nature. (The Saba 34:3-5)

[Prophet], if only you could see when they become terrified—there will be no escape, and they will be seized from a near place. They will say: We believe in it! But how will attaining (the faith) from a distant place be possible for them? (The Saba 34:51-52)

Stand aside today, oh guilty ones! Did I not charge you, oh Children of Adam, that you should not serve the Devil? Surely he is your open enemy. And that you should serve Me—this is the right way. Certainly he led astray numerous people among you. What, could you not then understand? This is the Hell with which you were threatened. Enter into it today, because you disbelieved. (Yasin 36:59-64)

On that Day, We will set a seal over their mouths, and their hands will speak to Us, and their feet will bear witness of what they earned. And if We pleased, We would certainly put out their eyes, and then they would strive to get to the way, first, but how could they see? And if We pleased, We would surely transform them in their places, and then they would not be able to proceed or return. Whomever We cause to live long, We reduce him to a low state of condition. Do they not then understand? (Yasin 36:65-68)

Jesus

Being asked by the Pharisees when the Kingdom of God would come, he answered them, "The Kingdom of God does not come with observation; neither will they say, 'Look, here' or, 'Look, there.' For look, the Kingdom of God is within you."[1] (Luke 17:20-21)

---

1 Wallerstedt et al., *Orthodox Bible,* 183. The Greek for "within you" can also be translated "among you" or "in your midst."

Muhammad ﷺ

This is a reminder; and most surely there is an excellent resort for those who guard (against evil)—The Gardens of Perpetuity, the doors are opened for them. Reclining there, calling for many fruits and drink. With them will be those restraining their eyes, equals in age. This is what you are promised on the Day of Reckoning. Most surely this is Our sustenance—it will never come to an end. This (shall be so). Most surely there is an evil resort for the disorderly ones: Hell. They will enter it—so evil is the resting-place. This (shall be so). So let them taste it: boiling fluid and [pus], and other (punishment) of the same kind—of various sorts. (Sad 38:48-58)

Exalter of the Degrees, Lord of Power, by His command, He inspires to light those whom He pleases of His servants, so that he may warn (men) of the Day of Meeting. (Of) the Day when they will come forth; nothing concerning them remains hidden to God. To whom belongs the Kingdom this day? To God, the One, the Subduer (of all). This day every soul will be rewarded for what it has earned; no injustice (will be done) on this day. Surely God is quick in reckoning. And warn them, [Prophet], of the Day that draws near, when hearts will rise up to the throats, [choking]. The [wrongdoers] will not have any compassionate friend nor any intercessor to be obeyed. (The Believer 40:15-18)

On the day that the enemies of God will be brought together to the Fire, they will be formed into groups. When they come to the Fire, their ears, eyes and skins will bear witness against them regarding what they did. They will say to their skins: Why have you borne witness against us? Their skins will say: God, Who makes everything speak, has made us speak. He created you at first, and you will be brought back to Him. You did not veil yourselves or fear that your ears, your eyes and your skins would bear witness against you—rather you thought that God did not know most of what you did. That was your (evil) thought that you entertained about your Lord, so that has tumbled you down into perdition. So you have become one of the lost ones. Then if they endure, the Fire is still their abode, and if they ask for goodwill, they will not be granted goodwill. (Ha Mim 41:19-24)

The knowledge of the Hour is referred to Him. None of the fruits come forth from their coverings, and no female bears or gives birth, without His knowledge. On the Day when He calls out to them: Where are (those whom you called) My partner-gods? They will say: We admit to You, we do not see them. What they called upon before will be vanished, and they will know for certain that there is no escape. (Ha Mim 41:47-48)

Jesus

Muhammad ﷺ

So have We revealed to you an Arabic Qur'an, so that you may warn the Mother City and those around it,[1] and so that you may give warning of the Day of Gathering Together, about which there is no doubt. A group will be in the Garden and (another) group in the Burning Fire. If God had pleased, He surely would have made them a single [community], but He makes whom He pleases enter into His mercy. The [wrongdoers] will have no guardian or helper. (The Counsel 42:7-8)

Keep waiting for the Day when the Heaven will bring [visible smoke] that will overtake the people; this will be a painful chastisement. Our Lord! Remove this chastisement from us—surely we are believers. How will they be reminded, when a Messenger came to them, making (the truth) clear, yet they turned their backs on him, and said: One taught (by others), a madman. We will remove the chastisement a little, (but) you will surely return (to evil). On the Day when We seize (them) with the most violent seizing: surely, We will inflict retribution. (The Drought 44:10-16)

Surely the Day of Separation is their appointed term, for all of them. The day on which a friend will not benefit (his) friend at all, nor will they be helped. Except those on whom God will have mercy; surely He is the Mighty, the Merciful. Surely the tree of the Zaqqum is the food of the sinful. Like dregs of oil; it will boil in (their) bellies, like boiling hot water. Seize him, and then drag him down into the middle of the Hellfire; and then pour above his head the torment of the boiling water. Taste; you indeed were the mighty, the honourable. Surely this is what you disputed about. Surely those who guard (against evil) will be in a secure place, in gardens and springs, wearing garments of fine, thick silk, (sitting) face to face. Thus (shall it be). We will unite them with pure, beautiful ones. They will call for every fruit there, in security. (The Drought 44:40-55)

So woe on that Day, to those who reject (the truth), those who sport, entering into vain discourse. The Day on which they will be driven away to the Fire of Hell, with violence. This is the Fire that you used to deny. Is it enchantment then, or do you not see? Enter into it, and then bear (it) patiently, or do not bear (it) patiently—it is the same to you. You will be recompensed only (for) what you did. (The Mountain 52:11-16)

So, [Prophet], turn (your) back on them (for) the Day when the Inviter invites them to a hard task, their eyes cast down, going forth from their graves as if they were scattered locusts, hastening to the Inviter. The unbelievers will say: This is a hard day. (The Moon 54:6-8)

---

1 Mecca—Ed.

Jesus

Then the Kingdom of Heaven will be like ten virgins, who took their lamps, and went out to meet the bridegroom. Five of them were foolish, and five were wise. For the foolish, when they took their lamps, took no oil with them, but the wise took oil in their vessels with their lamps. Now while the bridegroom delayed, they all slumbered and slept. But at midnight there was a cry, "Look. The bridegroom is coming. Come out to meet him." Then all those virgins arose, and trimmed their lamps. The foolish said to the wise, "Give us some of your oil, for our lamps are going out." But the wise answered, saying, "There will not be enough for us and you. Go rather to those who sell, and buy for yourselves." While they went away to buy, the bridegroom came, and those who were ready went in with him to the marriage feast, and the door was shut. Afterward the other virgins also came, saying, "Lord, Lord, open to us." But he answered, "Truly I tell you, I do not know you." Watch therefore, for you do not know the day nor the hour in which the Son of Man is coming. (Matthew 25:1-13)

Muhammad ﷺ

No, the Hour is their promised time, and the Hour will be most grievous and bitter. Surely the guilty are in error and distress. On the day when they will be dragged on their faces into the fire—taste the touch of Hell. (The Moon 54:46-48)

The flames of fire and smoke will be sent against [both] of you,[1] and then you will not be able to defend yourselves. Which then of the bounties of your Lord will you reject? And when the Heaven is split, it becomes red, like red hide. Which then of the bounties of your Lord will you reject? So on that Day, neither men nor Jinn will be asked about his sin. Which then of the bounties of our Lord will you reject? The guilty will be recognized by their marks—they will be seized by the forelocks and the feet. (The Beneficent 55:35-41)

The companions of the right; What are the companions of the right? Amid thornless lote-trees, and banana-trees (with fruits), one above another. And extended shade, water poured forth, and abundant fruit, neither intercepted nor forbidden, and resting places. Surely, we have created for them (new growth: We have made them virgins—loving, equals in age—for the companions of the right. And those of the left hand, how wretched are those of the left hand! In hot wind and boiling water, and the shade of black smoke, neither cool nor honourable. Before they lived in ease and plenty. They persisted in great violation. They used to say: What? When we die and have become dust and bones, will we indeed be raised? Or our fathers of yore? Say: The first and the last [generations] will most surely be gathered together for the Appointed Hour of a Known Day. (The Great Event 56:27-50)

On the Day, the hypocritical men and the hypocritical women will say to those who believe: Wait for us, that we may have light from your light. It will be said: Turn back and seek a light. Then separation will be brought between them, a wall having a door in it. On the inside of the wall will be mercy, and on the outside there will be chastisement before it. They will cry out to them: Were we not with you? They will say: Yes! But you caused yourselves to fall into temptation, and you waited and doubted. Vain desires deceived you, until God's threatened punishment came, while the arch-deceiver deceived you about God. So today ransom will not be accepted from you, nor from those who disbelieved. Your abode is the Fire; it is your friend, and evil is the destination. (The Iron 57:13-15)

---

1 Haleem, *The Qur'an*, 353. Mankind and Jinn.

Jesus

As the days of Noah were, so will be the coming of the Son of Man. For as in those days which were before the flood they were eating and drinking, marrying and giving in marriage, until the day that Noah entered into the ship, and they did not know until the flood came, and took them all away, so will be the coming of the Son of Man. (Matthew 24:37-39)

But in those days, after that oppression, the sun will be darkened, the moon will not give its light, the stars will be falling from heaven, and the powers that are in the heavens will be shaken. Then they will see the Son of Man coming in clouds with great power and glory. Then he will send out his angels, and will gather together his chosen ones from the four winds, from the ends of the Earth to the ends of the sky. (Mark 13:24-27)

Muhammad ﷺ

When the trumpet is blown with a single blast, and the Earth and the mountains are lifted away and crushed with a single crushing. On that day will the Great Event come to pass, and the Heaven will split, so that on that day it will be frail. The angels will be on its edges, and above them, eight will bear your Lord's throne.
(The Sure Calamity 69:13-17)

On that Day you will be exposed—no secret of yours will remain hidden. He who is given his record in his right hand will say: Lo! Read my record! Surely I knew that I would meet my account. So he will be in a life of pleasure, in a lofty garden, the fruits of which are near at hand: Eat and drink pleasantly, for what you did before, in the days gone by. But he who is given his record in his left hand will say: Oh! If only my record had never been given to me, and that I had not known what my account was. Oh! If only it had been the end (of me). My wealth has availed me nothing, and my authority is gone. Lay hold on him, and then put a chain on him, cast him into the burning Fire, and then thrust him into a chain with a length of seventy cubits. Surely he did not believe in God, the Great, nor did he urge the feeding of the poor. Therefore he has no true friend here today, nor any food except for the [pus of wounds], which only the [wrongdoers] eat. (The Sure Calamity 69:18-37)

Surely they think it to be far off, and We see it near. On the Day when the Heaven will be as molten brass, and the mountains will be as tufts of wool. Friend will not ask of friend, (though) they will be made to see each other. The guilty one will desire to redeem himself from the chastisement of that day by [sacrificing] his children, and his wife and his brother, and the nearest of his kinsfolk who gave him shelter, and all those who are on the Earth, (wishing) that this might deliver him.
(The Ways of Ascent 70:6-14)

If you disbelieve, how will you guard yourselves on the Day when we make children grey-headed? The Heaven will split. His promise is ever fulfilled. Surely this is a reminder: Let him, who will, take the way to his Lord.
(The Wrapped Up 73:17-19)

So when vision becomes confused, and the moon becomes dark, and the sun and the moon are brought together, man will say on that Day: To where can I flee? By no means! There is no place of refuge! The place of rest on that Day is only with your Lord. On that Day, man will be informed of what he sent forth and (what he) kept back. No! Man is a witness against himself! Even if he puts forth his excuses. No! But you love the present life and neglect the Hereafter. (Some) faces on that day will be bright, looking to their Lord. (Other) faces on that day will be gloomy, knowing that there a great calamity will befall them. (The Resurrection 75:7-15, 20-25)

Jesus

Then He will say also to those on the left hand, "Depart from Me, you cursed, into the eternal fire which is prepared for the devil and his angels; for I was hungry, and you did not give Me food to eat; I was thirsty, and you gave Me no drink; I was a stranger, and you did not take Me in; naked, and you did not clothe Me; sick, and in prison, and you did not visit Me." Then they will also answer, saying, "Lord, when did we see You hungry, or thirsty, or a stranger, or naked, or sick, or in prison, and did not help You?" Then He will answer them, saying, "Truly I tell you, inasmuch as you did not do it to one of the least of these, you did not do it to Me." These will go away into eternal punishment, but the righteous into eternal life. (Matthew 25:41-46)

So be careful, or your hearts will be loaded down with carousing, drunkenness, and cares of this life, and that day will come on you suddenly. For it will come like a snare on all those who dwell on the surface of all the Earth. Therefore be watchful all the time, praying that you may be counted worthy to escape all of these things that will happen, and to stand before the Son of Man. (Luke 21:34-36)

Muhammad ﷺ

We have prepared for the unbelievers chains and shackles and a burning fire. Surely, the righteous will drink from a cup with a mixture of camphor, and from a fountain that the servants of God will drink from, causing it to flow forth abundantly. They fulfil the vows and fear a day when evil is spreading far and wide. They give food to the poor, the orphan and the captive, out of their love for God—we feed you only for God's sake. We do not desire any reward or thanks from you. Surely we fear from our Lord a stern, distressful Day. (The Man 76:4-10)

God will guard them from the evil of that Day, and will cause them to meet with ease and happiness. And reward them, because they were patient, with a garden and silk. Reclining there on raised couches, they will not find there (the severe heat of) the sun or intense cold. Close above them (will be) the garden's shadows, and fruit will be made near (to them), in easy reach. And there will be circulating among them vessels of silver and glass goblets, (transparent as)glass, made of silver, and made to measure. They will be made to drink from a cup with a mixture of ginger, from a fountain there, named Salsabil. Immortal, young [boys] will circulate among them; when you see them, you will think them to be scattered pearls. And when you look, you will see blessings and a great Kingdom. Upon them will be garments of fine green silk and heavy brocade. They will be adorned with bracelets of silver, and their Lord will make them drink a pure drink. (The Man 76:11-21)

Walk on to what you called a lie. Walk on to the [shadow] having three [columns], neither having the coolness of the shade nor availing against the flame. Surely it sends up sparks, like palaces, as if they were tawny camels. Woe on that day to the rejecters. This is the Day of which they will not speak, and permission to offer excuses will not be given to them. Woe on that day to the rejecters. This is the Day of Decision. We have gathered you and those of yore. So if you have a plan, plan against Me (now). Woe on that day to the rejecters. Surely those who guard (against evil) will be amid shades and fountains and fruits such as they desire. Eat and drink pleasantly because of what you did. This is how We reward the doers of good. Woe on that day to the rejecters. (The Sent Forth 77:29-45)

Eat and enjoy yourselves for a little; surely you are guilty. Woe on that Day to the rejecters. When it is said to them, bow down, they do not bow down. Woe on that Day to the rejecters. Then, in what announcement after it will they believe? (The Sent Forth 77:46-50)

Jesus

Nation will rise against nation, and kingdom against kingdom. There will be great earthquakes, famines, and plagues in various places. There will be terrors and great signs from Heaven. But before all these things, they will lay their hands on you and will persecute you, delivering you up to synagogues and prisons, bringing you before kings and governors for my name's sake. It will turn out as a testimony for you. Settle it therefore in your hearts not to meditate beforehand how to answer, for I will give you a mouth and wisdom which all your adversaries will not be able to withstand or to contradict. You will be handed over even by parents, brothers, relatives, and friends. They will cause some of you to be put to death. You will be hated by all men for my name's sake. And not a hair of your head will perish. (Luke 21:10-18)

For as the lightning flashes from the east, and is seen even to the west, so will be the coming of the Son of Man. Wherever the carcass is, there is where the vultures gather together. (Matthew 24:27-28)

Muhammad ﷺ

But when the Deafening [Blast] comes, the day on which a man will flee from his brother, and his mother, and his father, and his spouse and his sons. Every man on that day will have an affair that occupies him. Faces on that day will be bright, laughing, joyous. And faces on that day will have dust on them. Darkness will cover them—these are the unbelievers, the wicked. (He Frowned 80:33-4)

When the sun is covered, when the stars [fall, and] darken, when the mountains are made to pass away, when the [pregnant] camels are left, when the wild animals are [herded together], when the seas swell, when [souls] are united, when the [female infant] buried alive is asked for what sin she was killed, when the records of deeds are spread open, when the Heaven has its covering removed, when Hell is kindled up, and when the Garden is brought near: every soul will (then) know what it has prepared. (The Folding Up 81:1-14)

When the Heaven becomes cleft asunder, and when the stars become dispersed, and when the [seas] are made to flow forth, and when the graves are laid open, every soul will know what it has sent before it and what it has left behind. (The Cleaving Asunder 82:1-5)

Oh, man! What has beguiled you from your Lord, the Gracious One, who created you, and then made you complete, and then made you symmetrical? He assembled you into whatever form He pleased. No! But you deny the Judgment, and most surely there are keepers over you, honourable recorders. They know what you do. Most surely the righteous are in bliss, and most surely the wicked are in burning fire. They will enter it on the Day of Judgment. And they will by no means be absent from it. (The Cleaving Asunder 82:6-16)

Surely, the guilty used to laugh at those who believe. When they passed by them, they winked at one another, and when they returned to their own [people], they returned exulting. When they saw them, they said: Most surely they are in error. But they were not sent to be keepers over them. So Today, those who believe will laugh at the unbelievers. On raised couches, they will observe. (The Defaulters 83:29-35)

Jesus

When, therefore, you see the abomination of desolation, which was spoken of through Daniel the prophet, standing in the holy place (let the reader understand), then let those who are in Judea flee to the mountains. Let him who is on the housetop not go down to take out things that are in his house. Let him who is in the field not return back to take his clothes. But woe to those who are with child and to nursing mothers in those days. Pray that your flight will not be in the winter, nor on a Sabbath, for then there will be great oppression, such as has not been from the beginning of the world until now, no, nor ever will be. Unless those days had been shortened, no flesh would have been saved. But for the sake of the chosen ones, those days will be shortened. (Matthew 24:15-22)

Muhammad ﷺ

Has the news of the Overwhelming Event not come to you? (Some) faces on that day will be downcast. Labouring, toiling. Entering into burning fire, made to drink from a boiling spring. They shall have no food except thorns, which will neither fatten nor satisfy their hunger. (Other) faces on that day will be happy, well-pleased because of their striving. In a lofty Garden, where you will not hear vain talk. There is a fountain flowing. There are thrones raised high, and drinking-cups ready, placed, and cushions set in a row, and carpets spread out. (The Overwhelming Event 88:1-16)

When the Earth is shaken with her (violent) shaking. The Earth brings forth her burdens, and man says: What has befallen her? On that Day, Earth will tell her news, as if your Lord had revealed to her. On that Day men will come forth in various groups, so that they may be shown their works. He who has done an atom's weight of good will see it. And he who has done an atom's weight of evil shall see it.
(The Shaking 99:1-8)

The Repelling Calamity! How terrible the Repelling Calamity! What will make you comprehend how terrible the Repelling Calamity is? The day on which men will be as scattered moths, and the mountains will be like loosened wool As for he whose measure of good deeds is heavy, he will live a pleasant life. But as for he whose measure of good deeds is light, his abode will be the Abyss. What will make you know what it is? A burning fire. (The Repelling Calamity 101:1-11)

Eternal Message

 Jesus

Heaven and Earth will pass away, but my words will not pass away. (Matthew 24:35)

Surely We have revealed the Reminder, and We will most surely be its guardian.

(The Rock 15:9)

My Wāy/Yȯur Wȧy

Other Faith Groups

 Jesus

Beware of false prophets, who come to you in sheep's clothing, but inwardly are ravening wolves. By their fruits you will know them. Do you gather grapes from thorns, or figs from thistles? Even so, every good tree produces good fruit; but the corrupt tree produces evil fruit. A good tree cannot produce evil fruit, neither can a corrupt tree produce good fruit. Every tree that does not grow good fruit is cut down, and thrown into the fire. Therefore, by their fruits you will know them. (Matthew 7:15-20)

Your father Abraham rejoiced to see my day. He saw it, and was glad. (John 8:56)

Muhammad ﷺ

Note: Muhammad refers to Christians and Jews as Followers of the Book, Followers of the Reminder, Those to whom a Portion of the Book Has Been Given, and Those Who Have Been Given the Book Before You.—Ed.

We gave Moses the Book, and We sent messengers after him, one after another. We gave Jesus the son of Mary clear arguments, and We strengthened him with the Holy Spirit. What? Whenever a messenger came to you with what your souls did not desire, you were insolent. So you called some liars, and some you slay. And when it is said to them: Believe in what God has revealed, they say: We believe in what was revealed to us—and they deny anything besides that, while it is the truth, verifying that which they have. Say: Then why did you kill God's prophets before (this), if you were indeed believers? (The Cow 2:87, 91)

They say: No one will enter the Garden (of Paradise) except Jews or Christians. These are their vain desires. Say: Bring your proof if you are truthful. Yes! Whoever submits himself entirely to God and does good (to others) has his reward from his Lord, and there is no fear for him, nor will he grieve. And the Jews say: The Christians do not follow anything (good), and the Christians say: The Jews do not follow anything (good), while they recite the (same) Book. Those who have no knowledge say similar things. So God will judge between them on the Day of Resurrection, about what they differ. (The Cow 2:111-113)

They say: God has taken to Himself a son. Glory be to Him! Rather, whatever is in the Heavens and the Earth is His. All are obedient to Him. (The Cow 2:116)

Were you witnesses when death visited Jacob, when he said to his sons: What will you serve after me? They said: We will serve your God and the God of your fathers, Abraham and Ishmael and Isaac, one God only, and to Him do we submit. (The Cow 2:133)

They say: Be Jews or Christians, you will be on the right course. Say: No! (We follow) the religion of Abraham, the upright one, and he was not one of the polytheists. (The Cow 2:135)

Say: Do you dispute with us about God, when He is our Lord and your Lord, and we will have our deeds and you will have your deeds, and we are sincere to Him? No! Do you say that Abraham and Ishmael and Isaac and Jacob and the tribes were Jews or Christians? Say: Who knows better, you or God? And who is more unjust than he who conceals a testimony that he has from God? God is not at all unmindful of what you do. (The Cow 2:139-140)

Jesus

Muhammad ﷺ

We made some of these messengers excel over others. Among them are those to whom God spoke, and some of them He exalted, by (many) degrees of rank. We gave clear proofs to Jesus son of Mary, and We strengthened him with the Holy Spirit. If God had pleased, those after them would not have fought one another, after clear proofs had come to them. But they disagreed, so there were some who believed, and others who denied. If God had pleased, they would not have fought one another, but God brings about what He intends. (The Cow 2:253)

When the angels said: Oh, Mary! Surely, God has chosen you, and purified you, and chosen you above the women of the world. Oh, Mary! Keep to obedience to your Lord, and humble yourself, and bow down with those who bow.
(The Family of Amran 3:42-43)

This We recite to you of the Verses and the Wise Reminder. With God, surely the likeness of Jesus is as the likeness of Adam—God created him from dust, and then He said to him, Be, and he was. (This is) the truth from your Lord, so do not be one of the disputers. (The Family of Amran 3:58-60)

Say, [Prophet]: Oh, Followers of the Book! Come to an equitable proposition between us, that we will not serve any but God, we will not associate anything with Him, and some of us will not take others for lords, besides God. But if they turn back, say: Bear witness that we are Muslims. (The Family of Amran 3:64)

A group of the Followers of the Book desire to lead you astray, but they lead astray only themselves, and they do not perceive. Oh, Followers of the Book! Why do you disbelieve in the Verses of God as you witness (them)? Oh! Followers of the Book! Why do you confound the truth with falsehood, and hide the truth, while you know?
(The Family of Amran 3:69-71)

A group of the Followers of the Book say: Avow belief in what has been revealed to [Muslims] in the first part of the day, and disbelieve at the end of the day, so that perhaps [the Muslims] will turn back. Believe only in he who follows your religion. Say: Surely the (true) guidance is the guidance of God—that God may give anyone the like of what you were given. Or they might contend with you, by an argument before your Lord. Say: Surely grace is in the hand of God: He gives it to whom He pleases, and God is Ample-giving, Knowing. He specially chooses for His Mercy whom He pleases. God is the Lord of Mighty Grace. (The Family of Amran 3:72-74)

Jesus

Muhammad ﷺ

There is a group among them who [distort] the Book [as they read from it], so that you may consider it to be (a part) of the Book, while it is not (a part) of the Book. They say: It is from God, but it is not from God. They lie against God, and they know it. (The Family of Amran 3:78)

Say: Oh, Followers of the Book! Why do you disbelieve in the Verses of God, while God is a witness of what you do? Say: Oh, Followers of the Book! Why do you hinder from the way of God he who believes? You seek (to make) it [seem] crooked, while you are witnesses, and God is not unaware of what you do. (The Family of Amran 3:98-99)

They are not all alike; there is an upright group among the Followers of the Book—they recite God's Verses in the night, [falling face-down in prayer]. They believe in God and the Last Day, and they abide by what is right and forbid the wrong. They strive with one another to hasten to good deeds. Those are among the good. Whatever good they do, they will not be denied it, and God knows those who guard (against evil). (The Family of Amran 3:113-115)

We will cast terror into the hearts of the disbelievers, because they set up [partners] alongside God, for which He has not sent down authority. Their abode is the Fire; evil is the abode of the [wrongdoers]. (The Family of Amran 3:151)

You will certainly be tried regarding your wealth and your souls, and you will certainly hear much abuse from Those Who Have Been Given the Book Before You, and from those who are polytheists. If you are patient and guard (against evil), surely that is one of the determining matters. God made this covenant with Those Who Were Given the Book: You will certainly make it known to men, and you will not hide it. But they cast it behind their backs, and they took a small price for it. So evil is what they purchased. (The Family of Amran 3:186-187)

Most surely, some of the Followers of the Book believe in God, and (in) what has been revealed to you, and (in) what has been revealed to them, being lowly before God. They do not take a small price in exchange for the Verses of God. These have their reward with their Lord. Surely God is quick in reckoning. (The Family of Amran 3:199)

Jesus

Muhammad ﷺ

Oh, You Who Were Given the Book! Believe what we have revealed, verifying what you have, before We [obliterate] faces and turn them on their backs, or curse them as We cursed the violators of the Sabbath. The command of God will be executed. Surely God does not forgive any thing being associated with Him, but He forgives other than that, for whomever He pleases. Indeed, whoever associates any thing with God devises a great sin. (The Women 4:47-48)

See how they invent the lie against God—this is sufficient as an obvious sin. Have you not considered Those to Whom a Portion of the Book Has Been Given? They believe in enchantment and idols, and they say that those who disbelieve are better guided in the path than those who believe [the Qur'an]. (The Women 4:50-51)

The Followers of the Book ask you to bring down to them a book from Heaven. Indeed, they demanded of Moses a greater thing than that, for they said: Show us God clearly. So the thunderbolt overtook them because of their injustice. Then they took the calf (for a god), after clear signs had come to them, but We pardoned this. We gave to Moses clear authority. We raised the mountain above them, at their covenant, and We said to them: Enter the door, making obeisance. We said to them: Do not exceed the limits of the Sabbath. We made a firm covenant with them. So, for their breaking their covenant, and their disbelief in the Signs of God, and their killing of the prophets wrongfully, and their saying: Our hearts are covered. No! God set a seal upon them because of their unbelief, so they have no faith, except a [few].
(The Women 4:153-155)

Oh, Followers of the Book! Do not exceed the limits in your religion, and do not speak (lies) against God, but (speak) the truth. The Messiah, Jesus son of Mary, was only a messenger of God. And he is God's Word, which God conveyed to Mary and to a [Spirit] from Him. So believe in God and His messengers, and do not speak of "Three."[1] Stop this, it is better for you! God is only one God. Far be it from His glory that He should have a son! Whatever is in the Heavens and whatever is on the Earth is His, and God is sufficient for a Protector. The Messiah does by no means disdain being a servant of God, nor do the angels who are near to God. God will gather together to Himself whoever is proud and scorns service to Him.
(The Women 4:171-172)

---

1 The Holy Trinity—Ed.

Jesus

Jerusalem, Jerusalem, who kills the prophets and stones those who are sent to her. How often I wanted to gather your children together, like a hen gathers her own brood under her wings, and you refused. Look, your house is left to you desolate. I tell you assuredly, you will not see me until you say, "Blessed is he who comes in the name of the Lord." (Luke 13:34-35)

Muhammad ﷺ

God made a covenant with the Children of Israel, and We raised up among them twelve chieftains. God said: Surely I am with you; if you keep up prayer, and pay the poor-rate and believe in My messengers, and assist them, and offer to God a good gift, I will most certainly cover your evil deeds, and I will most certainly admit you into gardens beneath which rivers flow. But whoever disbelieves among you after that will lose the right way. Because they broke their covenant, We cursed them, and made their hearts hard. They altered the words from their context, and they neglected a portion of what they were reminded. You will always discover treachery in them, except for a few of them. So pardon them, and turn away. Surely God loves those who do good. (The Food 5:12-13

We made a covenant with the Christians, but they neglected a portion of what they were reminded of. So We excited enmity among them, and hatred until the Day of Resurrection. God will inform them of what they did. (The Food 5:14)

Certainly those who say "God is the Messiah, son of Mary" disbelieve. Say [Prophet]: Then who could control anything against God when He wished to destroy the Messiah son of Mary and his mother and all of those on Earth? God's is the Kingdom of the Heavens and the Earth and what is between them. He creates what He pleases, and He has power over all things. (The Food 5:17)

The Jews and the Christians say: We are the sons of God and His beloved ones. Say: Then why does He chastise you for your faults? No, you are mortals from among those whom He has created. He forgives whom He pleases and chastises whom He pleases. God's is the Kingdom of the Heavens and the Earth and what is between them, and to Him is the Eventual Coming. (The Food 5:18)

For this reason, We prescribed to the Children of Israel that whoever slays a soul, unless it be for manslaughter or for mischief in the land, it is as though he slew all men And whoever keeps a soul alive, it is as though he kept alive all men. Certainly, Our messengers came to them with clear arguments, but even after that, many of them certainly act extravagantly in the land. (The Food 5:32)

We revealed the Torah, in which was guidance and light. With it, the prophets who submitted themselves (to God) judged (matters) for the Jews, and the rabbis and the scholars, because they were required to guard (part) of the Book of God, and they were witnesses. So do not fear the people, fear Me, and do not take a small price for My messages. Whoever does not judge by what God has revealed are the unbelievers. (The Food 5:44)

Jesus

No one puts a piece of unshrunk cloth on an old garment; for the patch would tear away from the garment, and a worse hole is made. Neither do people put new wine into old wineskins, or else the skins would burst, and the wine be spilled, and the skins ruined. No, they put new wine into fresh wineskins, and both are preserved. (Matthew 9:16-17)

Muhammad ﷺ

We sent Jesus son of Mary after them, in their footsteps, verifying what was before him of the Torah. We gave him the Gospel, in which was guidance and light, and verifying what was before it in the Torah—a guidance and an admonition for those who guard (against evil) (The Food 5:46)

Say, [Prophet]: Oh, Followers of the Book! Do you find fault with us (for anything) other than that we believe in God and in what has been revealed to us, and what was revealed before, and that most of you are disobedient? Say: Shall I inform you of (he who is) worse than this for retribution from God? (Worse is he) whom God has cursed and brought His wrath upon, and whom He made apes and swine,[1] and he who served the Devil: these are worse in rank, and more erring from the straight path. (The Food 5:59-60)

Why do the [rabbis] and the [religious scholars] not prohibit them from speaking sinfully and eating what is forbidden? Certainly they work evil. The Jews say: The hand of God is tied up! Their hands will be shackled, and they will be cursed for what they say. No, both His hands are spread out: He spends as He pleases. What has been revealed to you from your Lord will certainly make many of them increase in rebellion and unbelief. We have put enmity and hatred among them, until the Day of Resurrection. Whenever they kindle a fire for war, God puts it out, and they strive to make mischief in the land. God does not love the mischief-makers. (The Food 5:63-64)

Oh, Messenger! Deliver what has been revealed to you from your Lord. If you do not, then you have not delivered His message. God will protect you from the people. Surely God will not guide the unbelieving people. Say: Oh, Followers of the Book! You follow no good until you keep up the Torah and the Gospel and what is revealed to you from your Lord. Surely what has been revealed to you from your Lord will make many of them increase in rebellion and unbelief. So, do not grieve for the unbelieving people. (The Food 5:67-68)

---

1 Ali, M.M., *The Holy Qur'an*, 270. It is clear that those who are here spoken of as having been made apes and swine are the Jews.

2:65 also mentions apes: And certainly you have known those among you who exceeded the limits of the Sabbath, so We said to them: Be (as) apes, despised and hated. 7:166 says regarding the Tribe of Moses: Therefore when they revoltingly persisted in what they had been forbidden, We said to them: Be (as) apes, despised and hated.—Ed.

Jesus

Muhammad ﷺ

Those who say, "Surely God is the Messiah, son of Mary" certainly disbelieve. The Messiah said: Oh, Children of Israel! Serve God, my Lord and your Lord. Surely God has forbidden to the Garden whoever associates (others) with God, and his abode is the Fire. There will be no helpers for the [wrongdoers]. (The Food 5:72)

Those who say, "Surely, God is the third (person) of the three" certainly disbelieve. There is no god but the one God, and if they do not stop what they say, a painful chastisement will befall those among them who disbelieve. Will they not turn to God and ask His forgiveness? God is Forgiving, Merciful. The Messiah, son of Mary, is only a messenger. Messengers before him have indeed passed away. His mother was a truthful woman. They both ate food. See how We make the Signs clear to them, yet behold how they turn away. Say: Do you serve besides God that which does not control for you any harm or any profit? God is the Hearing, the Knowing. (The Food 5:73-76)

Say: Oh, Followers of the Book! Do not be unduly immoderate in your religion, and do not follow the low desires of people who went astray before, who led many astray and went astray from the right path. (The Food 5:77)

Those who disbelieved among the Children of Israel were cursed by the tongue of David and Jesus son of Mary. This was because they disobeyed and they exceeded the limits. They did not forbid each other the hateful things that they did—certainly they did evil. You will see many of them befriending those who disbelieve. Certainly their souls have sent evil before for them, so that God became displeased with them. They will abide in chastisement. Had they believed in God and the prophet and what was revealed to him, they would not have taken them for friends, but most of them are defiantly disobedient. (The Food 5:78-81)

Certainly you will find that the Jews and the polytheists have the most violent hatred for those who believe, and you will certainly find the nearest in friendship to those who believe are those who say: We are Christians. This is because there are priests and monks among them, and because they do not behave proudly. When they hear what has been revealed to the Messenger, you will see their eyes overflowing with tears because of the truth that they recognize. They say: Our Lord! We believe, so write us down with the witnesses (of truth). (The Food 5:82-83)

When God will say: Oh Jesus, son of Mary! Did you say to men: Take me and my mother for two gods besides God? Jesus will say: Glory be to You, it did not befit me that I should say what I had no right to (say). If I had said it, You would indeed have known it. You know what is in my mind, and I do not know what is in Your mind. Surely You are the great Knower of the unseen things. (The Food 5:116)

Jesus

Be careful that no one leads you astray. For many will come in my name, saying, "I am the Messiah,"[1] and will lead many astray. (Matthew 24:4-5)

Many false prophets will arise, and will lead many astray. (Matthew 24:11)

---

1 Messiah, meaning the anointed one of God as the subject of Hebrew Bible prophecies.—Ed.

Muhammad ﷺ

Wonderful Originator of the Heavens and the Earth! How could He have a son when He has no spouse, and He (Himself) created every thing, and He is the Knower of all things? (The Cattle 6:101)

The Jews say: Ezra is the Son of God. The Christians say: The Messiah is the Son of God; these are the words from their mouths. They imitate the saying of those who disbelieved before. May God curse them! How they are turned away! They have taken [rabbis] and their monks for Lords besides God, and (also) the Messiah son of Mary. They were ordered to serve one God only—there is no god but He. Far from His glory be what they associate (with Him). They desire to put out the light of God with their mouths, and God will not consent except to perfect His light, though the unbelievers are averse. It is He who sent His Messenger with guidance and the religion of truth, so that He might cause it to prevail over all religions, though the polytheists might be averse. (The Immunity 9:30-33)

Oh, you who believe! Most surely many of the [rabbis] and the monks eat away the property of men falsely, and turn (them) from God's way. Announce a painful chastisement to those who hoard up gold and silver and do not spend it in God's way. On the Day when it will be heated in the fire of Hell, their foreheads and their sides and their backs will be branded with it: This is what you hoarded up for yourselves, so taste what you hoarded. (The Immunity 9:34-35)

They say: God has taken a son (to Himself). Glory be to Him! He is the Self-sufficient. His is what is in the Heavens and what is on the Earth. You have no authority for this—do you say against God what you do not know? Say: Those who invent a lie against God will not be successful. (It is only) some enjoyment in this world, but then they will return to Us. Then We will make them taste severe chastisement because they disbelieved. (Jonah 10:68-70)

We certainly lodged the Children of Israel in a goodly abode, and We provided them with good things. They did not disagree until the knowledge came to them. Surely your Lord will judge between them, on Resurrection Day, concerning that in which they disagreed. (Jonah 10:93)

If your Lord had pleased, He certainly would have made people a single nation. They will continue to differ, except those on whom your Lord has mercy—He created them for this. The word of your Lord is fulfilled. Certainly I will fill Hell with the Jinn and the men, all together. (Hud 11:118-119)

Jesus

Muhammad ﷺ

Say: (All) praise is due to God, Who has not taken a son, Who has not a partner in the Kingdom, and Who has not a helper to save Him from disgrace. Proclaim His greatness, magnifying (Him). (The Israelites 17:111)

(All) praise is due to God, Who revealed the Book to His Servant and did not make any crookedness in it. Warn those who say: God has taken a son. They have no knowledge of it, nor had their fathers. It is a grievous word that comes out of their mouths; they speak nothing but a lie. Then maybe you will kill yourself with grief [Prophet], sorrowing after them, if they do not believe in this announcement. (The Cave 18:1, 4-6)

Mention Mary in the Book, when she drew aside from her family to an Eastern place. She took a veil (to screen herself) from them, and then We sent to her Our Spirit— it appeared to her as a well-made man. He said: I am only a messenger of your Lord! I will give you a pure boy. She said: [How] will I have a boy, when no mortal has touched me yet, nor have I been unchaste? He said: Even so! Your Lord says: It is easy for Me, so that We may make him a sign to men and a mercy from Us. It is a matter which has been decreed. So she conceived him, and then she withdrew with him to a remote place. (Mary 19:16-17, 19-22)

And she came to her people with him, carrying him (with her). They said: Oh, Mary! Surely you have done a strange thing. Oh, sister of Aaron, your father was not a bad man, nor was your mother an unchaste woman. But she pointed to him. They said: How can we speak to a child in the cradle? Jesus said: Surely I am a servant of God. He has given me the Book, and made me a prophet. He has made me blessed wherever I may be, and He has directed me to pray and give the poor-rate, as long as I live. He has made me dutiful to my mother, and not insolent, unblessed. Peace was on me on the day I was born, and peace will be on me on the day I die, and on the day I am raised to life. Such is Jesus son of Mary.[1] (This is) the truth about what they dispute. It is not proper for God to take to Himself a son, glory be to Him! When He has decreed a matter, He only says to it "Be," and it is. God is my Lord and your Lord, so serve Him; this the right path. But parties among them disagreed with each other, so woe to those who disbelieve, because of presence on a great Day. (Mary 19:27-37)

---

1 This story of Jesus speaking in his cradle is also in the *Syriac (Arabic) Infancy Gospel. See* page 487.—Ed.

Jesus

Muhammad ﷺ

And they say: The Beneficent God has taken (to Himself) a son. Certainly you have made an abominable assertion—the Heavens may almost be torn apart, and the Earth split asunder, and the mountains fall down in pieces, that they ascribe a son to the Beneficent God. It is not worthy of the Beneficent God that He should take (to Himself) a son. There is no one in the Heavens and the Earth who will not come to the Beneficent God as a servant. Certainly He has a comprehensive knowledge of them, and He has numbered them comprehensively. Every one of them will come to Him alone on the Day of Resurrection. (Mary 19:88-95)

We did not send before you any messenger to who We did not reveal that there is no god but Me, therefore serve Me. Yet they say: The Beneficent God has taken to Himself a son, glory be to Him. No! The messengers are honoured servants. They do not precede Him in speech, and they act (only) according to His commandment. He knows what is before them and what is behind them, and they do not intercede except for him whom He approves, and they tremble for fear of Him. We recompense with Hell whomever of them should say, "Surely I am a god besides Him." Thus do We recompense the [wrongdoers]. (The Prophets 21:25-29)

She who guarded her chastity—We breathed into her of Our [Spirit], and We made her and her son a sign for the nations. (The Prophets 21:91)

No! We have brought to them the truth, and most surely they are liars. God never took to Himself a son, and there was never any (other) god with Him—in that case, each god would have certainly taken away what he created, and some of them would have certainly overpowered others. Glory be to God, above what they describe! (The Believers 23:90-91)

Blessed is He Who sent down the Distinction upon His servant, that he may be a warner to the nations. He, Whose is the Kingdom of the Heavens and the Earth, and Who did not take to Himself a son, and Who has no associate in the Kingdom, and Who created every thing, and then ordained for it a measurement. (The Distinction 25:1-2)

Sincere obedience is due to God (alone). Those who take guardians besides Him, (say): We do not serve them, except that they may make us nearer to God. Surely, God will judge between them regarding their differences. Surely God does not guide a liar, ungrateful. If God desires to take a son to Himself, He will surely choose whom He pleases from those He has created. Glory be to Him: He is God, the One, the Subduer (of all). (The Companies 39:3-4)

Jesus

Muhammad ﷺ

Have they taken intercessors besides God? Say: What? Even though they did not ever have control over anything, nor do they understand? Say: Intercession belongs to God, altogether. His is the Kingdom of the Heavens and the Earth—you will be brought back to Him. (The Companies 39:43-44)

When an [example] of the son of Mary is given, lo! Your people, [Prophet], raise a clamour. They say: Are our gods better, or is he? They set forth [this objection] only to dispute. No, they are a contentious people! He was only a servant on whom We bestowed favour, and We made him an example for the Children of Israel.[1] (The Embellishment 43:57-59)

Have they settled an affair? Then surely, We are the Settlers.[2] Or do they think that We do not hear what they conceal and their private discourse? Yes! And Our messengers with them are recording. Say, [Prophet]: If the Beneficent God has a son, I am the foremost of those who serve. (The Embellishment 43:79-80)

Say [Prophet]: If the Beneficent God has a son, I am the first of those to serve him. Glory to the Lord of the Heavens and the Earth, the Lord of Power, from what they describe. So leave them plunging into false discourse and sporting, until they meet their Day, with which they are threatened. Those whom they call upon besides Him have no authority for intercession, except he who bears witness of the truth, and they know (him). If you asked them who created them, they would certainly say: God. So, from where are they turned back? Consider his cry: Oh, my Lord! Surely they are a people who do not believe. So turn away from them, and say, Peace, for they will soon come to know. (The Embellishment 43:81-83, 86-89)

Certainly, We gave the Book and the wisdom and the prophecy to the Children of Israel, and We gave them of the good things. We made them excel the nations. We gave them clear proofs of the affair. They did not differ until after knowledge came to them, out of envy among themselves. Surely, on the Day of Resurrection, your Lord will judge between them concerning that in which they differed. Then We put you on an [ordained] course in the matter—so follow it, and do not follow the low desires of those who do not know. (The Kneeling 45:16-18)

---

1 Ali, M.M., *The Holy Qur'an*, 949. When the case of Jesus was cited, the unbelievers objected to the respect shown to him when their own idols were condemned.

2 Ali, M.M., *The Holy Qur'an*, 952. The unbelievers should not think that they have settled the affair of the Holy Prophet with their plans to kill him, for it is God who settles all affairs.

Jesus

Then if any man tells you, "Look, here is the Messiah," or, "There," do not believe it. For there will arise false messiahs, and false prophets, and they will show great signs and wonders, so as to lead astray, if possible, even the chosen ones. See, I have told you beforehand. So, if they tell you, "Look, he is in the wilderness," do not go out; "Look, he is in the inner chambers," do not believe it. (Matthew 24:23-26)

Muhammad ﷺ

Then We sent Our Messengers to follow in their footsteps, and We sent Jesus son of Mary afterwards, and We gave him the Gospel. We put kindness and a mercy in the hearts of those who followed him. (As for) monasticism, they invented it, only to seek God's pleasure—We did not prescribe it for them. But they did not observe it with due observance. So, We gave reward to those of them who believed, but most of them are defiantly disobedient. (The Iron 57:27)

The Followers of the Book should know that they do not control any of the grace of God. That grace is in God's hand, and He gives it to whom He pleases. God is the Lord of Mighty Grace. (The Iron 57:29)

When Jesus son of Mary said: Oh, Children of Israel! Surely I am the messenger of God to you, verifying what came before me of the Torah, and giving the good news of a Messenger who will come after me, his name being Ahmad.[1] But when he came to them with clear arguments, they said: This is clear enchantment. (The Ranks 61:6)

Oh, you who believe! Be helpers (in the cause) of God, as Jesus son of Mary said to (His) disciples: Who are my helpers in the cause of God? The disciples said: We are helpers (in the cause) of God. So a group of the Children of Israel believed, and another group disbelieved. We aided those who believed, against their enemy, and they became predominant. (The Ranks 61:14)

The likeness of those who were charged with the Torah and then did not observe it is like the ass bearing books. Evil is the likeness of the people who reject the messages of God, and God does not guide the unjust people. Say: Oh, you Jews, if you think that you are the favourites of God to the exclusion of other people, then wish for death, if you are truthful. (The Congregation 62:5-6)

Mary, the daughter of Amran, guarded her chastity, so We breathed into [it] from Our [Spirit], and she accepted the truth of the words of her Lord, and His Books, and she was of the obedient ones. (The Prohibition 66:12)

---

1 Ali, M.M., *The Holy Qur'an*, 1071. Muhammad was also called Ahmad. Both names are derived from the same root, which is "praised." Muhammad meets all of the qualifications of the paraclete that Jesus prophesied in John 14:16-17, John 16:7 and John 16:12-14.

See John 14:16-17, John 16:7 and John 16:12-14 on page 460.—Ed.

Jesus

If anyone tells you, "Look, here is the Messiah," or, "Look, there," do not believe it. For there will arise false messiahs and false prophets, and they will show signs and wonders, so that they may lead astray, if possible, even the chosen ones. But you watch. Look, I have told you all things beforehand. (Mark 13:21-23)

Muhammad

Those who disbelieved among the Followers of the Book and the polytheists could not have separated [from their ways] until there had come to them the clear evidence: A messenger from God, reciting pure pages, wherein all the [writings are correct]. Those who were given the Book did not become divided until after clear evidence came to them. They were commanded only to serve God, be sincere to Him in obedience, upright, and keep up prayer and pay the poor-rate. That is the correct religion. (The Clear Evidence 98:1-5)

Say: He, God, is One. God is He on whom all depend. He begets not, nor is He begotten: And none is like Him.[1] (The Unity 112:1-4)

---

1 The Prophet said that this sura is equal to one-third of the Qur'an. (*The Hadith*, Sahih al-Bukhari, *Book of Oaths and Vows, Hadith 638*)—Ed.

The Way

 Jesus

Truly, truly, I tell you, one who does not enter by the door into the sheep fold, but climbs up some other way, the same is a thief and a robber. But one who enters in by the door is the shepherd of the sheep. The gatekeeper opens the gate for him, and the sheep listen to his voice. He calls his own sheep by name, and leads them out. Whenever he brings out his own sheep, he goes before them, and the sheep follow him, for they know his voice. They will by no means follow a stranger, but will flee from him; for they do not know the voice of strangers. (John 10:1-5)

I am the way, the truth, and the life. No one comes to the Father except through me. (John 14:6)

Say [Prophet]: Surely Gabriel revealed it to your heart by God's command, verifying what came before it, and a guidance and good news for the believers. So, whoever is the enemy of Gabriel and God and His angels and His messengers and Gabriel and Michael, surely God is the enemy of the unbelievers. Certainly we have revealed to you clear Verses, and none disbelieve in them except the defiantly disobedient. (The Cow 2:97-99)

Neither those who disbelieve among the Followers of the Book nor the polytheists want any good to be sent down to you from your Lord, and God especially chooses whom Be pleases for His mercy, and God is the Lord of mighty grace. Whatever verses We abrogate or cause to be forgotten, We bring one better than it or similar to it. Do you not know that God has power over all things? (The Cow 2:105-106)

Neither the Jews nor the Christians will be pleased with you, until you follow their religion. Say: Surely God's guidance is the (true) guidance. And if you follow their desires after the knowledge that has come to you, you will have no guardian from God, nor any helper. Those to Whom We Have Given the Book follow it as it ought to be followed. They believe in it. Whoever disbelieves in it are the losers. (The Cow 2:120-121)

(All) people were a single [community]; so God raised prophets as bearers of good news and as warners, and He revealed with them the Book with Truth, to judge between people regarding that in which they differed. After clear arguments had come to them, only the very people who were given it differed about it, out of [jealousy] among themselves. So, God has guided to the Truth, about which they differed, those who believe, by His will. God guides whom He pleases to the right path. (The Cow 2:213)

He revealed to you the Book with truth, verifying what came before it, and He revealed the Torah and the Gospel before, a guidance for the people, and He sent the Distinction.[1] Those who disbelieve in the Verses of God will have a severe chastisement. God is Mighty, the Lord of Retribution. (The Family of Amran 3:3)

Surely the (true) religion with God is Islam. Those to Whom the Book Had Been Given did not show opposition until after knowledge came to them, out of envy among themselves. Whoever disbelieves in the Verses of God—then surely God is quick in reckoning. (The Family of Amran 3:19)

---

1 Ali, M.M., *The Holy Qur'an*, 32, 140. Distinction between truth and falsity of the revelation.

Jesus

He who loves father or mother more than me is not worthy of me; and he who loves son or daughter more than me is not worthy of me. And whoever does not take his cross and follow after me, is not worthy of me. He who seeks his life will lose it; and he who loses his life for my sake will find it. (Matthew 10:37-39)

Muhammad ﷺ

Haven't you considered Those Who Are Given a Portion Of the Book?[1] They are invited to the Book of God so that it might decide between them. But some of them turn back and withdraw. This is because they say: The fire will touch us only for a few days. What they have created deceives them in the matter of their religion. So how will it be when We gather them together on a day about which there is no doubt, and every soul will be fully paid for what it earned? They will not be dealt with unjustly. (The Family of Amran 3:23-25)

Oh, Followers of the Book! Why do you dispute about Abraham, when the Torah and the Gospel were not revealed until after him? Do you not understand? Behold! You are those who disputed about that of which you had knowledge. So why do you dispute about that of which you have no knowledge? God knows, while you do not know. Abraham was not a Jew or a Christian: he was (an) upright (man), a Muslim, and he was not one of the polytheists. Most surely the nearest of people to Abraham are those who followed him, and this Prophet, and those who believe (in him). God is the guardian of the believers. (The Family of Amran 3:65-68)

God made a covenant through the prophets: Certainly what I have given you of Book and wisdom—then a messenger comes to you verifying that which is with you, you must believe in him, and you must aid him. He said: Do you affirm and accept My compact in this (matter)? They said: We do affirm. He said: Then bear witness, and I (too) am of the bearers of witness with you. Therefore, whoever turns back after this are the defiantly disobedient. (The Family of Amran 3:81-82)

Say: We believe in God and what has been revealed to us, and what was revealed to Abraham and Ishmael and Isaac and Jacob and the tribes, and what was given to Moses and Jesus and to the prophets from their Lord. We do not make any distinction between any of them, and we submit to Him. And whoever desires a religion other than Islam, it will not be accepted from him, and in the Hereafter, he will be one of the losers. (The Family of Amran 3:84-85)

[Believers], you are the best of the nations raised up for (the benefit of) men. You direct what is right, and forbid the wrong, and believe in God. If the Followers of the Book had believed, it would have been better for them. Some of them are believers, but most of them are defiantly disobedient. They will by no means harm you, except with slight [annoyance]. If they fight with you, they will turn (their) backs to you, and then they will not be helped. (The Family of Amran 3:110-111)

---

1 Christians and Jews.—Ed.

Jesus

I am the true vine, and my Father is the gardener. Every branch in me that does not bear fruit, he takes away. Every branch that bears fruit, he prunes, so that it may bear more fruit. You are already clean because of the word which I have spoken to you. Remain in me, and I in you. As the branch cannot bear fruit by itself, unless it remains in the vine, so neither can you, unless you remain in me. I am the vine. You are the branches. He who remains in me, and I in him, the same bears much fruit, for apart from me, you can do nothing. If a man does not remain in me, he is thrown out as a branch, and withers; and they gather them, throw them into the fire, and they are burned. (John 15:1-6)

Muhammad ﷺ

Whoever is hostile to the Messenger after guidance has become clear to him, and follows other than the way of the believers, We will turn him to what he has (himself) turned, and make him enter Hell. It is an evil destination. (The Women 4:115)

Surely those who disbelieve in God and His messengers, and (those who) desire to make a distinction between God and His messengers, and say: We believe in some and disbelieve in others, and we desire to take a course between (this and) that— these are truly the unbelievers, and We have prepared a disgraceful chastisement for the unbelievers. And We will grant due rewards to those who believe in God and His messengers and do not make a distinction between any of them. God is Forgiving, Merciful. (The Women 4:150-152)

There is not one of the Followers of the Book who will not most certainly believe in him before his death, and on the Day of Resurrection, he will be a witness against them. Because of their iniquity, We disallowed for the Jews the good things that had been made lawful for them, and for their hindering many (people) from God's way, and their taking usury—though indeed they were forbidden it—and their devouring the property of people falsely. We have prepared a painful chastisement for the unbelievers among them. But those firm in knowledge among them and the believers believe in what has been revealed to you, [Prophet], and what was revealed before you. We will give a mighty reward to those who keep up prayers and those who give the poor-rate and the believers in God and the Last Day. (The Women 4:159-162)

Ordain for us good in this world's life and in the Hereafter, for surely we turn to You. He said: (As for) My chastisement, I will afflict with it whom I please, and My mercy encompasses all things—I will ordain it (specially) for those who guard (against evil) and pay the poor-rate, and those who believe in Our Verses. Those who follow the Messenger-Prophet, the unlettered, whom they find mentioned in the Torah and the Gospel, (who) directs good and forbids them evil, and makes lawful to them the good things and makes unlawful to them impure things, and removes from them their burden and the shackles that were on them. So the successful are those who believe in him, and honour him, and help him, and follow the light that has been sent down with him. Oh, [mankind]! Surely I am the Messenger of God to you all, of Him whose is the Kingdom of the Heavens and the Earth, there is no god but Him. He brings to life and causes to die, so believe in God and His Messenger, the unlettered Prophet who believes in God and His words. Follow him so that you may walk in the right way. (The Elevated Places 7:156-158)

Jesus

He who is not with me is against me. He who does not gather with me, scatters. (Luke 11:23)

Jesus therefore said to them again, "Truly, truly, I tell you, I am the sheep's door. I am the door. If anyone enters in by me, he will be saved, and will go in and go out, and will find pasture." (John 10:7, 9)

Muhammad ﷺ

Oh, Prophet! Say to the captives who are in your hands: If God knows anything good in your hearts, He will give to you better than what has been taken away from you, and He will forgive you. God is Forgiving, Merciful. If they intend to act unfaithfully toward you, indeed they acted unfaithfully toward God before, but He gave (you) mastery over them. God is Knowing, Wise. (The Accessions 8:70-71)

I am God the Seeing. (This is) a Book, whose verses are [perfected], and then they are made plain, from One Wise, All-aware: (Hud 11:1)

He who has clear proof from his Lord, and a witness from Him recites it, and before it was the Book of Moses as a guide and a mercy—they believe in it. But whoever among the (different) groups disbelieves in it, the Fire is his promised place. So do not doubt it, surely it is the truth from your Lord, but most men do not believe. (Hud 11:17)

When We change (one) verse for (another) verse, and God knows best what He reveals, they say: You are only an inventor. No, most of them do not know. Say: The Holy Spirit has revealed it, with the truth from your Lord, so that it can establish those who believe, and as a guidance and good news for those who submit, [the Muslims].[1] (The Bee 16:101-102)

Surely this Qur'an guides to that which is the most upright, and it gives good news to believers who do good that they will have a great reward. (As for) those who do not believe in the Hereafter, We have prepared a painful punishment for them. (The Israelites 17:9-10)

We have revealed it with truth, and with truth it came. [Prophet], We have sent you only as the giver of good news and as a warner. It is a Qur'an that we have revealed in portions, so that you may read it to the people by slow degrees. Say, [Prophet]: Believe in it or believe not; surely Those Who Were Given the Knowledge Before fall down on their faces,[2] making obeisance when it is recited to them. They say: Glory be to our Lord! Most surely the promise of our Lord [is] fulfilled. They fall down on their faces weeping, and it adds to their humility. (The Israelites 17:105-109)

---

1 Ali, M.M., *The Holy Qur'an*, 555. In the Qur'an, the angel Gabriel is also called the Holy Spirit or the Faithful Spirit.

2 Christians and Jews.—Ed

Jesus

Muhammad ﷺ

Strive hard in (the way of) God, (such) a striving as is due to Him. He has chosen you and has not laid any hardship on you in religion—the faith of your father Abraham. He named you Muslims before and in this [Qur'an], so that the Messenger may be a bearer of witness to you, and you may be bearers of witness to the people. So keep up prayer and pay the poor-rate and hold fast by God. He is your Guardian; how excellent the Guardian and how excellent the Helper! (The Pilgrimage 22:78)

Surely this Qur'an declares to the Children of Israel most of what they differ about. Most surely it is a guidance and a mercy for the believers. Surely your Lord will judge between them with His judgment, and He is the Mighty, the Knowing. (The Naml 27:76-78)

No! These are clear Verses in the breasts of those who are granted knowledge. None reject Our Verses except the [wrongdoers]. (The Spider 29:49)

[Prophet], set your face upright for religion in the right state—the nature made by God, in which He made man. There is no altering of God's creation. That is the correct religion, but most people do not know. (The Romans 30:30)

Surely, there are those who disbelieve in the Reminder when it comes to them, and most surely it is a Mighty Book. Falsehood cannot approach it from before it or from behind it—it is a revelation from the Wise, the Praised One. Indeed, nothing is said to you besides what was said to the messengers before you. Surely your Lord is the Lord of Forgiveness and the Lord of Painful Retribution. (Ha Mim 41:41-43)

We have prepared burning fire for whoever does not believe in God and His Messenger, for the unbelievers. God's is the Kingdom of the Heavens and the Earth. He forgives whom He pleases, and He chastises whom He pleases. God is Forgiving, Merciful. (The Victory 48:13-14)

Jesus

It is done. I am the Alpha and the Omega, the Beginning and the End. I will give freely to him who is thirsty from the spring of the water of life. (Revelation 21:6)

I am the resurrection and the life. He who believes in me will still live, even if he dies. And whoever lives and believes in me will never die. Do you believe this?
(John: 11:25-26)

Muhammad ﷺ

It is He who sent His Messenger with the guidance and the true religion, so that He can make it prevail over all the religions. God is enough for a witness. Muhammad is the Messenger of God, and those with him are firm of heart against the unbelievers and compassionate among themselves. You see them bowing down, prostrating themselves, seeking grace from God, and pleasure. Their marks are on their faces because of the effect of prostration—that is their description in the Torah and their description in the Gospel. They are like seed-produce that puts forth its sprout, and then strengthens it, so that it becomes stout and stands firmly on its stem, delighting the sowers that God can enrage the unbelievers because of them. God has promised forgiveness and a great reward to those among them who believe and do good. (The Victory 48:28-29)

Say, [Prophet]: It has been revealed to me that a group of Jinn listened, and they said: Surely we have heard a wonderful Qur'an, guiding to the right way, so we believe in it, and we will not associate any one with our Lord: exalted is the majesty of our Lord— He has not taken a consort, nor a son. When we heard the guidance, we believed in it. So whoever believes in his Lord should neither fear loss nor being overtaken (by disgrace). Some of us submit, and some of us are the deviators. Whoever submits aims at the right way. The deviators are firewood for Hellfire. (The Jinn 72:1-3, 13-15)

Carry On with Hope

Holy Spirit and Rebirth

 Jesus

But the Helper, the Holy Spirit, whom the Father will send in my name, he will teach you all things, and will remind you of all that I said to you. (John 14:26)

If you love me, keep my commandments. I will pray to the Father, and he will give you another Helper, so that he may be with you forever—the Spirit of Truth. (John 14:15-17a)

Nevertheless I tell you the truth: It is to your advantage that I go away, for if I do not go away, the Helper won't come to you.[1] But if I go, I will send him to you. When he has come, he will convict the world about sin, and about righteousness, and about judgment; about sin, because they do not believe in me; about righteousness, because I am going to my Father, and you won't see me any more; about judgment, because the prince of this world[2] has been judged. (John 16:7-11)

If anyone loves me, he will keep my word; and my Father will love him, and we will come to him and make our dwelling place with him. (John 14:23)

When the Helper has come, whom I will send to you from the Father, the Spirit of Truth, who proceeds from the Father, he will testify about me. (John 15:26)

However when he, the Spirit of Truth, has come, he will guide you into all truth, for he will not speak on his own; but whatever he hears he will speak, and he will declare to you things that are coming. He will glorify me, for he will take from what is mine, and will declare it to you. (John 16:13-14)

John indeed baptized in water, but you will be baptized in the Holy Spirit.[3] (Acts 11:16)

---

1 Wallerstedt et al., *Orthodox Bible*, 255. The Helper, the Holy Spirit.

The Greek word "paraclete" most commonly refers to the Holy Spirit in the New Testament, and it has been translated into English as "Helper", "Counselor", "Advocate", or "Comforter."—Ed.

2 The Devil.—Ed.

3 John the Baptist—Ed.

We made some of the messengers excel over others. God spoke to some of them, and He exalted some of them, by (many) degrees of rank. We gave clear arguments to Jesus son of Mary, and We strengthened him with the Holy Spirit. If God had pleased, those after them would not have fought one with another after clear arguments had come to them, but they disagreed. Some of them believed, and others denied. If God had pleased, they would not have fought one another, but God brings about what He intends. (The Cow 2:253)

[Prophet], they ask you about the Spirit. Say: the Spirit is by the command of my Lord, and you are only given a little of the knowledge. (The Israelites 17:85)

Jesus

When they lead you away and deliver you up, do not be anxious beforehand, or premeditate what you will say, but say whatever will be given you in that hour. For it is not you who speak, but the Holy Spirit. (Mark 13:11)

"Truly, truly, I tell you, unless one is born again, he cannot see the Kingdom of God." Nicodemus said to him, "How can a man be born when he is old? Can he enter a second time into his mother's womb, and be born?" Jesus answered, "Truly, truly, I tell you, unless one is born of water and the Spirit, he cannot enter into the Kingdom of God. That which is born of the flesh is flesh. That which is born of the Spirit is spirit. Do not marvel that I said to you, 'You must be born again.' The wind blows where it wants to, and you hear its sound, but you do not know where it comes from and where it is going. So is everyone who is born of the Spirit." (John 3:3-8)

Which of you fathers, if your son asks fora a fish, he won't give him a snake instead of a fish, will he? Or if he asks for an egg, will give him a scorpion? If you then, being evil, know how to give good gifts to your children, how much more will your Heavenly Father give the Holy Spirit to those who ask him? (Luke 11:11-13)

Therefore I tell you, every sin and blasphemy will be forgiven men, but the blasphemy against the Spirit will not be forgiven men. And whoever speaks a word against the Son of Man, it will be forgiven him; but whoever speaks against the Holy Spirit, it will not be forgiven him, neither in this age, nor in that which is to come. (Matthew 12:31-32)

Muhammad ﷺ

Gather in Faith

 Jesus

But the hour comes, and now is, when the true worshippers will worship the Father in spirit and truth, for the Father seeks such to be his worshippers. God is spirit, and those who worship Him must worship in spirit and truth. (John 4:23-24)

Again, truly I tell you that if two of you agree on Earth concerning anything that they will ask, it will be done for them by my Father who is in Heaven. For where two or three are gathered together in my name, there I am in the midst of them. (Matthew 18:19-20)

Jesus entered into the temple of God and drove out all of those who sold and bought in the temple, and overthrew the money changers' tables and the seats of those who sold the doves. He said to them, "It is written, 'My house will be called a house of prayer,' but you have made it a den of robbers." The blind and the lame came to him in the temple, and he healed them. (Matthew 21:12-14)

The pilgrimage is (performed in) the well-known months. So whoever undertakes the pilgrimage, there will be no [sexual relations], abusing or disputing during the pilgrimage. Whatever good you do, God knows it. Make provisions, for surely the best provision is to guard yourselves, so be careful (of your duty) to Me, Oh men of understanding. There is no blame on you in seeking bounty from your Lord,[1] so when you hasten on from Mount Arafat, remember God near the Holy Monument—remember Him as He has guided you, even though you were certainly of the erring ones, before. Then hasten on from the place where the people hasten on, and ask the forgiveness of God. Surely God is Forgiving, Merciful. (The Cow 2:197-199)

Most surely the first House appointed for men is the Ka'ba, blessed and a guidance for the nations. In it are clear signs—the standing-place of Abraham—and whoever enters it is secure. Pilgrimage to the House is a duty upon men for the sake of God, (upon) every one who is able to undertake the journey to it. Whoever disbelieves—surely God is Self-sufficient, above any need of the worlds.
(The Family of Amran 3:96-97)

God has made the Ka'ba, the sacred house, an establishment for the people, and the sacred month, and the [sacrificial animal] offerings with garlands. This is so that you may know that God knows whatever is in the Heavens and whatever is on the Earth, and that God is the Knower of all things. (The Food 5:97)

The idolaters have no right to visit the mosques of God while bearing witness to unbelief, against themselves. Their deeds are null, and they will abide in the Fire. The only ones who can visit the mosques of God are those who believe in God and the Latter Day, and keep up prayer and pay the poor-rate and fear only God. It might be that they are [among the guided]. (The Immunity 9:17-18)

Oh, you who believe! The idolaters are nothing but unclean, so they shall not approach the Sacred Mosque after this year. If you fear poverty, God will enrich you out of His grace, if He pleases. Surely God is Knowing, Wise. (The Immunity 9:28)

---

1 Ali, M.M., *The Holy Qur'an*, 92. There is no harm in seeking an increase of wealth by trading in Mecca in the pilgrimage season.

Jesus

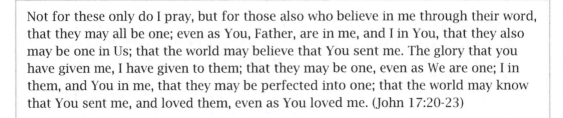

Not for these only do I pray, but for those also who believe in me through their word, that they may all be one; even as You, Father, are in me, and I in You, that they also may be one in Us; that the world may believe that You sent me. The glory that you have given me, I have given to them; that they may be one, even as We are one; I in them, and You in me, that they may be perfected into one; that the world may know that You sent me, and loved them, even as You loved me. (John 17:20-23)

The Sabbath was made for man, not man for the Sabbath. (Mark 2:27)

For the Son of Man is Lord of the Sabbath. (Matthew 12:8)

Muhammad ﷺ

Oh, our Lord! Surely I have settled a part of my offspring in a valley unproductive of fruit, near Your Sacred House, our Lord! So that they may keep up prayer. So make the hearts of some people yearn toward them, and provide them with fruits; by chance they may be grateful. Praise be to God, Who has given me in old age Ishmael and Isaac: most surely my Lord is the Hearer of prayer. My Lord! Make me keep up prayer, and my offspring, (too). Oh, our Lord—accept my prayer.[1]
(Abraham 14:37, 39-40)

Surely those who disbelieve and hinder (men) from God's way, and from the Sacred Mosque that We made for all men equally—(for) the dweller there and (for) the visitor—and surely whoever is inclined to wrong unjustly there, We will make him taste a painful chastisement. (The Pilgrimage 22:25)

Proclaim among men the Pilgrimage. They will come to you on foot and on every lean camel, coming from every remote path, so that they can witness advantages for themselves. Mention the name of God during stated days, over what He has given them of the cattle, and then eat of them and feed the distressed one, the needy. Then let them accomplish their needful acts of shaving and cleansing, and let them fulfil their vows, and let them go around the Ancient House. (The Pilgrimage 22:27-29)

Oh, you who believe! When the call is made for prayer on Friday, hasten to the remembrance of God, and leave trading; that is better for you, if you know. But when the prayer is ended, disperse in the land, and seek God's grace. Remember God much, so that you may succeed. (The Congregation 62:9-10)

---

1 Abraham's prayer, referring to Mecca and the Ka'ba—Ed.

Spread the Teachings

 Jesus

The Good News must first be preached to all the nations. (Mark 13:10)

Come after me, and I will make you fishers for men. (Matthew 4:19)

He who reaps receives wages, and gathers fruit to eternal life; so that both he who sows and he who reaps may rejoice together. (John 4:36)

Go therefore and make disciples of all nations, baptizing them in the name of the Father and of the Son and of the Holy Spirit, teaching them to observe all things that I have commanded you. (Matthew 28:19-20a)

And as you go, proclaim, saying, "The Kingdom of Heaven is near." And as you enter into the household, greet it. And if the household is worthy, let your peace come on it, but if it is not worthy, let your peace return to you. And whoever does not receive you, nor hear your words, as you leave that house or that city, shake off the dust from your feet. (Matthew 10:7, 12-14)

Being assembled together with them, he commanded them, "Do not depart from Jerusalem, but wait for the promise of the Father, which you heard from me. For John indeed baptized in water, but you will be baptized in the Holy Spirit not many days from now. You will receive power when the Holy Spirit has come upon you. You will be witnesses to me in Jerusalem, in all Judea and Samaria, and to the uttermost parts of the Earth."[1] (Acts 1:4-5, 8)

What I tell you in the darkness, speak in the light; and what you hear whispered in the ear, proclaim on the housetops. (Matthew 10:27)

---

1 The resurrected Christ, talking with his apostles about the upcoming Pentecost, when the Holy Spirit will descend on them.—Ed.

God's is the East and the West, so wherever you turn, there is God's purpose; surely God is Ample-giving, Knowing. (The Cow 2:115)

There is no compulsion in religion; truly the right way has become clearly distinct from error. So whoever disbelieves in the Devil and believes in God, indeed has laid hold on the firmest handle, which will not break off, and God is Hearing, Knowing. (The Cow 2:256)

Say, [Prophet]: What thing is the weightiest in testimony? Say: God is witness between you and me, and this Qur'an has been revealed to me so that I may warn you and whomever it reaches. Do you really bear witness that there are other gods with God? Say: I do not bear witness. Say: He is only one God, and surely I am clear of that which you associate (with Him). (The Cattle 6:19)

Those who guard (against evil) are not held accountable for the disbelievers—(theirs) is only to remind, that by chance the disbelievers may guard, also. (The Cattle 6:69)

Regarding the idolaters with whom you made an agreement, who have not failed you in anything and have not supported any one against you: fulfil their agreement to the end of their term—surely God loves those who are careful (of their duty). Then when the sacred months have passed, slay the idolaters wherever you find them, and take them captive and besiege them and lie in wait for them in every ambush. And then if they repent and establish the prayer and pay the poor-rate, leave their way free to them. Surely God is Forgiving, Merciful. (The Immunity 9:4-5)

Jesus

Jesus therefore said to them again, "Peace be to you. As the Father has sent me, even so I send you." When he had said this, he breathed on them, and said to them, "Receive the Holy Spirit. Whoever's sins you forgive, they are forgiven them. Whoever's sins you retain, they have been retained." (John 20:21-23)

Go into all the world, and proclaim the Good News to the whole creation. He who believes and is baptized will be saved; but he who disbelieves will be condemned. These signs will accompany those who believe: in my name they will cast out demons; they will speak with new tongues; they will pick up serpents with their hands; and if they drink any deadly thing, it will not harm them; they will lay hands on the sick, and they will recover. (Mark 16:15-18)

Everyone therefore who confesses me before men, him I will also confess before my Father who is in Heaven. But whoever denies me before people, him I will also deny before my Father who is in Heaven. (Matthew 10:32-33)

For whoever will be ashamed of me and of my words in this adulterous and sinful generation, the Son of Man also will be ashamed of him, when he comes in the glory of his Father with the holy angels. (Mark 8:38)

Whoever listens to you listens to me, and whoever rejects you rejects me. Whoever rejects me rejects Him who sent me. (Luke 10:16)

He who receives you receives me, and he who receives me receives Him who sent me. (Matthew 10:40)

Then Jesus said to his disciples, "If anyone desires to come after me, let him deny himself, and take up his cross, and follow me. For whoever desires to save his life will lose it, and whoever will lose his life for my sake will find it." (Matthew 16:24-25)

And Jesus went about all the cities and the villages, teaching in their synagogues, and preaching the Good News of the Kingdom, and healing every disease and every sickness among the people. But when he saw the crowds, he was moved with compassion for them, because they were harassed and scattered, like sheep without a shepherd. Then he said to his disciples, "The harvest indeed is plentiful, but the laborers are few. Pray therefore that the Lord of the harvest will send out laborers into his harvest." (Matthew 9:35-38)

Muhammad ﷺ

Fight Those Who Have Been Given the Book who do not believe in God or the Latter Day, or who do not prohibit what God and His Messenger have prohibited, or who do not follow the religion of truth. Fight them until they pay the tax in acknowledgement of superiority, while they are in a state of subjection. (The Immunity 9:29)

It is not fitting for believers to go forth [to battle] all together. A troop from every group should go forth, so that they can apply themselves to obtain understanding in religion, and so that they can warn their people, when they return, that they should be cautious. Oh, you who believe! Fight the unbelievers who are near to you, and let them find hardness in you. Know that God is with those who guard (against evil). (The Immunity 9:122-123)

Call to the way of your Lord with wisdom and goodly exhortation, and dispute with them in the best manner. Surely your Lord best knows those who go astray from His path, and He knows best those who follow the right way. (The Bee 16:125)

Do not dispute with the Followers of the Book except in the best manner—except with the [wrongdoers] among them. Say: We believe in what has been revealed to us and what was revealed to you, and our God and your God is One, and we submit to Him. Thus have We revealed the [Qur'an] to you. Those to whom We previously gave the Book believe in the [Qur'an], and so do some of these people. None deny Our Verses except the unbelievers. (The Spider 29:46-47)

He [Muhammad] frowned and turned (his) back when the blind man came to him. How could you have known, [Muhammad], whether he would have grown in spirit or profit from the Reminder? You address yourself to those who consider themselves free from need—there is no blame on you [Prophet] if they do not purify themselves. But you divert yourself from he who comes to you striving hard, with fears. No! Surely [this Qur'an] is (a source of) eminence. So let he who pleases mind it, on honoured pages, exalted and purified. In the hands of noble and virtuous scribes.[1] (He Frowned 80:1-16)

---

1 Ali, M.M., *The Holy Qur'an*, 1160. A blind man interfered with the Holy Prophet's conversation with some of the chiefs of the Quraish, and the Prophet frowned at this interference.

Jesus

So when they had eaten their breakfast, Jesus said to Simon Peter, "Simon, son of Jonah, do you love me more than these?" He said to him, "Yes, Lord; you know that I have affection for you." He said to him, "Feed my lambs." He said to him again a second time, "Simon, son of Jonah, do you love me?" He said to him, "Yes, Lord; you know that I have affection for you." He said to him, "Tend my sheep." He said to him the third time, "Simon, son of Jonah, do you have affection for me?" Peter was grieved because he asked him the third time, "Do you have affection for me?" He said to him, "Lord, you know everything. You know that I have affection for you." Jesus said to him, "Feed my sheep." (John 21:15-17)

You did not choose me, but I chose you, and appointed you, that you should go and bear fruit, and that your fruit should remain; so that whatever you ask of the Father in my name, he may give it to you. (John 15:16)

Truly I tell you, there is no one who has left house, or wife, or brothers, or parents, or children, for the Kingdom of God's sake, who will not receive many times more in this time. And in the world to come, eternal life. (Luke 18:29-30)

The harvest is indeed plentiful, but the laborers are few. Pray therefore to the Lord of the harvest, that he may send out laborers into his harvest. (Luke 10:2)

Muhammad ﷺ

All is Possible with Faith

 Jesus

Jesus rebuked him, the demon went out of him, and the boy was cured from that hour. Then the disciples came to Jesus privately, and said, "Why weren't we able to cast it out?" So Jesus said to them, "Because of your little faith. For truly I tell you, if you have faith as a grain of mustard seed, you will tell this mountain, 'Move from here to there,' and it will move; and nothing will be impossible for you." (Matthew 17:18-20)

If you can believe, all things are possible to him who believes. (Mark 9:23)

Truly I tell you, whoever may tell this mountain, "Be taken up and cast into the sea," and does not doubt in his heart, but believes that what he says will happen, it will be done for him whatever he says. (Mark 11:23)

If you had faith like a grain of mustard seed, you would tell this mulberry tree, "Be uprooted, and be planted in the sea," and it would obey you. (Luke 17:6)

The things which are impossible with men are possible with God. (Luke 18:27)

For a woman whose young daughter had an unclean spirit heard of him came and fell at his feet. Now the woman was a Greek, a Syrophoenician by race. She begged him that he would cast the demon out of her daughter. But Jesus said to her, "Let the children be filled first, for it is not appropriate to take the children's bread and throw it to the dogs." But she answered him, "Yes, Lord, but even the dogs under the table eat the children's crumbs." He said to her, "For this saying, go your way. The demon has gone out of your daughter." And when she went away to her house, she found the demon gone out, and the child lying on the bed.[1] (Mark 7:25-30)

---

1 Wallerstedt et al, *Orthodox Bible: Old and New Testaments* 2008, 1298. Having evoked this woman's love and persistent faith, Christ now reveals her humility.

Prayer

 Jesus

Therefore, you should pray this way: "Our Father in Heaven, hallowed be your name. Let your Kingdom come. Let your will be done, on Earth as it is in Heaven. Give us today our daily bread. And forgive us our debts, as we also forgive our debtors. And lead us not into temptation, but deliver us from the evil one. For yours is the Kingdom, the power, and the glory, forever. Amen."[1] (Matthew 6:9-13)

Therefore I tell you, whatever you ask for in prayer, believe that you have received it, and it will be yours. (Mark 11:24)

All things, whatever you ask in prayer, believing, you will receive. (Matthew 21:22)

---

1 The Christian Lord's Prayer—Ed.

In the name of God, the Beneficent, the Merciful. (All) Praise is due to God, the Lord of the Worlds. The Beneficent, the Merciful, Master of the Day of Requital. You [alone] do we serve, and You [alone] do we beseech for help. Guide us on the right path, the path of those upon whom You have bestowed favours, not the path of those upon whom You brought down wrath, or those who go astray.[1]
(The Opening 1:1-7)

Indeed, [Prophet], we see the turning of your face to Heaven, so we will surely turn you to the direction of prayer that you like. So turn your face toward the Sacred Mosque, and wherever you are, turn your faces toward it. Those who have been given the Book most surely know that it is the truth from their Lord. God is not at all heedless of what they do. (The Cow 2:144)

When you have performed your devotions, laud God as you lauded your fathers, rather a greater lauding. But there are some who say: Our Lord! Give us in the world—they will have no portion in the Hereafter. There are some who say: Our Lord! Grant us good in this world and good in the Hereafter, and save us from the chastisement of the Fire! They will have (their) portion of what they have earned, and God is swift in reckoning. (The Cow 2:200-202)

Attend constantly to prayers and to the most excellent prayer, and stand up truly obedient to God. But if you are in danger, (say your prayers) on foot or on horseback; and then when you are secure, remember God, as He has taught you what you did not know. (The Cow 2:238-239)

Surely, those who believe and do good deeds and keep up prayer and pay the poor-rate will have their reward from their Lord, and they will have no fear, nor will they grieve. (The Cow 2:277)

---

1 Ali, M.M., *The Holy Qur'an*, 3. These verses have a special importance as a prayer, being an essential part of every prayer, whether offered in congregation or in private. Its Oft-repeated Seven Verses constitute the prayer for guidance of every Muslim, at least thirty-two times a day, and therefore it has a much greater importance for him than the Lord's Prayer for a Christian.

Jesus

But I tell you who hear: love your enemies, do good to those who hate you, bless those who curse you, and pray for those who mistreat you. (Luke 6:27-28)

Whenever you stand praying, forgive, if you have anything against anyone; so that your Father, who is in Heaven, may also forgive you your transgressions. (Mark 11:25)

In that day you will ask nothing of me. Truly, truly I tell you, whatever you may ask of the Father in my name, he will give it to you. Until now, you have asked nothing in my name. Ask, and you will receive, so that your joy may be made full. (John 16:23-24)

And when you pray, you are not to be as the hypocrites, for they love to stand and pray in the synagogues and in the corners of the streets, that they may be seen by others. Truly, I tell you, they have received their reward. But you, when you pray, enter into your inner chamber, and having shut your door, pray to your Father who is in secret, and your Father who sees in secret will reward you openly. (Matthew 6:5-6)

Muhammad ﷺ

When you journey on the Earth, there is no blame on you if you shorten the prayer, if you fear that those who disbelieve will cause you distress. Surely the unbelievers are your open enemies. When you [Prophet] are among [believers] and you lead the prayer for them, let a group of them stand up with you, and let them take their arms. Then when they have prostrated themselves, let them go to your rear, and let another group who have not prayed come forward and pray with you, and let them take their precautions and their arms. (For) those who disbelieve desire that you may be careless of your arms and your luggage, so that they may turn upon you with a sudden united attack. There is no blame on you, if you are annoyed with rain or if you are sick, that you lay down your arms, and take your precautions. Surely, God has prepared a disgraceful chastisement for the unbelievers. (The Women 4:101-102)

When you have finished the prayer, remember God standing and sitting and reclining. But when you are secure (from danger), keep up prayer. Surely, prayer is a timed order for the believers. (The Women 4:103)

When you call to prayer, they make it a mockery and a joke; this is because they are a people who do not understand. (The Food 5:58)

Say, [Prophet]: 'Shall we call on that besides God, which does not benefit us nor harm us, and shall we be turned back on our heels after God has guided us, like he whom the devils have made fall down perplexed on Earth? He has companions who call him to the right way, (saying): Come to us. Say: Surely the guidance of God is the (true) guidance, and we are commanded to submit to the Lord of the Worlds. You should keep up prayer and be careful of (your duty to) Him. It is Him to whom you will be gathered. (The Cattle 6:71-72)

Say: My Lord has ordered justice, and set upright your faces at every time of prayer. Call on Him, being sincere to Him in obedience; He brought you forth in the beginning, so shall you also return. (The Elevated Places 7:29)

Call on your Lord humbly and secretly. Surely He does not love those who exceed the limits. (The Elevated Places 7:55)

Keep up prayer in the two parts of the day, and in the first hours of the night. Surely, good deeds take away evil deeds—this is a reminder to the mindful. (Hud 11:114)

Jesus

And in praying, do not use vain repetitions, as the Gentiles do; for they think that they will be heard for their much speaking. Therefore do not be like them, for your Father knows what things you need, before you ask him. (Matthew 6:7-8)

If you remain in me, and my words remain in you, you will ask whatever you desire, and it will be done for you. In this is my Father glorified, that you bear much fruit and so prove to be my disciples. (John 15:7-8)

And whatever you ask in my name, this I will do, that the Father may be glorified in the Son. If you ask anything in my name, I will do it. (John 14:13-14)

Muhammad ﷺ

True prayer is due to Him. Those to whom they pray besides God give them no answer, but (they are) like one who stretches forth his two hands toward water that it may reach his mouth, but it will not reach it. The prayer of the unbelievers is only in error. (The Thunder 13:14)

Keep up prayer from the declining of the sun until the darkness of the night, and the morning [Qur'an] recitation. Surely, the morning recitation is witnessed. During part of the night, forsake sleep for prayer, beyond what is obligatory for you; maybe your Lord will raise you to a position of great glory. (The Israelites 17:78-79)

[Prophet], order prayer on your followers, and steadily adhere to it. We do not ask you for subsistence—We give you subsistence, and the (good) ending is for guarding (against evil). (Ta Ha 20:132)

Recite what has been revealed to you of the Book, and keep up prayer. Surely prayer keeps (one) away from indecency and evil, and certainly the remembrance of God is the greatest, and God knows what you do. (The Spider 29:45)

Those who believe in Our Verses are only those who, when reminded of them, fall down making obeisance and celebrate the praise of their Lord—they are not proud. Their sides draw away from (their) beds, and they call upon their Lord in fear and in hope, and they spend (benevolently) out of what We have given them. (The Adoration 32:15-16)

Oh, you [Prophet], who have wrapped up yourself![1] Rise to pray in the night, all but a little, half of it, or lessen it a little. Or add to it, and recite the Qur'an, well-arranged. Surely We will make a weighty word light upon you. Surely the rising by night is the firmest way to tread, and the best corrective of speech. Surely you have a long occupation in the daytime. Remember the name of your Lord, and devote yourself to Him with (exclusive) devotion. (The Wrapped Up 73:1-8)

Glorify the name of your Lord morning and evening. And during part of the night [bow to] Him, and give glory to Him (a) long (part of the) night. (The Man 76:25-26)

Surely, We have given you abundance of good, therefore pray to your Lord and make a sacrifice. Surely your enemy is the one cut off (from good). (The Abundance of Good 108:1-3)

---

1 Haleem, *The Qur'an*, 397. After his first encounter with the Angel of Revelation in the Cave of Hira, the Prophet went home trembling and asked his wife to cover him with his cloak.

Appendices

Contents

A. Religion Development

 ## Christianity Timeline

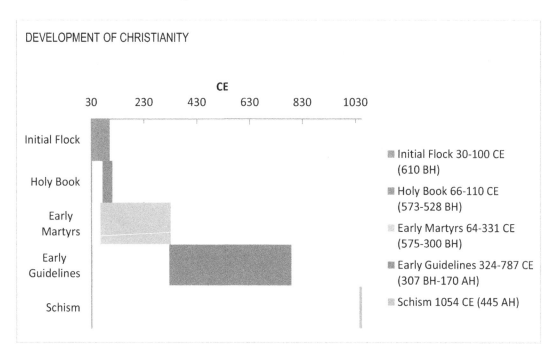

DEVELOPMENT OF CHRISTIANITY

- Initial Flock 30-100 CE (610 BH)
- Holy Book 66-110 CE (573-528 BH)
- Early Martyrs 64-331 CE (575-300 BH)
- Early Guidelines 324-787 CE (307 BH-170 AH)
- Schism 1054 CE (445 AH)

Initial Flock

The Religion Begins

- Christ preaches from around 30 CE (610 BH) until his death in 33 CE (607 BH).
- After His death, Christ physically appears to his apostles and tells them to "Therefore go, and make disciples of all nations." (Matthew 28:19)
- In front of his apostles, Christ ascends to Heaven. (Luke 24:50-51)
- In Jerusalem, the Holy Spirit descends on 120 gathered disciples as "a rushing, mighty wind and tongues like fire." They speak in languages that they do not know, covering all languages of the 3,000 people who are present. Those 3,000 become followers of Christ. (Acts 2:1-15, 41) The Church is born.

The Religion Spreads

• Apostles spread Christianity from Jerusalem throughout the Hellenized Empire to Jews, Gentiles and Pagans.

• The apostle Paul, the last to die, dies around 100 CE (538 BH).

• In roughly the first 100 years after Christ's death, Christianity spreads to regions that are in modern-day Bosnia, Cyprus, Egypt, Ethiopia, Greece, Herzegovina, Hungary, India, Iran, Iraq, Italy, Jordan, Kuwait, Lebanon, Montenegro, Palestine, Russia, Serbia, Syria, Turkey, Ukraine and the West Bank.[1]

• The Church continues to gradually spread via preaching and writing, throughout the Roman Empire and beyond.

Holy Book

SOME BOOKS IN THE CHRISTIAN BIBLE

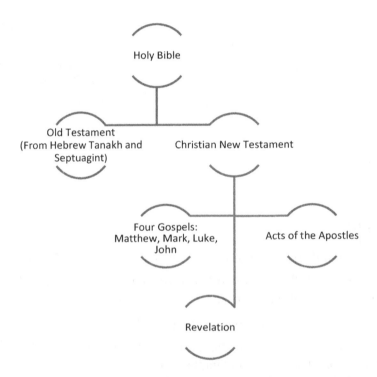

• In the New Testament Bible, the four Gospels (Matthew, Mark, Luke and John) in the New Testament chronologically describe Christ's life and mission. They are written between 32-78 years after Christ dies.[2]

---

1 Eusebius, *The History of the Church*, (Caesaria: fourth century), Rev. Arthur Cushman McGiffert, trans., Kindle Edition (Stilwell: Digireads.com, 2005) 34,41-42,60, 63, 70, 82, 85, 90-91, 229; Galatians 1:17, Acts 13:4-13.

2 Raymond E. Brown, *An Introduction to the New Testament*, Chapter 1, Section B, (New Haven: Yale University Press, 1997).

- Tradition holds that the apostle Matthew (one of the Twelve Apostles, a tax collector) writes the Gospel of Matthew, and the apostle John (one of the Twelve Apostles, a fisherman) writes the Gospel of John and Revelation.[1] They write based on their witnessing Christ's life and ministry. Scholars date the writings around 70-110 CE (569-528 BH).

- Luke (a physician) and Mark are early apostles, possibly part of the Seventy Apostles.[2] Tradition holds that they write the Gospel of Luke and the Gospel of Mark, and that Luke also writes the Acts of the Apostles. Scholars date the writings around 65-85 CE (574-554 BH).

- The oldest discovered fragment of the New Testament is five verses from the Book of John, found on a fragment of papyrus from Egypt. It is dated 100-150 CE (538-487 BH), which is 15-65 years after John wrote it. The Codex Sinaiticus, a complete copy of the New Testament, is dated 350 CE (280 BH). 5,644 manuscripts record portions of the New Testament in Greek, its original language.[3]

- Other than minor copying errors that do not affect Christian doctrine, there are no discrepancies among the manuscripts.[4]

- Early Church Fathers reject certain gospels that circulate in the early centuries of Christianity as non-canonical, because they do not agree with the four Gospels. They are considered to have been anonymously written and sometimes falsely attributed to apostles of Christ. Here are three examples:

The *Infancy Gospel of Thomas* describes miracles from Jesus' childhood that are undocumented elsewhere, such as a five-year-old Jesus fashioning twelve sparrows from clay that flew away. This writing has been described as perhaps being written by someone (not the disciple Thomas) in the second century CE (554-462 BH). Perhaps the writer yearned for more miracle stories in Jesus' youth. It presents the Christ child as sometimes malevolent, comparable to the trickster nature of the god-child in many Greek myths.[5]

The *Syriac (or Arabic) Infancy Gospel* describes the infant Jesus speaking to his mother Mary from his cradle. It dates back to the fifth or sixth century CE (246-23 BH).[6]

The *Questions of Bartholomew* describes Satan explaining how he fell from Heaven. The oldest existing manuscript is dated in the fifth century CE (246-130 BH). In this writing,

---

1 Wallerstedt et al., *Orthodox Bible*, 588.

2 Philip Schaff, *Ante-Nicene Fathers Volume 5 - Enhanced Version (Early Church Fathers)* Kindle Edition (Grand Rapids: Christian Classics Ethereal Library, June 2009), "Appendix to the Works of Hippolytus."

3 Lee Strobel, *The Case for Christ* (Grand Rapids: Zondervan, 2008, Kindle Edition), 79-81, via interview with Bruce Metzger, renowned Biblical Scholar.

4 Ibid., 82-85.

5 "Infancy Gospel of Thomas," *Wikipedia*, https://en.wikipedia.org/wiki/Infancy_Gospel_of_Thomas (accessed December 2017).

6 "Syriac Infancy Gospel," *Wikipedia*, https://en.wikipedia.org/wiki/Syriac_Infancy_Gospel (accessed December 2017)

God created man in His image, and the archangel Michael requested the angel Satanael (now Satan) to worship man. Satan cried: "I am fire of fire, I was the first angel formed, and shall I worship clay and matter? God will not be wroth with me; but I will set my throne over against his throne, and I will be as he is. Then was God wroth with me and cast me down.[1]

Early Martyrs

Note: Christian martyrs are people who are killed or persecuted for following Christianity, throughout time. Christianity embraces the sanctity of life: therefore Christianity does not condone suicidal martyrdom or offensive warfare.

The Sanctity of Life

• Humans are created in the image of God. Therefore, life is sacred:

"And God said, 'Let Us make man in Our image, after Our likeness; and let them have dominion over the fish of the sea, and over the birds of the sky, and over the livestock, and over all the Earth and over every creeping thing that creeps on the Earth.' And God created man in His own image. In God's image He created him; male and female He created them." (Genesis 1:26-27)

• God lives within humans, in the form of the Holy Spirit. Therefore, life is sacred:

"Do you not know that you are the temple of God and that the Spirit of God dwells in you? If any man destroys the temple of God, God will destroy him, for the temple of God is holy, and that is what you are." (1 Corinthians 3:16-17)

Preparing to Defend Yourself

• When Christ sends out his apostles into harms way, just before Roman authorities crucify Him, he tells them "But now, whoever has a money bag must take it, and likewise a pack. Whoever has none, must sell his cloak, and buy a sword. For I tell you that this which is written must still be fulfilled in me: 'He was numbered with the transgressors.' For that which concerns me has an end." They said, "Lord, look, here are two swords." He said to them, "That is enough." (Luke 22:36-38)

Non-Resistance

• Yet, when Jesus' apostle begins to attack the Roman soldier who had apprehended Jesus, He says this:

"Put your sword back into its place, for all who take the sword will die by the sword. Or do you think that I could not ask My Father, and He would even now send me more than twelve legions of angels? How then would the Scriptures be fulfilled, that it must be so?" (Matthew 26:52-54)

---

1 M.R. James, "The Apocryphal New Testament " (Oxford: Clarendon Press, 1924).

"While he was still speaking, look, a crowd came, and he who was called Judas, one of the Twelve, was leading them. He came near to Jesus to kiss him, but Jesus said to him, 'Judas, do you betray the Son of Man with a kiss?' When those who were around him saw what was about to happen, they said, 'Lord, should we strike with the sword?' A certain of them struck the servant of the high priest, and cut off his right ear. But Jesus answered, 'Let me at least do this'—and he touched his ear, and healed him."[1]
(Luke 22:47-51)

- "You have heard that it was said, 'An eye for an eye and a tooth for a tooth.' But I tell you, do not set yourself against the one who is evil. But whoever slaps you on your right cheek, turn to him the other also. And if anyone sues you to take away your coat, let him have your cloak also." (Matthew 5:38-40)

- "But I tell you who hear: love your enemies, do good to those who hate you, bless those who curse you, and pray for those who mistreat you." (Luke 6:27-28)

- "Blessed are those who are persecuted for righteousness' sake. Blessed are you when men insult you, and persecute you, and say all kinds of evil against you falsely, for My sake." (Matthew 5:10-11)

- "Look, I send you out as sheep in the midst of wolves. Therefore be wise as serpents, and harmless as doves." (Matthew 10:16)

First Martyrs

- During the first three centuries of Christianity (in the Roman Empire), Roman authorities martyr Christians for not worshipping Roman gods or paying homage to the Roman Emperor as divine.

- In 313 CE (319 BH), Emperor Constantine I, the founder of the Byzantine Empire, becomes a Christian and stops Christian oppression and martyrdom via the Edict of Milan.

---

1 Judas (a Disciple of Christ) betrayed Jesus to the high priest, who was among the Roman soldiers who came to arrest and crucify him.—Ed.

Early Guidelines

Ecumenical Councils

The first seven Ecumenical Councils gather to settle matters of church doctrine and practice. The Eastern Orthodox Church and the Catholic Church accept all seven of these councils as ecumenical.

Because of doctrinal differences, the Nestorian Church (Church of the East) accepts only the first two councils and the Oriental Orthodox Church accepts only the first three.

COUNCIL (YEAR CE/BH or AH)	DOCTRINAL CONCLUSIONS
First Council of Nicaea (325 CE/306 BH)	• Emperor Constantine I convenes this council to settle a controversial issue, the relation between Jesus Christ and God the Father. • The council describes "God's only-begotten Son, Jesus Christ, as of the same substance with God the Father. Thus Arian beliefs are heretical.[1] This becomes a criterion for the Christian Holy Trinity.
First Council of Constantinople (381 CE/248 BH)	• The council approves what is the current form of the Nicene Creed. • The council condemns the teaching that there is no human mind or soul in Christ. Thus Apollinarism is heretical.[2]
Council of Ephesus (431 CE/197 BH)	• The council proclaims the Virgin Mary as the Theotokos (God-bearer). Thus Nestorian beliefs are heretical.[3]
Council of Chalcedon (451 CE/176 BH)	• The council concludes that Christ is in two natures: both fully human and fully divine, united in one individual person and existence. Thus Nestorian beliefs are heretical.The Oriental Orthodox reject the council's conclusion.[3]
Second Council of Constantinople (553 CE/71 BH)	• The council confirms that Christ has two natures, one divine and one human, united in one person with neither confusion nor division. Thus Nestorian beliefs are heretical.[3] • The council confirms that the Virgin Mary can be called the Mother of God (Theotokos). Thus Nestorian beliefs are heretical.[3]
Third Council of Constantinople (680 CE/60 AH)	• The council affirms that Christ has both human and divine energies and wills. Thus monoenergism and monothelitism are heretical.[4]

▶

COUNCIL (YEAR CE/BH or AH)	DOCTRINAL CONCLUSIONS
Second Council of Nicaea (787 CE/170 AH)	• The council restores the veneration of icons (holy images) and ends the first iconoclasm. • The council establishes that people who contemplate icons are moved to fervent memory of the icons' prototypes. • The council concludes that it is proper to fervently and reverently adore icons, but not to worship them. Worship belongs to the Divine Being alone. • The council clarifies that when people honor and adore an icon, the honor and adoration passes over to the icon's prototype.

---

1 G.C. Stead, "The Thalia of Arius and the Testimony of Athanasius," *Journal of Theological Studies* 39, no. 1 (April 1978): 48–50. Arians believed that Christ was created and not always present with God.

2 Alister McGrath, *Historical Theology, An Introduction to the History of Christian Thought*, (Oxford: Wiley-Blackwell,1998), Chapter 1, Apollinaris believed that Jesus had a divine mind and a lower soul (emotions).

3 Nestorius, *The Bazaar of Heracleides*, (Constantinople: fifth century), translated from Syriac, (Eugene: Wipf and Stock, 2002), xxix, Nestorians believe that Mary was Christ-bearer vs. God-bearer and that Christ is two persons, human and divine.

T.H. Bindley and F.W. Green, T*he Oecumenical Documents of the Faith*, (London: Methuen & Co.,1950), 91-92) The Oriental Orthodox would accept only that Christ is "*of or from* two natures" but not "*in* two natures".

Dialogue toward restoring communion between the Oriental Orthodox church and the Eastern Orthodox and Catholic churches began again in the mid-20th century and continues.—Ed.

4 John B. Bury, *A History of the Later Roman Empire from Arcadius to Irene, Volume II* (Chestnut Hill: Adamant Media, 2000), 249-253, Monoenergism holds that Christ had two natures but one energy. Monothelitism that Christ had two natures, but only one will.

Schism

BRANCHES OF CHRISTIANITY[1]

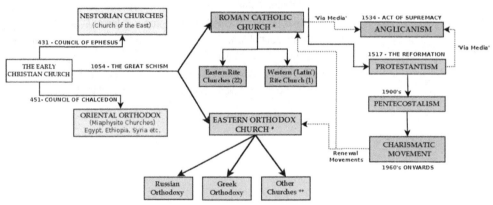

* Both Eastern Orthodox and Roman Catholic Churches claim the title of the 'One True Church'.
** There are several other autonomous and autocephalous churches within Eastern Orthodoxy.

- Due to institutional and theological differences, the Early Christian Church breaks apart into Eastern Orthodox Christianity and Western Catholicism. The official schism occurs 1,021 years after Christ dies, in the year 1054 CE (445 AH).

- Prominent issues are these:

  The Filioque: Does the Holy Spirit proceed both from the Father and the Son (Catholic), or is the Father alone the source of the Holy Spirit (Orthodox)?

  Leadership: The Pope's claim to universal jurisdiction and Constantinople's place in relation to the five Patriarchates

---

1 erasercrumbs, "Branches of Christianity," reprinted by permission from *WaitingTillMarriage*, http://forums.waitingtillmarriage.org/topic/1664-what-exactly-are-denonimations/ (accessed March, 2016).

ﷺ Islam Timeline

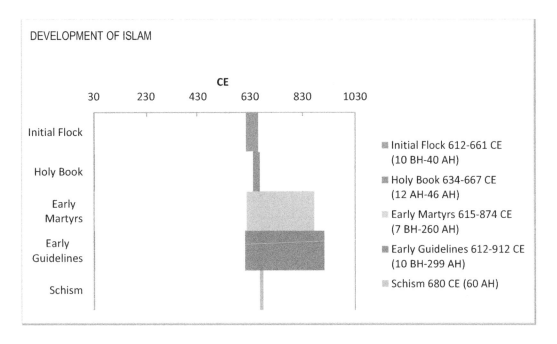

DEVELOPMENT OF ISLAM

CE

Initial Flock 612-661 CE (10 BH-40 AH)

Holy Book 634-667 CE (12 AH-46 AH)

Early Martyrs 615-874 CE (7 BH-260 AH)

Early Guidelines 612-912 CE (10 BH-299 AH)

Schism 680 CE (60 AH)

Initial Flock

The Religion Begins

- Muhammad preaches from 613 CE (9 BH) until his death in 632 CE (11 AH).[1]

- Leaders of the Muslim community disagree over who should succeed Muhammad as leader. Since none of Muhammad's sons survive into adulthood, direct hereditary succession is not an option.[2]

- Umar (Umar ibn al-Khattab), a prominent companion of Muhammad, nominates Muhammad's father-in-law and trusted advisor, Abu Bakr. Others add support, and Abu Bakr becomes the first caliph.[3] Some of Muhammad's companions dispute the choice, preferring Ali, Muhammad's cousin and son-in-law.

---

1 Ira M. Lapidus, *A History of Islamic Societies*, (Cambridge: Cambridge University Press, 2002) 14, (Hereafter cited as Lapidus, *History Islamic Societies*).

2 Ibid., 23.

3 Ibid., 38.

The Religion Spreads

- Beginning with Abu Bakr, a series of four Caliphs (the Rashidun) governs the Islamic state from 632 CE (11 AH) through 661 CE (41 AH).[1]

- The Rashidun oversee the initial phase of the Muslim conquests, advancing through Syria, Kourasan (parts of Persia, Afghanistan, Turkmenistan), Egypt and Iraq.[2]

Holy Book

SURAS AND TOPICS IN THE QUR'AN

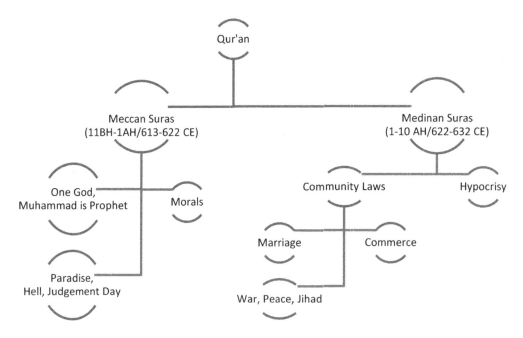

- Over a period of 23 years, through the angel Gabriel, God first reveals the suras to Muhammad in Mecca, and then in Medina after the migration.

- People memorize things that Muhammad says, and scribes write his message on palm leaves and stones. (Bukhari[3] vol. 6:509)

- There is no organized manuscript of the Qur'an before Muhammad dies in 632 CE (11 AH). Shortly after his death, some who have memorized parts of the Qur'an die in battle. Thus, some ayat (verses) do not survive, or are otherwise lost. (Bukhari vol. 6:509)[4]

---

1 Albert Hourani, *A History of the Arab Peoples*, (London: Faber & Faber, 2002) 25 (Hereafter cited as Hourani, *History Arab Peoples*).

2 Ibid., 23-24.

3 Saḥīḥ al-Bukhārī is one of the six major Hadith collections (prophetic traditions) of Sunni Islam. It is also used as an authentic Hadith collection by Zaidi Shia Muslims.—Ed.

4 Some Shia believe that the Qur'an was gathered and compiled by Muhammad during his lifetime.—Ed.

- Concerned that the message will be lost, Abu Bakr (the first appointed Caliph) appoints Zayd ibn Thabit (a scribe during Muhammad's lifetime) to collect and preserve the book in one volume. (Bukhari vol. 6:509)

- In about 650 CE (29 AH), as Islam expands beyond the Arabian Peninsula into Persia, the Levant, and North Africa, Uthman ibn Affan (the third Caliph) notices slight differences in pronunciation of the Qur'an. To preserve the sanctity of the text, he orders a committee headed by Zayd to use Abu Bakr's copy and prepare a standard copy of the Qur'an. Uthman has rival texts of the Qur'an burned. (Bukhari vol. 6:510)

- The suras (chapters) are not compiled and arranged in the Qur'an by chronological revelation. According to tradition, Muhammad told his companions the traditional placement as he revealed them.[1] They are generally in order from the longest to the shortest.

- 86 suras are classified as Meccan (revealed to Muhammad while he was living in Mecca), and 28 are Medinan (revealed after his migration to Medina).

- Meccan suras generally deal with faith and the Hereafter. Medinan suras are more concerned with organizing Muslim society and showing strength toward achieving the goal of Dar al-Islam (ruling countries by Sharia Law).

- With regard to the Qur'an, abrogation (Naskh) is this principle in Islamic law: When there is a contradiction in the Qur'an, the later revealed ayat (verses) cancel out, or at least modify, earlier revealed ayat.[2] Four ayat in the Qur'an actually discuss substitution. (2:106, 13:39, 17:86, 16:101)

- Traditional Muslims believe that the Qur'an can only be understood in classical Arabic, which Islamic tradition says is the language of Heaven. Without special training, Arabic speakers cannot understand classical Arabic. Thus, to understand the Qur'an, most Muslims rely on commentaries and what they learn at the mosque or through Muslim media.[3]

Early Martyrs

Note: Islam views a martyr as one who "dies" while conducting jihad (Holy Struggle for divine truth). Death can be off the battlefield (simply *willing* to defend and die for the truth) or on the battlefield (literally die).[4] The Qur'anic Arabic word for martyr is "shaheed," which means "one who is witness, of God and His religion."[5] Opinions in the Muslim world vary on whether suicide attacks count as martyrdom. Qur'an aya 2:195 says, in part, "Do not throw yourselves to perdition with your own hands." This is understood by some translators to outlaw suicide and self-harm, whereas other translators view this, taken in context, as meaning that withholding monetary aid to Islam could endanger Islam, thus casting the community into perdition.

---

1 Israr Ahmed, Introduction in *Bayan-ul-Qur'an—In English Tafsir*, 3 Mp3 CDs, (ASIN: B017BOTANA).

2 David S. Powers, "On the Abrogation of the Bequest Verses," *Arabica* Journal 29, no. 3 (Sept, 1982): 246-247, 249-287.
Some Shia do not accept the principle of abrogation.—Ed.

3 Mark A. Gabriel, *Jesus and Muhammad: Profound Differences and Surprising Similarities*, (Lake Mary: Frontline, 2004), 220 (Hereafter cited as Gabriel, *Jesus and Muhammad*).

4 A. Ezzati, "The Concept Of Martyrdom In Islam," *Al-Serat*, Vol XII (1986).

5 Khalid Zaheer, "Definition of a Shaheed," *Dawn*, www.Dawn.com, (November 22, 2013) (accessed December, 2017).

Martyrdom Leads to Heaven

A shaheed (martyr) is one whose place in Paradise is promised. These ayat in the Qur'an discuss a shaheed's place in Paradise:

- "Do not speak of those who are slain in God's way as dead. No, (they are) alive, but you do not perceive it." (2:154)

- "Do not think of those who are killed in God's way as dead. No, they are alive, and they are provided sustenance from their Lord, rejoicing in what God has given them of His grace. They rejoice for those who are (left) behind, who have not yet joined them, that they will have no fear, nor will they grieve." (3:169-170)

- "Those who fought and were slain, I will most certainly cover their evil deeds, and I will most certainly admit them to gardens, beneath which rivers flow—a reward from God." (3:195)

- "If you are willing to trade the life of this world for the Hereafter, fight in God's way, for great reward. Whoever fights in the way of God, be he slain or be he victorious, We will grant him a mighty reward. Fight in the way of God for the weak men, women, and children who cry out, 'Lord, cause us to go forth from this town, whose people are oppressors!' Fight against the friends of the Devil." (4:74-76)

- "God has bought the lives and wealth of the believers in return for the Garden—they fight in God's way: they slay and are slain—this is a binding promise given by Him in the Torah, the Gospel, and the Qur'an. Who could be more faithful to his covenant than God? So rejoice in the pledge that you have made: that is the mighty achievement." (9:111)

- "God will most certainly grant a good sustenance to those who fled in God's way and then were slain or died. Most surely God is the best giver of sustenance. He will certainly admit them to an entrance that they will be well pleased with." (22:58-59)

- "Regarding those who are slain in the way of God—He will by no means cause their deeds to perish. He will guide them and improve their condition and admit them to the Garden." (47:4-6)

- "Struggle hard in God's way with your wealth and your lives. That is better for you, if only you knew! He will forgive you your faults and admit you into gardens, beneath which rivers flow, and goodly dwellings in gardens of eternity; that is the mighty achievement." (61:11-12)

Preparing to Defend Yourself

- "Prepare against them what force you can. Tie horses at the frontier, to frighten the enemy of God and your enemy and others besides them whom you do not know. God knows them; and any thing that you spend in God's way, it will be paid back to you fully, and you will not be dealt with unjustly. If they incline to peace, then you also incline to it, and trust in God. Surely He is the Hearing, the Knowing." (8:60-61)

Resisting Enemies through Jihad

Muslims and scholars disagree on the definition of jihad. In Arabic, jihad means "striving, applying oneself, struggling, persevering."[1] Some define jihad as having two meanings: an inner spiritual struggle (the "greater jihad") and an outer physical struggle against the enemies of Islam (the "lesser jihad"), which can take a violent or non-violent form.[2]

- When angels asked God why He would place one on Earth who would make mischief and shed blood, He said "I know what you do not know." (2:30)

- "Fight in the way of God with those who fight you, and do not exceed the limits. Surely God does not love those who exceed the limits. And kill them wherever you find them, and drive them out from wherever they drove out you. Persecution is more severe than slaughter. Do not fight them at the Sacred Mosque until they fight with you in it, but if they do fight you, slay them. Such is the recompense of the unbelievers. But if they cease, surely God is Forgiving, Merciful. Fight them until there is no persecution and religion is only for God. But if they cease, there should be no hostility except against the oppressors. The sacred month for the sacred month, and all sacred things are (under the law of) retaliation. So whoever acts aggressively against you, inflict injury on him according to the injury that he inflicted on you, and [fear] God." (2:190-194)

- "Fight in the way of God, and know that God is Hearing, Knowing. Who will offer to God a goodly gift, so that He will multiply it to him in many ways? God restricts and amplifies, and you will be returned to Him." (2:244-245)

- "Your Lord revealed to the angels: I am with you, so make firm those who believe. I will cast terror into the hearts of those who disbelieve. So strike off their heads and strike off every finger-tip of them. This is because they acted adversely to God and His Messenger; surely God is severe in repaying (evil) for whoever acts adversely to God and His Messenger." (8:12-13)

- "If they break their oaths after their agreement and (openly) revile your religion, fight the leaders of disbelief—surely their oaths are nothing—so that they may cease. Fight them; God will chastise them by your hands, bring them to disgrace, assist you against them and heal the hearts of a believing people." (9:12, 14)

- "Fight those who have been given the Book who do not believe in God or the Latter Day, or who do not prohibit what God and His Messenger have prohibited, or who do not follow the religion of truth. Fight them until they pay the tax in acknowledgement of superiority, while they are in a state of subjection." (9:29)

- "If you do not go forth, He will chastise you with a painful chastisement, and replace you with a people other than yourselves, and you will do Him no harm. God has power over all things." (9:39)

- "Say to those of the Bedouins who were left behind: 'You will soon be invited (to fight) against a people possessing mighty prowess. You will fight against them until they

---

1 Khaled M. Abou El Fadl, *The Great Theft: Wrestling Islam from the Extremists*, (New York: HarperOne, 2007), 221;

2 Gabriel, *Jesus and Muhammad*, 126.

submit. If you obey, God will grant you a good reward, but if you turn back as you turned back before, He will chastise you with a painful chastisement.'" (48:16)

- "Oh, you who believe! Fight the unbelievers who are near to you, and let them find hardness in you. Know that God is with those who [fear Him]." (9:123)

- "God will certainly help whoever retaliates, in like manner, to his own affliction and oppression. Most surely God is Pardoning, Forgiving." (22:60)

- "God loves those who fight in His way in ranks, as if they were a firm and compact wall." (61:4)

First Martyrs

- The first martyr of Islam is a woman named Sumayyah bint Khayyat, who is murdered by Meccans for her beliefs, in the early days of Islam.[1]

- Hamza, a noted warrior of the early community and the uncle of Muhammad, is slain in Battle of Uhud in 625 CE (3 AH).[2]

- Ja'far, Muhammad's cousin who leads the first group of Muslim refugees to Abyssinia, is martyred fighting the Byzantines in the Battle of Mu'tah in 629 CE (8 AH).[3]

- The final three of the four Rightly-guided Caliphs (the first Sunni caliphs) are martyred while serving as caliph. Caliph Umar by Persians in response to the Muslim Conquest of Persia (644 CE/23 AH), Caliph Uthman by Muslim rebels, and Caliph Ali by a member of an early sect of Islam, during prayer.

- Eleven of the Twelve Infallible Imams (Shia Twelver branch religious leaders) are martyred, most on the order of opposing caliphs.[4] An important Shia holiday, the Day of Ashura, commemorates the martyrdom of Husayn (the Third Imam) at Karbala.

Early Guidelines

Sunni Guidelines

After Muhammad dies, Sunni followers compile three guides to the spiritual, ethical, and social life of an orthodox Sunni Muslim:[5] Shia doctrines solidify later.

1. **Qur'an**: Words regarded as coming from God, through the angel Gabriel, to Muhammad. The Qur'an is the holy scripture of Islam.

---

1 Aloys Sprenger, M.D., *The Life of Mohammad, From Original Sources* (Godabad: Presbyterian Mission Press, 1851), 182.

2 A Guillaume, *The Life of Muhammad: A Translation of Ibn Ishaq's Sirat Rasul God*, (Oxford: Oxford University Press, 2004),

3 Ibid., 535.

4 "The Fourteen Infallibles," *Wikipedia*, https://en.wikipedia.org/wiki/The_Fourteen_Infallibles, (accessed December 2017).

5 Helen Chapin Metz, *Saudi Arabia, a country study*, (Washington D.C.: Library of Congress, Federal Research Division, 1992), 75 (Hereafter cited as Metz, *Saudi Arabia*).

2. **Hadith:** Muhammad's sayings and teachings, recalled by those who knew Muhammad, and compiled generations after his death. Some scholars also include Muhammad's actions.

3. **Sunnah:** Religious practices and the exemplary way of life established by Muhammad among his companions. The Sunnah pass to Muslims by the consensus of generations, and they draw from the Qur'an and the Hadith.

Sharia Law

- During his life, Muhammad is both spiritual and political leader of the Muslim community; he establishes Islam as an all-encompassing way of life for individuals and society.

- Islam traditionally recognizes no distinction between religion and state, religious and secular life or religious and secular law.[1]

- A comprehensive system of religious law (Sharia) develops during the first four centuries of Islam, primarily through precedence and interpretation by judges and scholars.

- In Sunni Islam, during the tenth century (200s AH), legal opinion begins to harden into authoritative doctrine, and flexibility in Sunni Islamic law gradually closes.[2]

- Yet in Shia Islam, at the end of the eighteenth century (around 1200 AH), religious courts begin to increase, and authorities deem legal scholars and tradition scholars the *new* producers of Islamic law (ijtihad).[3]

- Ijtihad is an Islamic legal term that means "independent reasoning" or "the utmost effort an individual can put forth in an activity." It is recognized as a decision-making process in Islamic law (Sharia) through personal effort that is completely independent of any school of law.[4]

- Today, progressive Muslims "want to recover the freedom of the mind," and they have re-opened ijtihad to accommodate Islam with modern society. Interestingly, modern independent thinkers such as Osama Bin Laden and the Muslim Brotherhood also embrace(d) ijtihad.[5]

- Many conservative, literalist institutions impose harsh restrictions on ijtihad and its modern-day application. They are against modifying and individually interpreting Islam to surrender to westernization and secularization, which they deem evil.

---

1 Metz, *Saudi Arabia*, 75.

2 Ibid., 75.

3 Moojan Momen, *An Introduction to Shi'i Islam: The History and Doctrines of Twelver Shi'ism.* (New Haven: Yale University Press, 1985), 186.

4 John L. Esposito, ed, "Ijtihad" in *Oxford Islamic Studies Online*, (Oxford University Press USA, 2007) http://www.oxfordislamicstudies.com/browse (accessed December, 2017).

5 "Mujtahid," World Heritage Encyclopedia Edition, *World Library*, http://www.netlibrary.net/articles/eng/Mujtahid (accessed December 2017).

Schism

BRANCHES OF ISLAM[1]

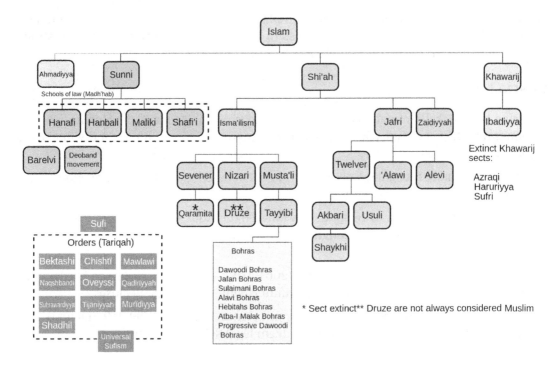

- After the Prophet Muhammad dies, believers divide over the question of who takes over the leadership of the Muslim nation.

- Muhammad has no surviving sons, so direct succession is not possible. Sunni Muslims want the new leader to be elected from among the Prophet's capable companions. However, Shia Muslims believe that leadership should pass directly to the Prophet's cousin (and son-in-law, married to daughter Fatimah), Ali bin Abu Talib.

- The Sunni prevail, and Abu Bakr, the Prophet's close friend and adviser, becomes the first Caliph of the Islamic nation. Sunni Muslims consider the first four caliphs to be models of righteous rule, and they refer to them as the Rightly Guided Caliphs.

- Muhammad's cousin and son-in-law, Ali bin Abu Talib, whom the Shia had wanted to be the first caliph, later becomes the Fourth Caliph of the Rightly Guided Caliphs. However, most Shia consider him to be their *First* Caliph, and they regard the first three caliphs of the Rightly Guided Caliphs as usurpers.

---

1 Chart shared by Angelpeream - Own work, CC BY-SA 3.0, "Islam Branches and Schools," *Wikimedia Commons*, https://commons.wikimedia.org/w/index.php?curid=12871191 (accessed December 2017)

- The Shia begin their own line of ruling caliphs, beginning with Ali, the Fourth Caliph. The following eleven Shia caliphs are from the genetic line of Ali and Fatimah. The Twelver branch of Shia (The Ithna Asharis) refer to these Imams as The Twelve Infallibles. The Twelvers believe that Muhammad's religious leadership, spiritual authority, and divine guidance were passed on to the Twelve Imams.[1]

- The division in Islam crystallizes when the ruling Sunni Caliph's troops kill Ali's son Husayn, the third of the Twelve Infallibles, at The Battle of Karbala, in Iraq. The split occurs 48 years after Muhammad's death, in the year 680 CE (61 AH). After Husayn's killing, the Sunni Caliphs seize and consolidate their political power, leaving the Shia marginalized.

---

1 John L. Esposito, ed, "Shii Islam" in *Oxford Islamic Studies Online*, (Feb 8, 2017) http://www.oxfordislamicstudies.com/browse (accessed December, 2017).

B. Followers

 Christians

Early Christians

Pentecost

- The Christian Church traces its development back to the earliest church established by Saint Paul and the apostles almost 2,000 years ago, through the ancient Roman Empire and its continuation in the Byzantine Empire.[1] It regards itself as the historical and organic continuation of the original Early Church founded by Christ and His apostles.

- The first church is where Jesus and His Twelve Apostles meet in the "Upper Room" of a house (Acts 1:13), traditionally believed to be where the Cenacle is today, in Jerusalem.[2] Here they experience three powerful events: the Last Supper and the institution of Holy Communion, Christ's appearance while resurrected (before Ascension), and the Holy Spirit's descent on the day of Pentecost.

- About 120 followers gather for the Jewish Pentecost feast, which is days after they witness Christ's ascension to Heaven. Participants include the Disciples, apostles, Christ's mother Mary, and His his brothers. (Acts 1:13-15) The Holy Spirit descends upon all present. Pentecost is generally considered the "Birthday of the Church."

- "Now when the day of Pentecost had come, they were with one accord in one place. Suddenly there came from the sky a sound like the rushing of a mighty wind, and it filled all the house where they were sitting. Tongues like fire appeared and were distributed to them, and one sat on each of them. They were all filled with the Holy Spirit, and began to speak with other languages, as the Spirit gave them the ability to speak. Now there were dwelling in Jerusalem Jews, devout men, from every nation under the sky. When this sound was heard, the crowd came together, and were bewildered, because everyone heard them speaking in his own language." (Acts 2:1-6)

- The apostle Peter states that Pentecost is the beginning of a continual outpouring that will be available to all believers from that point on, Jews and Gentiles alike. (Acts 2:39) "Then those who gladly received his word were baptized. There were added that day about three thousand souls." (Acts 2:41)

- Thus begins Christ's commission to "Therefore go, and make disciples of all nations, baptizing them in the name of the Father and of the Son and of the Holy Spirit, teaching them to obey all things that I commanded you." (Matthew 28:19).

---

1 John Binns, *An Introduction to the Christian Orthodox Churches*, (Cambridge: Cambridge University Press, 2002), 3.

2 "The Cenaculum," *Tourist Information Israel*, https://info.goisrael.com/en/the-coenaculum (accessed Feb, 2017).

Acts of the Apostles

- The Book of Acts (Acts of the Apostles) in the New Testament recounts the verbal spread of Christianity by Christ's apostles and the expansion of many small congregations. Acts 1-28 describes many miracles that the apostles witness and perform through the Holy Spirit in the first 26 years after Christ's death. The miracles include prophecies, visions, the gift of tongues, resuscitations from the dead, cures and healings, exorcisms, sudden penalties or temporary afflictions by God, and natural or cosmic miracles.

- The Book of Acts includes this story: Saul of Tarsus, a Roman citizen dedicated to the persecution of the early disciples of Jesus in the area of Jerusalem, travels the road from Jerusalem to Damascus on a mission of persecution. Jesus appears to him in a great Light. He falls to the earth, and he hears a voice saying, "Saul, Saul, why do you persecute me?" Saul replies, "Who are you, Lord? Christ says, "I am Jesus whom you persecute." Saul is struck blind, but after three days his sight is restored, and he begins to preach that Jesus of Nazareth is the Jewish Messiah and the Son of God. He becomes the apostle Paul, and he is generally considered one of the most important figures of the Apostolic Age [mid-30s to the mid-50s CE (605-584 BH)]. He establishes churches in Asia Minor and Europe, taking advantage of his status as both a Jew and a Roman citizen to minister to both Jewish and Roman audiences.

- The apostle Paul exalts the Christian Church as the Body of Christ. (1 Corinthians 12:27) The ministry of the church evolves to nurturing and serving others in love and charity, through the prayer, free will and faith of the participants, via the mercy of God and with the assistance of the Holy Spirit. (Romans 12:4-8, 2 Corinthians 13) By imitating Christ and becoming the vessels of His love and mercy to all whom Christians encounter, Christians are called to spread God's Light and "come home to God," which is God the Father's greatest desire.[1]

---

1 Matthew 18:11-14; John 1:7; 1 Corinthians 6:19-20, 1 Corinthians 11:1; 2 Corinthians 4:6; Ephesians 5:8

Early Worship

- For the first 300 years of early Christianity, people meet in homes, partially because of intermittent persecution. (Romans 16:3-5; 1 Corinthians 16:19; Colossians 4:15)[1]

- The Roman authorities persecute Christians, because like Judaism, its monotheistic teachings are fundamentally foreign to the polytheistic traditions of the ancient world and a challenge to the imperial cult.

- Christian groups first organize themselves loosely. While certain decisions by elders and apostles are binding, there are no precise functions yet for bishops, elders and deacons.[2] Each Christian community has presbyters, as was the case with Jewish communities, who were also ordained and who assisted the bishop. As Christianity spreads, presbyters exercise more responsibilities and take shape as priests. Deacons and deaconesses perform certain duties, like tending to the poor and sick.

- The first bishops reportedly knew and studied under the apostles personally. A church hierarchy develops by the late 1st century and early 2nd century. A structure based on apostolic succession develops, where a bishop becomes the spiritual successor of the previous bishop in a line tracing back to the apostles themselves.[3]

- At numerous times beginning in the second century CE (538 BH), alternative theological ideas arise to challenge the Early Church. At these times, the Church convenes Ecumenical Councils of all available bishops, ecclesiastical dignitaries and theological experts throughout the world to discuss and settle matters of church doctrine and practice.

- Roman Emperor Constantine I convenes the first Ecumenical Council, the Council of Nicea in 325 CE (538 BH), which attempts to provide the first universal creed of the Christian faith.

- According to Eastern tradition, the Divine Liturgy's roots go back to Jewish worship and the adaptation of Jewish worship by Early Christians. The most celebrated Liturgy in the Orthodox Church is attributed to Saint John Chrysostom, an Early Church Father (349-407 CE/281-214 BH). The Liturgy is seen as transcending time and the world. Participants are united in worship in the Kingdom of God, along with departed saints and the celestial angels.[4]

- In the 4th century, Emperors Constantine and Theodosius I legalize the Church and then promote it as the state church of the Roman Empire (Edict of Milan).

---

1 John Fenn, "House Churches in the New Testament," *The Church without Walls International*, https://churchwithoutwallsinternational.org/what-is-house-church/ (accessed March, 2016).

2 Stephen L. Harris, *Understanding the Bible*. (Palo Alto: Mayfield, 1985).

3 Eusebius, *The Church History*, (Caesaria: fourth century), Paul L. Maier, trans., (Grand Rapids: Kregel Academic & Professional, 2007) 21, 339-343.

4 Emmanuel Hatzidakis, *The Heavenly Banquet: Understanding the Divine Liturgy*, (Clearwater: Orthodox Witness, 2013), 59.

Early Writers

Early Church Fathers

Much of the information in this section is summarized from the source cited, below.[1]

- The Early Church Fathers are ancient and generally influential Christian theologians and scholars. They are respected teachers, great bishops and archbishops, monastics, hymnographers, iconographers, translators, and extensive writers of poetry, prose and liturgies still used today. Many are considered saints.

- They were from present-day Afghanistan, Armenia, Cyprus, Egypt, England, France, Greece, Iraq, Ireland, Italy, Lebanon, North Africa (Tunisia, Algeria), Palestine, Portugal, Romania, Russia, Serbia, Spain, Syria and Turkey.

- The earliest Fathers, the Apostolic Fathers, lived within two generations of the Twelve Disciples of the living Christ. The Greek (Church) Fathers wrote in Greek. The Cappadocians were fourth century monastics. The Latin (Church) Fathers wrote in Latin. A few Church Syriac Fathers wrote in Syriac; many of their works were also widely translated into Latin and Greek. The Desert Fathers were early monastics living in the Egyptian desert.

- The Fathers often addressed heretical movements and attacked them. They considered Christian unity and often argued doctrine at the Ecumenical Councils. Some denounced abuse of authority by ecclesiastical and political leaders.

- The Eastern Orthodox Christian view is that humans need not agree on every detail, much less be infallible, to be considered Church Fathers. Orthodox doctrine is determined by the *consensus* of the Holy Fathers—those points on which they agree.[2] This guides the church in dogma, interpretation of scripture, and authentic sacred tradition (vs. false teachings).

Saints

Much of the information in this section is summarized and used courtesy of the source cited, below.[3]

- The only true "saint," or Holy One, is God Himself.

- The Hebrew Bible states For I am the Lord your God. Sanctify yourselves and be holy; for I am holy. (Leviticus 11:44; 19:2, 20:7)

---

1 "Church Fathers," *Wikipedia*, https://en.wikipedia.org/wiki/Church_Fathers (accessed July, 2016).

2 (Protopresbyter) Michael Pomazansky, *Orthodox Dogmatic Theology*, (Platina: Saint Herman of Alaska Brotherhood, 1984, English translation from Russian), 37.

3 George Bebis, PhD, "The Saints of the Orthodox Church," *GREEK ORTHODOX ARCHDIOCESE OF AMERICA*, http://www.goarch.org/ourfaith/ourfaith8044 (accessed July, 2016).

- "You therefore are to be perfect, as your Heavenly Father is perfect." [1] (Matthew 5:48)

- "A disciple is not above his teacher, but everyone when he is fully trained will be like his teacher." (Luke 6:40)

- Man becomes holy and "sainted" by participation in the holiness of God. Saints imitate God and live the life of theosis (the process of coming into union with God).

- Saints are people who apply in their lives the scriptural virtues of "righteousness, godliness, faith, love, patience, and gentleness." (1 Timothy 6:11)

- Through their genuine piety and absolute obedience to God, saints please God, and God then "sanctifies" their souls and bodies.

- God gives the gift of holiness or sainthood through the Holy Spirit. A saint's effort to become a participant in the life of divine holiness is indispensable, but sanctification is the work of the Holy Trinity, especially through the sanctifying power of Jesus Christ.

- God gives many saints special "grace" or "favor" to perform miracles on Earth or after their departure. God grants them the special gift to pray and intercede for those still living in this world.

- Orthodox Christians honor the saints to express their love and gratitude to God, who has "perfected" the saints. Saints are venerated but not worshipped.

- Many Orthodox Christian theologians classify the saints in six categories:

  1. The Prophets: Predicted and prophesied the coming of the Messiah.

  2. Christ's Apostles: The first to spread the message of the Incarnation of the Word of God and of salvation through Christ.

  3. The Martyrs for Christ: Sacrificed their lives and fearlessly confessed Jesus Christ as the Son of God and the Savior of humankind.

  4. The Fathers and Hierarchs of the Christian Church: Excelled in explaining and defending, by word and deed, the Christian faith.

  5. The Christian Monastics: Live(d) in the desert and dedicated themselves to spiritual exercise (askesis), reaching, as far as possible, perfection in Christ.

  6. The Just: Live in the world, leading exemplary lives as clergy or laity with their families, becoming examples for imitation.

---

1 Wallerstedt et al., *Orthodox Bible*, 17. This verse summarizes Jesus' teaching on God's standards. The Christian should grow into the perfection of the Father. Christ is our guide, and He is able to bring us to participate in the very life of God, which is love.

 Muslims

Early Muslims

Early Caliphs & Umayyads (610-750 CE/12-132 AH)

- After Muhammad dies, the first four caliphs govern the Islamic state: Abu Bakr (632-634 CE/10-12 AH), Umar ibn al-Khattab (634-644 CE/12-22 AH), Uthman ibn Affan, (644-656 CE/22-34 AH), and Ali ibn Abi Talib (656-661 CE/34-39 AH). They are the "Rashidun" or "Rightly Guided" Caliphs in Sunni Islam. Shia Muslims consider only the fourth caliph, Ali, legitimate.

- The Rashidun oversee the initial phase of the Muslim conquests, advancing through Persia, Levant, Egypt, and North Africa.

- Islamic missionary and military activities expand the Arab Empire and lead to caliphates and dynasties in North, West and East Africa; the Middle East (Syria, Egypt, Iran, Iraq); and Spain.

- There are two strands of converts to early Islam: (a) animists and polytheists of tribal societies of the Arabian peninsula and the Fertile Crescent, and (b) monotheistic populations (Christian, Jewish and Zoroastrian) of the Middle Eastern agrarian and urbanized societies.

- The Arab conquerors do not require the conversion as much as the subordination of non-Muslim peoples, because new Muslims dilute the economic and status advantages of the Arabs.[1]

- Islamic conquests stretch from the Iberian Peninsula (modern-day Spain, Portugal, Gibraltar and Andorra) to parts of Egypt, Carthage (modern-day Tunisia) and east to the Indus Valley (India).

- At its largest extent, the Umayyad dynasty covers more than 5,000,000 square miles (13,000,000 km^2) making it one of the largest empires the world has yet seen.[2]

- However, the Byzantines drive back the Umayyads, and they cannot hold any territory in Anatolia. The Berbers attack and drive Muslims from North Africa for a period. Weakened by civil wars, the Umayyad lose supremacy at sea and abandon the islands of Rhodes and Crete. In 732 CE (113 AH), the Franks defeat the Muslims at the Battle of Tours.

- Caliphs establish the first schools, which teach Arabic language and Islamic studies.

---

1 Lapidus, *History Islamic Societies*, 200.

2 Khalid Yahya Blankinship, *The End of the Jihad State, the Reign of Hisham Ibn 'Abd-al Malik and the Collapse of the Umayyads.* (Albany: State University of New York Press, 1994) 37.

They build mosques across the empire.

- In the Muslim world, the Umayyads make Islamic currency exclusive, transform agriculture and commerce, make Arabic the state language, and organize a regular postal service.

- The Umayyads ask new converts to pay a poll tax to assist with welfare state expenses, but the Umayyad rulers' wealth and luxury increase discontent among the converts, poor Arabs and some Shia. Anti-Umayyad feeling is prevalent, especially in Iran and Iraq.

- At the end of the Umayyad period, less than 10% of the people in Iran, Iraq, Syria, Egypt, Tunisia and Spain are Muslim.

The Abbasids (750-1258 CE/132-656 AH)

- The descendants of Muhammad's uncle Abbas ibn Abd al-Muttalib rally the discontented against the Umayyads and overthrow them, inaugurating the Abbasid dynasty in 750 CE (132 AH).[1]

- The Abbasids distinguish themselves from the Umayyads by attacking the Umayyads' moral character and administration. The Abbasids develop initiatives aimed at greater Islamic unity.

- Initially expansion ceases and gradual conversions of the populations within the empire occur through growth of Islamic philosophy, theology, law and mysticism.

- Islamic civilization flourishes. Arabic prose and poetry, commerce and industry and the arts and sciences prosper.

- Expansion continues, sometimes by force, sometimes by peaceful proselytizing.

- The Abbasids conquer Mediterranean islands, including the Balearics and Sicily. Through contact with Muslim traders and Sufis, conversions expand to the Turkic tribes and South Saharans in Africa. These initial conversions are flexible: inhabitants are not forced to convert, but they are charged a special tax, their clothing colors are restricted, and men may not marry Muslim women.[2]

- Shariah law codifies, and the four Madhabs (schools of thought) are established. Classical Sufism rises. Sahih Bukhari and others complete the canonical collections of Hadith.[3]

- The doctrines of the Sunni and Shia, two major denominations of Islam, solidify, and the divisions form.

- The cost of running a large empire becomes too great.[4] The Turks, Egyptians, and Arabs adhere to the Sunni sect; the Persians, a great portion of the Turkic groups, and several of the princes in India are Shia. The political unity of Islam begins to

---

1 H. U. Rahman, *A Chronology of Islamic History, 570-1000 CE*, (London: Ta-Ha Publishers Ltd , 1999), 106, 129.

2 Hourani, *History Arab Peoples*, 47.

3 Seyyed Hossein Nasr, *Islam: Religion, History and Civilization*, (New York: HarperOne, 2002), 121.

4 Lapidus, *History Islamic Societies*, 129.

disintegrate. Independent dynasties appear in the Muslim world, and the caliphs recognize them as legitimately Muslim.

Seljuks and Ottomans (950-1450 CE/338-853 AH)

- Early on in this period, conversions in the Muslim heartland accelerate.

- The Turkish tribes conquer Asia Minor, the Balkans, and the Indian subcontinent.[1] Newly conquered regions retain significant non-Muslim populations.

- Some boundaries of the Muslim world contract, such as Sicily and Al Andalus, where Muslim populations are expelled.

- Later, the Mongol Invasion occurs (particularly the Siege of Baghdad in 1258). Eventually the invaders convert to Islam.

Early Worship

Much of the information in this section is summarized from the citation, below.[2]

- In accordance with Arab tribal customs, the Prophet holds community meetings in the courtyard of his house. They begin with a call to prayer and are followed by counsel and community business. He develops the Friday Day of Prayer, after a Jewish example.

- Upon Muhammad's victorious return to Mecca in 630 CE (8 AH), he and his son-in-law break the idols in and around the Ka'bah and end its pagan use. This begins Islamic rule over the Ka'bah. Later, after Muhammad dies, it is renovated into the first mosque, the Masjid al-Haram.

- In the Umayyad Period (661 CE-750 CE/40-132 AH), caliphs build major mosques in great army camps of conquered provinces. The camp meeting place is linked to the governor's tent, and later his rooms. Negotiations between Muslim commanders and Arab tribal leaders take place here, preceded by prayer. The caliphs appear with their portable thrones to give lectures about current politics.

- In 691 CE (71 AH), the Caliph Abd al-Malik orders the building of The Dome of the Rock, a shrine located on the Temple Mount in the Old City of Jerusalem.

- In 705 CE (86 AH), Caliph al-Walid I finishes the building of Al-Aqsa Mosque, opposite his father's Dome of the Rock. He also renovates the Prophet's courtyard area in Medina, now known as Al-Masjid an-Nabawi, the Prophet's Mosque.

- Once the empire is stable, caliphs no longer need to influence tribal chieftains with political or religious lectures. Bureaucracy governs the state, and the social function of the mosque gives way to the religious one.

- By 750 CE (132 AH), at Friday services, imams instead of provincial governors begin

---

1 Hugh Goddard, *Christians and Muslims: From Double Standards to Mutual Understanding*, (London: Routledge, 1995), 131.

2 C.H. Becker, "On the History of Muslim Worship," lecture at the Fourth International Congress on the History of Religion in Leiden, September 1912, http://www.islam-and-muslims.com/Becker-history-of-muslim-worship.pdf (accessed December, 2017).

to occupy pulpits in mosques. However, the custom of announcing political decrees, appointments, etc. in provincial towns on the occasion of the Friday service survives until at least the 900s CE (286-390 AH).

- During the Abbasids Period (750-1258 CE/132-655 AH), the mosque becomes exclusively the house of God. The mihrab, a Mecca-facing niche in the wall, toward which the congregation faces to pray, is well-established. The minaret is used for the call to prayer five times per day.

Early Writers

Hadith

Hadith are second only to the Qur'an in developing Islamic jurisprudence (law).

- There are two differing understandings of Hadith collections:

  They are verbatim quotes of Muhammad regarding any matter.[1]

  They are reports, stories or traditions of Muhammad's statements or actions, or reports of his tacit approval or criticism of something.[2]

- Hadith are spoken reports in circulation in society after Muhammad dies. Hadith are evaluated and gathered into large collections during the 8th and 9th centuries, generations after Muhammad's death, but not by central authority.

- Some Muslim scholars question and critique the Hadith literature throughout its history, including questions about authenticity,[3] theology and philosophy. Qur'anists, a small heterodox group, reject the authority of the Hadith collections.[4]

- Each Hadith is based on two parts: a chain of narrators reporting the Hadith, and the text itself.[5]

- Muslim clerics and jurists classify each Hadith as sahih ("authentic"), hasan ("good") or da'if ("weak").[6] However, different groups and scholars do not necessarily agree on the classifications.

- Sunni and Shia branches refer to different collections of Hadith. Shia prefer Hadith attributed to the Ahl al-Bayt (family and close associates of Muhammad and the Twelve Imams), and they have their own separate collection of Hadiths.

- Like the Qur'an, the Hadith are written in classical Arabic. To understand the Hadith,

---

1 Khaled Abou El Fadl, "What is Shari'a?" (16 Jan 2012) in ABC *RELIGION AND ETHICS*, http://www.abc.net.au/religion/articles/2012/01/16/3170810.htm (accessed December, 2017).

2 Juan Eduardo Campo, "*Hadith*," *Encyclopedia of Islam*, (New York: Checkmark Books, 2009), 278.

3 Wael B. Hallaq, "The Authenticity of Prophetic Hadîth: A Pseudo-Problem," *Studia Islamica*, No. 89 (1999): 75–90.

4 Aisha Y. Musa, "The Qur'anists," *Religion Compass*, Volume 4, Issue 1 (January 2010), 12–21.

5 Gordon D. Newby, *A Concise Encyclopedia of Islam* (London: Oneworld Publications, 2002), 70.

6 Ziauddin Sardar, *The Future of Muslim Civilisation* (Kent: Croom Helm,1979) 26.

most Muslims rely on commentaries and what they learn at the mosque or through Muslim media.[1]

Saints

- The Qur'an states the following regarding participants in other religions who pray to saints or intercessors: "Have they taken intercessors besides God? Say: What? Even though they did not ever have control over anything, nor do they understand? Say: Intercession belongs to God, altogether. His is the Kingdom of the Heavens and the Earth—you will be brought back to Him." (39:43-44)

- However Sufis practice pre-Islamic customs that incorporate saints and miracles, under the cover of mysticism.[2]

- Sufi orders are largely Sunni and follow one of the four schools of Sunni Islam, but various Sufi orders have been influenced by and adopted into various Shi'ite movements.

- Sufis believe that their Shaikhs (saints) receive knowledge directly from God, and that even after death, the Shaikhs can hear, see, communicate and help the living.[3]

- Sufism is generally understood by scholars and Sufis to be the inner, mystical, or psycho-spiritual dimension of Islam. Today, however, many Muslims and non-Muslims believe that Sufism is outside the sphere of Islam.[4]

---

1 Gabriel, *Jesus and Muhammad*, (Lake Mary: Frontline, 2004), 220.

2 Annemarie Schimmel, "Sufism | Islam," *Encyclopaedia Britannica*, https://www.britannica.com/topic/Sufism (accessed December, 2017).

3 Sajid Abdul Kayum, *The Jamaat Tableegh and the Deobandis*, First Edition (AHYA Multi-Media, 2001), "Chapter 4: Life of the Barzakh," 66, http://memberfiles.freewebs.com/27/59/52445927/documents/Jamaat%20e%20Tableeq%20Teaching%20Shirk%20and%20Bidah.pdf (accessed December, 2017).

4 Alan Godlas, *Sufism's Many Paths*, University of Georgia, http://islam.uga.edu/Sufism.html (accessed December, 2017).

C. Traditional Teachings

 ## Jesus in Context

Who Was He?

- Christ is a descendant of Abraham/Sarah and Isaac, with whom God made a covenant. (Genesis 17:19, Matthew 1:1-16)

- Christ is born of the Virgin Mary, and He is the Son of God.[1] He performs miracles.[2] He is not of this world. (John 8:23)

- Christ is The Messiah (the anointed one of God), as He explains: "The woman said to Him, 'I know that Messiah comes' (he who is called Christ). 'When He has come, He will declare to us all things.' Jesus said to her, 'I am He, the one who speaks to you.'" (John 4:25-26).

- Christ is crucified, dies and is buried. (Luke 23:44-47) He resurrects from the dead and walks among His Disciples for 40 days.[3] He ascends into Heaven. (Luke 24:50-53) He sits at the right hand of the Father.[4]

- Christ was with God since the beginning of time, and He will be with Him eternally.[5] He will come again with glory to judge the living and the dead.[6]

Why Did God Provide Him?

- God created only good: God did not create evil. (Genesis 1:31) Satan, an angel in Heaven, was good. However God cast him from Heaven because he desired to ascend in Heaven, to be like the Most High. (Isaiah 14:12-14, Luke 10:18, Revelation 12:8-9)

- God created humankind in His image (Genesis 1:26-27, 5:1, 9:6), with the gift of free will. God respects and does not violate peoples' free will, so people can choose to follow God or to be influenced by Satan.[7]

- Christ came, suffered and died to abolish the choke hold of evil and death. (John 8:51,11:25-26) Since Christ's coming, Satan and death no longer rule the world. (John 12:31)

---

1 Matthew 14:24-33, 16:15-17, 17:1-6; Luke 1:35,10:22, 22:67-71; John 3:16-17, 5:19-21, 5:40-44, 10:25-30, 14:7-11, 16:28

2 Matthew 8:3-6, 8:13, 9:2-7, 9:18-25, 9:28-30, 12:10-13; Mark 7:32-36, 8:2-9, 8:22-26, 10:51-52; Luke 5:3-11, 7:12-15, 17:12-19; John 2:1-9, 4:49-53, 9:1-7, 11:39-44

3 Matthew 28:1-20; Luke 24:36-43; John 20:11-29, 21:3-14

4 Matthew 26:64; Mark 14:61-62; Luke 22:69

5 Luke 10:18; John 8:23, 8:58, 17:4-5, Revelation 22:13

6 Matthew 16:27, 24:30-31, 25:31-46; Luke 21:34-36; John 5:28-30

7 Matthew 5:29-30, 16:23; Luke 11:27-28; John 3:20-21, 8:31-34; 2 Corinthians 3:17

- To remind people to love God with all their hearts, with all their souls, and with all their minds, and to worship only God.[1]

- God sent Christ, His only begotten Son, because He loves the world and wants to offer a peaceful life and everlasting life after death to those who believe in Him.[2]

- To seek and to save those who are lost.[3] God is saddened when we do not choose The Way (Matthew 10:12-14), and He rejoices when people do. (Luke 15:8-24)

- As a light into the world, so that whoever believes in Him should not live in darkness.[4]

- Christ describes God and His relationship with people: Do not worry or fear, be at peace.[5] All is possible with faith in God. (Mark 9:23, 11:23) God is a merciful and loving Father, Who's good pleasure it is to give people everlasting life. (Luke 12:32) God comforts people and answers every personal prayer.[6]

- To emphasize loving one another, including enemies, as God loves Christ and us.[7] To guide people to give to the less fortunate.[8]

- To emphasize this message: Pray for your enemies (Luke 6:27-28), judge not,[9] forgive others,[10] and turn the other cheek when persecuted. (Matthew 5:38-39; Luke 6:29) Blessed are the peacemakers. (Matthew 5:9) All who take the sword will die by the sword. (Matthew 26:48-52; Luke 22:47-51)

- To set an example for humankind to follow, including to lead by following.[11]

---

1 Matthew 22:37-38, 23:9; Mark 10:18; Luke 4:5-8; John 13:16-17

2 John 3:16-17, 4:14, 5:24, 6:27, 6:47-50, 10:11-18, 10:27-29

3 Matthew 18:11; Luke 9:56, 19:10

4 John 8:12, 9:5, 12:35-36, 12:46, 20:21; Luke 11:33-36

5 Matthew 6:25-34; Mark 5:36; Luke 4:16-21, 8:22-25, 12:4-7, 12:32; John 14:27-28, 16:33 Revelation 2:10

6 Matthew 5:3-5, 7:7-10, 11:28-30; Mark 11:24; John 14:14, 16:24

7 Matthew 5:43-48, 22:37-40; Luke 6:31-32, 7:44-48; John 13:34-35, 15:9-15, 17:26

8 Matthew 5:41-42, 19:21; Mark 12:43-44; Luke 6:34, 10:30-37, 14:13-14, 16:19-31; Acts 20:35

9 Matthew 7:1-2, Luke 6:37, John 7:24, 8:15

10 Matthew 6:14-15, 18:21-22, 18:35; Luke 17:3-4

11 Matthew 5:48, 20:26-28; Mark 9:35; Luke 6:40, 22:27; John 13:12-16

- To explain that we all sin (miss the mark).Through repentance, people now have everlasting life after death. God accepts repentance until the very last moments of our lives.[1]

- To save the world, not to judge the world. (John 12:47-50) But people must attempt to abide in God and Christ to protect their souls from sin and Hell and to enter Heaven.[2]

- To introduce people to the Holy Spirit, who guides people and gives them peace if they keep Christ's commandments.[3]

- Christ is the way, the truth, and the life. No one comes to the Father except through Christ.[4]

- Christ tells His followers to preach the Gospel to all nations. (Matthew 28:19-20, Mark 16:15, Luke 24:46-47)

- Christ warns of false prophets and false messiahs who will come after him: people will know them by their fruits.[5]

Relationship to Earlier Faiths

- Jewish Levitical priests taught regulations and laws for the Jewish people.

- The Jewish Prophet Jeremiah discusses a future New Covenant with God: "Look, the days come," says the LORD, "when I will make a New Covenant with the house of Israel, and with the house of Judah: not according to the covenant that I made with their fathers in the day that I took them by the hand to bring them out of the land of Egypt; which my covenant they broke, and I disregarded them," says the LORD. "But this is the covenant that I will make with the house of Israel after those days," says the LORD: "I will put my law in their minds, and write it on their hearts; and I will be their God, and they shall be my people: and they shall teach no more every man his neighbor, and every man his brother, saying, 'Know the LORD'; for they shall all know me, from their least to their greatest," says the LORD: "for I will forgive their iniquity, and their sins I will remember no more." (Jeremiah 31:30-33)

- Jewish Prophets foretell a messiah[6]: He is from the seed of Isaac and King David. (Genesis 17:19, Jeremiah 23.5) A man of the wilderness, a messenger, prepares the way for him. (Isaiah 40:3) He is born from a virgin[7], in Bethlehem. (Isaiah 7:14; Micah 5:1-2) The government is upon his shoulder, and his name is Everlasting Father, Prince

---

1 Matthew 3:2, 9:12-13, 20:1-16; Luke 13:4-5, 24:46-47; Revelation 3:19

2 Matthew 7:21, 12:43-45, 13:41-43, 16:26, 25:41-46; Luke 13:24-30; John 15:1-6

3 John 7:37-38, 14:15-17, 14:26, 15:26, 16:13-15

4 Luke 11:23; John 10:7-9, 14:6, 15:1-5

5 Matthew 7:15-16, 24:4-5, 24:11, 24:24-26; Mark 13:21-22

6 These passages from the Old Testament are cited by Christians as pointing to Christ as the Messiah. Please note that Hebrew scholars usually view the significance of these passages differently from many Christian scholars.—Ed.

7 The Hebrew Bible reads "young woman," whereas the Greek Septuagint version of the Old Testament reads "virgin."

of Peace. (Isaiah 9:5-6) He spends a season in Egypt. (Hosea 11:1) He is the son of man, given everlasting dominion, glory, and a kingdom that all the peoples, nations, and languages should serve him. His kingdom will not be destroyed. (Daniel 7:13-14) The Lord tells Him, "You are My son." (Psalm 2:6-7) He preaches good tidings to the poor, heals the brokenhearted, proclaims liberty to captives, opens the eyes of the bound, and comforts all who mourn. (Isaiah 61:1-2) He performs miracles. (Isaiah 35:4-6) He rides victorious into Jerusalem on a lowly donkey. (Zechariah 9:9) He is betrayed by thirty pieces of silver, which is cast back to the treasury. (Zechariah 11:12-13) He is oppressed but does not complain, we are healed with his stripes, he is led to slaughter, bears the sin of many, and dies for our transgressions, He is buried with the wicked and laid to rest in a rich man's tomb. (Isaiah 53:3-12) They give him gall and vinegar. (Psalm 69:21-22) They cast lots for his garments. (Psalm 22:18-19) The House of David pierces him and then mourns him. (Zechariah 12:10) His bones are not broken. (Psalm 34:20-21)

- Christ comes to fulfill (not destroy) the law of Moses, the prophets and the Psalms. (Matthew 5:17, Luke 24:44) Father Abraham rejoices to see Christ's coming to Earth. (John 8:56) Christ is saddened that the Jewish people do not believe He is the Messiah. (Luke 13:34-35)

- The New Covenant involves following His message and embracing God's Holy Spirit, who personally guides you and makes a home in you, along with Christ and God. Thus you enter God's Kingdom after death. Christ asks you to make disciples of all nations, baptizing them in the name of the Father and of the Son and of the Holy Spirit.[1] (Matthew 28:19-20, John 3:3-15; John 14:23)

- Christ's New Covenant with humankind is represented by the Eucharist (Holy Communion), as presented by Christ at the Last Supper. (Matthew 26:26-28)

- God sent Christ to do God's will and to *finish* God's work.[2]

---

1 The Christian Holy Trinity: Father, Son and Holy Spirit—Ed.

2 John 4:34, 7:16, 8:29, 17:4-5

 Muhammad in Context

Who Was He?

- Muhammad is the final prophet, as prophesied in the Hebrew Bible. (33:40)
- Muhammad is held in honor by the Lord of the Dominion, and he is to be obeyed. (81:19-21)
- Muhammad is a mortal. (18:110) He does not perform miracles (17:90-93), and he sins like any other man.[1]
- Muhammad does not know what those on high discuss. (38:65-70) Muhammad was not present on Mt. Sinai when God called out to Moses. (28:44-46)

Why Did God Provide Him?

- As a messenger among his people, to whom no messenger had come before. To teach, warn them, and purify them because they were astray.[2]
- To clearly warn that there is no god but God the One, and God will judge you if you worship more than Him.[3]
- To bring guidance and good news to those who believe in God, His angels and His messengers, those who obey and swear allegiance to Muhammad and submit to, serve, praise and fear God (Muslims), those who patiently take the way of their Lord, who do good and give alms, who fast, pray and repent. These will receive God's blessings, mercy, reward and favor, they will have no fear, no grief, and they will have firm footing and be successful with their Lord.[4]
- To bring good news of the Garden—gardens, with pure springs and rivers of milk, wine and honey. Pavilions with green cushions and fine carpets. Sitting on couches, clothed in silk and brocade, without weariness or bitterness. Never-ending dishes and gold goblets are passed around, with abundant fruit and meat. Men unite with nubile maidens, untouched (by men or Jinn), with large, dark eyes, maidens restraining their glances, like rubies and brilliant pearls. Pure ones are confined to the pavilions, there are loving virgins, fresh ones, equal in age. All are reunited with offspring who followed them in faith. Devoted boys wait on you.[5]

---

1 40:55; 47:19; 48:1-2, 110:1-3

2 2:128; 3:164; 28:46; 35:24

3 3:151; 4:47-48; 16:2; 23:116-117; 28:88; 29:8; 38:65

4 2:215; 2:223; 2:271; 3:92; 3:132; 6:48; 7:156; 9:112; 10:1-2; 16:71; 16:97; 16:101-102; 17:26-28; 18:46; 22:37; 24:52; 30:39; 41:30-32; 48:8-10; 49:14; 51:15-19; 67:12

5 15:45-48; 43:71-73; 44:51-55; 47:15; 52:20-28; 55:56-59; 55:62-76; 56:27-40; 58:8-26; 76:11-21; 78:31-37

- To bring people from darkness to light, with God's mercy.[1]

- To provide a guiding light to the Straight Path.[2]

- To warn only those who fear God and believe in the Qur'an's ayat (verses). (30:53; 36:10-11) Unbelievers will not believe, because God seals their hearts, covers their eyes and ears, incites them to err, appoints a devil to them and leaves them to stray.[3]

- To explain that if you do not believe, honor and obey Muhammad and his message, God is your enemy, you are a loser, and you will burn in Hell.[4]

- To warn people to submit to and obey God, or go wrong and be fuel for Hell.[5]

- To call for all to believe, do good deeds and repent for God's mercy.[6] But mercy is not guaranteed after repentance. At the end of your life, God weighs your good works against your bad works: if your good works are heavy, you go to Heaven.[7] God lets in whom he chooses, and last-minute repentance is not accepted.[8] Muhammad himself expressed doubts about his own salvation. (46:9)

- To enter Heaven, believe and do good works,[9] fight, die or spend in God's way,[10] emigrate to flee persecution,[11] obey and believe in God and His Messenger,[12] guard against evil, fear and submit to God.[13]

---

1 14:1-2, 24:35; 33:43; 57:9

2 4:174-175; 5:15-16; 42:52

3 2:6-7; 3:178; 4:88; 6:25-26; 6:125; 7:186; 10:11; 16:37; 16:107-108; 17:45-46; 19:83; 27:4-5; 35:8; 35:19-23; 39:23; 39:36; 40:35; 42:44; 43:36-37

4 2:97-99; 3:3; 3:19; 3:81-85; 4:41-43; 4:47; 4:115; 5:78-81; 6:49; 7:36; 9:61; 9:63; 11:17; 22:72; 31:6-7; 33:56-57; 34:5; 35:24-26; 48:13-14; 58:8

5 2:208-209; 6:15; 39:11-16; 39:54; 72:13-15

6 3:135-136; 5:39-40; 11:3; 16:97; 20:82; 25:71; 50:32-35, 51:15-19, 66:8; 110:1-3

7 7:6-9; 23:102-104; 101:1-11

8 4:17-18; 7:156-157; 9:102-103; 17:54; 28:67-69; 48:13-14

9 2:81-82, 4:122-124, 4:57, 9:72, 16:30-32, 17:19, 22:23, 41:30-32, 47:12, 64:8-10

10 2:154; 2:244-245; 3:146-148; 3:157; 3:169-170; 3:195; 4:77, 9:38-39, 9:111; 22:58-59; 47:4-6; 48:16-17, 57:10

11 3:195, 4:77, 4:100, 16:41-42, 22:58-59

12 4:13, 6:126-127, 14:27, 57:21, 61:11-12, 64:8-9

13 3:198, 10:62-64, 12:108-109, 39:73-75, 43:69-70, 79:40-41

Relationship to Earlier Faiths

- Muhammad brings guidance and the religion of Truth that is above all false religion.[1]

- Muhammad's message supersedes Christian and Jewish messages, which were distorted by the people, and from which they stray.[2]

- Most Followers of the Book (Jews and Christians) deny, rebel against and spread corruption about God's revelation to Muhammad.[3] God could make humanity all one community, but He chooses not to. (2:253; 11:118-119)

- Most of the Jews exchanged their oaths and covenant with God for a small price.[4]

- The Christians distorted God's message about Jesus' inception. God breathed on Mary from His Spirit, and Mary begat Jesus as a virgin, but Jesus is her son, and he is a man, not the Son of God.[5]

- Christ was not killed, and He did not resurrect on Earth. God simply raised him up to Himself. (4:156-158)

- God did perform miracles through Christ, and if anyone saw them and still disbelieved, God punished them like no others on Earth. (5:110-115)

- Muhammad preached that Christians worship Jesus and Mary as partners to God by embracing the Holy Trinity, which the Muslims describe as God/Jesus/Mary.[6]

- Muhammad came as Christ predicted: that a messenger would follow Christ, and his name would be Ahmad. (61:6)

---

1 3:3; 3:19; 3:65-68; 3:84-85; 9:33; 16:101-102; 48:28; 61:7-9

2 2:105-106; 2:120-121; 2:135; 2:139-140; 3:64; 3:78; 4:50-51; 5:48; 5:63; 5:65-66; 5:77; 10:68; 25:1-2; 27:76-78

3 2:91; 2:139-140; 3:69-71; 3:98-99; 4:150-151; 5:12-14; 5:17; 5:59-60; 5:64; 5:67-68; 29:46-47

4 2:40-42; 3:75-77; 3:186-187; 3:199

5 2:116; 3:58-60; 6:100-101; 10:68-70; 17:111; 18:4-5; 19:16-21; 19:27-35; 21:91; 23:90-91; 25-1-2; 39:4; 43:57-60; 43:81-82; 112:1-4

6 4:47-48; 4:171-172; 5:72-76; 5:116; 9:30-33

D: Doctrine

 ## Christian Doctrine

Definitions

The Holy Trinity

- Father, Son and Holy Spirit. One God, undivided. The Holy Trinity is three, distinct, divine entities without overlap among them, who share one divine essence (Greek ousia).[1]

- The Father is the Godhead, eternal and not begotten. The Son (the Logos, the Word of God) is eternal and begotten of the Father. The Holy Spirit is eternal and proceeds from the Father.[2]

- Eastern Orthodox doctrine regarding the Holy Trinity is summarized in the Nicene Creed (Symbol of Faith). Christ, the only begotten Son of God, became man by the good will of the Father and by the cooperation of the Holy Spirit who proceeds from the Father. Christ prays for God to send the Holy Spirit to help people, and the Holy Spirit forms Christ's words and example to live in their hearts—thus God the Father is glorified.[3]

Commandments

- God gives the Ten Commandments to Moses on Mount Sinai, accompanied by smoke, thunder and lightning and the blast of a trumpet, to emphasize the importance of these laws. Moses records God's words in Exodus 20 and recounts the event again in Deuteronomy 5. Here is a list of the commandments in short form:

  1. You shall have no other gods before Me.

  2. You shall not make idols.

  3. You shall not take the name of the Lord your God in vain.

  4. Remember the Sabbath day, to keep it holy.

  5. Honor your father and your mother.

  6. You shall not murder.

  7. You shall not commit adultery.

  8. You shall not steal.

  9. You shall not bear false witness against your neighbor.

  10. You shall not covet.

---

1 Bishop Kallistos (Timothy) Ware, *The Orthodox Church*, (New York: Penguin Books, 1993) 22-23, 202, 207-211.

2 John 1:14, 8:23, 8:58, 14:28, 15:26, 16:28, 17:4-5; 1 Corinthians 2:12; Revelation 22:13

3 Matthew 28:19-20; Luke 11:13; John 3:16; 8:42, 14:16-17, 14:26, 15:26

- Christ discusses the commandments in the following passages of the New Testament:

"You are to love the Lord your God with all your heart, with all your soul, and with all your mind. This is the first and great commandment. A second likewise is this: You are to love your neighbor as yourself. The whole Law and the Prophets depend on these two commandments." (Matthew 22:37-40)

You know the commandments: "Do not commit adultery, Do not murder, Do not steal, Do not give false testimony, Do not defraud, Honor your father and your mother." (Mark 10:19)

Creed

Bishops at the first Ecumenical Council in Nicea (325 CE/306 BH) and at the second Ecumenical Council in Constantinople (381 CE/248 BH) formally drew up the Nicene Creed. Today, Orthodox Christian faithful recite this "symbol of faith" at baptisms, during every Divine Liturgy and during daily prayers.

The Nicene Creed

I believe in one God, Father Almighty, Creator of Heaven and Earth, and of all things visible and invisible.

And in one Lord Jesus Christ, the only-begotten Son of God, begotten of the Father before all ages: Light of light, true God of true God, begotten not created, of one essence with the Father, through Whom all things were made.

Who for us men and for our salvation came down from Heaven and was incarnate of the Holy Spirit and the Virgin Mary and became man.

He was crucified for us under Pontius Pilate, and suffered and was buried;

And He rose on the third day according to the Scriptures.

He ascended into Heaven and is seated at the right hand of the Father;

And He will come again with glory to judge the living and the dead; His Kingdom will have no end.

And in the Holy Spirit, the Lord, the Creator of Life, Who proceeds from the Father,[1] Who together with the Father and the Son is worshipped and glorified, Who spoke through the Prophets.

In one Holy, Catholic and Apostolic Church.

I acknowledge one baptism for the forgiveness of sins.

I expect the resurrection of the dead, and the life of the age to come. Amen.

---

1 The Catholic Nicene Creed uses the words "Father and Son" here, instead of "Father." This discrepancy (the Filioque) contributed to the Orthodox/Catholic schism in 1054 CE (445 AH).—Ed.

Prayer

Types of Prayer

Christian prayer includes public and private prayer. Public prayer is shared within the worship setting or other public places.

- In the Orthodox tradition, public prayer occurs in the Divine Liturgy, which consists of specific prayers geared to the season of the Liturgical Year, such as Advent, Christmas, Lent and Easter. The Liturgy revolves around an offering of Holy Communion. It includes blessings, processions, chanted and read hymns, litanies, prayers and the Lord's Prayer, the Nicene Creed, Old Testament and New Testament Bible readings and (sometimes) a sermon by a priest.

- Private prayer occurs when individuals pray silently or aloud, and it can be spontaneous or reading of written prayers. The Jesus Prayer ("Lord Jesus Christ, have mercy on me") is esteemed by the spiritual fathers as a method of opening the heart and bringing about the Prayer of the Heart (considered to be the Unceasing Prayer that the apostle Paul advocates in the New Testament).

- The ancient church developed a tradition of asking for the intercession of (deceased) saints and intercessory prayer by believers praying on behalf of individuals, groups or even nations.

- Orthodox monks and devout believers pray the Hours of Prayer (a schedule of specific Psalms) at sundown, before sleep, at dawn, at 9:00 A.M., at noon, and at 3:00 P.M.

The Lord's Prayer

This is the most common prayer among Christians. According to Matthew 6:9-13, Jesus taught his disciples to pray this prayer:

Our Father in Heaven, hallowed be your name.

Let your Kingdom come, let your will be done, on Earth as it is in Heaven.

Give us today our daily bread.

And forgive us our debts, as we also forgive our debtors.

And lead us not into temptation, but deliver us from the evil one.

For Yours is the Kingdom, the power, and the glory, forever.

Amen.

Seven Sacraments

The "Mysteries of the Church," otherwise known as the Sacraments, remind Christians that God is truly near to them. Although He cannot be seen, God is not detached from His creation. Through the risen Christ and the Holy Spirit, God is present and active in our lives and in creation.[1]

God's presence and actions are heightened and celebrated during the events of the church called the Sacraments, where God discloses Himself through the prayers and actions of His people.

By participating in the Sacraments, Christians receive the gifts of the Holy Spirit and grow closer to God and other people.

The Sacraments

Information for this section is summarized and used courtesy of the source listed, below.[2]

1. **Holy Eucharist (Communion):** It is the mystical communion of humans with God and with each other, through Christ and the Holy Spirit. The eucharistic liturgy is celebrated in the church every Sunday and on feast days.

   At the end of His life, Christ ate the Passover meal with his apostles. He transformed the Passover meal, a ritual supper to commemorate the liberation of the Israelites from slavery in Egypt, into an act done in remembrance of Him: of his life, death and resurrection as the new and eternal Passover Lamb who frees humanity from the slavery of evil, ignorance and death and transfers them into the everlasting life of the Kingdom of God.

   At their Last Supper together, Christ discusses the New Covenant with his apostles: And as they are eating, Jesus takes bread, gave thanks for it and breaks it. He gives it to the disciples, and says, "Take, eat; this is My body." He takes the cup, gives thanks, and gives it to them, saying, "All of you drink it, for this is My blood of the new covenant, which is poured out for many for the remission of sins." (Matthew 26:26-28)

2. **Baptism:** Baptism means "immersion in water." It was practiced among the people of the Hebrew Bible as well as the people who belonged to pagan religions. The universal meaning of baptism is "starting anew," of dying to an old way of life and being born again into a new way of life. Thus, baptism is and was connected with repentance, which means a moral conversion, a "change of mind," a change in living from something old and bad to something new and good.

   Christian baptism is a "new birth by water and the Holy Spirit" into the Kingdom of God. (John 3:5)

---

1 Reverend Thomas Fitzgerald, "The Sacraments," *St. George Antiochian Orthodox Church*, http://www.stgeorgenj.com/the-seven-sacraments-of-the-orthodox-church.html (accessed August, 2016).

2 "The Sacraments," *The Orthodox Faith Volume II - Worship*, Orthodox Church in America, http://oca.org/orthodoxy/the-orthodox-faith/worship/the-sacraments (accessed December, 2016).

3. **Chrismation:** The sacrament of chrismation is performed in the Orthodox Church together with baptism. Chrismation is performed by anointing the person's body with the special oil called Holy Chrism, whereby the person is given the "power from on high," the gift of the Holy Spirit, to live the new life received in baptism. (2 Corinthians 1:21-22)

4. **Penance (Confession):** Christians living in communion with Christ periodically humble themselves consciously before God and receive guidance in the Christian life from their pastor in the church. Translated from the Greek, "amartia" (sin) means "missing the mark." Christ forgives any confessed sins. "Confess your transgressions to one another, and pray for one another, so that you may be healed. The prayer of the righteous person is powerfully effective." (James 5:16) "If we confess our sins, He is faithful and righteous to forgive us the sins, and to cleanse us from all unrighteousness." (1 John 1:9)

5. **Unction:** One of the signs of Christ's messiahship was to heal the sick. The power of healing remains in the Church because Christ remains in the Church through the Holy Spirit. The sacrament of the Unction of the sick is the Church's specific prayer for healing. If the faith of the believers is strong enough, and if it is the will of God, there is every reason to believe that the Lord can heal those who are diseased. Holy Unction is the sacrament of the spiritual, physical, and mental healing of a sick person, whatever the nature or the gravity of the illness may be.

6. **Matrimony:** Christian marriage reflects the created image of God's love, which is eternal, unique, indivisible and unending. In marriage, a couple can become one spirit and one flesh in a way that no human love can provide by itself. In Christian marriage, the Holy Spirit is given so that what is begun on Earth does not "part in death," but is fulfilled and continues most perfectly in the Kingdom of God.

7. **Ordination:** In Orthodox Christianity, Christ is the only priest, pastor and teacher of the Christian Church. He alone guides and rules his people, forgives sins and offers communion with God.

However, Christ remains present and active in the Church through the Holy Spirit. Christ is present now, always, and forever in His Church. Through ordination, the bishops, priests, and deacons of the church receive the gift of the Holy Spirit to clearly show Christ, in the Spirit, to humanity.

 Muslim Doctrine

Definitions

Islam

Islam means to surrender, commit or resign oneself to the will of God. Islam is the act or state of submission.[1]

Muslim

Muslim, the word for an adherent of Islam, is from the same root as Islam. A Muslim is one who submits and totally surrenders to the will of God.

Commandments

Some Muslim scholars maintain that the following ayat (verses) in the Qur'an contain the content of the Ten Commandments:[2]

"Say, Prophet: Come! I will recite what your Lord has forbidden you. Do not associate anything with God, show kindness to your parents, do not slay your children for (fear of) poverty—We provide for you and for them—and do not draw near to apparent or concealed indecencies. Do not kill the soul, which God has forbidden, except for the requirements of justice. This He orders you, so that you may understand. Do not approach the property of an orphan, except in the best manner, until he attains his maturity. Give full measure and weight, with justice. We do not impose on any soul a duty, except to the extent of its ability. When you speak, be just, even if it is (against) a relative. Fulfil God's covenant—with this He commands you, so that you may be mindful. (Know) that this is My path, the right one. So follow it, and do not follow (other) ways, for they will lead you away from His way. He has directed you with this, so that you may guard (against evil)." (6:151-153)

"Do not associate any other god with God, lest you sit down despised, neglected. Your Lord has commanded that you not serve (any) but Him, and that you show goodness to your parents. If either or both of them reach old age with you, do not say to them (so much as) 'Ugh,' or chide them, and speak a generous word to them. Make yourself submissively gentle to them with compassion, and say: 'Oh, my Lord! Have compassion on them, as they brought me up (when I was) little.' Your Lord knows best what is in your

1 Barnard Lewis and Buntzie Ellis Churchill, *Islam: The Religion and the People*, (Upper Saddle River: Financial Times Prentice Hall, 2015) 8.

2 Liyakat Takim, "The Ten Commandments and the Tablets in Shi'i and Sunni Tafsir Literature: A Comparative Perspective," *The Muslim World*, 101, no.1 (2011): 94-109.

minds. If you are good, then He is surely Forgiving to those who turn (to Him) frequently. Give the near of kin his due, and also the needy and the wayfarer, and do not spend wastefully. Surely the wasteful are the fellows of the devils, and Satan is ever ungrateful to his Lord. If you turn away from the needy, seek mercy from your Lord, which you hope for, and speak a gentle word to them. Do not make your hand shackled to your neck like a miser or stretch it forth to the utmost reach, lest you sit down blamed, destitute. Surely your Lord makes plentiful means of subsistence for whom He pleases, and He also restricts it. Surely He is ever Aware of, Seeing, His servants. Do not kill your children for fear of poverty—We give them sustenance, and yourselves (too)—surely to kill them is a great wrong. Do not go near fornication; surely it is an indecency, and evil is the way. Do not kill any one whom God has forbidden, except for a just cause. We have indeed given authority to the heir of whomever is slain unjustly, but do not let the heir exceed the just limits in slaying; surely he is aided. Do not draw near to the property of the orphan, except in a goodly way, until he attains his maturity. Fulfil your promises; surely, (every) promise will be questioned about. Give full measure when you measure out, and weigh with a true balance; this is fair and better in the end. Do not follow that of which you have no knowledge. Surely the hearing, the sight and the heart—you will be questioned about all of these. Do not go about the land exultingly, for you can not cut through the Earth, nor can you reach the mountains in height. All of this—the evil of it—is hateful in the sight of your Lord. This is what your Lord has revealed to you of wisdom. Do not associate any other god with God, lest you should be thrown into Hell, blamed, cast away." (17:22-39)

Creed

The Cow 2:285

According to Martin Lings in *Muhammad, His Life Based on the Earliest Sources* (page 105), this revelation in the Qur'an contains the Creed of Islam:

"The Messenger believes in what has been revealed to him from his Lord, and (so do) the believers. They all believe in God and His angels and His Books and His messengers: We make no difference between any of His messengers. They say: 'We hear and obey, our Lord! Your forgiveness (do we crave), and to You is the eventual course.'" (2:285)

Aqidah

Systematic statements of belief became necessary, from early Islam on, initially to refute heresies, and later to distinguish points of view and to present them, as the divergences of schools of theology or opinion increased.[1]

Here are fundamental statements of belief, or Aqidah (Creed):

---

1 Cyril Glasse, *The New Encyclopedia of Islam: A Revised Edition*, (Lanham: Rowman & Littlefield Publishers, 2001), 105.

Articles of Faith

The Articles of Faith are derived from the Qur'an and Sunnah.

1. Belief in God, the One and Only One worthy of all worship
2. Belief in the angels
3. Belief in the Books sent by God (including the Qur'an)
4. Belief in all the Prophets and Messengers sent by God
5. Belief in the Day of Judgment and in the Resurrection (life after death)
6. Sunni only: Belief in Destiny (Predestination or Fate)

   The Shia do not subscribe to Article 6, because they believe that in human life, there is both free will and predestination. Shia stress God's boundless justice over predestination.

Five Pillars/Principles of Religion

These are the mandatory foundations of Islam.

- Sunni Five Pillars:
  1. The Declaration of Faith (There is one God and Muhammad is His messenger)
  2. Formal prayer (5 daily salat)
  3. Fasting from dawn to dusk (obligatory during the month of Ramadan)
  4. Paying the alms tax (zakat) for charity within the giver's community
  5. Pilgrimage to Mecca (obligatory at least once in a lifetime)

- Shia Principles of Religion (Twelvers, the largest sect):
  1. The Oneness of God
  2. Divine Justice
  3. Prophethood
  4. Succession: Political leadership and spiritual supremacy of the Prophet's successors
  5. Day of Judgment and the Resurrection

  Shia additional Ten Ancillaries (Obligatory Practices):
  1. Prayer
  2. Fasting
  3. Charity
  4. Tithing 20% of annual income
  5. Pilgrimage to Mecca at least once in a lifetime

6. Jihad: two meanings—the "greater jihad" (an inner spiritual struggle), and the "lesser jihad" (an outer physical struggle against the enemies of Islam)

7. Enjoin what is right. Urge others to take the Straight Path.

8. Forbid what is reprehensible. Urge others to abstain from reprehensible acts.

9. Express love toward the divinely appointed individuals and teachers of the Islamic faith after Muhammad.

10. Disassociate from those who oppose God or Muhammad and those who were enemies of Muhammad or his family.

Prayer

Five salat prayers

- Daily ritual prayer is obligatory worship, performed at dawn, immediately after noon, mid-afternoon, sunset, and early night.

- Ritual cleanliness, washing, clean clothes and removal of shoes are required before prayer. One may pray individually or communally, at home, outside, virtually any clean place, as well as in a mosque, though the latter is preferred.

- Friday congregational noon prayer in a mosque is also obligatory. It is accompanied by a sermon.

- Prayers are led by any learned person who knows the Qur'an and is chosen by the congregation. He (or she, if the congregation is all-women) is called the imam.

- Prayer consists of ayat (verses) from the Qur'an and other prayers, accompanied by standing, bowing, prostrating and sitting. They are said in Arabic, the language of the revelation, though personal supplications can be offered in one's own language. Worshippers face the Qiblah, the direction of the Ka'bah in the city of Makkah (Mecca).

Sura Fatiha: The Islamic Lord's Prayer

In the name of God, the Beneficent, the Merciful.

(All) Praise is due to God, the Lord of the Worlds. The Beneficent, the Merciful, Master of the Day of Requital.

You alone do we serve, and You alone do we beseech for help. Guide us on the right path, the path of those upon whom You have bestowed favours, not the path of those upon whom You brought down wrath, or those who go astray. (The Opening 1:1-7)

The Mahdi

Today approximately 80% of world Muslims are Sunni and 15% are Shia. Approximately 85% of the Shia are Twelver Shia.[1]

A point of departure between the Sunni and the Shia branches of Islam is the Shia belief that individuals in Muhammad's line of descendents possess the legitimate political, spiritual and religious guidance over Islam on Earth.[2] This Shia line of descendents is the Twelve Infallible Imams.

The line of Twelve Infallibles ends with Muhammad al-Mahdi, born in 869 CE (255 AH). He is the Twelfth Imam, and the Twelvers believe that he is currently still alive, and hidden "in Occultation" since 874 CE (261 AH).[3]

The Qur'an does not explicitly reference the Mahdi, but the Hadith (the reports and traditions of Muhammad's teachings collected after his death) reference him.

Twelvers believe that The Mahdi will return at the end time to bring justice to the world by establishing Islamic State and applying Islamic laws.[4] Some believe that the Mahdi, together with Jesus, will fight and kill the AntiChrist (al-Dijjal).[5]

Some Sunni Muslims believe that the Mahdi is the Muslims' future leader who is yet to come, but they do not believe the Mahdi to be the Twelfth Imam, divine or someone who is already born. They believe that he will simply be a rightly guided Muslim from Muhammad's family, from the line of Muhammad's daughter, Fatimah. However, some more Orthodox Sunni Muslims dispute the concept of the Mahdi because there is no mention of it in the Qur'an or Sunnah.[6]

Both Shia and Sunni also hold to the stories of Christ's return that are described in the Qur'an.

---

1 Mathieu Guidère, *Historical Dictionary of Islamic Fundamentalism.*, (Lanham: Scarecrow Press, 2012), 319, 331.

2 Ibid, 320.

3 Ibid., 320.

4 Sayyed Hossein Nasr, *Expectation of the Millennium: Shiism in History,* (Albany: SUNY Press, 1989), 19.

5 Tamara Sonn, *A Brief History of Islam* (Hoboken: Wiley-Blackwell, 2004), 102.

6 "Sunni and Shia," *BBC,* 2009, http://www.bbc.co.uk/religion/religions/islam/subdivisions/sunnishia_1.shtml (accessed December 2017).

Index

"Guide me in Your truth, and teach me,
for You are the God of my salvation;
I wait for You all day long." (Psalm 25:5)

RISING MYRRH

Thank you for reading our book. We hope that you enjoyed it! **We would be honored if you left your impressions in a review on Amazon.com.**

Contact@risingmyrrhpress.com

Made in the USA
Las Vegas, NV
09 May 2024

89755817R00295